MW01098178

GLOBAL JUSTIC
CHRISTIAN ETHICS

Global realities of human inequality, poverty, violence, and ecological destruction call for a twenty-first century Christian response that links cross-cultural and interreligious cooperation for change to the gospel. This book demonstrates why just action is necessarily a criterion of authentic Christian theology and gives grounds for Christian hope that change in violent structures is really possible. Lisa Sowle Cahill argues that theology and biblical interpretation are already embedded in and indebted to ethical-political practices and choices. Within this ecumenical study, she explores the use of the historical Jesus in constructive theology; the merits of Word and Spirit christologies; the importance of liberation and feminist theologies as well as theologies from the global south; and the possibility of qualified moral universalism. The book will be of great interest to all students of theology, religious ethics and politics, and biblical studies.

Lisa Sowle Cahill is J. Donald Monan, S.J., Professor of Theology at Boston College. Her most recent publications include *Sex, Gender and Christian Ethics* (1996), *Bioethics and the Common Good* (2004), and *Theological Bioethics: Participation, Justice and Change* (2005). She is currently a member of the Catholic Common Ground Initiative, the Advisory Board of the Public Religion Research Institute, the Board of Directors of the international journal *Concilium*, and the Catholic Peacebuilding Network.

NEW STUDIES IN CHRISTIAN ETHICS

General Editor

ROBIN GILL

Editorial Board

STEPHEN R. L. CLARK, STANLEY HAUERWAS, ROBIN W. LOVIN

Christian ethics has increasingly assumed a central place within academic theology. At the same time the growing power and ambiguity of modern science and the rising dissatisfaction within the social sciences about claims to value-neutrality have prompted renewed interest in ethics within the secular academic world. There is, therefore, a need for studies in Christian ethics which, as well as being concerned with the relevance of Christian ethics to the present-day secular debate, are well informed about parallel discussions in recent philosophy, science or social science. *New Studies in Christian Ethics* aims to provide books that do this at the highest intellectual level and demonstrate that Christian ethics can make a distinctive contribution to this debate – either in moral substance or in terms of underlying moral justifications.

GLOBAL JUSTICE, CHRISTOLOGY, AND CHRISTIAN ETHICS

LISA SOWLE CAHILL

Boston College

CAMBRIDGE
UNIVERSITY PRESS

32 Avenue of the Americas, New York NY 10013-2473, USA

Cambridge University Press is part of the University of Cambridge.

It furthers the University's mission by disseminating knowledge in the pursuit of education, learning and research at the highest international levels of excellence.

www.cambridge.org
Information on this title: www.cambridge.org/9781107515321

© Lisa Sowle Cahill 2013

First published 2013
First paperback edition 2015

A catalogue record for this publication is available from the British Library

Library of Congress Cataloguing in Publication data
Cahill, Lisa Sowle, author.
Global justice, Christology and Christian ethics / Lisa Sowle Cahill.
pages   cm. – (New studies in Christian ethics)
Includes bibliographical references and index.
ISBN 978-1-107-02877-7 (hardback)
1. Christianity and justice.   2. Globalization–Religious aspects–Christianity.
3. Jesus Christ–Person and offices.   4. Christian ethics.   5. Bible–Theology.   I. Title.
BR115.J8C33   2013
241–dc23   2012040415

ISBN 978-1-107-02877-7 Hardback
ISBN 978-1-107-51532-1 Paperback

To my father,
Donald Edgar Sowle, 1915–

Contents

General Editor's Preface

After a gap of seventeen years, it is a great pleasure to have another contribution to *New Studies in Christian Ethics* from Lisa Sowle Cahill. Her first contribution, *Sex, Gender and Christian Ethics*, was, as expected, very well received. She combined critical Catholic feminism with a theological realism that was committed to both ecumenical dialogue and compassionate social activism with those who were economically and socially marginalized. In her subsequent writings she developed a particular interest in issues within bioethics, especially in areas that involve sharp questions about social justice such as the global challenge of AIDS and novel developments in biotechnology. In this new book she is less concerned with particular social issues. Her aim now is to supply a sustained theological basis for global justice.

Critics of theological realism have long argued that it is short of theology and fatally shaped by the secular world. For many of them it is the bible alone, or perhaps the bible together with certain favored theologians (from Augustine to Barth), that must form the *only* basis for Christian ethics. Writing from a theological position committed to natural law – albeit a reconstructed vision of natural law to that understood by Aquinas – she dissents radically from this dogmatic claim. She contends that "certain goods for humans can be universally known, most obviously those based on the physical conditions of human survival, and on our natural sociality and need for cooperative relationships." Such a perspective gives Christian theologians a basis for dialogue with both secularists and followers of other faith traditions. For her, the christological commitments enshrined in the New Testament and historic creeds give a distinctive Christian shape to and strong support for otherwise ubiquitous natural laws.

As the chapters of this new book unfold, it becomes clear that for Lisa Sowle Cahill a number of key theological concepts shape a distinctively

Christian concept of global justice. Among these are the kingdom of God from the synoptic gospels; Word christology, especially from John 1, combined with Spirit christology from Luke, Acts, and parts of Paul; and the cross and atonement properly understood. In the process, she develops an understanding of global justice that is both passionate and compassionate.

This is a rich theological offering that makes a major contribution to theological and moral realism, as well as to *New Studies in Christian Ethics*, now in its twenty-first year. I recommend it without hesitation.

ROBIN GILL

Acknowledgments

My numerous intellectual and personal debts will be evident in the pages of this book, especially in Chapter 1, where I name several of my teachers and colleagues at the University of Chicago. The example of my dissertation director, James Gustafson, has continually led me to consider and reconsider the interface of systematic or dogmatic theology and theological ethics, and to probe the questions they raise for one another. I was inspired to return to serious study of christology when I read my friend Roger Haight's *Jesus: Symbol of God* in 2003. Tatha Wiley gave me my first opportunity to publish on ethics and christology by contributing an essay to her edited volume, *Thinking of Christ* (2003). Gustafson taught his students not to make facile theological claims about the nature of the moral life and its possibilities, unbacked by any sort of practical evidence, and I have tried to take that lesson seriously here, in drawing connections between christology and global social ethics.

My dependence on and gratitude to fellow teachers and learners at Boston College will be less obvious but just as important. The Theology Department, particularly my colleagues in the ethics doctoral seminar (which includes faculty and students from the B.C. School of Theology and Ministry), has been for me a community of friendship, of scholarship, and of genuine inquiry about what Christianity really means. I could not function as a theologian at all without the companionship of my fellow ethicists Ken Himes, David Hollenbach, Jim Keenan, John Paris, Steve Pope, and Andrea Vicini. Doctoral candidates Sarah Moses, Autumn Ridenour, Jill O'Brien, and Kate Ward have been exemplary research assistants and wise advisers. Many, many more students have challenged, enlarged, and improved my theological framework. Theology faculty members who have most frequently been the patient objects of my importunate pleas for help are Steve Pope, David Hollenbach, Pheme Perkins, Charles Hefling, Nancy Pineda-Madrid, and Bob Daly. My close friend Anthony J. Saldarini supported me for many years in the study of

Jesus, early Christianity, and Judaism. Since his passing in 2001, I have continued to learn from one of Tony's best friends, Daniel Harrington. My remedial forays into biblical scholarship and christology were aided immensely when I sat in on graduate classes taught by Charles, Pheme, Michael Buckley, and the late Frederick J. Murphy (Joseph Visiting Professor).

It is *de rigueur* to mention one's family in naming one's blessings, and I happily do so here: my husband, Larry, and Charlotte, James, Don, Will, and Ae. There is nothing like a spouse and five adult children – with their own lives, disappointments, accomplishments, sorrows, and joys – to remind one that writing books should not be equated with "the real world" and also to occasion the profound human experiences that nourish, shape, and test our notions of God. Lastly I thank my dad, Donald E. Sowle, who at this writing had recently celebrated his ninety-seventh birthday. Dad is a faithful, traditional Catholic whose trust in God, dedication to the Catholic sacraments, and personal generosity have been an inspiration to my sister and me, even when the "institutional Church" has not. He is also a great supporter of daughters getting PhDs and producing books. I dedicate this one to him.

July 29, 2012

CHAPTER I

The politics of salvation

Global realities of human inequality, poverty, violence, and ecological destruction call for a twenty-first-century Christian response that can link the power of the gospel to cross-cultural and interreligious cooperation for change. The aims of this book are to give biblical and theological reasons for Christian commitment to justice, to show why just action is necessarily a criterion of authentic Christian theology, and to give grounds for Christian hope that change in violent structures is really possible.

The premise of this work is that religious experience of God carries a moral way of life as its equally original counterpart. This is because inclusive community with other human beings is a constitutive dimension of community with God. "Love the Lord your God with your whole heart, mind, and soul; and your neighbor as yourself" (Mark 12:28–34). Love God *and* neighbor – not God, *then* neighbor. To experience salvation is to have one's life completely reoriented in relation to God and simultaneously, integrally, in relation to other human beings. Authentic religious experience – salvation – is inherently transformative and political. Reconciled human relations are lenses through which we glimpse the goodness and power of God.

In the words of Gustavo Gutiérrez – almost four decades ago – "to know God *is* to do justice."[1] Jürgen Moltmann voices the theological corollary: "christopraxis is the source from which Christology springs."[2]

---

[1] "Conversion means a radical transformation of ourselves ... To be converted is to commit oneself to the process of the liberation of the poor and oppressed, to commit oneself lucidly, realistically, and concretely." Gustavo Gutiérrez, *A Theology of Liberation: History, Politics, and Salvation*, trans. and ed. Sister Caridad Inda and John Eagleson; rev. edn., with new introduction, trans. Matthew J. O'Connell (Maryknoll, NY: Orbis Books, 1988), p. 118. Originally published by CEP, Lima, 1971; original English translation published by Orbis Books, 1973.

[2] Jürgen Moltmann, *The Way of Jesus Christ: Christology in Messianic Dimensions*, trans. Margaret Kohl (Minneapolis: Fortress Press, 1993). See also Jürgen Moltmann, *Jesus Christ for Today's World*, trans. Margaret Kohl (Minneapolis: Fortress Press, 1994), p. 47: "There is no Christology without christopraxis, no knowledge of Christ without the practice of Christ. We cannot grasp Christ

I

Elisabeth Schüssler Fiorenza makes the same point with specific reference to feminist theology: "we must ground feminist theology in wo/men's struggles for the transformation of kyriarchy."[3] I agree with Paul Murray that "Christian faith is not primarily a way of thinking or speaking … but a lived, communal praxis of living in accordance with and out of God's transforming action in Christ and the Holy Spirit."[4] David Tracy explains that "the criteria of theology are ethical-political criteria because … there is no revelation without salvation."[5] Therefore, in the words of Jon Sobrino, *orthodoxy* must meet the criterion of *orthopraxis*, because it is the experience of resurrection life, the proximity of God's reign in our historical existence, that gives rise to worship and theology in the first place.[6]

The term "salvation," derived from the Latin word for health, *salus*, connotes an actual healing of sin as idolatry, selfishness, and violence.[7] If God's full incarnation in human existence is a fact, and resurrection life a present reality, then Christian politics must be, can be, and is transformative of its social world. To proclaim that God is truly present in Jesus Christ, and that in Christ humans are reconciled to God, is to commit oneself to personal and political ways of life coherent with the reign of God that Jesus inaugurates.

Furthermore, the sociopolitical dimension of salvation has consequences for the purposes and criteria of theology. Theology is systematic, intellectual reflection on the experience of salvation; to be adequate to that experience, theology must incorporate and foster salvation's relational and social dimensions. To the extent that theological concepts and systems foster historical injustice, they are inauthentic and false to the

---

merely with our heads or our hearts. We come to understand him through a total, all-embracing practice of living … Discipleship is the holistic knowledge of Christ, and for the people involved it has a cognitive as well as an ethical relevance; it means knowing and doing both."

[3] Elisabeth Schüssler Fiorenza, *Jesus: Miriam's Child, Sophia's Prophet: Critical Issues in Feminist Christology* (New York: Continuum, 1994), p. 48.

[4] Paul D. Murray, *Reason, Truth and Theology in Pragmatist Perspective* (Leuven: Peeters, 2004), p. 9. Murray references John W. de Gruchy, "Christian Witness and the Transformation of Culture in a Society in Transition," in Hilary D. Regan and Alan J. Torrance (eds.), *Christ and Context: The Confrontation Between Gospel and Culture* (Edinburgh: T & T Clark, 1993), pp. 131–52.

[5] David Tracy, "The Uneasy Alliance Reconceived: Catholic Theological Method, Modernity, and Postmodernity," *Theological Studies*, 50 (1989), p. 569.

[6] Jon Sobrino, *Christ the Liberator: A View from the Victims*, trans. Paul Burns (Maryknoll, NY: Orbis Books, 2001), p. 157.

[7] The New Testament provides many metaphors for the restoration of right relationship of humans to God in Jesus Christ, all of which disclose dimensions of an ultimately mysterious reality. They include salvation (biological or organic), redemption (economic), justification (legal or forensic), and purification (cultic or ritual). Salvation as healing suggests the real change in believers and in the community that is essential to a transformative Christian politics.

experience of salvation in Jesus Christ. Theology must be tested by its effects in human life, judged not only in terms of spiritual conversion and the formation of religious community, but also in terms of the well-being of humans and other creatures. Theology is accountable to the normative claims of a moral realism that defines justice as practical recognition of basic human goods, human equality, respect for other species, and participation of all in the common good.

In the face of the evils of poverty, war, gender-based violence, and environmental destruction, Christians must proclaim in deed and word the cosmic span of God's creating power and the transformative possibilities of redemption. We must not give up the fight for justice as ultimately nonsensical, historically doomed, or outside the vocation of Christian discipleship. Indeed, Christian justice work is a testimony to the authenticity and power of the gospel. Good Christian practices and true Christian theologies display salvation as love of God and neighbor, forgiveness, reconciliation, resurrection, and the power of the Holy Spirit in history. This is why moral and political practices are criteria of theological truth.

Finally, it is vital to my project not only that biblical narratives of the life, death, and resurrection of Jesus shape Christian social ethics, but also that the key formulations of Nicaea and Chalcedon furnish its inspiration and rationale. The recovery of the humanity of Jesus, his ministry of the reign of God, and salvation through the resurrection have been dominant and vital concerns in recent Christian ethics and in liberation theologies. Yet more traditional affirmations of the divinity of Christ, salvation through the cross, and the real presence of God's Spirit in the church are equally crucial to a confident Christian politics of liberation and justice. Both biblical and creedal sources must be interpreted flexibly, receptive to Christianity's internal pluralism, today and in ages past. Diversity within Christian theology and its sources reflects diversity within the biblical canon, within the viewpoints in union at Nicaea and Chalcedon, and among the sites of global Christianity.

The reality of reconciliation and renewal in Jesus Christ, with its practical and political ramifications, will be guiding concerns of later chapters, especially Chapter 4 ("Christ"), Chapter 5 ("Spirit"), and Chapter 6 ("Cross"). The present chapter will concentrate on the case that the relation between theology and ethics is a two-way street. Not only do biblical and theological claims about salvation in Jesus Christ require active commitment to social justice; the practices in which Christians are already engaged shape their theological vision, and the just or unjust practical consequences of Christian concepts and doctrines are indicators of the latter's truth and adequacy.

This chapter will expand on the basic interdependence of theology and ethics in several steps. The section to follow will examine the mutual formation of morality, politics, and religion, and hence of interpersonal ethics, social ethics, and theology ("The Necessary Interdependence of Theology and Politics"). The link of sociopolitical realities and theoretical knowledge is now well established by philosophers from Marx to Nietzsche to Wittgenstein to Foucault to Irigaray and Chandra Mohanty. In *Sources of the Self* and *A Secular Age*, Charles Taylor reveals the cultural and intellectual heritages culminating in a Western ethos of individuality, "inwardness," agency, and equal respect, as well as a worldview that allows only for historically "immanent" but not "transcendent" meaning.[8] His diagnosis of the ways historical realities enable and constrain the possibilities of thought and imagination for their participants may be applied analogously to theology and theologians – emphasizing more strongly than Taylor, however, the fact that worldviews are created at least as much by social and material practices, and by the quality of human relationships, as by their intellectual and artistic streams. The codetermination of Christian theology and practices will be illustrated at the end of this chapter by a liturgy honoring the Virgin of Guadalupe and, in Chapter 6 ("Cross"), by the Roman Catholic Tridentine Good Friday liturgy and its depiction of the Jews.

In the next section of this chapter ("Pragmatism: A Resource for Theology and Ethics"), I will turn to an aspect of my own cultural heritage, the American philosophical tradition of pragmatism, to explicate further how ethical and theological truths have practical origins, practical meaning, and practical criteria of verification, even though they can also be true across particular communities or "universally." Varieties of realist Christian ethics are numerous and may be defended in many ways. My own approach is indebted to the revised "natural law" tradition rooted in Aquinas and developed primarily by Roman Catholic authors (see Chapter 7, "Nature"). It also bears affinities with several other thinkers associated with the University of Chicago, such as James Gustafson, David Tracy, Robin Lovin, Douglas Ottati, William Schweiker, Stephen Pope, Cristina Traina, and Kevin Jung.[9] In Lovin's words, the Christian

---

[8] Charles Taylor, *Sources of the Self: The Making of the Modern Identity* (Cambridge, MA: Harvard University Press, 1989); and *A Secular Age* (Cambridge, MA: Harvard University Press, 2007).
[9] See James M. Gustafson, *Ethics from a Theocentric Perspective*, vol. 1: *Theology and Ethics* (Chicago and Oxford: University of Chicago Press and Basil Blackwell, 1981); and *Ethics from a Theocentric*

realist's complex and culturally pliable conception of human nature is compatible with the conviction that "the human good is the proper subject of ethics, and that we cannot settle our disagreements about what we ought to do without reference to our understandings of a fully human life."[9] My appropriation of pragmatism is carried forward in this spirit.

After laying out the political side of all theology and making a neo-pragmatist case for the practical character of truth claims, I will argue that, consequently, religion and politics are not separate spheres but interdependent ("Christian Identity and Public Politics"). Most if not all societies are colored by the religious dimensions of human experience. Moreover, the religious identities of Christians are thoroughly intertwined with their other identities and communities, and this holds for Christian theology and ethics too. This has been the case from biblical times onward, since Christianity began as a Jewish reform movement, incorporated Gentiles, adapted Greco-Roman social and household structures, and continually found new cultural and philosophical forms in which to cast its experiences of God. Paul Ricoeur captures this dynamic by speaking of the "narrative unity" of a life. Selves, living "with and for others," gather together multiple relationships and spheres of belonging in identities constituted over time.[11] The diachronic and dynamic nature of identity applies to communities as well.

Perspective, vol. 2: *Ethics and Theology* (University of Chicago Press, 1984); David Tracy, *The Analogical Imagination: Christian Theology and the Culture of Pluralism* (New York: Crossroad, 1981); Robin W. Lovin, *Christian Realism and the New Realities* (Cambridge University Press, 2008); Douglas F. Ottati, *Hopeful Realism: Reclaiming the Poetry of Theology* (Eugene, OR: Wipf & Stock, 2009); William Schweiker, *Theological Ethics and Global Dynamics: In the Time of Many Worlds* (Oxford: Blackwell, 2004); Stephen J. Pope, *Human Evolution and Christian Ethics* (New York: Cambridge University Press, 2008); Cristina L. H. Traina, *Feminist Ethics and Natural Law: The End of the Anathemas* (Washington, DC: Georgetown University Press, 1999); and Kevin Jung, *Moral Realism and Christian Ethics* (manuscript submitted to Cambridge University Press). Gustafson, strongly influenced by the Reformed tradition and H. Richard Niebuhr, taught at the University of Chicago from 1972 to 1989 and mentored myself, Ottati, Schweiker, Pope, and Traina. Niebuhr's interest in pragmatism influenced Gustafson and was transmitted to several of his students. Lovin, a scholar of the thought of Reinhold Niebuhr, taught for thirteen years at the same institution. Jung is a student of Schweiker. For all of these, moral discernment is situated and thus partial, is often biased, must be accountable to evidence about basic human and moral goods, must be informed by accurate and adequate descriptions of the "facts" of human life, and should be guided by the well-being of humans and other species, in relation to God and God's purposes. Tracy, who taught at Chicago during Gustafson's tenure, brings a Catholic perspective on the "sacramentality" of ordinary life and on justice, and a critical yet realist hermeneutic of knowledge.

[10] Robin W. Lovin, *Reinhold Niebuhr and Christian Realism* (Cambridge University Press, 1995), p. 240.

[11] Paul Ricoeur, *Oneself as Another*, trans. Kathleen Blamey (University of Chicago Press, 1992), pp. 139, 158.

Christian theology and Christian ethics are not insulated from other traditions of belief, practice, and theory. This is one of the main factors that give Christian ethics social and political traction. "Other" identities do not necessarily dilute Christian commitment; on the contrary, they can provide important insight into what is humanly good and to be affirmed, what is evil and to be rejected. For example, modern equality and respect have made it possible to recognize more clearly that Jesus' "kingdom or reign of God" requires inclusive community and social justice as universal participation in the common good. Patriarchy and slavery are recognized as deformations of the Christian life. In addition, the flexibility and porousness of human identities, and the potential to share practices and values across groups, make it possible to work with others toward moral and political aims. Later in this chapter, efforts to combat rape and sex trafficking will provide illustrations ("Christian Politics and Global Justice: Sex Trafficking"), while a celebration of the feast of Guadalupe will connect transformative politics to Christian ritual, showing that the meaning of the ritual is both dependent on and refracted through ordinary social life ("Guadalupe: Ritual, Conversion, and Transformation").

These two examples in particular illustrate an argument central to the book as a whole: personal, communal, social, and political transformations are real possibilities, despite the intransigence of sin and evil. Political realism, not otherworldliness, liberal individualism, or secularism, is the biggest contemporary threat to Christian ethics and the preferential option for the poor. Political realism is the idea not only that the overriding motive of moral and political behavior is self-interest, but that self-interest is politically normative. While self-interest is indeed a powerful (and often valid) motivator, human beings and societies are capable of altruism and solidarity. It is these capabilities that salvation regenerates and to which Christian ethics appeals. Christian faith in the incarnation, atonement, and resurrection – as well as in Jesus' inauguration of the kingdom of God – require hope that change is possible and that hope takes root in real experiences of salvation as reordered relationship. These ideals have resonance in global, interreligious movements to alleviate human suffering and make societies more just.

To be practically effective, theological and ethical ideals must grip people and communities at more than an intellectual or theoretical level. They must have imaginative and affective appeal. Jon Sobrino accompanies orthodoxy and orthopraxis with *orthopathy*.[12] To understand in the

---

[12] Sobrino, *Christ the Liberator*, pp. 209–10, 213.

right way requires doing in the right way; to do what is right requires an attraction to the good, commitment to its reality, and the imagination to see possibilities of goodness that stretch beyond present conditions. The aesthetic dimensions of truth and of "beautiful" relationships account for the importance of story, symbol, ritual, music, and art in conveying the truth of theology and the goodness of Christian practices or, for that matter, the real presence of God in human existence.

THE NECESSARY INTERDEPENDENCE OF THEOLOGY AND POLITICS

Theology aims to orient humans rightly, in relation to the divine. As Elizabeth Johnson repeatedly declares, "The symbol of God functions."[13] Thus feminist theology explores multiple images of God to orient humans more justly to God, other persons, and all creation. In the estimation of James Gustafson, "Theology primarily is an activity of the practical reason. This it shares with ethics."[14] He sees the task of theological ethics as "the interpretation of God and God's relations to the world, including human beings."[15] Miroslav Volf agrees: theology is more a practical than a theoretical science; it aims not only "to deliver 'knowledge,' but serve a way of life."[16] Christian transformation in community is the proving ground of theological formulations.

Why and how theology is embedded in and interdependent with social and political practices is clarified by the modern social sciences. Building on Ernst Troeltsch's sociological approach to ecclesiology,[17] H. Richard Niebuhr first showed how Christian denominations in North America are captive to and distorted by all sorts of national, regional, racial-ethnic, and economic forces; he then proposed more constructively that different church stances toward culture represent recurrent and perhaps complementary ways of experiencing, understanding, and enacting the significance of Jesus Christ for "the world."[18] To see the church and theology as

---

[13] Elizabeth A. Johnson, *She Who Is: The Mystery of God in Feminist Theological Discourse* (New York: Crossroad, 1996), p. 5.

[14] Gustafson, *Ethics from a Theocentric Perspective*, vol. 1, p. 158.

[15] Ibid., vol. 2, p. 144.

[16] Miroslav Volf, "Theology for a Way of Life," in Miroslav Volf and Dorothy C. Bass (eds.), *Practicing Theology: Beliefs and Practices in Christian Life* (Grand Rapids, MI: Eerdmans, 2001), p. 246.

[17] Ernst Troeltsch, *The Social Teaching of the Christian Churches*, trans. Olive Wyon, new edn., 2 vols. (original translation 1931; reprint Louisville, KY: Westminster John Knox Press, 1992).

[18] See H. Richard Niebuhr, *The Social Sources of Denominationalism* (originally published 1929; reprint La Vergne, TN: Lightning Source, 2004); and *Christ and Culture* (New York: Harper & Row, 1956).

culturally embedded and as constituted in response to historical realities does not equate to reductionism. Rather, the churches are historical sites where the contingent encounters the eternal; God is present to human beings in and through their historical communities and relationships. To be determined by, yet responsive to, God is to be determined by and responsive to the historical communities, relationships, and structures in which God is actively present. The role of theology is to articulate the significance of the inner dynamic presence of the divine to, and sometimes over against, humanity and human societies.

The economist Margaret Archer offers a "morphogenetic" approach to social structures and human agency that sheds light on culture and church, politics and theology.[19] Archer's main concern is to show how, within a temporal process, individual human agency is always shaped by preexisting structures and forms of social agency; yet the "social self" as an emergent entity still has the capacity to transform systemic features, which in turn guide new social formations and new agency.[20] An important point that Archer does not emphasize is that emergent agency and structures are more than constraining forces that future agency has some freedom to reinscribe or escape. Emergent structures can enable greater human freedom, more complete instantiations of justice, and more authentic patterns of relating to the transcendent and divine. Examples might be systems of democratic government and the rule of law, the Christian eucharistic liturgy and its cultural variations, Catholic social tradition, and Caritas Internationalis.

Not only theology but the Christian churches, and the Christian experience of God in Jesus Christ itself, are "morphogenetic" in that they depend on and are even constituted by structures and practices (such as "the body of Christ"); yet they also constantly recreate and reinvent what has nurtured them. Going beyond sociology, however, Christian faith and theology pose a normative test for the adequacy of any Christian reality that emerges morphogenetically: analogical resemblance to the good news of salvation embodied in Jesus Christ. This resemblance must be real and practical, not just conceptual or theoretical.

David Tracy shows that the theological enterprise is shaped by its historical circumstances and its three "publics" of church, academy, and world, making theology accountable both to the real presence of a loving

---

[19] Margaret S. Archer, *Realist Social Theory: The Morphogenetic Approach* (Cambridge University Press, 1995).
[20] Ibid., pp. 75, 255, 257.

God and to the test of transformative praxis.[21] Church, academy, and
society provide for theology some of the inevitable "social-political realities embedded in all discourse."[22] They also enable theology's voice and
vitality. When Christians proclaim Jesus Christ as Lord or explicate that
confession theologically, they are witnessing to the "fundamental existential truth" that human life has meaning in light of the gracious power
of a loving God, who breaks the power of sin and makes a new existence
possible.[23] The theologian conveys this meaning to the three publics shaping his or her dynamic and sometimes conflicted identity.[24]

The final norm of theology is "the risen, exalted Jesus present now"
in Christian community and its texts, rituals, and practices – not apart
from "social-political realities" but in and through their renegotiation.[25]
The cognitive status of the truth claims of Christianity cannot be resolved
by "better theories" alone. It requires verification in the authenticity and
transformative capacity of the combined "intellectual, moral and religious praxis of concrete human beings in distinct societal and historical
situations."[26]

That practical results test theology is not a new idea; in fact it is a very
old one. Nicaea and Chalcedon were driven by debates over what theological expressions of Jesus' identity best suit the *fact* of salvation in Jesus
Christ, a fact also of reordered relationships. It was and is assumed that the
practical quality of Christian community as mediating the gospel anew
depends on the answer. For example, for Gregory of Nyssa, the church as
body of Christ mediates salvation and presupposes union with the person of Christ. To faithfully sanctify its members, it must derive from the
intimate union of the Word with the Father and their sharing of a single
divine power.[27] For Augustine similarly, Christian practice and identity
are shaped by the presence in Christ and in the church of the coeternal Word of God.[28] For the defenders of the Nicene legacy generally, the

[21] See in particular David Tracy, *Blessed Rage for Order: The New Pluralism in Theology* (University of Chicago Press, 1996; originally published 1975); *Analogical Imagination*; and *Plurality and Ambiguity: Hermeneutics, Religion, Hope* (University of Chicago Press, 1994); see also T. Howland Sanks, S.J., "David Tracy's Theological Project: An Overview and Some Implications," *Theological Studies*, 54 (1993), pp. 698–727.
[22] Tracy, "Uneasy Alliance," pp. 548–70, 569.
[23] Tracy, *Blessed Rage for Order*, pp. 221, 223.
[24] Tracy, *Analogical Imagination*, pp. 30–1.
[25] Ibid., p. 272.   [26] Ibid., p. 70.
[27] Lewis Ayres, *Nicaea and Its Legacy: An Approach to Fourth-Century Trinitarian Theology* (Oxford University Press, 2004), p. 307.
[28] Ibid., p. 311.

Christian life is possible due to the action of the "consubstantial Word drawing Christians towards God in union with him."[29]

The dominant theological traditions pursuant to the early christological formulations affirmed the identity of Jesus Christ as the incarnation of the divine Word in order to account for and mediate experiences of authentic human existence, salvation, and sanctification. However, as later critics were to note (and as will be developed in Chapters 3 ("Kingdom of God") and 4 ["Christ"]), the theologies of Jesus Christ as Word incarnate tended to downplay the humanity of Jesus, the moral and political content of his ministry of the reign of God, and the eschatological conviction that God's transformative reign is even now affecting history.

In the twentieth century, some of the spiritualizing trajectories of Word christologies were held up to scrutiny in light of theology's recovery of the social dimensions of salvation. In 1917, Walter Rauschenbusch took to task "the individualistic gospel" and its "doctrinal theology" for not rendering faithfully the social nature of salvation and the effects of salvation on social institutions.[30] The next one hundred years were to see variants and improvements on the social gospel in the form of liberation theologies, feminist theologies, Latina and womanist theologies, and Christian theologies from Asia and Africa. Also driven by ethical and political concerns are critiques of soteriologies interpreting the cross as the penal substitution of an innocent man for unrepentant sinners (the subject of Chapter 6, "Cross"). Influential alternative interpretations see the cross as God's solidarity with the victims of historical evil or as a historically evil consequence of Jesus' unfailing and self-sacrificial commitment to his mission.

The "bottom line" is that both humanity and divinity, both cross as historical evil and cross as divine salvation, are essential to Christian experience and to practices of salvation and liberation. Bad theologies can engender practices that have a negative effect on the community's relation to God; social effects that are patently out of line with the gospel are very reliable symptoms of inadequate or unfaithful theologies.

PRAGMATISM: A RESOURCE FOR THEOLOGY AND ETHICS

Some insights of pragmatist philosophy help clarify not only why theological claims should issue in a coherent ethics and politics, but why ethics

---

[29] Ibid., p. 312.
[30] Walter Rauschenbusch, *A Theology for the Social Gospel* (Nashville: Abingdon, 1945), pp. 5–6. Originally delivered as the Taylor Lectures, Yale School of Religion, 1917.

and politics are key to the generation of theological claims and why the test of theological truth is practical. David Tracy believes "we are all the heirs of William James's insistence on the criteria of ethical, humane fruits, or consequences for action, for praxis, both individually and societ-ally."³¹ Leading up to a defense of a pragmatist model of rationality within Christian theology, Paul Murray observes that two "postmodern" themes have contributed over the past century and a half to a reevaluation of the relation of reason to practice. These are the absence of any neutral per-spective on reality and the constructive role of humans in actually shaping reality.³² In the rallying call of William James, the pragmatist "turns away from abstraction" and "closed systems." He or she "turns toward concrete-ness and adequacy, towards facts, towards action, and towards power."³³

Pragmatism is set over against an epistemology in which individ-ual agents build up knowledge of the world by taking in information and forming inner representations of what is external. This traditional, "objectivist" type of epistemological realism assumes that knowledge of self is prior to knowledge of external reality; that factual knowledge of reality comes before the attribution of value or disvalue; and that know-ledge of the natural comes before knowledge of transcendent realities³⁴ (which must be inferred from the natural).³⁵ The pragmatic critique is that these are actually simultaneous processes.

Charles Taylor captures the central conviction of pragmatist philoso-phers in this way: "We are from the very beginning at grips with the world … our entire understanding of things comes to be framed only within this committed and active perspective."³⁶ Not only is reason necessarily situated, understanding (or misunderstanding) depends on the actions we take or the practices in which we are engaged. Hence, the understanding of Christian truth depends on "the conformity of life to God's practice in Christ and the Spirit" rather than on the "intellect alone."³⁷

Taylor pulls in the "Augustinian insight" that to understand certain things (like love or God) we have to be open to them³⁸ – as well as open to

³¹ Tracy, "Uneasy Alliance," p. 569.
³² Murray, *Reason, Truth and Theology*, p. 4.
³³ William James, *"Pragmatism" and "The Meaning of Truth,"* intro. A. J. Ayer (Cambridge, MA: Harvard University Press, 1975; originally published 1907 and 1909, respectively), p. 31.
³⁴ Charles Taylor, "What Is Pragmatism?" in Seyla Benhabib and Nancy Fraser (eds.), *Pragmatism, Critique, Judgment: Essays for Richard J. Bernstein* (Cambridge, MA: MIT Press, 2004), pp. 73–92, at 74.
³⁵ Ibid., p. 81.   ³⁶ Ibid., p. 74.
³⁷ Murray, *Reason, Truth and Theology*, pp. 193, 152.
³⁸ Ibid., p. 82.

a variety of ways in which we might connect existentially with their reality. Connection requires certain dispositions and affections in the knower, but this does not necessarily reduce realities known to the knower's desires. Yes, some truths can be discovered only by those who desire them – but the discovery connects nevertheless with "how things really are."[39]

The communities to which we belong make a difference. If understanding arises only within commitment and action, then we are open only to those realities with which we are at least inchoately engaged. This implies socially symbolized, narrated, and practiced worldviews, shared with others. Openness to transcendence depends in large part on collective belonging within which opportunities for transcendence are structurally supported and practically conveyed.[40]

The pragmatist tradition includes theologian H. Richard Niebuhr; George Herbert Mead, who is cited by Niebuhr in *The Responsible Self*;[41] Charles Sanders Peirce, the "founder" of American pragmatist philosophy; and William James, who wrote extensively about religion and who is frequently taken (I suspect incorrectly) to reject moral and religious realism.[42] Current reinterpretations of the pragmatist tradition include those of Donald MacKinnon,[43] Charles Taylor,[44] Jeffrey Stout,[45] and Robin

---

[39] Ibid., p. 90.

[40] The collective nature of religious belief is noted by Taylor as a correction of William James's *The Varieties of Religious Experience* (New York: Longmans, Green, 1902); but, oddly, communal belonging and shared praxis are not much invoked as a solution to the problem of constricted religious belief in the time of the "immanent frame." See the review of *Sources of the Self* by Frances S. Adeney, *Theology Today*, 48/2 (1991), pp. 204–10; and Peter Steinfels, "Modernity and Belief: Charles Taylor's 'A Secular Age'," *Commonweal*, 135 (May 9, 2008), pp. 14–21.

[41] H. Richard Niebuhr, *The Responsible Self: An Essay in Christian Moral Philosophy* (New York: Harper & Row, 1963).

[42] A. J. Ayer, for instance, does not regard James as an epistemological realist, despite some of James's own statements to the contrary. Ayer seems to regard the deciding consideration to be James's view that truth depends on verification. However, this does not exclude a realist view, inasmuch as James sees truth as inhering in a statement about a reality (as correspondence to reality), not as a property of realities known. It is not "objective reality" that cannot exist without verification, but the truth of our ideas and proposals about it. These depend on actually engaging with the reality, which is what constitutes the process of verification. See A. J. Ayer, "Introduction," in William James, *"Pragmatism" and "The Meaning of Truth,"* pp. xxvii–xxviii. Charles Taylor claims of James that "it cannot really be sustained that we have here a sense of things 'working' that really displaces the center of gravity away from truth as usually understood" (Taylor, "What Is Pragmatism?" p. 90). Michael Slater makes, to me, a convincing case in favor of James's realism and cites a good deal of the philosophical debate over this question. See Michael R. Slater, "Pragmatism, Realism, and Religion," *Journal of Religious Ethics*, 36/4 (2008), pp. 653–81.

[43] Donald M. MacKinnon, *Borderlands of Theology and Other Essays*, ed. George W. Roberts and Donovan E. Smucker (London: Lutterworth Press, 1968); and *The Problem of Metaphysics*, Gifford Lectures, 1965–6 (Cambridge University Press, 1974).

[44] Charles Taylor, *Varieties of Religion Today: William James Revisited* (Cambridge, MA: Harvard University Press, 2002); and "What Is Pragmatism?"

[45] Jeffrey Stout, *Ethics After Babel: The Languages of Morals and Their Discontents* (Boston: Beacon Press, 1988); and *Democracy and Tradition* (Princeton University Press, 2005).

Lovin,[46] all of whom connect pragmatism to the contemporary prospects of religion, religious belief, and Christian politics. Pragmatist insights are also useful to liberationist theologians, like Alejandro García-Rivera[47] and Nancy Pineda-Madrid,[48] and to some interested in the question of inter-religious dialogue and truth, like Robert Cummings Neville.[49] Pragmatist philosophy is quite an amorphous tradition; its key proponents disagree with one another on major points. The landmark essay by Peirce, "How to Make Our Ideas Clear,"[50] seems more to name an aspiration than furnish a prescription for success. My approach aims to incorporate pragmatist insights within a realist view of truth, both moral and religious.

Three possible contributions of pragmatism are especially important for theology and ethics. First, selves are socially constituted, their identities formed within particular worldviews and their attendant practices. The social status of women, for instance, is perceived only within structures, roles, and relationships that are already conferring identity and creating both men's and women's expectations. Niebuhr cites "the social psychology of G. H. Mead and his successors" in support of his view of the self as itself a social structure, arising in social experience and "born in the womb of society as a sentient, thinking, needful being with certain definitions of its needs and with the possibility of experience of a common world."[51] (As a social ethicist whose watchword was "responsibility," Niebuhr would certainly agree with Margaret Archer that the emergence of agency out of social structures need not be construed deterministically.)

In Mead's own words, the social process is not derived from individual selves, but vice versa. Selves derive "from the social process in which they are implicated and in which they empirically interact with one another."[52]

[46] Lovin, *Reinhold Niebuhr and Christian Realism.*
[47] Alejandro R. García-Rivera, *The Community of the Beautiful: A Theological Aesthetics* (Collegeville, MN: Liturgical Press, 1999); and *A Wounded Innocence: Sketches for a Theology of Art* (Collegeville, MN: Liturgical Press, 2003).
[48] Nancy Pineda-Madrid, "Interpreting Our Lady of Guadalupe: Mediating the Christian Mystery of Redemption," PhD dissertation, Graduate Theological Union, Berkeley, CA (2005).
[49] Robert Cummings Neville, *The Truth of Broken Symbols*, SUNY Series in Religion (Albany: State University of New York Press, 1996); and *Symbols of Jesus: A Christology of Symbolic Engagement* (Cambridge University Press, 2001).
[50] Charles Sanders Peirce, "How to Make Our Ideas Clear," in Nathan Houser and Christian Kloesel (eds.), *The Essential Peirce: Selected Philosophical Writings*, vol. 1: *1867–1893* (Bloomington: University of Indiana Press, 1992), pp. 124–41.
[51] H. Richard Niebuhr, *The Responsible Self*, pp. 72–3.
[52] George Herbert Mead, "A Contrast of Individualistic and Social Theories of the Self," in Louis Menand (ed.), *Pragmatism: A Reader* (New York: Random House, 1997), p. 296. Mead proposes a "social theory of mind," in which "mind can never find expression and could never have come

It is precisely this interactive dynamic among the experience of salvation, religious symbols, stories, and practices, theological clarifications, and transformation of believers or disciples that drives traditional and conciliar concerns for adequate doctrinal expressions. Religion is a "cultural system," in the sense of a pattern of symbols, concepts, and practices by which people sustain, communicate, and develop their knowledge and attitudes about life.[53] Our communal vocabularies shape our religious experience, however "subjective," "spiritual," or "interior" our relation to the divine may seem.[54]

The constitution of the individual person by relationships is better appreciated within communitarian cultures than within political liberalism with its prioritization of freedom and autonomy as defining experience and norm. Examples are abundant in Latin America, Asia, and Africa, but they also thrive in subcultures within liberal societies. Roberto Goizueta highlights a "relational anthropology" as distinctive of Latino Catholicism. Just as human worlds of meaning and identity are relationally constituted, shared norms or truths are mediated by active relationships among persons and groups.[55] As Ada María Isasi-Díaz contends, "Community is not something added on, but a web of relationships constitutive of who we are."[56]

Second, however, pragmatist truth is not the mere creation of a symbol system and set of practices, be they political or religious. The word "truth" refers to the *correspondence* between reality and a perception of or statement *about* reality. Philosophical backing is provided by William James. "Truth" is a relation of agreement between an idea or statement and its object. "Realities are not true, they *are*; and beliefs are true *of* them."[57] Truth means "agreement ... with reality."[58] James denies the accusation that pragmatism is incompatible with being an epistemological realist; in fact, he claims that tag for himself.[59]

into existence at all, except in terms of a social environment; that an organized set or pattern of social relations and interactions (especially those of communication by means of gestures functioning as significant symbols and thus creating a universe of discourse) is necessarily presupposed by it and involved in its nature." Ibid., p. 297.

[53] Clifford Geertz, *The Interpretation of Cultures: Selected Essays* (New York: Basic Books, 1973), pp. 89–90.

[54] Taylor, *Varieties of Religion Today*, p. 28.

[55] Roberto S. Goizueta, *Caminemos con Jesús: Toward a Hispanic/Latino Theology of Accompaniment* (Maryknoll, NY: Orbis Books, 1995), p. 153.

[56] Ada María Isasi-Díaz, *En la Lucha / In the Struggle: A Hispanic Women's Liberation Theology* (Minneapolis: Fortress Press, 1993), p. 171.

[57] James, *"Pragmatism" and "The Meaning of Truth,"* p. 272.

[58] Ibid., p. 169.   [59] Ibid., p. 272.

Truth has both a relatively subjective referent (in the knower or knowers) and a relatively objective referent (in the reality known). Yet for pragmatists, truth is a type of correspondence in which the mind or knower, or knowing community, is not passive.[60] Instead truth is established by interacting with reality in a "process of validation."[61] The truth relation can be and must be experienced in "events," in order to have "cash value,"[62] that is, the practical worth and efficacy without which objects of knowledge cannot really be true for human knowers. Any idea "that fits, in fact, and adapts our life to the reality's whole setting ... will be true of that reality."[63]

In other words, truths can be known only on the basis of participation in the realities they indicate. Truths are constituted within one's local environment, by engagement with what is personally, practically, and communally available. For instance, it is taken for granted in theologies of liberation that the true identity of Jesus as the Christ can be known only on the basis of practices of discipleship, commitment to the inbreaking reign of God.[64] Such practices reflect and embody a local community's worldview, but they also connect to and embody the universal reality of God and of divine salvation.

James seems not to note or at least emphasize an aspect of pragmatism's realism that is vital for social ethics. This is that dimensions of local realities necessarily cross-cut and intersect with other locales "universally" because human beings as such share basic characteristics, including a human body and the minimal requirements of physical and psychosocial survival and function. Whatever the practices in which one engages, the realities that absorb one's particular attention, one is always susceptible, like other human beings, to fear, injury, or death at the hands of a violent aggressor or a hurricane or to comfort, trust, and joy in friendship or in natural abundances beneficent to human needs. (The universalistic

---

[60] Slater, "Pragmatism," p. 658, n. 6.

[61] James, *"Pragmatism" and "The Meaning of Truth,"* pp. 169–70.

[62] Ibid., pp. 173, 169, and 32, respectively.

[63] Ibid., p. 170. In a chapter originally published in William James's *The Principles of Psychology*, "The Perception of Reality," James distinguishes "metaphysical reality, reality for God," from the reality that human truth accesses, which is "practical reality," "reality in a relative sense." In the practical and relative sense, "reality means simply relation to our emotional and active life." Reality is "that which excites and stimulates our interest," that which demands our attention so that we "accept it," "believe it," and "practically take account of it": William James, "The Perception of Reality," in *The Heart of William James*, ed. Robert Richardson (Cambridge, MA: Harvard University Press, 2010), pp. 46–78, at 56.

[64] Sobrino, *Christ the Liberator*, pp. 1, 21–22; Roger Haight, S.J., *The Future of Christology* (New York: Continuum, 2005), p. 27.

dimensions of experience, and hence of truth and morality, will be illustrated in relation to sexual violence and will be discussed more extensively in Chapter 7, "Nature.") In addition, humans and their shared psychosocial and bodily realities are now connected by "glocal" lines of communication and social institutions.

Third, truths engage with, affect, and are affected by particular and universal realities of human being and relationality. This implies a contribution of pragmatism that goes beyond James. Truth claims are not morally neutral, precisely because they do engage and shape the realities in which humans exist. Insofar as realities grasped involve human beings in relationship, all truths about those practical realities tacitly reference their moral aspects. Truth claims must therefore be evaluated in moral terms. The moral aspects of truths (as engaged characterizations of reality) should be evaluated explicitly as good or bad, as to be approved and reinforced, or as to be repudiated and resisted.

But James does not explicitly apply moral standards to reality proposals validated as true by human belief and action. A missing dimension in James's scheme – or at least one that must be further explicated – is the *goodness or badness* of realities, over and above whether they exist and engage us. James seems to assume that to dispatch with philosophical and religious shibboleths, and to turn to the worth of ideas for the real human condition, will lead to beneficial results for individuals and for the human race. But his own grounds for so believing and the standards by which he would define what constitutes good practical results are underdeveloped.

A 2010 discussion of the highlights of James's philosophy on National Public Radio (U.S.), featuring the scholar Robert Richardson, brought to the surface the importance of understanding James's claims (and their limits) in historical context.[65] As a mid-nineteenth-century writer, James was concerned primarily with countering idealism (and its accompanying dogmatisms), which as a philosophy divorces ideas from actual life and the results that ideas may or may not have. Moreover, he is part of a North American scientific age of enlightenment and progressivism. James's attention was not directed to the concerns of later ethicists who witnessed two world wars, the persistence of global poverty in a scientific age, or the clashes of culture, ethnicity, and religion that produced recurrent modern conflicts and genocides. According to Richardson, James continually asserts or at least supposes that pragmatists will judge actions

---

[65] See "On Point," hosted by Tom Ashbrook, National Public Radio (90.9 WBUR), January 3, 2011, featuring Robert Richardson, editor of *The Heart of William James*, onpoint.wbur.org/2011/01/03/william-james-pragmatism (accessed May 14, 2011).

by all of their consequences, not just by what "works for me," aiming at "a better actual world," the betterment of human life. Yet "better" is not well defined. James's tacit message in the moral realm is simply that we must not think of the good as an ideal Platonic form or idea only dimly reflected in the world as we know it.[66] Because he was confident about the possibility of progressive human reasonableness and welfare, he was not as concerned as many later ethicists with the ways biased notions of progress can trend toward greater evils rather than toward the "better."

Finally, James more assumed than defended a utilitarian philosophy of "the greatest good for the greatest number," which to him was a support to democracy and an antidote to the tyranny of elite interests, as well as to the ease with which human beings ignore the interior lives and interests of those they consider their inferiors. In fact, James was insistent that class distinctions are irrelevant to moral worth and wrote a passionate defense of the importance of what we would today call compassionate empathy and solidarity with those whose inconsequential-seeming lives are bearers of moral virtue and nobility.[67]

Developing a philosophy that is responsive to these values and concerns, James does not then focus on questions that were to become vital for later generations of philosophers (especially ethicists). These include the danger of relativism, the need to make cogent moral judgments on evil "truths" that may work pragmatically and have "cash value" for some people, and the possibility that the "lesser number" excluded by the utilitarian principle might not be greedy elites but oppressed minorities, possibly under corrupt or fascist regimes. These possible sources of critique show why it is necessary to build into pragmatism a moral standard that judges moral results by well-substantiated interpretations of what is good for and due to human beings, incorporating an explicit principle of equality. If the moral quality of local realities and concrete states of affairs is controversial, it may be evaluated in light of more general or constitutively human realities, respect for which is required by human well-being.

Consider the examples of rape, prostitution, and sex trafficking. Women's status and the sexuality of women may be perceived and enacted differently in particular moral contexts. It may be true that in a given social context women are inferior and degraded. But truths about particular realities must be distinguished from moral judgments about the value or goodness of those realities for human persons, and such

[66] Ibid.
[67] James, "On a Certain Blindness in Human Beings," in *The Heart of William James*, pp. 145–63.

judgments can be made in light of more comprehensive discernment of what human beings do and do not deserve. Moral judgments go beyond particular social enactments of relationship, to reference goods and evils that are widely or even universally recognized by human beings, whatever their particular circumstances and practices. A case in point is that there is a reality of female embodiment and of basic psychosocial well-being against which contextually defined gender identity must be evaluated.[68]

If moral proposals and judgments have practical meaning and power only when they are genuinely understood, then seeing the moral quality of rape and torture as evil, for example, means entering at some level into the relation between the perpetrator and victim. It means grasping the violation of the human good that takes place on both sides and acting in aversion to the evil that results. The making of claims and their validation are social, practical, and lead to further interaction.

Through ritual and moral practice, religions "constitute communal and individual ways or patterns of life for living engaged with the ultimate." For instance, "All three Abrahamic religions strongly emphasize the moral virtues of love, justice, and mercy, virtues believed to be divine as well as binding on human beings."[69] Inauthentic patterns of religious life can engage practitioners with ultimacy, but the results are demonic and idolatrous – as in the religious validation of patriarchy or the Christian endorsement of Nazism. This conviction motivates the massive turn of theology to concern with the concrete quality of human social life, so evident in the revisionist theologies and ecclesiologies that sprang up in the late nineteenth and early twentieth centuries – Catholic social teaching and the social gospel, above all. These arose just a few decades after the emergence of pragmatist philosophy. Not only are religion and theology inevitably historical and communal, they have responsibilities to histories and communities.

[68] For a provocative yet nuanced discussion, see Sandra D. Lane and Robert A. Rubinstein, "Judging the Other: Responding to Traditional Female Genital Surgeries," *Hastings Center Report*, 26/3 (1996), pp. 31–40. For a critique of the very concept "gender" and its use, see Jeanne Boydston, "Gender as a Question of Historical Analysis," *Gender & History*, 20 (2008), pp. 558–83.
[69] Robert Cummings Neville, "How to Read Scriptures for Religious Truth," in Alan J. Avery-Peck, Daniel Harrington, and Jacob Neusner (eds.), *When Judaism and Christianity Began: Essays in Memory of Anthony J. Saldarini*, vol. 2: *Judaism and Christianity in the Beginning* (Leiden: Brill, 2004), p. 606. Neville proposes a "pragmatic semiotic theory" of religion, based on the work of Charles S. Pierce (pp. 603–4, n. 3).

CHRISTIAN IDENTITY AND PUBLIC POLITICS

If the realities we call "faith," "discipleship," and "church" are formed interactively with other human identities, practices, and communities, then Christian politics is not confined within the church, nor is it limited to a countercultural witness. Christian communities are not insular or impermeable, but interactive, dialogical, even "hybrid."[70] The morality, politics, and imaginative worldview of any community will interweave with, be affected by, and shade off into the practices and ideas of other communities networked in the same social space – increasingly a global space. Within and across communities, humans share certain basic experiences, needs, goods, relationships, and possibilities of transcendence, making moral and religious understanding and shared commitment possible. Christians are and should be part of debates about shared public goods. In the process, it is important for Christian ethics to bring its characteristic convictions, insights, and practices to bear on public life. In so doing, Christian ethics must maintain its integrity, but its practical requirements will not necessarily be unique.[71]

The twentieth-century rediscovery of the symbol "reign of God" as central to the teaching of Jesus gained momentum with global movements for decolonization, democracy, and human rights, benefiting from modern papal social encyclicals and the Second Vatican Council, and liberation theologies from every continent. The fundamental challenge these theologies posed to traditional Christianity was to recover the social and political dimensions of spirituality and salvation. But this reappropriation of the symbol "kingdom of God" benefited from modern insights into human equality, equal respect, and the possibility of revolutionizing age-old structures of inequality and exclusion. Reciprocally, Christian traditions of inclusion and compassion support recognition of the truths of respect and equality.

Religion should not be juxtaposed to the concept of a majority secular culture, to which religion is an outsider. Individual human persons, social groups, and even whole cultures regularly claim experience of the divine as a constitutive feature of their identities. World religions such as Daoism, Buddhism, Hinduism, Zoroastrianism, Judaism, Christianity,

---

[70] Jeannine Hill Fletcher, "As Long as We Wonder: Possibilities in the Impossibility of Interreligious Dialogue," *Theological Studies*, 68 (2007), pp. 531–54.
[71] Nigel Biggar, *Behaving in Public: How to Do Christian Ethics* (Grand Rapids, MI: Eerdmans, 2011), pp. 8–9, 45–8. Biggar is informed by the thought of his mentor, James M. Gustafson, as am I. See James M. Gustafson, *Can Ethics Be Christian?* (University of Chicago Press, 1975).

and Islam, as well as ancient Greek and Roman religions and the indigenous religions of Africa, Asia, and the Americas, all express some conception of the cosmos as a whole that includes a creator, ground, or transcendent ordering principle.[72] Readers in North America and Western Europe, particularly those in the "academy" of humanistic higher education and scholarship, may readily object that religious belief is a cultural artifact and one that is being quickly left behind by modern, liberal, scientific cultures. Following the "masters of suspicion" Nietzsche, Freud, and Marx, they may dismiss religion as an illusory or oppressive projection of human desires. And they may hope and indeed trust that as science and democracy spread worldwide, the need for religion will disappear along with alchemy and the divine right of kings.

An oft-noted fact is that secularizing trends in Western postindustrial cultures have been fed by modern science and scientific criteria of truth, as well as by the availability of scientific and technological means of explaining and controlling the world. In addition, economic modernization and prosperity seem to diminish the importance of religious reassurances and hopes in democratic, capitalistic cultures. As Charles Taylor has elucidated – brilliantly and at length – the modern (Western) "social imaginary" circulates an "immanent frame" of meaning, whose symbols actively discourage, if not exclude, openness to the transcendent.[73] Taylor maintains that post-Reformation Christianity itself has been a contributing factor in growing secularity, since by valorizing ordinary life and endorsing the goal of historical human flourishing (commendable developments in themselves), Christianity has made it more possible to conceive of meaning and fulfillment apart from transcendent values and ends.[74]

Secularization is not equally prevalent, however, in cultures not controlled by modern science and the market or in those where a vibrant culture of religion and transcendence still maintains deeply embedded religious symbols and rituals, despite scientific and economic development. This actually describes much, even most, of U.S. culture. Very few Americans identify themselves as "secular" and "unaffiliated" with any religion.[75] Ninety-two percent of Americans say they believe in God or a "universal spirit."[76] What humans share across cultures and eras are not

[72] See Neville, "How to Read Scriptures for Religious Truth," p. 605.
[73] Taylor, *Secular Age*, p. 542.   [74] Ibid., pp. 77–84.
[75] Only 4% say they are atheist or agnostic, according to 2007 data of the Pew Forum on Religion & Public Life, Religious Landscape Survey, "Key Findings," religions.pewforum.org/reports (accessed April 28, 2012).
[76] Pew Forum on Religion & Public Life, Religious Landscape Survey, "Full Report," religions.pewforum.org/reports (accessed April 22, 2012), p. 164.

only some aspects of human moral experience, but experiences of the divine as well. The cultural chauvinism of intellectual elites who dismiss as unenlightened the religious worldviews of most of the world's peoples is veiled by their advocacy for human rights and their aesthetic taste for exotic, quaint, or colorful religious manifestations. But modern science and secularity have not in fact eliminated the plausibility of experiences of the divine. Such experiences are still mediated by complex cultures whose meaning extends beyond the purview of scientific assessment. Globally, human cultures certainly affirm such experiences.[77]

The quest for conformity to or union with the powers that sustain life is as old as the species and shapes humanity's most sublime music, art, and literature. When Christians interface with other communities and identities, they also interact with, benefit from, and challenge other kinds of religious experience. Christians and members of other religious traditions learn from and shape one another when they share practices and cultural symbol systems. When creative works correspond to deeply shared human questions, quests, yearnings, and fulfillments, they can function as culture-crossing "classics."[78] Many such classics are religious in inspiration. Michelangelo's *Pietà*, Bach's *St. Matthew Passion*, the Cambodian temple Angkor Wat, and the "flower and song" poetry of ancient Mexico's Nahuatl sages are eloquent across time and place. We might even speak of religion's moral and political "classics" – practical exemplars whose pathway to transcendence illumines a way beyond boundaries. The loyalty of the biblical Ruth to Naomi, Jesus' parable of the Good Samaritan, Siddhartha's quest for an end to suffering, St. Francis's embrace of "Lady Poverty" and "Sister Moon," Gandhi's commitment to nonviolence, Nelson Mandela's courage under persecution, and Mother Teresa's dedication to the poor – all inspire seekers beyond their own faiths.

CHRISTIAN POLITICS AND GLOBAL JUSTICE: SEX TRAFFICKING

To grasp the importance of making religiously inspired, theologically grounded, practically located, yet normatively comprehensive judgments

---

[77] On the actual increase of religiosity across the world, see John Micklethwait and Adrian Wooldridge, *God Is Back: How the Global Revival of Faith Is Changing the World* (New York: Penguin Press, 2009); Peter L. Berger (ed.), *The Desecularization of the World: Resurgent Religion and World Politics* (Grand Rapids, MI: Eerdmans, 1999); José Casanova, *Public Religions in the Modern World* (University of Chicago Press, 1994); and Robert D. Putnam and David E. Campbell, *American Grace: How Religion Divides and Unites Us* (New York: Simon & Schuster, 2010).

[78] Tracy, *Analogical Imagination*, p. 163.

that can back cross-cultural and interreligious moral action, one has only to consider the example of rape, including the kidnapping and prostitution of young girls. Rape is a form of violence that demands a Christian, a political, and a global response. The reality of rape demonstrates the moral importance of defending nonrelative moral realities, of holding all religious traditions accountable to such realities, and of marshaling religious resources to accomplish moral and political change. As a human reality, rape has a universal meaning: violent sexual assault. As a moral reality, rape is universally wrong. Cultural and "religious" narratives can bring into being evil moral states and relationships the affirmation of which is "true" insofar as they define and describe the realities of those subject to them. But the evil or goodness of such realities can still be measured in terms of dimensions of human flourishing and suffering that cut across and judge communal stories.

Despite its universally destructive character, rape as a social practice is condoned or approved in some moral narratives, including religious ones, which prioritize other agendas or values over the dignity and integrity of rape victims and rapists. Such narratives interface with and expand a moral reality in which evil is done and good avoided. Yet diverse religious traditions, post-Enlightenment philosophies, and global social movements hold up ideals of common humanity and of beneficent compassion as representing the best potential of human existence and as morally compelling. These ideals furnish moral grounds for the universal condemnation of practices like sexual violation. If the truth of the ideals is recognized not only as theoretically true, but as personally and culturally meaningful "for us," they will inspire mobilization for change.

On New Year's Day 2009, the *New York Times* published "The Evil Behind the Smiles," Nicholas Kristof's account of sex trafficking in Cambodia.[79] Kristof begins with a compelling narrative whose human dimensions resonate widely and engage the emotions as well as the intellect. He follows the work of a Vietnamese activist, Sina Vann, who was kidnapped at age thirteen, imprisoned in a fancy hotel with a subterranean dungeon, and sold to wealthy Cambodian men and visiting Westerners. Sina was tortured "many, many times." If she resisted sex, she was beaten, shocked with 220-volt wires, and locked naked in a tight wooden coffin full of biting ants for days at a time. The ants were kept from her eyes by her tears. Kristof concludes, "I hope Barack Obama and Hillary

---

[79] Nicholas D. Kristof, "The Evil Behind the Smiles," *New York Times*, January 1, 2009. See also Nicholas D. Kristof and Sheryl WuDunn, *Half the Sky: Turning Oppression into Opportunity for Women Worldwide* (New York: Knopf, 2009).

Clinton will recognize slavery as unfinished business on the foreign policy agenda,"[80] a hope obviously premised on the tradition-transcending moral truths that rape, torture, and slavery are wrong; that common humanity demands practical, political intervention; and that narratives can engage audiences more effectively than logical arguments. If we grasp the moral truth of Kristof's article, it is because we can connect to the human evil of the experiences he describes by drawing analogies to other experiences we have had or know about. When we do so, the truth of Kristof's vision is validated, and the scope and effect of the evils named are reduced.

Kristof's essay can have an impact on readers who have not personally interacted with anti-trafficking activists but who recognize the human goods at stake. Kristof aims at moral persuasion regarding these goods and their violation within a particular narrative: the worldview and practices of modern equality, women's rights, global human rights, and solidarity for practical change. But Kristof also assumes common human dimensions in the experiences he describes. By concretely portraying the physical and emotional suffering of prostituted girls, as well as by invoking a moral worldview centered on compassion, equality, and solidarity, Kristof aims not only to get readers to recognize in the abstract that sex trafficking is evil, but to engage them in resisting that evil, whether through personal activism, teaching and preaching, philanthropy, or responsible voting.

Tellers of the Christian story in the theological academy discern the moral messages of our narratives out of much the same worldview and practices as Kristof. Partly because of our "modern" or "liberal" values of equality and global solidarity, we discern Jesus' inclusive preaching of the kingdom or reign of God to be basic to our scriptural narrative. We let this center define how we interpret the authority and relevance of competing moral messages within scripture and tradition. And both modern respect for the individual person and the biblical mandate to care for the poor help inspire the compassion we feel for Sina Vann and the girls she describes. Identity-conferring stories (like Jesus' parables) attune our hearing to the truth or falsity of competing moral proposals; but, conversely, the human realities to which the stories refer suggest experiential criteria of good and evil to which we must hold our stories accountable.

Our scriptures, interpreted within the ongoing history of the church and of Christian practices, become a resource from which we join with

[80] At the time, Obama was the U.S. president-elect, and Clinton was his nominated secretary of state.

others to end the sexual exploitation of girls. Of course, this happens if and only if the truth of women's equality, the moral goodness of equal respect in the practical domain, and the special moral claim of the poor are intellectually, morally, and affectively compelling.

GUADALUPE: RITUAL, CONVERSION, AND TRANSFORMATION

Modern ideals of equality, respect, and compassion inform Christians' moral judgments and call their attention to universal realities of human well-being that sit in judgment of particular cases. Yet Christians also locate their moral and political convictions within the practices of the church. Informing the life of the church – when it is authentic – is the present experience of resurrection life in the Spirit of Christ. From a complementary perspective, human experience is united with God in Christ in a saving way in the incarnation. Christian ethics and politics are not matters of argument and logic alone, not even if solidly anchored in scriptural principles, natural law, humanistic values, the enumeration of moral and theological virtues, or even the preservation of a narrative that is demonstrably consistent with the bible. Rather, the ethics and politics of salvation point to a living experience of God's presence that transcends our moral knowledge even while it lends certainty to our convictions and unites our efforts to God's reign.

Following James, Charles Taylor suggests that confirmation of the truth of religious experience is "precisely the transformation it wreaks in the convert." "We are empowered" because we "have an experience of deliverance, of assurance of the meaningfulness of things, of the triumph of goodness"; and "the entire superiority of this state is bound up with its being seen to be in more profound contact with reality."[81]

From the Christian perspective, reconciled community is not merely an ideal, a fleeting possibility, a religious exception, or a future state. As an eschatological gift, it is a transforming reality with global promise here and now. Biblical and theological themes of incarnation and resurrection underwrite reconciliation as a historical possibility. Because in Christ humanity is united with divinity, because the faithful share resurrection life, and because the Spirit is present in our relationships, we affirm that kingdom life is present now, even though awaiting future fulfillment. Because the reality of salvation affects all our relations and communities,

---

[81] Taylor, "What Is Pragmatism?" pp. 90–1.

it also affects those with whom we share social and political life, as they affect us. A central task of theology is the creation not only of an eschato-logical *vision* of a new reality, but of an *actual* alternative space that is both ecclesial and sociopolitical.[82]

The concrete symbol of Our Lady of Guadalupe provides Nancy Pineda-Madrid with an opportunity to illustrate the theological value of Josiah Royce's pragmatist approach to community formation.[83] Her treatment demonstrates the practical, engaged nature of religious truth and theological reflection, as well as its moral-political ramifications. The focus of her argument is a liturgy honoring Guadalupe, a concerted unity of religious truth claims, moral practices, and artistic imagery, music, and ritual.

The Virgin of Guadalupe traces back to a sixteenth-century image of Mary in a blue-green cloak and clay-pink robe, also said to be the colors of the ancient Aztec goddess Tonantzin. According to traditional Mexican Catholic lore, this image represents a sixteenth-century apparition of Mary to a peasant named Juan Diego. Speaking in the local language, Nahuatl, she asked him to build a church, then miraculously gave him a cloak full of Spanish roses with which to prove to his bishop the man-date's supernatural origin. When the roses were presented to the bishop, the image of the Virgin of Guadalupe appeared where the roses had been, on the inside of Juan Diego's cloak.

The interpretation of Guadalupe is contested. Seen by indigenous Mexicans as a sign of divine favor, Our Lady of Guadalupe almost from the beginning raised official suspicion that she was but a "Christianized" version of Tonantzin. Some have suggested that Guadalupe was an inven-tion of sixteenth-century priests who were trying to "tame" Tonantzin and bring her devotees more into line with Catholic doctrine, and hence with colonial rule.[84] Today some see her as a liberating indigenous figure

---

[82] Rosemary Carbine, "Ekklesial Work: Toward a Feminist Public Theology," *Harvard Theological Review*, 99/4 (2006), pp. 433–55, at 452. See Schüssler Fiorenza, *Jesus: Miriam's Child, Sophia's Prophet*; and *Discipleship of Equals: A Critical Feminist Ekklesia-logy of Liberation* (New York: Crossroad, 1993).

[83] Nancy Pineda-Madrid, "Traditioning: The Formation of Community, the Transmission of Faith," in Orlando O. Espín and Gary Macy (eds.), *Futuring Our Past: Explorations in the Theology of Tradition* (Maryknoll, NY: Orbis Books, 2006), pp. 204–26.

[84] See Virgil Elizondo, *Guadalupe, Mother of the New Creation* (Maryknoll, NY: Orbis Books, 1997); Patricia Harrington, "Mother of Death, Mother of Rebirth: The Mexican Virgin of Guadalupe," *Journal of the American Academy of Religion*, 56/1 (1988), pp. 25–50; Jeanette Rodriguez, *Our Lady of Guadalupe: Faith and Empowerment among Mexican-American Women* (Austin: University of Texas Press, 1994); Louise M. Burkhart, *Before Guadalupe: The Virgin Mary in Early Colonial Nahuatl Literature* (Austin: University of Texas Press for the Institute of Mesoamerican Studies, State University of New York, Albany, 2001); D. A. Brading, *Mexican Phoenix: Our Lady of*

of Mexican popular religion, while others see her as yet another means of capturing women's meaning and agency for patriarchal control. Historically, as now, Guadalupe has had meaning in relation to political realities and action-guiding interests. The truth of the different Guadalupe cults is tested by the relations they enact.

Pineda-Madrid recounts her experience in a Guadalupe festival in which the main rituals were the offering of flowers and song (including choir and mariachis) in a Catholic church in Chihuahua, Mexico. Midway, a procession of *cantineras* (barmaids) entered the church, carrying armloads of fresh roses; they were regarded disdainfully by some members of the congregation, more sympathetically by others. "Throughout the year these women remained unseen, indoors, waiting for their mostly US male clients in one of the bedrooms attached to the local bars." Like the girls in Kristof's Cambodia, these women had been forced, though perhaps not as violently, into prostitution by poverty and gendered expectations that they would and should sell their bodies when "there was no other way to feed and clothe their extended family."[85]

Through their intrusive presence at the annual celebration, the *cantineras* affirmed their own dignity and that of others whom poverty had pushed past the margins of social respectability. In enacting their relation to Guadalupe as protector and benefactor, they exposed publicly the question of their role in the church and the justice of their circumstances. The other members of the congregation could not avoid them. These women strategically manipulated a local ritual practice to transform their experience of self, challenge and alter community relations, and restore their own agency and authority.[86]

This example shows how "alternative spaces" are possible even within communities marked by exclusionary assumptions and practices. Alternative spaces are also mainstream spaces and compromised spaces to the extent that participants bring different interpretations to shared activities. These very same ambivalences provide axes of influence from the alternative spaces to larger public spheres. In the Chihuahua ritual, participants bring clashing frameworks to define belonging in the worshipping community, frameworks strongly dependent on social location

---

Guadalupe: Image and Tradition across Five Centuries (New York: Cambridge University Press, 2001); and Timothy Matovina, "Theologies of Guadalupe: From the Spanish Colonial Era to Pope John Paul II," *Theological Studies*, 70/1 (2009), pp. 61–91.

[85] Pineda-Madrid, "Traditioning," p. 207.
[86] Ibid., p. 209. Here Pineda-Madrid relies on Catherine Bell's *Ritual Theory, Ritual Practice* (New York: Oxford University Press, 1992).

and status. Community understanding is renegotiated ritually and aes-
thetically, rather than through theoretical argument or direct political
confrontation; yet evaluation of moral and political practices is key to the
whole process and motivates the assent most readers will give to the incident Pineda-Madrid describes .

The Guadalupe example focuses attention on a theological and practical issue of extreme importance for the two chapters to follow, on creation and the kingdom of God. This is the issue of who does and does
not belong to the community of salvation, who is or is not recognized in
the community's practices. The inclusivity of salvation is a difficult and
unresolved point in bible and tradition, both because experiences of God
originate in particular communities and because human beings exploit
the power of religious symbols to validate particular, self-interested goals.

For example, in the book of Genesis, the cosmic providence of the
Creator stands in tension with the particular election of Israel and the
seeming validation by both the narrator and God of violent tactics to
further Israel's calling. In the New Testament, the inclusiveness of Jesus'
kingdom preaching is key to the agenda of contemporary liberation theology and of much in Christian social ethics. Yet we must remember the
likelihood that Jesus himself saw his primary mission as reform of Israel,
the possibility that the mission to the Gentiles was not yet on his agenda,
and the certainty that already in the early church and the canonical
scriptures a polemic against "the Jews" was unfolding to later murderous
results. Still, by the time of Paul, author of the earliest New Testament
writings, the self-understanding of Christ's followers had expanded to
include non-Jews. A second-century letter written in Paul's name even
sees God's saving will as universal (1 Tim. 2:3).

Rituals within a community, referring to its history and traditions,
allow present identities to be formed by events beyond one's memory and
lifetime. Identity, destiny, and legacy borrow from collective meaning,
mediated in the commemoration of an event or events that the community and all its members see as community-forming and constitutive.
Such events form the community as a community of memory and also
of hope.[87] But a constant danger is the formation of community around
selective memories and hope for a future that decisively validates one
group over another.

---

[87] Pineda-Madrid, "Traditioning," pp. 216–17. Pineda-Madrid refers primarily to Josiah Royce's
The Problem of Christianity (Washington, DC: Catholic University of America Press, 2001; originally published 1913).

The *cantineras* challenge the imbalance of power within their own community by engaging the ritualization of identity-constituting events in a way that is both disruptive and consequential for the self-understanding of participants. They blur the boundary between insiders and outsiders, asserting not only the inclusivity of salvation, but the normative inclusivity of Christian social practices. Though not all accepted their presence, the ritual event opened to accommodate the *cantineras*. Through their gift of roses, the *cantineras* reinterpreted their relation to Guadalupe and created hope for their future and that of the community, as a community of reconciliation.[88]

CONTEXTS, CAVEATS, AND HOPES

As a project in twenty-first-century theological ethics, written by a white, academic, feminist, Catholic theologian in the United States, this book will participate in some discourses more than others, necessarily privileging some moral questions and claims. Still, its "social location" not only affords but demands intersection with the circumstances, voices, and practices of people who are situated quite differently. The identity of a theologian today is circumscribed but porous, her work and claims produced by a limited experience and agenda, but taking shape in dialectical relation with the attestations, contestations, innovations, and revisions of others. In particular, assertions about values and justice that come from the standpoint of privilege easily elide the real differences in particular experiences and situations. With mixed trepidation and courage, I embark on a mission to probe Christian convictions about Christ, church, and politics that are central and evangelical, yet pluralistic and ambiguous. The results are offered in hope of the reader's generosity, and in expectation of productive critique.

Forces on the contemporary theological landscape are multiple and culturally variant. It is tempting and almost unavoidable to confine one's range to interlocutors who read the same sources, work in similar structures of church, academia, activism, or culture, and share convergent social agendas. As a result, theologians frequently fail to notice and learn from discourses relevant to their own work but carried on in the theological equivalent of parallel universes. Unnecessary separations have grown among doctrinal theology, biblical research, and theological ethics, but even within ethics the communities of discourse can be unduly

---

[88] Pineda-Madrid, "Traditioning," pp. 221–2.

insular. While some debate the connections among Aquinas, Catholic
social teaching, and liberation theology, others train their sights on
Augustine, the Niebuhr brothers, and Christian "realism." Some debate
the prospects for Christian participation in liberal polities; others worry
about how to proceed from postmodern and postcolonial critiques to the
possibility of real emancipation for the global poor. Some reinterpret the
theological classics for a modern age; others celebrate the originality of
womanist, *mujerista*, or Dalit politics.[89]

There are also generational differences. Younger theologians, like other
so-called Millennials (born from 1981 to 2000), have grown up in pluralistic and shifting religious and moral landscapes, where religious diversity
and moral idiosyncrasy are taken for granted. Many seek ways to reinvigorate rather than deconstruct religious belief and belonging, and to revitalize spiritual and liturgical practices.

When one turns to liberationist movements within North America,
and certainly when one attends to the theologies of Latin America, Asia,
and Africa, the Christian call to affirm common humanity and justice is
clarion. From the standpoint of those who cry out from "the underside
of history" (Frantz Fanon), theoretical debates about whether humanity
and justice can have common meanings are virtually irrelevant. The issue
is, rather, to take seriously their human situations, call the privileged to
account, and seek solutions that empower local agency, community, and
well-being.[90] Deconstruction can and should unmask "colonizing" gener-
alizations about the human reality. But the emancipatory practices rightly

---

[89] See Michelle A. Gonzalez, *Created in God's Image: An Introduction to Feminist Theological Anthropology* (Maryknoll, NY: Orbis Books, 2007), pp. 96–103. Gonzalez opposes the search for "commonality" by white Euro-American women. (In fact, not all Latina women embrace the designation *mujerista*.) Gonzalez follows Jeanette Rodriguez in posing the alternative question, "'What is that we can all stand behind?'" Ibid., p. 102. I agree that this is the right question.

[90] See Linda Martin Alcoff and Eduardo Mendieta (eds.), *Thinking from the Underside of History: Enrique Dussel's Philosophy of Liberation* (Oxford: Rowman & Littlefield, 2000). The contribu-tors advance the reconstruction of global ethical understanding and action, especially a prefer-ential option for the poor, after absorbing the impact of postmodern and postcolonial critique of Eurocentric "universality." In their introduction the editors state, "Dussel insists that our primary concern must be nothing less than the ongoing global genocide. An estimated 20 million persons die each year from starvation and malnutrition perpetrated by the new world order of global capitalism." The philosophical result is an approach to common morality and politics that takes seriously differences in experiences and starting points, and builds common ground from dialogue among local realities. "Dussel calls such an approach, which revises universality by combining it with a recognition of irreducible difference, a 'diversality.'" Ibid., p. 2.

demanded by those newly claiming their voices require that utopias be envisioned and cross-cultural bridges be built.[91]

These gestures toward the complicated background of our enterprise are overly broad, partial, and in obvious ways simplistic. Still, they are sufficient to illustrate the daunting complexity of any attempt to reconnect ethics, scripture, and theology and to make a case for moral common ground and a hopeful, transformative Christian global politics. To ground ethics in a religious tradition is to give it concreteness and particularity, to engage the imagination with specific formative narratives, and to form the agent in coherent practices. At the same time, it is important to insist that the normative content of ethics is in important ways shared. Christians can and must join with members of many moral, religious, and cultural traditions to relieve human suffering, enable human agency, and build just institutions. It is not enough that local practices stay vibrant, as though universal commitments could be effective while abstract. The kind of universality that is dialectical and hybrid also depends on real practices of interconnection and recognition, in the sorts of mediating structures and institutions that have proliferated in the age of modern communication.[92]

A public Christian theology today must work in the practical spaces linking church and polis in and through the multiple identities and activities of its members, local, midlevel, and global. The interaction of theology, ethics, and politics in these practical spaces likewise transforms theology. True understanding of God and of humanity before God may inform practice before it is recognized theologically; critical practices motivate the revision of theological claims. In fact, changing global patterns of social interaction and the liberation movements they have birthed are challenging Christian beliefs and institutions in a way that theology has yet to absorb fully.

The next chapter, on the biblical creation narratives, will confront in more depth the reality of evil in the world, asking why it has such a strong hold on human nature and how its grip can be loosened. It will propose that the creation stories look forward to redemption as renewed relationships among God and human beings, beginning a trajectory of salvation that is realized within the history of Israel and continued in the ministry of Jesus.

---

[91] Wonhee Anne Joh, *Heart of the Cross: A Postcolonial Christology* (Louisville, KY: Westminster John Knox Press, 2006), p. 13.
[92] Robert J. Schreiter, *The New Catholicity: Theology between the Global and the Local* (Maryknoll, NY: Orbis Books, 1997), pp. 108–10; see also pp. 74–81 on hybri

A public Christian theology today must work in the practical spaces linking church and polis in and through the multiple identities and activities of its members, local, midlevel, and global. The interaction of theology, ethics, and politics in these practical spaces likewise transforms theology. True understanding of God and of humanity before God may inform practice before it is recognized theologically; critical practices motivate the revision of theological claims.

The next chapter, on the biblical creation narratives, will confront more fully the reality of evil in the world, asking why it has such a strong hold on human nature and how its grip can be loosened. It will propose that the creation stories look forward to redemption as renewed relationships among God and human beings, beginning a trajectory of salvation that is realized within the history of Israel, and continued in the ministry of Jesus.

CHAPTER 2

Creation and evil

The biblical story of creation is poetic: it celebrates the beauty of the natural universe and of humanity's place within it. Simultaneously, it centers the human gaze on a divine Creator. God, not human beings, is the
unifying center. The poetry and theology of creation place human existence against the magnificent horizon of God's sovereignty, glory, goodness, and justice. Creation places humans within an array of other beings
who exist prior to humanity, who do not exist only to serve humanity,
and who are, in God's word, "good." It shows God to be interactive with
creation. God empowers the oceans and the earth to "bring forth" other
creatures. God permits the needs of the first human being to inspire the
creation of a second and works with the first's own body to fashion a
companion. God continues to speak with humans and care for humans
even after they have rejected the life-giving message of previous divine
words. The God of the first two chapters of Genesis is an immanent God,
an active God, a provident God, a God who is near, even while mysterious and awesome. God's enfolding power, shared creativity, and gracious
blessing nourish a vibrant resonance among all that exists and God's own
life, a unity in which every unique and varied creature delights in common praise of God.

Nevertheless, the biblical creation narratives (Gen. 1 and 2) form a
unity with the story of "the fall" (Gen. 3). In other words, already within
the paradigmatic biblical account, evil and suffering mark the glorious
God-inhabited world. In Genesis, evil comes upon creation, not as an
inherent flaw, but as a disastrous interruption for which humans bear

Parts of this chapter are based on the following works: "Creation and Ethics," in Gilbert Meilaender
and William Werpehowski (eds.), *The Oxford Handbook of Theological Ethics* (Oxford University
Press, 2005), pp. 7–24; "Embodying God's Image: Created, Broken, and Redeemed," in William
Schweiker, Michael A. Johnson, and Kevin Jung (eds.), *Humanity Before God: Contemporary
Faces of Jewish, Christian, and Islamic Ethics* (Minneapolis: Augsburg Fortress, 2006), pp. 55–77;
"Nature, Change, and Justice," in Cabell King and David Albertson (eds.), *Without Nature? A New
Condition for Theology* (New York: Fordham University Press, 2009), pp. 282–303.

responsibility. Seen from the standpoint of the pervasive existential reality of evil, the narratives and theology of creation judge evil to be non-normative and non-necessary, as contrary to God's will, as resistible, and as ultimately defeated by God's saving action. And, as we shall see, Genesis itself provides a response to evil that is not an explanation. The answer of Genesis is to project the formation of right relationships along a trajectory of history and hope, leading to covenant and new creation.

When the first three chapters are read as part of the entire book of Genesis and linked to the Pentateuch, creation becomes an integral component of the story of salvation focused through Abraham and Moses, to be carried forward, according to Christian faith, in Jesus Christ. "Creation," from the standpoint of faith traditions, is not some prehistoric event that constitutes a temporal prelude to the human history of sin and redemption. Creation is not "over," in the past, but a continuing reality in the present and for the future. Creation speaks to humanity's entire existence before God. It is one symbolic strand in a multilayered narrative of human blessedness, suffering, guilt, and hope, a narrative to which creation, redemption, church, and moral transformation afford interdependent points of entry. Each of these will provide subject matter for chapters of this book, beginning with creation later in the present chapter. However, before delving into the positive resources of creation theology, I want to confront one intransigent reality that underlies the potency and power of the creation narratives: evil and the suffering evil causes.

At face value, the narratives and theology of "creation" are about divinely bestowed goodness, blessing, and calling. The practical human situations to which creation replies are strife, oppression, and pain. Biblical accounts of creation function precisely to remind us that even radical evil is not ultimate. They urge us to protect, sustain, and restore all the good that evil wrecks. These accounts assure us that God is greater than evil, that God's presence persists despite evil, that created beings are not doomed to evil, and that our battle against evil will eventually pay off.

Historically, the Genesis creation stories reflect a search for solace and solutions in a time of suffering for the people of Israel. Following the conquest of Jerusalem and the destruction of the Temple by the Babylonians in 597 BCE, the nationhood of Israel and its identity as God's chosen people were called into question. The two versions of creation in Genesis 1 and 2 originated at different periods of Israel's history (probably in the sixth and tenth centuries BCE, respectively). Though the two stories should not be conflated, they may be seen as deliberately juxtaposed and complementary. Common to the situation of many in the twenty-first century and to Israel at the time of the Priestly author is the experience of devastating loss and suffering. Evil brings anguished questioning of divine justice, God's plan for history, and the possibility of salvation from overwhelming adversity and guilt. The communities addressed by the Priestly author search for ways not only to reconstitute the people around new rituals and institutions, but also to vindicate divine purposes behind historic events and to encourage hope of deliverance. Then and now, the creation stories are not just a celebration of life. Though they do affirm that life and all that exists are the objects of divine valuation and care, they also confront, lament, judge, and resist existential evil. This is not to avoid either the fact that the bible as a whole presents an ambivalent God who is capable of violence or the fact that evil is often not resisted successfully. These problems will be given more attention later, especially as intruding on the stories of Hagar and Job.

The purpose of this chapter is to show that the biblical creation narratives display the dynamics of evil and point the way to God's redemption. The Hebrew Bible (Christian Old Testament) has thereby integrity of its own and not only as a "prelude" to redemption in Christ. Christian theology has also interpreted creation to back affirmations about God that develop in response to alternatives that threaten the coherence of evolving Christian orthodoxy. One outstanding example is the doctrine of *creatio ex nihilo*, which combated the encroaching dualism of ancient cosmologies depicting the divine ordering of a preexistent formless matter or envisioned the contest of plural deities in authority over different spheres. As formulated by Irenaeus, Tertullian, and Augustine there is one omnipotent Creator, "maker of all things seen and unseen" (Nicaea), whose goodness is manifest in the goodness of the entire creation.[1] In these authors, the doctrine of creation is formulated in the light of christology and in light of redemption from evil in Jesus Christ. In fact, second- and third-century attempts to formulate creedal confessions of Christian faith involved refinements of belief in creation that aimed to safeguard the reality of the temporal world as distinct from God, as dependent on God,

---

[1] See Gerhard May, *Creatio Ex Nihilo: The Doctrine of 'Creation out of Nothing' in Early Christian Thought*, trans. A. S. Worrall (Edinburgh: T & T Clark, 1994); Colin Gunton (ed.), *The Doctrine of Creation: Essays in Dogmatics, History and Philosophy* (Edinburgh: T & T Clark, 1997); David B. Burrell, Carlo Cogliati, Janet M. Soskice, and William R. Stoeger (eds.), *Creation and the God of Abraham* (Cambridge University Press, 2010); and Brian D. Robinette, "The Difference Nothing Makes: *Creatio ex nihilo*, Resurrection, and Divine Gratuity," *Theological Studies*, 72 (2011), pp. 525–57.

as having both a beginning and an end, as nevertheless not only good but related to the triune life of God, and as an arena of divine action and divine–human interaction.[2]

Rather than tracing the theological history of the doctrine of creation, my current program is to probe Genesis 1–3 in relation to some historical-critical proposals about circumstances of the narratives' composition and explore their interplay with other texts in the canon, mindful of existential, moral, and political problems that challenge our appreciation of creation's goodness and our expectation of evil's ultimate defeat. An important point is that the creation trajectory within the Hebrew Bible itself already refers to God's redeeming action in history.

The proportions of evil in our own time hardly need enumeration. No one escapes life without suffering physical pain and personal loss; death is an ultimate, certain, and terrifying prospect that all must confront. Yet even more impressive is the unprecedented magnitude of global injustice, whether the structurally embedded suffering of the majority that lives on less than two dollars a day (more than 3 billion people) or the directly inflicted suffering of those who are raped, tortured, and murdered in ethnic, religious, and military conflicts. Though science and technology bring life-enhancing marvels to the self-absorbed few, the miserable majority struggles against death-dealing violence, selfishness, and apathy. War, genocide, torture, illegal incarceration and execution, human trafficking, domestic abuse of women and children, and commercial exploitation of the natural environment all come readily to mind. More than one-third of the world's population (2 billion people) live in failed or failing states – countries where the state deprives them of basic rights and access to necessary goods, and sometimes engages in mortal violence against its own citizens.[3]

Under discussion here is not the numeric, historical, or geographic extent of evil and suffering or the naming of all types of affliction. Rather, I want to consider some of the dynamics by which humanly caused evil takes hold, persists, and grows. Natural disasters, in the increasingly rare

[2] Robert W. Jenson, "Aspects of a Doctrine of Creation," in Gunton (ed.), *The Doctrine of Creation*, pp. 17–28.
[3] "Failed States Index 2010," published by Foreign Policy and the Fund for Peace, Foreign Policy, March 31, 2011, www.foreignpolicy.com/articles/2010/06/21/the_failed_states_index_2010 (accessed March 31, 2011).

event that they are not exacerbated by human activity, constitute a problem for "theodicy," a point to which we shall return later. However, I maintain that the primary and most pervasive cause of radical suffering is humanly caused evil. Human betrayal of God's purposes, resulting in personal violence and structural injustice, is the focus of the Hebrew prophets and the authors and editors of the biblical stories of creation, the exodus from Egypt, and the rise and fall of the monarchy. The heart of the theological problem of evil is the *moral* dimension, a dimension with huge religious significance. Our relations to one another reflect and embody our relation to God. The challenge the moral problem of evil presents is conversion, transformation, and change, both personal and social. But does a "realistic" appraisal of the human situation demand stoicism, nihilism, or despair rather than hope?

The bible and Christian theology can provide a positive, hopeful response to evil, consisting in divinely empowered action to change relationships. Before validating this claim by an analysis of Genesis and creation theology, it is important to gain more insight into the human situations to which this response is addressed. How do human relations go wrong? What is the corporate nature of evil? How does individual evil interact with corporate identities and social structures?

These are certainly not new questions; they are addressed by ancient philosophers such as Plato and the Stoics. They must be reconsidered under conditions of human suffering that change in every age, yet remain discouragingly familiar. In 1932, Albert Einstein wrote to Sigmund Freud soliciting wise counsel on an "insistent" problem: "Is there any way of delivering mankind from the menace of war?"[4] Einstein opines that an international governing body – by whose decisions each nation would voluntarily abide – would be the obvious solution. However, he also remarks on the exceeding ease with which a "small clique" of greedy power-holders "bend the will of the majority" to favor war – and enthusiastically sacrifice their lives – even though war does not serve the majority's interests. Mentioning the inadequacy of his own insight into "the dark places of human will and feeling," as well as the evident "impotence" of professional statesmen to deal with the problem, Einstein appeals to Freud as an expert on human psychology. "Is it possible to control man's mental

---

[4] "Albert Einstein and Sigmund Freud: Why Are There Wars?" in Amélie Oksenberg Rorty (ed.), *The Many Faces of Evil: Historical Perspectives* (London: Routledge, 2001), pp. 253–64. Originally published in *The Standard Edition of the Complete Psychological Works of Sigmund Freud*, vol. 22 (London: Hogarth Press and Institute of Psycho-analysis, 1975).

evolution so as to make him proof against the psychoses of hate and destructiveness?"

Freud is not very reassuring. In his view, not only war but states, governments, and indeed all social relations develop out of the "original" human state in which humans, like other animals, dominate by force or violence. Might makes right, though muscular strength was in our evolutionary past soon supplanted by tools and superior intelligence. In Freud's view, it remains true that the rule of law is simply "the might of a community." "Laws are made for and by the ruling members," and the ruling class subjugates the less strong – including the vanquished, slaves, women, and children. Of course, changes in the balance of power may occur, since the "oppressed members" of any group are constantly agitating for leverage, sometimes managing to impose their own will by force.

Domination and aggression are not the only motivators Freud discerns in human relationships. In addition to the "instinct for hatred and aggression," he identifies an instinct "to preserve and unite." However, the so-called death instinct and erotic instinct are usually mixed together in any human action. In his view it is the task of culture or civilization to enhance the erotic impulse, altruism, and "love of neighbor." But the complete subjugation of baser instincts is regarded by Freud as "Utopian."

From a twenty-first-century philosophical and practical perspective, there are limits to the terms of this analysis. Freud does not recognize the potential of fellow feeling to work in favor of collective violence, a major cause of war. He separates the emotions or "instinct" from reason (reflecting Kant), rather than seeing how they are interdependent. He does appreciate the (utilitarian) role of religion in fostering concern for the other and peaceful coexistence, but does not offer any philosophical or theological basis for maintaining that altruism and peace are demanded by "reason" and morality. In other words, Freud does not answer why might *should* not make right or why it *would* be a good thing to move persons and groups away from the motive of self-interest and toward justice as "equality" or "inclusion." At the same time, both Einstein and Freud take as their point of departure a very important human problem: the proclivity to violence and the apparent impotence of "moral" ideals to reduce violence, whether personal or social.

It must be conceded that, speaking in purely factual terms, there is a "natural" human disposition to evil as well as to good. This is quite obvious whether we consider history or the world presently around us. Competition, violence, and destruction are part of the human condition. Augustine rightly named the *libido dominandi* (the lust to dominate or rule) as the root of social evil, a root whose tentacles grip every human heart.[5]

The contemporary human sciences, especially sociobiology and evolutionary psychology, help shed explanatory light on the dismal reality of evil as a fact of human life. Despite a tendency to explain human nature in reductionist terms, evolutionary sciences can offer the ethicist greater understanding of the fact that humans display a great and complex variety of traits and behaviors. A significant proportion of human traits evolved because they were supportive of the goals of reproduction and survival. Yet they are still evolving in interaction with our environment, including the social networks and institutions that humans have designed. The given and the chosen are inextricable and mutually interdependent parts of human nature. Together, they explain human existence as we know it and indicate opportunities for change.

To generalize, evolutionary psychology explains certain basic tendencies in human behavior in terms of the natural selection of biologically and genetically grounded (not necessarily determined) traits that enabled humans to solve adaptive problems faced by our hunter-gatherer ancestors.[6] For the great majority of our history, humans have existed in small nomadic bands, foraging for food. Forming protective alliances, hoarding resources, and taking aggressive action against outsiders provided evolutionary advantages. Humanity's evolutionary past provides us with certain species-typical bodily components, needs, and capacities; cognitive capabilities; emotional and psychological ranges and responses; and capacities and desires for social interaction and connection.

The moral agency characteristic of and unique to humans takes shape on the basis of increasingly complex cognitive and emotional capacities, as well as on the basis of goals and inclinations that, as Freud already saw, will inevitably conflict with one another.[7] Moral agency is grounded on an inclination of humans to seek out social membership and to depend on networks of reciprocal cooperation and commitment, but reciprocity

[5] Augustine, *The City of God*, trans. Marcus Dods (New York: Random House, 1950), book I, preface, p. 3.
[6] James Waller, *Becoming Evil: How Ordinary People Commit Genocide and Mass Killing* (Oxford: Oxford University Press, 2002), pp. 145–9. Waller cites as his key sources on evolutionary psychology two "pioneers" in the field: psychologist Leda Cosmides and anthropologist John Tooby, both at the University of California at Santa Barbara (p. 145). For present purposes, I am presenting this field of research very schematically. For an extensive treatment in relation to religion and ethics, see Stephen J. Pope, *Human Evolution and Christian Ethics*, New Studies in Christian Ethics (Cambridge University Press, 2007).
[7] Pope, *Human Evolution and Christian Ethics*, pp. 143, 262.

is selective.[8] In fact, reciprocity can work to increase rather than diminish the innate human drive to dominate and control, by validating, magnifying, and collectivizing it. Meanwhile, the institutions through which individual agency is organized and coordinated can lessen individual accountability while magnifying the effects of many concerted individual choices. Humans "naturally" reconcile evolved inclinations to engage in pro-social behavior with other human inclinations to behave selfishly and aggressively. They often do this by forming groups that promote self-interest via intra-group cohesion and dominance of outsiders. This is not the only type of moral behavior that is natural to humans and societies, but it is a very familiar one.

Reinhold Niebuhr identified this tendency of group behavior as "collective egotism."[9] By dedicating oneself to the ideology and agenda of a group, one can align one's fragile and finite self with a transcendent cause and, in the name of that cause, seek power and prerogatives, in effect overcoming anxiety about one's own finitude. Groups and their elites play on this tendency to conscript the loyalty of individuals to serve the aims of the larger group and to protect the authority and interests of elite control. In Niebuhr's view, this whole process is a symptom of sin in the world, and the cause of injustice and violence. To call a social pattern sinful, of course, is also to deem it non-normative and to admonish us to moral responsibility. Despite the determinism of some sociobiology, humans are not fated to act always for reasons that are primarily selfish. Nature may provide parameters and conditions of our freedom, but freedom is part of nature nonetheless. Indeed, Niebuhr himself envisioned the potential of societies to develop not only "collective egotism" but "structures of brotherhood," a side of his thought for which he does not receive enough credit.[10]

In his treatment of the social factors that help marshal human behavior around evil and genocide, James Waller lights specific paths to change, and does so more confidently than Augustine, Freud, or Niebuhr. Waller's first contribution is the use of social and evolutionary psychology to clarify the origin of the social dynamic that leads to evil as destructive social

---

[8] Ibid., pp. 150–1, 251–3.

[9] Niebuhr, *Moral Man and Immoral Society*; and *The Nature and Destiny of Man*, vol. 1: *Human Nature* (New York: Charles Scribner's Sons, 1941), pp. 218–19.

[10] See Reinhold Niebuhr, *The Nature and Destiny of Man*, vol. 1: *Human Nature* (Louisville, KY: Westminster John Knox Press, 1996), p. 212, on collective egotism; and *The Nature and Destiny of Man*, vol. 2: *Human Destiny* (Louisville, KY: Westminster John Knox Press, 1996), pp. 95, 248–9, on the spirit and structures of brotherhood; and p. 308, n. 10 on politics as fashioning "the brotherhood of the Kingdom of God."

violence, its frequency, and the difficulty of countering it. His second contribution is to understand the steps necessary to reverse the process.

According to Waller, three evolved tendencies of human nature are conducive to a human "capacity for extraordinary evil – ethnocentrism, xenophobia and the desire for social dominance."[11] These are inclinations that our nature has handed us – not determinants of moral outcomes. However – and here it is salutary to keep in mind Niebuhr's "collective egotism" – there is a powerful impetus for groups to rationalize such behavior as good, necessary, and fair, and for individuals to seek belonging in groups that help aggrandize their own claims. This works especially well when individuals or groups feel under threat, real or perceived. Of course, it is in the interests of both individuals and groups to exaggerate threat in order to justify aggression and the expropriation of more goods.

Waller argues that the likelihood of enacting extraordinary violence is much greater when personal self-interest or advancement is involved, when cultural belief systems encourage obedience to authority and a high degree of ideological commitment, and when a "culture of cruelty" is created in the immediate social context. A culture of cruelty requires and builds on socialization to engage in violence against others, often via professional roles. This socialization is accomplished by means of escalating commitments to participate in violence, ritual conduct legitimizing violence or the roles entailing it, and the repression of individual conscience. Cruelty is bolstered by group bonds that diffuse responsibility, deindividuate agency, and enforce conformity to peer pressure, and by the merger of role and person in such a way that an individual agent comes to believe that acting morally consists in fidelity to one's role, often one's professional role. Finally, extraordinary violence depends on us–them thinking, that is, seeing adversaries as guilty and deserving of persecution, as nonhuman, or as both.[12]

Waller exposes readers to several horrifying first-person accounts of instances of genocide and murder, taken from Nazi death camps, Vietnam, Cambodia, East Timor, Kosovo, Srebrenica, Rwanda, and Guatemala. He shows that these crimes were not committed by psychopaths or monsters but by ordinary people for whom evolutionary, personal, and social factors came together in a perfect storm to create a capacity, indeed an eagerness, to do extraordinary evil. This kind of evil is not even rare. Though most societies do not in fact commit genocide, Waller reminds us that "buried in the midst of all our progress in the twentieth century are well

---

[11] Waller, *Becoming Evil*, p. 153.   [12] Ibid., p. 20.

over 100 million persons who met a violent death at the hands of their fellow human beings. That is more than five times the number from the nineteenth century and more than ten times the number from the eighteenth century."[13] It is not hard to imagine that hundreds of millions more have seen early deaths due to the institutionalized violence of poverty; lack of access to food, clean water, and sanitary living conditions; and minimal health care.

Sometimes monstrous social evil is orchestrated through direct tactics of group chauvinism, ideologies of past victimization, fearmongering, mass hysteria, and stigmatization or "scapegoating" of outsiders, or weak insiders, as demonic or subhuman.[14] Twentieth- and twenty-first-century genocides provide ample evidence of the capacity of the few to mobilize the many for direct participation in violence and killing, even face-to-face torture and killing of neighbors, friends, and family members. Modern, technologically advanced societies also provide opportunities for mass killing in more detached modes. As a journalist witnessing the 1961 trial in Jerusalem of the Nazi murderer Adolf Eichmann, Hannah Arendt arrived at her insight into the "fearsome, word-and-thought-defying *banality of evil*."[15] With this phrase, Arendt answers the question of how an apparently "decent" and "respectable" man like Eichmann, a student of Kant and a man in all ways devoted to his duty and the law, could have been conscripted into a system perpetrating hideous crimes. Of course, this question applies equally well not only to the millions of "ordinary" Germans who either cooperated with or tolerated systematic murder, but also to the millions of people today who facilitate global structures enabling death and destruction, or simply refrain from making interference a personal priority.

Evil can be "banal" to the extent that evil agency is encrypted in socialization processes that encourage individuals in unreflective obedience to the "ordinary" and "expected." Arendt's and Waller's analyses agree on how useful the professionalization and routinization of roles, and the subordination of conscience to role conformity, are to the mass perpetration

[13] Ibid., p. x.
[14] René Girard elucidates one such type of dynamic; see his *Violence and the Sacred*, trans. Patrick Gregory (Baltimore: Johns Hopkins University Press, 1977).
[15] Hannah Arendt, *Eichmann in Jerusalem: A Report on the Banality of Evil*, rev. edn. (New York: Penguin Books, 1994), p. 252; emphasis in original. For the development of Arendt's analysis, see Peg Birmingham, "Holes of Oblivion: The Banality of Radical Evil," *Hypatia*, 18/1 (Winter 2003), pp. 80–103. Birmingham also suggests, following leads in Arendt, that friendship may be a remedy for radical evil. This is similar to my proposal that the creation stories and other biblical resources offer relationships to God and others as responses to evil.

of evil. People who do not reflect on the ultimate consequences of quo-
tidian duties and routines and avoid introspection easily stifle the self's
incipient protest. At the extreme, Eichmann seemed to look only for a
"script" to follow, whether as an official of the Third Reich, a compliant
"model" defendant, or a condemned man bidding a platitudinous farewell in the incongruous phrases of funeral oratory.

For extraordinary evil, direct or indirect, socialization maneuvers
have to be strong and well executed. Yet ordinary social evil is enabled
in a similar if less coercive way. The "professions" and "discourses" of science, business, academia, and even religion involve participants in strategies that rationalize, ritualize, and disguise self-interested practices that
are detrimental to other persons, other groups, and the common good.
Sometimes religious ideologies and fanaticism perpetrate violence as a
direct effort to conquer and exterminate. But even "mainstream" and
"responsible" churches, believers, and theologians often focus their attention only on problems that seem to pose direct threats to themselves and
their communities. This makes us "guilty bystanders," in the phrase of
social psychologist Ervin Staub, a child Holocaust survivor. A "bystander"
to social evil is an individual – or a collection or organization of individuals – who witnesses what is happening, but remains passive. "This passivity encourages perpetrators."[16]

Arendt's report on the Eichmann trial evoked an unanticipated level
of Jewish protest.[17] Resistance to her analysis of Eichmann's "banality"
focused on two sticking points. First, moral monstrosity, not banality,
is required to account for evil perceived by its victims to be not only
extraordinary, but even exceptional and unique. Second, it is necessary
to attribute full moral intention and responsibility to the perpetrators in
order to do justice to the magnitude of their guilt. But the Eichmann
story reminds us that the self's identity, his or her behaviors, and the
shaping social practices of which they form a part, are interdependent.
Moral responsibility does not require (nor can it attain) a pristine, free,
existentialist choice that is fully "self"-determined. Rather, selves – moral
selves – are constituted interactively by personal agency and personal history, as well as by the relationships, communities, and structures in which
the self is embedded. Moral freedom consists in exercising responsibility for the good within these structures. Social conditions can influence

[16] Ervin Staub, *The Psychology of Good and Evil: Why Children, Adults, and Groups Help and Harm
Others* (Cambridge University Press, 2003), p. 4.
[17] See Jerome Kohn, Introduction to Hannah Arendt, *Responsibility and Judgment*, ed., Jerome
Kohn (New York: Schocken Books, 2003), pp. xi–xv.

the likelihood of an "anti-social" or "pro-social" decision. They either increase the likelihood of aggression and conflict or encourage affiliative and reconciliatory behaviors,[18] guiding and sometimes even overriding the individual's contextual judgment. Aggression or altruism is more than a simple moral "choice."

As feared by Arendt's critics, this kind of analysis does in fact lead to the conclusion that some moral agents are more responsible for their actions – good or bad – than others. In fact, Arendt's own solution to the Eichmann problem – to "think for oneself," to resist received wisdom in favor of one's own moral sense – does not do full justice to the implications of her report on Eichmann. The self and its thinking can never, after all, completely free themselves from their formative contexts. Agents have differing abilities and opportunities to grasp the tools of critical intro-spection and to accept, control, or resist the biological and social condi-tions of their identity. While at first this may seem to undermine the very idea of moral responsibility, it really sets responsibility in perspective and allows a more effective antidote to irresponsibility. It makes responsibility a collective project as well as a personal one. The realization that agency is always socially contextualized and at least in part socially constituted urges upon both individuals and communities the moral obligation to create life-giving practices in which all share. These include practices of accountability, mutual responsibility, equitable distribution of social ben-efits and burdens, and not least of all dialogic critical inquiry directed at both self and *polis*. Such practices must be concrete, consistent, and mor-ally formative in order to bring social behavior under the aegis of reliable and just ideals.

It is not necessarily true, then, that groups behave less morally than individuals. Sometimes groups are catalysts for social justice and social change, and may even oppose destructive collective behavior. Waller takes issue with part of Reinhold Niebuhr's analysis on this point.[19] True, Niebuhr identifies a dynamic of group solidarity often found when groups adopt oppressive or violent policies and actions. Groups can bind people together around shared grievances and lead them to engage in more extreme behavior than they would as individuals. Yet the same bonding and concerted strength occur when groups form identity around coopera-tive or humanitarian aims.[20]

---

[18] Pope, *Human Evolution and Christian Ethics*, p. 144.
[19] Waller, *Becoming Evil*, pp. 33–5. [20] Ibid., p. 35.

The analyses of James Waller, Stephen Pope, and Ervin Staub confirm those of Einstein and Freud. We as humans are equipped "naturally" – by genes and by many other dimensions of our history – for social behavior that can be either inclusive and cooperative or aggressive and discriminatory. Yet, despite the apparent odds in favor of the latter, we need not despair. On one hand, Einstein sees the dual motivations of the human spirit as an "enigma," while Freud rather pessimistically calls for "reason" and "culture" to restrain instincts. Waller, on the other hand, uses social science in a way that would support Niebuhr's hope for greater "structures of brotherhood." Waller appreciates that cultures work precisely to channel and validate instincts and that "rationality" does not operate apart from social practices and institutions that socialize both reason and emotions to favor certain ends. Yet Waller does not accept that aggressive instincts will necessarily become dominant over cooperation and altruism.

By understanding the conditions that make humans more likely to exhibit fear, aggression, and dominance, we will learn how to inspire compassion, cooperation, and concern for those beyond our sphere of self-interest. In Pope's words, "We have the capacity to act in ways that transcend what accords with our fitness interests."[21] We are equipped naturally (by evolution) with dispositions toward love of kin, kin altruism, reciprocal altruism, and enduring reciprocal alliances in the form of friendships and civic and political membership. Our capacities for empathy and our contextual freedom permit us to encourage and enhance such alliances and even extend them.

The evolved human ability to respond with empathic identification to the feelings and needs of those to whom our own self-interest is bound (kin and allies) is the basis of our ability to recognize the needs and feelings of everyone as part of a moral program of universal dignity and equality. I concur with Staub that ideologies and worldviews can be constructive as well as destructive, enabling followers to assume risk for those outside the group and work together "for a shared cause."[22] Individuals, organizations, and communities, including religious communities, are capable of "active bystandership."

The central moral challenge posed by the reality of evil is to extend human beings' naturally self-serving emotions and preferences to non-kin, non-members, "strangers," and even "enemies," and even when it does not serve their immediate success strategy or that of their group. This

---

[21] Pope, *Human Evolution and Christian Ethics*, p. 263.
[22] Staub, *Psychology of Good and Evil*, p. 547.

is precisely the function of religious narratives, stories, and practices oriented around maxims such as "All are made in the image of God," "Love your neighbor as yourself," or "Do unto others as you would have others do unto you." Though the absolute claims of religions can be co-opted for violent ends, I submit that the heart of true religiosity, as demonstrated in all the major world religions, is humility and gratitude before God; unity of all in the name of God; and, in moral terms, mutual forbearance, a spirit of reconciliation, inclusive cooperation, and compassionate action against suffering.

GENESIS CREATION NARRATIVES

Christian faith puts love and mercy at the center of the narrative of redemption culminating in Jesus Christ. Readers of the bible and theologians alike often see creation as mere background to the story of salvation carried forward by Abraham, Moses, Exodus, Sinai, and Jesus. They understand God's liberation of Abraham's descendants and God's covenant at Sinai as signs of saving love. A sort of prelude to God's action in history, creation is but the first chapter of a human career that went horribly wrong with the "fall." Theologians like Aquinas, Luther, and Calvin understand creation to have established a certain ordering of human life and of nature in general that continues to guide ethics and politics. Yet the real concern of Christian faith is subsequent actions of the covenanting God to redeem God's people from the calamity by which, as Calvin put it, we are no longer able to see in creation the "mirror" of God's glory.[23]

To so view creation is to misunderstand its scope and to short-circuit the redemptive significance of Genesis. There has been a recent move by biblical theologians to reconnect creation theology to salvation history, and even to see salvation in terms of God's continuing creative action. Here again, ethical practices and aims influence theological perspectives and priorities. The creation texts are works of moral and religious imagination that shape a communal ethos.[24] Interest in creation is strong among scholars committed to ecology and to dialogue among the world's religions. But sometimes ethical categories, salutary in themselves, have left creation in the shadows.

[23] John Calvin, *Institutes of the Christian Religion*, vol. 1, trans. Henry Beveridge (Grand Rapids, MI: Eerdmans, 1981), book I.V.1–4.
[24] See William P. Brown, *The Ethos of the Cosmos: The Genesis of Moral Imagination in the Bible* (Grand Rapids, MI: Eerdmans, 1999).

In fact, the twentieth-century marginalization of creation by influential Europeans such as Gerhard von Rad and Karl Barth was itself ethically inspired. Despite Barth's prima facie claim that theology is simply a response to God's unilateral self-revelation, neo-orthodoxy was motivated in no small part by the need to reinvigorate the gospel's countercultural edge. Midcentury theologies of election and of God's historical command to the church were part of a struggle against the so-called theology of creation devised by National Socialism to legitimize its ideology.[25] In the 1950s, G. Ernest Wright's *God Who Acts* lifted up God's historical activity as central to the bible, again at the expense of nature and creation. Other factors diminishing attention to creation have been anthropocentrism, existentialism, and liberalism, all of which privilege the human perspective and especially human freedom and choice. More recently, political and liberation theologies have rightly accented oppressive social forces, but neglected the rest of nature and humanity's place within it.[26]

In the past decade or two, many biblical theologians have come to "regard creation as the very foundation upon which all other foundations of biblical faith rest (e.g., election, covenant, salvation, and eschatology)."[27] God's creative presence in the world is as real and dynamic as God's redemption of a people. In fact, the two cannot be separated. Terence Fretheim maintains that the present organization of the biblical canon indicates a distinct theological orientation and judgment, as of at least 500 BCE, and most probably centuries earlier. The bible places creation before exodus and redemption precisely because, from the perspective of Israelite faith, the experience of salvation refers to creation as a basic and integral part.[28] Creation lends depth to redemption and suggests its universal frame of reference.[29]

The biblical creation narratives establish the essential *goodness* of existence (as over against existential suffering and guilt). They portray *relationship* as the divinely modeled form that created goodness takes. Moreover, the creation narratives fill out the substance of good and divinely blessed relationship as mutuality, generosity, and *life-givingness* ("fruitfulness").

[25] See William P. Brown and S. Dean McBride, Jr., Preface to William P. Brown and S. Dean McBride, Jr. (eds.), *God Who Creates: Essays in Honor of W. Sibley Towner* (Grand Rapids, MI: Eerdmans, 2000), pp. xi–xiii; and Terence E. Fretheim, *God and World in the Old Testament: A Relational Theology of Creation* (Nashville: Abingdon Press, 2005), pp. ix–xi.
[26] See Fretheim, *God and World*, pp. ix–x.
[27] Brown and McBride, Preface to *God Who Creates*, p. xiv. For contributions to the literature, see Fretheim, *God and World*, pp. xi–xiv.
[28] Fretheim, *God and World*, pp. xiv–xvi.
[29] Ibid., pp. xiv, xvi.

First, creation is *good*. In the vision of the biblical creation narratives, what exists is made, validated, and blessed by God. This is not a particularly iconoclastic point; familiar to most are the repeated declarations of Genesis 1, "God saw that it was good," culminating in "God saw everything that he had made, and indeed, it was very good" (Gen. 1:31). More interesting to the careful reader are the ways in which this verdict can be complexified. It is useful to compare creation in Genesis with other ancient, more prevalent Near Eastern myths of "creation by combat," like the *Enuma Elish*. The trouble with such myths is that they "ontologize" evil, see it as primordial, and vindicate violence as God's way of dealing with it.[30] The combat myth, probably in a Canaanite (Ugaritic) version, did leave its mark on the biblical narrative (e.g., Job 26:7–14; Ps. 74:12–17, 89:5–14), but in a minority voice. According to the prevailing witness, God creates with remarkable ease, even empowering ("letting") the waters and the earth to share in the process[31] and commissioning all living things to "be fruitful" in their own ways.

It is intriguing, therefore, that the God of Genesis 1 says to humans not only that they should be fruitful, multiply, and fill the earth, but also that they must "subdue" it and, in troublesome wording, "have dominion" over all that lives (Gen. 1:28). Chaos, perhaps not; but is there some hint here of unruliness, of disorder, in the world as originally made, even before the fall? And is there some way to think of a "not yet ordered quality" without pulling that quality into an Augustinian framework, in which the systematic ordering of all things is constitutive of the very meaning of goodness? Catherine Keller notes that chaos precedes the Creator's activity (Gen. 1:2). The Creator's action models creative responsiveness to "chaos" as "uncertainty, unpredictability, turbulence, and complexity."[32] Problematizing "order" in nature harks back to the discussion of evolution and the prospect that nature may be inherently multivalent and multidirectional.

Disorder, the unpredictability of complex interactions, and divergent natural needs and purposes may not be evil in themselves. They may be the necessary conditions of growth and creativity. Yet they do require certain human responses. There will be competitive goods and goals

[30] J. Richard Middleton, *The Liberating Image: The Imago Dei in Genesis 1* (Grand Rapids, MI: Brazos Press, 2005), p. 254. See also J. Richard Middleton, "Created in the Image of a Violent God? The Ethical Problem of the Conquest of Chaos in Biblical Creation Texts," *Interpretation*, 58/4 (October 2004), pp. 341–55.

[31] Middleton, *Liberating Image*, pp. 264–5. See also W. Sibley Towner's review of Middleton's *Liberating Image* in *Interpretation*, 59/4 (October 2005), pp. 408–11.

[32] Catherine Keller, "The Lost Chaos of Creation," *Living Pulpit*, 9:2 (2000), pp. 4–5.

within humans, among humans, and among different forms of life. These cannot always be "harmonized," and perhaps they should not be. Still, humans are called to enhance life and diminish suffering. The command to humans to take responsibility for creation's unsynchronization, even when they are not to blame for it, even in some way to "subdue" it, discloses the nature of "evil" as responsibility's converse. Moral evil is the failure to avoid or minimize the harm that plurality and contingency can cause, to manipulate contingent drives and ends for selfish advantage, and to resolve conflicts through domination of perceived competitors. Genesis does not answer the question of why aspects of creation as humans know it should be liable to causing harm. It does answer the question of the fitting human response, the response that images God.

The Lord permits the first human to name the other creatures, connoting God-given power and authority. In the ancient world and in the Hebrew Bible, names indicate the essential quality of something; to know someone's name is to have (or to be given) power in relation to that person. The naming of the animals by the human suggests a process of understanding, familiarizing, and assuming power as responsibility. Humans within the world are to take responsibility for "every living creature" (a mandate that seems to call for the addition of a "helper" and "partner"; v. 18). Together, human beings, as commissioned by God, are to help *bring beneficent order* to a creation that is not already orderly and harmonious in every way.

This approach does not explain the origin of disorder or the rationale, if any, behind it. It simply accepts that unorderedness and potential conflict do exist, that creation is good nonetheless, and that the goodness of creation includes human responsibility to "subdue" at least some aspects of earthly existence as we are given it. In this frame, "dominion" does not mean destructive or prideful domination, but "ruling" that emulates God's wisdom and care. Because all humans are in God's image, this ruling is democratized to all, not merely to a kingly or royal subset.[33] The purpose of the special role with which God commissions humanity is "rule within the ecosphere in God's manner."[34]

The picture of creation's goodness receives still another nuance from the story of humanity's sequential fabrication by God from preexisting materials. God personally fashions and gives life to each human being.

---

[33] Fretheim, *God and World*, pp. 50–3.
[34] W. Sibley Towner, "Clones of God: Genesis 1:26–28 and the Image of God in the Hebrew Bible," *Interpretation*, 59/4 (October 2005), p. 348.

Yet, at stage one, humanity is determined by its maker to be "not yet good" – a fact expressed by God in view of the human's loneliness. The human needs a suitable kind of "helper" and "partner." Together, God and creature venture an unsuccessful trial of various candidates for the position (Gen. 2:18–20). Although the animals are already "good," none are a good "fit" with the needs and capacities of the human. The search process and eventual creation of the woman as a solution to the man's "not good" solitude reinforce the point that created goodness and responsibility take the form of relationship – between God and the first human, between the two humans together, and finally between the pair and God. And the humans are always envisioned as part of a larger created environment with which they are also in relation and which even constitutes them (humanity derives from "dust of the ground"; Gen. 2:7).

From the beginning, whether in Genesis 1 or 2, God creates in multiples. "In the beginning ... God created the heavens and the earth" (Gen. 1:1; cf. 2:4). And creatures generate their own relationships. All living creatures, and in Genesis 1 even nonliving ones, have a generative relation to successive creations. "Let the waters bring forth swarms of living creatures" (1:20). Among living things, fruitfulness is premised upon multiplicity and relationship within every distinct kind or species. Likewise, the creation of humans is complete and good, as indicated in both Genesis creation stories, when there is more than one of them. The first sexually undifferentiated "earth creature" (*ha-'adam*) (2:5) is soon joined by a partner. The creation of humanity is complete when there is a pair of sexually different humans, a man (*'iss*) and woman (*'issa*) (2:21–4).[35]

Together the female and male are created in the image of God (1:27). Unique among creatures, they disclose in a special way the reality of One who remains "wholly other."[36] The aspect of humanity that constitutes the image is mutual and creative relationship, not intelligence, freedom, or a human soul. Humans, in the image of God, are fulfilled in relationship to others. Humans are essentially social creatures. Together the first pair takes up the commands to "be fruitful" of their own kind and to assume responsibility for fellow humanity and for creatures of other kinds (1:28;

---

[35] The first human is called *ha-'adam* in a play on the word for the earth or ground, from which "it" was taken: *ha-adamah*. After the creation of the second human, distinct words for male and female are employed (*'iss* and *'issa*). See Phyllis Trible, *God and the Rhetoric of Sexuality* (Philadelphia: Fortress Press, 1978), pp. 76–80, 94–105.

[36] For a review of interpretations of the image and of current proposals, see Towner, "Clones of God;" and Janell Johnson, "Between Text and Sermon: Genesis 1:26–28," *Interpretation*, 59/2 (April 2005), pp. 176–9.

2:15, 18). The "complicated responsibility" of humanity, "for and with the Other," and for the earth, "mediates the very presence of God."[37]

The image as personal, relational, and reciprocal is supported by the "let us" rhetoric in Gen. 1:26 (see also 3:22, 11:7). The Priestly author and editor does not, of course, refer ahead to the doctrine of the Trinity. Most scholars agree that the plural divine subject reflects an earlier polytheistic notion of a retinue of divine beings, a "Divine Council," clustered around a heavenly king (see also 1 Kings 22:19–23; Job 1:16, 2:1; Ps. 82, 89: 5–7; Isa. 6:1–8; and Jer. 23:18). Yet this plurality can be recaptured within monotheistic faith as implying that "whatever it is in human beings that mirrors God mirrors the divine realm as a whole."[38]

Undeniably, the nature of divine relations with humanity is in the Hebrew Bible a complex matter, even in Genesis. "At times the reader finds a God who is angry, jealous, and a deliverer of death and destruction against those who obstruct the divine plan. At other times, God appears compassionate and forgiving."[39] But the fundamental and overarching role of the creation narrative in the Pentateuch makes it plausible for communities of faith to select its depiction of God as the one that ultimately controls the interpretation of other narratives of divine activity. The ethical and political test elaborated in the first chapter of this book is operative in the discernment process. In Genesis 1 and 2, God does not rule as a despot or as an angry monarch, but with love, life-givingness, and generosity. God even acts as the "servant" of the human image in creation by determining to make for the first human a most suitable partner and permitting the human to test whether the goal has been achieved.[40] The human image of God takes shape in relation to this model. God is mirrored in human dialogue, joint decision making, and active cooperation to create and sustain life.

The image of God in humanity is found in relationship that recognizes the "other" as a suitable partner for companionship and help.[41] The imaginative device of God taking the woman from the man's rib

---

[37] Kristin M. Swenson, "Care and Keeping East of Eden: Gen 4:1–16 in Light of Gen 2–3," *Interpretation*, 60/4 (October 2006), p. 373.
[38] Towner, "Clones of God," 3.
[39] Johnson, "Between Text and Sermon," 1. This complexity will be addressed later in the chapter.
[40] Fretheim, *God and World*, pp. 48–60.
[41] The Hebrew word for "helper" (*'ezer*) should be understood to mean, not a subordinate, but an equal companion, a "suitable counterpart." In fact, the word can even be used to refer to God as the savior of Israel. See Trible, *God and the Rhetoric of Sexuality*, p. 90; and Carol Meyers, *Discovering Eve: Ancient Israelite Women in Context* (Oxford: Oxford University Press, 1988), p. 85.

underscores the unity of two differentiated creatures in a single embodied nature, a one-flesh unity and a *social* unity. Two human beings not joined by "blood ties" or kinship, nor yet in sexual union, nor certainly by the (later) "institution" of marriage, are drawn together as "one." Proclaims the first human in recognizing a counterpart: "This at last is bone of my bones, and flesh of my flesh" (2:23). The first man compares the woman to the animals, after all, not to human males. He recognizes her not specifically as a "woman," but as first and foremost a human being, much better than any other "living creature" to remedy his loneliness (2:18–20).

The second human's creation is a model for human relationships in general, as constituted by a sort of "different sameness." Human beings are irreducibly unique but called to mutuality in one-flesh relationship. They are to be "helpers" and partners for one another. As constitutively different human individuals, they are constitutively destined for fellowship. Their sociality is not merely psychological or spiritual; it has an inherent reference to shared life in the material world. Materiality or physicality is a necessary condition of human personhood. Embodiment is a quality not shared with God, but it is still necessary for humans to "image" God. In Genesis 2, it is specifically their embodiment that distinguishes the woman and man as "different" partners in relationship, and it is their embodiment as "same" that allows mutual recognition (though the story is told from the man's point of view).

The exclamation of the first man, when presented with the first human "other," represents the capacity for fellowship of all human beings, inherent in our embodied connectedness and communicative capacity: "This at last is bone of my bones, flesh of my flesh" (2:23). Karl Barth sees image as our call to "fellow-humanity," to "freedom in fellowship."[42] "God created man in His own image in the fact that He did not create him alone but in this connexion and fellowship," for God, like humanity, "is not solitary," but properly "in connexion and fellowship."[43]

The human body establishes basic needs that society is meant to serve for everyone in every culture. The body also makes it possible to communicate and cooperate with others, and to express our spiritual capacities in art and religious practices. Above all, the human body makes it possible to recognize and acknowledge other human beings as like ourselves, with the same essential needs and vulnerabilities, and as persons with whom we can enter into relationship. Human embodiment and

[42] Karl Barth, *Church Dogmatics* III/4 (Edinburgh: T & T Clark, 1961), p. 117.
[43] Karl Barth, *Church Dogmatics* III/2 (Edinburgh: T &T Clark, 1960), p. 324.

inherent sociality make it possible to name some fundamental and universal goods that every human seeks in cooperation with other humans.
Among the most obvious are food, shelter, and the labor that provides
these; reproduction of the species and the institutions that organize and
socialize reproduction, that is, marriage and family; and political organization that arranges social roles to the mutual benefit of society's members and defines means of access to the basic goods. (The universality of
basic goods will be elaborated in Chapter 7).

The embodied differences of the first two, accentuated by their nakedness, are part of their creation for embrace and partnership. They are not
yet cause for suffering or strife (2:25). "Bone of my bones, flesh of my
flesh" fellowship is the moral ideal or criterion that should structure all
human differences in relationships that image God. From the beginning
of their existence, God is in beneficent relation to humans; so to be in
God's image, humans are to be in similar relations with each other. In
Genesis, the two most fundamental of all embodied social endeavors are
family and work. Each is connected to the creation of the human body
in God's image, because each constitutes a basic form of relationship, in
which bodily needs and capacities bring people together cooperatively, in
joint projects. Together, humans are charged to care for and work with the
rest of creation and to be the parents and educators of future generations.

Though the creation stories deal directly with only two individuals,
these stories implicitly refer "image" to larger communities and society.
The mandates to be fruitful by bearing children and to work project forward to human community, to social identities created through shared
practices. A collective sense of humanity and of the image is conveyed
in the first version by the terms of God's decision to create ("let us make
humankind in our image"; 1:26), by the double use of the plural "them"
to indicate both "humankind" and "image" (1:27), and by God's decision
to "let them have dominion" (1:26). In the second version, the collective is
suggested by the Hebrew word for the first human being ("*ha-'adam*" in
2:7), which can be used either singly or collectively.[44] The collective image
of God in humans begins with the first pair, expands via intergenera-
tional relations, and moves outward to all the forms of collective human
endeavor necessary to sustain human goods and fulfill human potentials.

In Genesis, creation is neither static nor a past event. Creation has a
forward momentum, evident in the command to "subdue the earth" and
in the blessing of fertility (1:28), as well as in the idea that the humans

[44] Towner, "Clones of God," pp. 3–4.

are not only to "keep" or preserve the garden, but also to "till" or culti-
vate it (2:15). Humans are not placed in creation as a completed paradise
for their passive enjoyment, or even for protective conservation. Work, as
endowing human life with purpose and fulfillment and as an activity that
images God's own creating, is a fundamental aspect of human existence.[45]
Throughout the book of Genesis, work on the land, tilling the land, and
reaping the bounty of the land are part of God's promises. As humans create and nurture the next generation, they contribute "procreatively" to the
future of all for which God continues to provide interactively. Procreation
establishes the family and kin groups that carry God's promises forward,
in Abraham, Isaac, and Jacob. The embodied work of procreation, par-
enthood, and contribution to the ongoing life of extended families blesses
humans with their most fundamental and universal experiences of love,
out of which they learn concern for others and the discipline of cultivat-
ing goods and wholes other than or larger than the self.

Two literary devices in Genesis link originally diverse sources. They are
the "generations" formula, which occurs eleven times in Genesis, and the
divine "promises" of blessing, beginning immediately after the creation
of male and female in God's image (1:28), and eventually extended to "all
the families of the earth" through Abraham (12:3).[46] The generations and
promises themes extend the relation and calling of two first *individuals*
into *communal* vocations, linking the creation of humanity with family histories and community, with the well-being of the earth and of the
earth's diverse peoples, concretizing the universality of God's continuing
creation.

Though all creation remains under the active reign of God,[47] creation
is vulnerable to human misdoing. Humans as in God's image must fulfill
a moral mandate. They are to unite differences in fellowship, fulfilling
God's promises through family, social cooperation and work, and productive stewardship of the environment.

THE FALL

Into this dynamic of promise intrudes "the fall," dramatized in Genesis
3. This story is often interpreted as a straightforward narrative of willful

[45] Claus Westermann, *Creation*, trans. John J. Scullion, S.J. (Philadelphia: Fortress Press, 1974),
pp. 80–2.
[46] Thomas W. Mann, " 'All the Families of the Earth': The Theological Unity of Genesis,"
Interpretation, 45/4 (1991), p. 343.
[47] Fretheim, *God and World*, pp. 4–5, 53, 272–3.

ingratitude and disobedience to God. Yet the story of Eve and Adam's expulsion from the garden is actually complex and ambiguous. Feminist scholar Phyllis Trible noted long ago that, just as the creation story has been misconstrued to validate the inferiority of women, so the fall story has been misread to set trouble in paradise on Eve's side of the ledger.[48] In fact, when the woman interacts with the serpent (3:1–5), the man is also present (3:6). Both the active and the passive sinner are equally guilty, and the consequences of their sin bring an ironic reversal. The passive partner in crime will be forced to earn a living with toil and exertion (3:17–19). The active agent will be subject to the uncontrollable pain of childbirth and to the "rule" of the man (3:16).[49]

In addition to the question of relative human guilt and punishment, the narrative of Genesis 3 suggests further perplexing questions. Indeed, the story does not come together in a clear picture of created harmony, willful wrongdoing, and unequivocal guilt and responsibility. Instead, it reflects evil's enigmatic and even absurd quality, as well as the blurry boundaries of moral agency and the ineluctable quality of sin. The story is highly suggestive and rich with layers of psychological and social meaning. No one reading can resolve its contradictions or do justice to its symbolic depth.

One common interpretive mistake is, in my view, to try to explain the origin of evil in terms of some "necessary" aspect of God's good creation. For instance, the humans' liability to sin is sometimes seen as an unavoidable concomitant of human freedom.[50] Such explanations reflect a perceived need to vindicate the Creator's goodness and justice. But Genesis really offers no such explanation, for it does not conceive of the divine ways as in need of justification. I agree with theologian Terrence Tilley that "theodicy is legerdemain." Theodicies attempt unbiblical and unpersuasive "rational" answers, while "the testimonies of scripture and tradition about God and suffering are obscured."[51] The testimony of the creation narratives about evil and suffering is that humans should respond to it in the way the Creator does and should do so in relationship with God. Terence Fretheim wisely entitles his chapter on the fall "Creation at

[48] Trible, *God and the Rhetoric of Sexuality*, pp. 72, 112–14, 126–32.
[49] Ibid.
[50] Even Fretheim makes an uncharacteristic departure from the content of Genesis on this score. He speculates, "For God to have forced compliance to the divine will and not allowed creatures the freedom to fail would have been to deny any genuine relationship"; *God and World*, p. 70.
[51] Terrence W. Tilley, Prologue to Anthony J. Tambasco (ed.), *The Bible on Suffering: Social and Political Implications* (New York: Paulist Press, 2001), p. 1.

Risk: Disrupted, Endangered, Restored (Genesis 3–11)."[52] This title makes two important points.

First, the fall portrays the reality of human sin but does so from the standpoint of the possibility of salvation, not from the standpoint of its ultimate origin and rationale. Second, the fall must be seen in light of the first eleven chapters of Genesis, the "primeval history" (and indeed of the whole Pentateuch). Seen as a whole up to the calling of Abraham (Gen. 12), the narrative does not explain *why* evil exists, so much as examine its dynamics, implying strategies of reform. Evil exists primarily as disruption of relationships; the proper response is to restore those relationships in alignment with God's continuing activity as Creator, Savior, and Sustainer.

Genesis 3 makes it hard to pinpoint the precise origin or "first moment" of moral evil. It also makes it hard to see the sin of the first humans as truly "original" or as an entirely "free" choice. The role of the serpent is especially puzzling. Why does the serpent suggest to the woman that the fruit of the tree in the middle of the garden would be good to eat (3:1–4), even though God has apparently forbidden it (2:9, 2:17), all creatures are "good," and "sin" has not yet occurred?[53] Genesis 1 already intimates that creation is not "naturally" orderly in every respect – hence humans are to subdue, name, and exercise dominion over destructive varieties of disorder. But the serpent, described as "crafty" (3:1), seems bent on inducing in the woman a process of rationalization or self-deception toward very questionable ends. She does not come up with this herself.

The humans are portrayed as "naked" and "not ashamed" (2:25). This characterization, albeit with sexual overtones, connotes a more general state of innocence and defenselessness.[54] The serpent, in contrast, comes across as manipulative, unaccountably insinuating doubt, suspicion, and disharmony into the human–divine relationship. Though not overtly "evil," the serpent is not neutral either. The serpent is disruptive. He is immediately successful in destabilizing the woman's trusting relation to

---

[52] Fretheim, *God and World*, p. 69.

[53] Genesis 2:9 actually mentions two trees in the middle of the garden, the tree of life and the tree of the knowledge of good and evil. In Genesis 2:17, God tells the first human (before the creation of the second) not to eat of the latter, the former having apparently dropped out of the picture. Genesis 3 mentions only a singular "tree in the middle of the garden," but the serpent's predictions about the consequences of eating, "You will not die ... and you will be like God, knowing good and evil" (3:4–5), allude to both. Moreover, the two are sent away from the garden lest they "take also from the tree of life, and eat, and live forever" (3:22). The story is likely a combination of two versions or two traditions about the trees, borrowing from other ancient myths.

[54] Trible, *God and the Rhetoric of Sexuality*, p. 109.

God. "You will not die ... you will be like God, knowing good and evil" (3:4). The intelligence of their conversation is ironic. The woman's first and fatal mistake is to not *name* the serpent for what he is, not *subdue* his promptings, and not assume rightful *dominion* as one made in the divine image.

Yet it is not without cause that the woman, questioned by the Lord, tries to evade responsibility with the rejoinder, "The serpent tricked me" (3:13). The man's similar excuse is that "she gave me fruit from the tree, and I ate," but he points out even more boldly that it was the same woman "whom you gave to be with me" (3:12). Of course, the woman could just as easily have taken God to task for creating the serpent. God does not accept the blame game and declares the serpent cursed for having started the process (3:14). But this only reinforces the impression that moral evil and responsibility originate prior to human choices. And it certainly does not resolve the issue of why God so made the world in the first place.

If the fall narrative is not an account of the *origin* of evil, it does capture evil's captivating *dynamics*, the dynamics of what later came to be called "original" sin. Genesis 3 shows us how evil entraps human agency. Once evil has blighted our relationships, it becomes unavoidable for each of us. The inevitability of sin is not due to a blot on the soul, a defect inherited through sexual reproduction, or a twist in the wills of individual agents. It is due to a combination of factors: the evolved and "natural" instinct of every living thing (and group) to preserve itself and its advantages, an instinct that is not morally wrong in itself; the social and practical ways in which identity and selfhood necessarily are constituted; the gradual development of moral awareness in all persons; and the de facto pervasiveness of biased social behavior.

"Social" explanations of original sin have often been rejected as not doing justice to sin's universality and necessity. This line of critique, however, rests on the wrong assumption that the self is essentially independent of its social environment and able in principle to resist mere "socialization." As has been shown by pragmatists like Charles Sanders Peirce, G. H. Mead, and William James, and more recently by Catherine Keller and Charles Taylor, identity, agency, and freedom always arise within a context of interactions among selves and all the aspects of their environments.[55] Solidarity,

[55] The pragmatists and Taylor were discussed in the preceding chapter. See also Catherine Keller, *From a Broken Web: Separation, Sexism and Self* (Boston: Beacon Press, 1986); and *Face of the Deep: A Theology of Becoming* (London: Routledge, 2003).

not individuality, is the most illuminating framework for understanding sin[56] – as it will be also for salvation.

Perhaps the serpent stands for the *preexisting* and the *practical* character of human implication in waywardness, in guilty relationships in which one seems to be caught even before recognizing them for what they are. While yet in a state of innocence, the woman is drawn into a process of rationalization, impairing her capacity for clear-eyed and responsible judgment. The story presents human evil as somehow tied to knowledge, specifically moral knowledge ("knowledge of good and evil") and to the conditions under which moral knowledge is obtained. Moral knowledge concerns right relationships, relationships that humans can affect and for which they have responsibility. The woman desires such knowledge but adopts a strategy to acquire it that compromises her relationship to God and consequently her moral relationships. She allows the serpent to shape her understanding of what she can, does, and should know.

Rationalization is not just a willful, self-generated series of intellectual contortions. It is a biased yet plausible interpretation of events and possibilities, pulled together from among options, within an environment, by an interested agent, to constitute a viewpoint that legitimates action. Rationalization is a strategy of self-deception. Rationalization depends on preexisting contexts and relationships, and on already being invested in certain outcomes. It is a warped exercise of practical reason about real goods to be achieved, an exercise in which the self averts attention from the real worth of various goods, the relation among the goods, and the effects that seeking a good, at a certain time, in a certain way, will have on other beings.

Interaction with the serpent, which the story portrays as initially unexceptional, gradually induces the woman to reason in the wrong way about goods available to her. She privileges a perceived opportunity for wisdom (3:6) over her trusting relation with God and over her vocation to image God's rule, a vocation she should be fulfilling in partnership with her (silent) partner. The crux of the woman's sin is forgetting her own dignity within creation. In addition to her failure to order her decision rightly regarding the serpent, the man, and wisdom, the woman also fails to

---

[56] Ted Peters, *Sin: Radical Evil in Soul and Society* (Grand Rapids, MI: Eerdmans, 1994), p. 30. On sin, original sin, and the social nature of sin, see Peters, *Sin*; Andrew Sung Park, *The Wounded Heart of God: The Asian Concept of Han and the Christian Doctrine of Sin* (Nashville: Abingdon Press, 1992); Tatha Wiley, *Original Sin: Origins, Developments, Contemporary Meanings* (New York: Paulist Press, 2002); and Darlene Fozard Weaver, "How Sin Works: A Review Essay," *Journal of Religious Ethics*, 29 (2001), pp. 473–501.

order her relation to the "good" tree and its attractive fruit. Instead, her sense experience, her affections, and her reasoning process all confirm the serpent's enticements.

Though the woman's moral state in the process prior to eating the fruit could be termed "temptation" but not yet sin, the matter is not so simple. In fact, the woman, by conversing with the serpent, is already participating in a social interaction that has power to draw her consciousness, her thoughts, her emotions, and her imagination away from God's life-giving activity. Responsibility, accountability, and guilt emerge in a process, not at a "point." What is true of the woman is also true of all other humans. We develop moral consciousness already within social relations that are dangerous if not already damaging. We understand what is "good and evil" within contexts that potentially distort our evaluation of goods and of how prioritization of goods for ourselves affects others with whom we are in relationship (personally or through social structures).

Though the serpent encourages the woman to adopt a distorted perspective on knowledge and its fruits, the serpent's predictions are not entirely wrong. A symbol in the ancient Near East of wisdom and immortality, the serpent delivers on half of his promise that the woman will enjoy both. The humans will in fact die after their eating, but they do gain knowledge: "the eyes of both were opened" (3:7). Even God concedes that the humans had "become like one of us, knowing good and evil" (3:22). But did they know "good and evil" like God – as the serpent had predicted?

Some interpreters see the fall as a fall "upward" into maturity and understanding.[57] Perhaps the first pair needed to change, and "should" have. "They had to enter the world of work, sweat, and tears, of childbearing and the joys and frustrations of sexual relations (Gen. 3:16–19), and they had to do so at the price of surrendering a life without risk and without end."[58] But the details of the story do not support this view. After all, life in the garden before the fall was already not risk-free, nor had immortality been explicitly promised (though threat of death was part of God's warning to obey; 2:17). In fact, death is presented as a consequence of the man's having been taken out of dust in the first place (3:19). It is

---

[57] See Fretheim, *God and World*, p. 71.

[58] Joseph Blenkinsopp, *Treasures Old and New: Essays in the Theology of the Pentateuch* (Grand Rapids, MI: Eerdmans, 2004), p. 101. The chapter is titled "Gilgamesh and Adam: Wisdom through Experience in *Gilgamesh* and in the Biblical Story of the Man, the Woman, and the Snake."

hard to claim either that the garden was a fool's paradise or that the narrative itself presents the fall in a positive light.

By eating the fruit, the first humans do come to know what good and evil are, and in this way they are more like God. But Eve is *unlike* God in that, when she reaches the capacity and the duty to recognize evil, she is already involved in its processes. In their state of original nakedness, the couple is naive and vulnerable, like children whose moral sense and sense of self are not far developed. Infants and children naturally, innocently, and unconsciously seek to have their own needs met, and only gradually become aware that others have similar needs and that others are affected by one's choices. (This is why Augustine's illustration of original sin with a "greedy" nursing infant is ludicrous and unconvincing.)[59] By the time moral awareness emerges, a child is already involved in practices that prioritize the needs of the self. It is then difficult to reverse the pattern. One's emergent moral sense is already biased to continue pre-moral behavior of advantage to the self. It is much easier and more attractive to "justify" ongoing or accustomed behaviors and rationales that work to one's advantage than to widen the scope of moral consideration.

The environment is not just an environment; it is a constituting aspect of the self and its habits. To say that selfish behavior is irresponsible and sinful is not to say that the good of the self is not a proper end among others. It is often morally necessary to assert the needs and goods of the self (or of a group) over against oppressive relations and structures.[60] Also, one has an obligation to advocate for those for whom one is most responsible by virtue of special relations, such as children in one's care. But at the root of all oppressive structures is disproportionate self-interest that has successfully arranged the social system in its service. Moral evil and oppression may be described very simply as the violation of some relationships or persons, so that different persons can lay claim to more power, goods, and benefits than they deserve.

It is not only the relation between the serpent and the woman that is problematic even before the fatal decision to take and eat. The relation of the two humans is equally indicative of the impending disaster. The two are to embody God's image as together ordering in a life-giving way. Yet Genesis never depicts the couple as actually engaging in activities that fulfill this calling. The first active move after the woman's

[59] Augustine, *Confessions*, I.vii.
[60] Valerie Saiving Goldstein, "The Human Situation: A Feminine View," *Journal of Religion*, 40 (April 1960), pp. 100–12.

creation is her solo rejoinder to the serpent, repeating God's command. From there the conversation goes downhill. The man and woman do not react together at all, much less demonstrate equality, reciprocity, and mutual care. The woman and man are both in the garden when the serpent approaches (3:6), but they do not reflect together about God, the garden, the tree, the serpent, their own relationship, or the proposal before them. The woman is reflective with the serpent, who is not her "helper"; if the man is reflective he certainly keeps quiet about it. She talks, he sits, she takes and eats and gives, he eats. Then their eyes "were opened" – passive voice. Their first joint actions seem to be making loincloths (3:7) and hiding from God (3:8). Questioned, they hurl accusations rather than face up to their shared vocation and their failure to assume it.

Even before the pair disobeys the tree command, they are already exhibiting a "fall" from unified relationship. Though created "good," the human beings did not waste much time in destabilizing the situation. Separately eating the fruit, the two fall definitively out of order to God, each other, and the other aspects of creation. "Life has lost to Death, harmony to hostility, unity and fulfillment to fragmentation and dispersion. The divine, human, animal, and plant worlds are all adversely affected … Truly a love story gone awry."[61]

As God announces (not commands),[62] the human body will now resist the blessings of fruitfulness and land, turning blessings into the painful labor of childbirth and agriculture (3:16–19).[63] The woman will "desire" her lost union with the man, but he will now "rule over" her, in a fallen way (3:16). The man soon names "his wife," as he did the animals (3:20). Patriarchy designates the rule of man over woman, but patriarchy is much more than the institution of marriage, a family system, or a system of sexual subordination. "It is a domination system. Such systems, then and now, are characterized … by 'unjust economic relations, oppressive political relations, biased race relations, patriarchal gender relations, hierarchical power relations, and the use of violence to maintain them

---

[61] Trible, *God and the Rhetoric of Sexuality*, p. 139.
[62] There is a modern consensus, stimulated not least of all by feminist biblical interpretation, that the so-called curses and punishments of Genesis 3 are not divine decrees to be observed forever. They are God's announcement or declaration of the consequences that Eve and Adam (and the serpent) have brought on themselves and the rest of creation. These consequences are to be resisted and transformed as part of the process of redemption. See Fretheim, *God and World*, p. 75.
[63] Carol Meyers proposes that the Hebrew phrasing suggests Eve is not destined to suffer in childbirth specifically, but through a greater number of pregnancies, stress and grief in parenting, and toil in general. See Meyers, *Discovering Eve*, pp. 103–9, 118.

all.'"[64] Patriarchy exemplifies and is the first instance of all social domination systems, especially ones built around ideologies that inscribe social inequality in the innate differences of human bodies. Rather than reconciling conflicts and rectifying harms among creatures, such systems exploit them to the advantage of a few. Domination systems are the deplorable result of human betrayal of God's image.

Following on their parents' choice, Cain and Abel present an almost immediate and ultimate destruction of God-imaging relationship. In a corruption of the embodied "generations" trajectory of creation, which ought to be the basis and school of fellowship, Adam and Eve's children pull their parents' legacy into the future in terrifying ways. The brothers divide in conflict over the value and rights of their work on the land, and its social and religious significance. Their fraternal and human one-flesh unity ends in fratricidal violence, causing further alienation from the earth itself and exile from kindred and community (4:1–14). The later bestowal of blessing on Noah and his sons in Genesis 9, with its companion outlawing of murder, confirms that human life in the image of God especially excludes the killing of other human beings (9:6).

Sin consists not in wanting to know good and evil, but in seeking undue control over the conditions and results of this knowledge, without humility about the scope of one's power or the justice of one's vision. Cain is understandably disappointed that God does not look favorably on his offering, preferring that of his brother. This preference seems arbitrary. Cain's real fault is in reacting with rage and not accepting that God's ways are not always explained.[65] Humans and their communities sin when they, like Cain, make themselves and their particular projects the center of religion and morality, justifying the destruction of their competitors.

BETWEEN SIN AND REDEMPTION: ABRAHAM, SARAH, AND HAGAR

The story of redemption through God's chosen people Israel begins with the call of Abraham (Genesis 12), a character whose trust in God amidst uncertainty and "unfair" demands contrasts strongly with Cain. The story begins abruptly, as the Lord simply and suddenly speaks to Abraham (Abram), summoning him to abandon all that is familiar and

---

[64] Wiley, *Original Sin*, p. 27, citing Walter Wink, *Engaging the Powers: Discernment and Resistance in a World of Domination* (Minneapolis: Fortress Press, 1992), p. 107.
[65] See Fretheim, *God and World*, p. 78.

journey into the unknown. "Go from your country and your kindred and your father's house to the land that I will show you ... So Abram went" (Gen. 12:1, 4). Abraham leaves his home in southern Mesopotamia ("Ur of the Chaldeans"; 11:28) and travels into the "promised land" of Canaan, where he makes a covenant with the Lord (Gen. 121:6–8). With divine help, Abraham and his wife, Sarah, already past childbearing age, establish a family line through which God's plan of redemption will be realized (Gen. 21:1–3).

Abraham's trust in the ways of the unknowable God is proved in his obedience to the command to sacrifice his son, Isaac, the child through whom Abraham had expected God to fulfill the promise to "make of you a great nation." This demand is no more intelligible in human terms than God's command not to eat of the tree of the knowledge of good and evil, God's creation of a world that humans need to "subdue" lest they fall into evil, or God's preference for Abel's offering over that of Cain. In fact, this and other commands of God deserve to be questioned from a moral standpoint. But the point of the story is that Abraham does not falter in his relation to God or his confidence in God's agenda: "I will bless you, and make your name great, so that you will be a blessing ... and in you all the families of the earth shall be blessed" (12:2–3).

The story of Abraham, Sarah, and Isaac, however, is no more a story of unambiguous faith than is the story of Adam and Eve a story of unambiguous sin. While Abraham is usually remembered as a paragon of trust, first he and then Sarah doubt the predicted miracle birth, laughing at the news (17:17, 18:12). And Abraham eventually goes along with Sarah's plan to take the matter into their own hands. Thus commences an incident that shows that even the patriarchs and matriarchs of God's chosen live in a world marked by evil and are not immune to its perverse practices or exempt from its "domination systems." The couple's wrongdoing does not stop with their determination to control a course of events that God is inexplicably allowing to go "off course." Confronted with continuing "barrenness," Sarah proposes to use her foreign slave, Hagar, as surrogate mother, and Abraham approves (16:2).

On the surface, it may look like all the evil plans are motivated by Sarah. No doubt the narrative was recorded by a male editor interested in protecting Abraham as a model of faith. Yet the editor of Genesis has also placed the story of Abraham under the judgment of the story of Adam. Ironically, Abraham repeats Adam's sin by not making this a well-considered, truly joint, and much more prudent decision. The pair's actions also illustrate the way patriarchy structures the institutions of childbearing, as projected by Genesis 3. Rather than patiently wait for the blessing of fruitfulness to be fulfilled through their own one-flesh partnership, they exploit Hagar's powerlessness and fertility. She is ordered to have sex with Abraham, producing a child for his benefit and that of Sarah. Hagar is not envisioned to share in the Lord's "blessings," but expected merely to serve as their unconsenting instrument.

Hagar does become pregnant. But almost immediately, the arrangement unravels, for now Hagar "looked with contempt on her mistress" (16:4). Hagar is only too eager to take advantage of the cultural equation of women's value with childbearing to turn the tables on her abuser. Rather than rectify any of the accumulating injustices, Abraham underwrites the dynamics of the power game, reminding his wife of her superior status: "'Behold, your maid is in your power; do to her as you please'" (16:6). So Sarah "dealt harshly" with Hagar, and Hagar runs away. In one of the few places in the bible where God appears directly to a woman and speaks to her, God tells Hagar to go back to Sarah, assuring Hagar that "the Lord has given heed to your affliction" and promising that she will bear a son, Ishmael (16:7–13).

For good reason, some African American womanist theologians find in Hagar a sort of "patron saint" of those triply exploited by race or ethnicity, gender, and slavery. Ante-bellum U.S. slaves were forced to accept the sexual advances of masters and bear them children, while suffering the abuse of harsh and jealous plantation wives. Like Hagar, they longed for escape, fleeing into great danger, little refuge, and unknown futures. Delores Williams, in *Sisters in the Wilderness*, acclaims the Hagar story as a rich resource for a long tradition of African American biblical interpretation, a story that is particularly apt for the expression of the experience of women.[66] She points out that Hagar does exert her own agency and escapes into freedom, but that action brings her into very precarious straits, a situation that persisted for American slaves even after the Civil War. God does not exactly "liberate" Hagar, but does provide the necessities of survival.

At God's instruction, the pregnant Hagar returns to the household, where she can at least be assured of security in giving birth and nursing her infant. But after Sarah has her own baby, Isaac, she sees Ishmael and Isaac play together and becomes angry. She wants to ensure that no "son of this slave woman" will "inherit along with my son Isaac." Since

[66] Delores S. Williams, *Sisters in the Wilderness: The Challenge of Womanist God-Talk* (Maryknoll, NY: Orbis Books, 1993).

women's lives are defined largely through their sons and the sons' fathers, the women compete. Sarah fully intends to protect her own son's priority over that of her rival. At her insistence and over Abraham's reluctance to repudiate a son, he accedes to Sarah's demand to send Hagar and Ishmael away from the family (21:8–14).

The Lord's actions pose questions of their own, for God compensates Hagar without directly challenging the patriarchal structures, or even taking Abraham and Sarah to task for their unjust manipulation of them. It is not clear whether God really has compassion on Hagar or is only concerned about the safety of Ishmael, the offspring of Abraham.[67] The Lord assures Abraham that though Isaac will be the heir of the promise, God will "make a nation" of his other son too. Therefore, it is apparently not a problem that Sarah is demanding they be ousted (21:12–13). Giving Hagar bread and water, Abraham sends her into the wilderness. Hagar has not been apprised of the plans God has disclosed to Abraham. Her suffering is great, and her desperation grows. When the water is gone, she casts her child under a bush and retreats, pleading, "Let me not look on the death of the child" (21:16). What more onerous suffering than that of a mother unable to save her baby from starvation at human hands, a mother also lacking any human offer of consolation in her sorrow? But God hears the baby crying. God tells Hagar to pick him up and shows Hagar a well of water – now revealing that he is going to give Ishmael descendants too. Ishmael is finally saved by the mercy of God (21:17–19).

The story of Hagar is a puzzle. It provides such a good model for the experience of oppressed women today because it reflects entrenched injustices with which women must cope – with the help of their own courage and God's guidance, but not always with the result of true liberation. Sometimes the best that can be achieved is mere survival; Hagar and her child come close enough to destruction that we are reminded how often survival is out of reach. Why does God permit and even encourage the unjust treatment of Hagar by her "owners"? Why does God not denounce their sinfulness and call them to repentance?

One way to understand the tale of Abraham, Sarah, Hagar, and their children is in relation to Israel's process of identity formation. It reflects, if ambivalently, on the dynamic of particularity and universality, the problematic of us–them thinking, and the human realities of self-assertion and attempted dominance, that thread through both the Hebrew Bible

---

[67] Mignon R. Jacobs, *Gender, Power, and Persuasion: The Genesis Narratives and Contemporary Portraits* (Grand Rapids, MI: Baker Academic, 2007), pp. 147–9, 154.

and the Christian New Testament. "Hagar the Egyptian" is an outsider (Gen. 16, 21) whose origin recalls the tempting power of a wealthy people where Abraham temporarily settled (after passing Sarah off as his sister to Pharaoh) and where Joseph took refuge and became prosperous. The family of Abraham becomes entangled with the family of a foreign woman, whose son with Abraham it must reject or "abject" in order to assert its own permeable and insecure identity.[68] Hagar ultimately asserts her own identity, in a parallel contrast to Abraham: she procures a wife for her own son from among her people, Egypt.[69] Ishmael, however, remains at the borders of Israel's consciousness, never fully separated and unwilling to be tamed. The identities of Abraham and Hagar, Isaac and Ishmael, are established, but the connection is never entirely broken: Ishmael goes back to bury his father, though he remains an outsider to the family history (Gen. 25:9).

The process of establishing identity for these figures and the peoples they represent is hazardous and conflictual, even violent. Secure identity seems to require self-definition "over against" others, implying exclusion if not dominance. The story leaves unsettled the divine reaction to this situation. It is clear that Abraham and his descendants are God's favored people and that the son of Sarah is the true link to the future of Israel. Yet Israel seems unable to pursue her destiny in full separation from other peoples. Relationships with other people are relationships that Israel both chooses and abjures, both exploits and repents. Even though God sets Israel apart, God too is related to other peoples and takes steps toward their protection. The book of Genesis still has religious authority and appeal because its mediation of the divine is rich, complex, and ultimately redemptive. The creation stories set a tone for what follows. The universal presence and providence of God in creation are echoed in Israel's stories of redemption, even though Israel's election is the prominent theme.

The bible construes great continuity between creation and redemption. Redemption is the restoration of the image of God and liberation for ever new and greater human community, fruitful interdependence with nature, and personal intimacy with God. The universality of God's creating and saving acts is established in creation, reestablished in God's covenant with Noah (Gen. 8:21, 9:11), reaffirmed in God's promise to bless all peoples of the earth through Abraham (Gen. 12:3), focused through

---

[68] J. Cheryl Exum, "Hagar *en Procès*: The Abject in Search of Subjectivity," in Peter S. Hawkins and Lesleigh Cushing Stahlberg (eds.), *From the Margins 1: Women of the Hebrew Bible and Their Afterlives* (Sheffield: Sheffield Phoenix Press, 2009), pp. 1–16.

[69] Ibid., p. 16.

Israel's election as "light to the nations" (Isa. 49:6), and cosmically expansive. The liberation of Israel from Pharaoh's cruelty is depicted as a universal victory, demonstrating "the reign of God over the entire cosmos (15:18)" and the promise of a new heaven and a new earth (Isa. 65:17; 2 Cor. 5:17).[70] Redemption is a continuation of God's creative power, a reclaiming of humans to fulfill the image of God as they were given life to do. As illustrated in the wilderness events, redemption is also a restoration of the life-giving abundance of the land and of nature.[71] "God who created continues to create – not abandoning the primal cosmic design ... but renewing, adjusting, and amplifying it (e.g., Isa. 34–35; 40–45; Ezek. 34:25–31; Rom. 1–11; Rev. 21–22; cf. Sir. 24)."[72]

On the assumption, then, that the central messages of Genesis are the righteousness and beneficence of the Creator, the mandate that all humanity embody the image of God, and God's redeeming covenant, the following conclusions may be drawn. First, the image of God is reflected in human relationships. If relationships truly image God, they will not violate the one-flesh union of spouses, of women and men, and of every human with every other. The true humanity of all must be respected, even when needs conflict. The eloquent "subtext" in the story of Hagar is that her situation is unjust and deserves compassion, as interpretations and artistic portrayals over the centuries have accentuated.[73] Second, when relationships are subject to violence and exploitation, the redemptive response follows the lead of God's compassion for the powerless. God includes Hagar as a beneficiary of the saving actions directed in the story primarily to the good of Ishmael. Third, despite redemptive experiences, relationships, and practices, evil remains. The destructive force of evil, especially evil against the most vulnerable, must be confronted. It can be resisted but not explained in any satisfactory moral or religious terms. Hence the ambiguity of the story of Hagar. Fourth, historical human relationships inevitably take shape within structures of personal and social sin, but that does not mean the end of responsibility. Nor does God cease to act redemptively for and with humans, even when they remain captive to those structures and even when God's intentions seem opaque. Neither patriarchy nor unjust treatment of outsiders is overturned in Hagar's story, but their effects are alleviated, and their victims given a future.

---

[70] Fretheim, *God and World*, p. 111.   [71] Ibid., p. 125.
[72] S. Dean McBride, Jr., "Divine Protocol: Genesis 1:1–2:3 as Prologue to the Pentateuch," in Brown and McBride (eds.), *God Who Creates*, p. 40.
[73] J. Cheryl Exum, "The Accusing Look: The Abjection of Hagar in Art," *Religion and the Arts*, 11 (2007), pp. 143–71.

NEW CREATION

As we have seen, the Genesis creation stories concern primarily two human individuals within a cosmos made up of other natural formations, forces, and life forms. [The dreadful consequence of sin as depicted in Genesis 3 is that human relationships, families, communities, practices, and structures are undermined and perverted by conflict, violence, and domination.] God calls the covenant people to enact a way of life under divine rule, a communal way of life with social and political dimensions that should reflect the effects of salvation from human sin and slavery.

These political themes are carried forward from Jewish tradition and scripture in Jesus' proclamation of the advent of God's reign or kingdom (Mark 1:14). As the new creation of God's image (Col. 3:10), Christ brings about a new way of being human (Col. 1:15, 17). This new way is corporate or collective, a communal antidote to sin. Differences may remain, but divisions and structures of exclusion and oppression are overcome in communities united in Christ (Gal. 3:28; Col. 3:11). The complete healing of social and political relations is an eschatological reality, only partly realized now. But its effects in history are real.

Jesus teaches an alternative way, contrasting the material image of Caesar on a coin with God's rule. "There is another reality, God's reality, and humankind created by God bears the image of the creator of all that is real." "Giving to God what is God's" does not mean giving spiritual praise to God, while serving Caesar's will in society and politics. It means acknowledging that social and political structures provide the essential conditions of human identity, agency, and association; and believing that those who live in God's image and under God's rule can give a different moral quality to practices, structures, and politics. In God's image and God's kingdom, the one-flesh partnership of all humans is on the way to renewal.[74]

Feminist theologians such as Elizabeth Johnson and Elisabeth Schüssler Fiorenza celebrate the figure of Wisdom, or Sophia, to show that the creative and saving work of the Creator, that of Christ, and of Spirit are interdependent and effective throughout the cosmos.[75] In the wisdom literature, God the Creator is praised as ordering creation and as present

---

[74] See Deborah Krause, "Keeping It Real: The Image of God in the New Testament," *Interpretation*, 59/4 (October 2005), p. 367.
[75] Elizabeth A. Johnson, *She Who Is: The Mystery of God in Feminist Theological Discourse* (New York: Crossroad, 1994); Elisabeth Schüssler Fiorenza, *Jesus: Miriam's Child, Sophia's Prophet: Critical Issues in Feminist Christology* (New York: Continuum, 1994).

throughout creation, delighting in its beauty and guiding those who love God. God is personified as Lady Wisdom, or Sophia.[76] The longest speech of Wisdom concerning creation is found in Proverbs 8. "Take my instruction instead of silver, and knowledge rather than choice gold" (8:10). "I walk in the way of righteousness, along the paths of justice, endowing with wealth those who love me" (8:21). "The Lord created me at the beginning of his work, the first of his acts of long ago" (8:22). "I was daily his delight, rejoicing before him always, rejoicing in his inhabited world and delighting in the human race. … For whoever finds me finds life and obtains favor from the Lord; but those who miss me injure themselves; all who hate me love death" (8:30, 35–6).

The image of Wisdom will influence depictions of Jesus in the New Testament, including the prologue to John's gospel, where "Word" replaces "Wisdom." Feminine imagery is not only appropriate but necessary to appreciate the extent and effects of God's cosmic creativity. Johnson discerns a "trinitarian pattern of experience" in biblically based, dialectical models of God as "Mother-Sophia," "the absolute mystery of unoriginate origin;" "the conflictual, liberating story of Jesus-Sophia ongoing as the Christ," and "Spirit-Sophia present and absent in the world."[77]

The Genesis creation stories set all that exists under the creative rule of God and urge human beings to fulfill the divine image of reciprocity, life-givingness, and healing. Creation, sin, and salvation have personal and corporate dimensions. Human beings are to honor their one-flesh partnership, to care for the earth, and to turn back evil through hopeful and compassionate action. These practices restore the image of God and constitute communities where redemption from evil is tasted.

THE PERSISTENT AMBIGUITY OF EVIL AND REDEMPTION

The realities of human evil and the hope of salvation have been presented in relation to creation and in light of the biblical narratives as offering a response to evil rather than an explanation of why evil exists. God's decisive saving actions in the covenant with Israel and in Jesus Christ signify that the transformative power of salvation is real, that this power can upset the powers of evil and suffering.

Yet evil is pervasive, and not even the scriptures give complete assurance that God will bring it under control or that God's mercy

[76] Ibid.   [77] Johnson, *She Who Is*, p. 187.

is inclusive. For example, though God saves his chosen people from oppression, he also exerts his power over Pharaoh by killing innocent children, down to and including "the firstborn of the female slave who is behind the handmill" (Exod. 11:5) and "the firstborn of the prisoner who was in the dungeon" (12:29). Such texts can be chalked up to the biases and hyperbole of human authors expressing a religious point long before the era of modern equality and rights. Nevertheless, they remind the theological ethicist, and all believers for that matter, that not even an authentic religious worldview can neatly tie up the problem of evil.

In particular, two difficult problems that surfaced earlier have not gone away. I return to and even accentuate these problems in conclusion, because too often triumphalist Christian theologies offer proclamations of redemption that do not look contradictions in the face. One problem is the fact that God's own actions as narrated biblically do not always appear to be unambiguously good. The other is that, in fact, an unbearable load of suffering is not overcome in history. Radical evil can destroy human beings, depriving them of agency and even of identity. These problems do not have easy solutions.

On the first problem, consider the puzzling character of God, already evident in the story of Hagar. Even more challenging texts are those in which God directly exhorts his people to violence and destruction, as in the conquest of Canaan (Exod. 23:23; Num. 33:52, 53; Deut. 20:16, 17), or in which biblical characters, even those most favored by God, commit violence and injustice. We have seen Abraham and Sarah's treatment of their "slave girl." Even more horrifying are "texts of terror," like the victorious general Jephthah's sacrifice of his young daughter (Judg. 11:28–40), in which atrocities against women go completely unremarked upon by biblical narrators.[78] While one biblical theologian asserts that "the proper outcome of the idea of *imago dei* in Genesis is an ideology that is democratic and nonviolent,"[79] another protests that "the variety of ways God acts in the Bible gives Christians legitimate cause to wonder what behavior is appropriate for them."[80] Still another notes that many aspects of the biblical narrative are of a "problematic nature," then remarks rather laconically that there are "higher ideals" in the bible that remain "compelling,"

---

[78] Phyllis Trible, *Texts of Terror: Literary-Feminist Readings of Biblical Narratives* (Philadelphia: Fortress Press, 1984).
[79] Towner's review of Middleton's *Liberating Image*, 3.
[80] Johnson, "Between Text and Sermon," 2.

such as "the command to love our neighbor as ourselves, or the calls for justice in the prophets."[81]

I have already suggested, following several biblical scholars, that the Creator God of Genesis provides an overarching standard for the interpretation of God's actions in other narratives. If God's saving and liberating purpose, as continuing and restoring creation, is the bible's overarching message, then texts seeming to condone or urge violence can be understood as a narrator's way of expressing God's absolute determination to show favor to his people, despite all opposition and odds. But certainly violent texts, particularly those that ascribe violence to God, can be, have been, and are taken out of context to validate violence at the hands of supposedly religious people who claim to be acting in God's name. Therefore, it is not enough to say simply that such texts are not "central."

More must be done to show how biblical faith and the communities that transmit it can, should, and do repudiate violence and foster human dignity, peace, and justice. This also begins a reply to the second problem, the continuing hold of evil on the world, despite the supposed fact of redemption. The centrality of reconciliation to the Christian message and the Christian claim that reconciliation is a historical possibility ultimately rely on Christian practices, the practical politics of salvation, to demonstrate their truth and validity. What cannot be argued conclusively at the theoretical level must be proved by the difference that Christian politics actually makes against specific, concrete forms of suffering and violence. Following chapters develop further the teaching and example of Jesus, christological approaches to salvation, the work of the Spirit in the church, and the practical ways in which Christians and others turn aside violence and advocate peace and justice.

Despite these efforts, evil and suffering are too frequently radical and unrelieved. We turn to biblical narratives for the illumination of intractable human misery, recognizing the unacceptability of characterizations of God's justice that facilely reconcile radical suffering with divine goodness or offer false assurances that all kinds of injustice fit into God's "plan." Like the problem of God's character, hopeless suffering calls for a practical over a theoretical response.

---

[81] John J. Collins, "Old Testament in a New Climate," in Yale Divinity School's *Reflections* (Spring 2008), p. 6.

JOB: A PRACTICAL RESPONSE TO THE MYSTERY OF EVIL

The biblical story of Job never explains adequately, from a theoretical or theological perspective, why Job has to suffer and whether he is finally rescued. Instead it offers a specific, ongoing relationship among Job, God, and Job's friends.

Job suffers not only because he has lost his livelihood, health, and family, but because he is isolated and criticized by his spouse and friends, and because God is silent. It seems that even God has turned against him, is set to destroy him, and there is no refuge to be found (10:7–8). Job has reached the point where he sees no meaning or purpose in having been born (3:1, 11; 10:1, 18). The reader learns that Job's suffering is permitted by God at "Satan's" ("the satan's") instigation. The Lord is allowing Job's faithfulness to be tested, even though he has never given God cause for doubt (2:1–6). When God does respond to Job's protests, it is in a tone more of accusation than of comfort.

The unwillingness of God to give Job any reassurance should be understood in light of Satan's original challenge: Will "righteous" humans still worship God with piety and devotion if they receive no reward for it and have no punishment to fear (1:9–11, 2:5)? Perhaps the author of Job has this question come from Satan because it would make an unseemly premise of divine behavior. The question of why humans are motivated to "fear" and adore the Lord is a very human question about the real grounds on which we believe in and trust God; but it is a question that can finally be answered under conditions that God alone can create. The drama setting this question on the table raises many further questions about God's justice, questions that are in fact taken up by Job and his friends.

Once the drama is under way, it is clear that Job's faith will have not met Satan's challenge if God repays Job's loyalty or leaves with him any good whose loss might motivate continued piety. To prove the "purity" of Job's faithfulness, he must be utterly beaten down and forsaken. Job, however, does not reach the ultimate depths; he does not lose his agency, integrity, or openness to God's voice. To the contrary, Job continues to question God and to defend his own record (27:5–6). He keeps demanding that his relationship to God be recognized. The fact that God does finally reply and Job eventually accepts God's answer, desisting from further questioning, suggests that their relationship has been sustained and has reached equilibrium.

God has not really explained his ways to Job or given a rationale for Job's suffering. But God directs Job's attention away from his plight and

toward God's creative power. Creation contains incredible and dangerous beasts, natural forces, and events that are far from orderly and for
which God makes no apology. "Where were you when I laid the foundation of the earth? ... Have you commanded the morning since your
days began ... ?" (38:4, 12). Just as Job does not understand or control the
awesomeness of nature, he does not understand or control his own place
in God's design. But Job has a relationship with God. It is a relationship
of personal presence and exchange ("now my eye sees you"; 42:5), and that
relationship lies within the cosmic work of God.

God personally seals their relationship by informing Job and his
friends that only one person has spoken rightly of God: God's "servant
Job" (42:7). Therefore, God recognizes the power of Job's prayer to save
the friends from punishment and accepts that prayer (42:9), reinstating
Job's status in others' eyes as righteous before God. By mandating and
accepting Job's petition for his friends, God even confers power on Job –
power not only over the friends, but also over the divine dispositions.
With regard to its central question – why Job suffers – this narrative is
inscrutable and ultimately "resists closure."[82]

The story of Job is admirably complicated. It manages to communicate
simultaneously that God is powerful and provident, that neither innocent suffering nor God's responsibility for it can be fully understood, and
that a personal and reciprocal relationship to the Creator can provide a
resolution – affirmed from God's side as well as Job's – that questioning
inquiry cannot. Perhaps "the point of Job is not to solve the problem of
suffering but to illustrate what a person of integrity does in the face of
it: cling to God in faith and continue to serve God for nothing save that
relationship."[83]

From his side, Job persistently questions God, and even accuses God, a
way of sustaining relationship that is also represented in the biblical genre
of lament. In the heartfelt words of African American theologian Bryan
Massingale, "Laments are cries of anguish and outrage, groans of deep
pain and grief, utterances of profound protest and righteous indignation
over injustice, wails of mourning and sorrow in the face of unbearable
suffering ... Laments ... are uncivil, strident, harsh, and heart-rending."[84]

[82] Alissa Jones Nelson, "Job in Conversation with Edward Said: The 'Outsider' as Ethical and Pedagogical Dilemma in Biblical Interpretation," *SBL Forum, SBL E-Newsletter*, January 23, 2009, www.sbl-site.org/publications/article.aspx?articleId=797 (accessed January 23, 2009), 7.
[83] Susan F. Mathews, "Job," in Tambasco (ed.), *The Bible on Suffering*, p. 68.
[84] Bryan N. Massingale, *Racial Justice and the Catholic Church* (Maryknoll, NY: Orbis Books, 2010), p. 106.

Sunken in suffering on the cross, Jesus laments in the words of Psalm 22, "My God, my God, why have you forsaken me?" (Mark 15:34). Though laments express desperate distress, they are also a form of protest that calls God or the universe to account, at least suggesting that a hearing and a response are possible.[85] Interpreting the book of Joel, womanist theologian Emilie Townes provides a reflection on the power of "communal lament" to transform a desperate situation by recognizing, grieving, and complaining to God. Lament is an established tradition in the cries and songs of American slaves. Lament cries out against tragedy, calamity, or "impending doom" with no way out and no way forward. Lament forms community and makes suffering bearable, whether or not the community "understands" or has a "solution."[86]

From God's side, there is no direct accounting for Job's suffering. But God does maintain relationship, not with Job only, but with a reestablished community of Job and friends. Even in solitary suffering, strength is found in mindfulness of relations past and present, especially those that mediate and reinforce the reality of the divine for and with us. Tormented Job recalls when he lived in "righteousness," delivering the poor, the widow, and the orphan, just as the Hebrew prophets had demanded (29:7–17). He is mindful of the oppressed even when his ability to help is undercut, relating his own spiritual crisis to injustices in landownership (9:24), treatment of the poor (24:2–4), and benefit allocation within social structures (29–30).[87] The role of "father to the needy," of having "championed the cause of the stranger" (29:16), is still part of who he is, allowing Job to place his own tribulations alongside others' suffering. Relationships among persons and in community are the most fitting and effective response to evil and suffering that we cannot directly alleviate. They are the moral response, the deepest response of which humans are capable, and the response that most enacts the divine image. In the book of Job, God's own response to suffering is precisely to sustain relationship.

To be in relation with God is to be in relation with one another: that is important to the message of the creation story. Whatever the folly of their counsel, their attitude of blame, and the self-justifying subtext of their advice, the friends of Job are still "there for him" as he struggles on. Though God in the end rebukes them, God also speaks directly to them

---

[85] Ibid.

[86] Emilie M. Townes, *Breaking the Fine Rain of Death: African American Health Issues and a Womanist Ethic of Care* (New York: Continuum, 1998), p. 23.

[87] Mathews, "Job," p. 68.

and allows them to be pardoned through their friendship with Job. It is a three-way relationship among God, Job, and friends.

Citing Simone Weil, Elizabeth Johnson writes of "affliction" whose effect is to "squeeze out life, dry out power, introduce unwarranted guilt and self-hatred, plunge the sufferer into darkness."[88] Hagar seems to have reached this point when she casts away her baby, so desolate, in pain, and abandoned that she cannot even abide in love with her son as together they face death. Fortunately for them, God comes to the rescue. But this does not always occur. Many face death alone, afraid, bewildered, unnoticed, and unremembered. Where is their hope? As Johnson observes, that there is no hope for them is a terrible possibility that theology cannot completely penetrate.

CONCLUSION

We live in a world in which suffering is pervasive, much of it at human hands. Yet "the world is charged with the grandeur of God."[89] The creation narratives direct attention to a transcendent power on which we are dependent, and judge human actions that participate in violence, collude in suffering, or destroy relationships among God, humans, and fellow humanity. The creation accounts tell us that although discord may result from variance in our own natures and in the world around us, humans are charged to take responsibility, and God's continuing presence enables conversion. Genesis as a whole and the trajectory of blessing in the Pentateuch depict the kinds of relationships to God and others that turn aside the harmful effects of disharmony and interrupt the structural perpetration of evil. Creation gives hope by lighting another path in conformity to God's glory, justice, and life-giving power. God as Creator, Savior, and Sustainer continues at work in the world. The one God who creates also renews.

> Oh, morning, at the brown brink eastward, springs –
> Because the Holy Ghost over the bent
> World broods with warm breast and with ah! bright wings.[90]

---

[88] Johnson, *She Who Is*, p. 261.
[89] Gerard Manley Hopkins, "God's Grandeur," 1918, in Bartleby's Books Online, at www.bartleby.com/122/7.html (accessed September 3, 2008).
[90] Ibid. The entire poem reads:

> THE WORLD is charged with the grandeur of God.
> It will flame out, like shining from shook foil;
> It gathers to a greatness, like the ooze of oil
> Crushed. Why do men then now not reck his rod?

The next chapter will pursue the Christian hope of personal and communal renewal as captured in the biblical metaphor "kingdom of God," a way of describing salvation that has clear political overtones. The kingdom or reign of God is key to the mission and message of Jesus. It is his answer to the problem of evil, specifically of the suffering that humans inflict. Jesus' embodiment of the kingdom led to his death. Through a share in his resurrection, Christians hope to experience and to spread the good news of evil's defeat and creation's renewal, beginning even now in the midst of tribulation.

> Generations have trod, have trod, have trod;
> And all is seared with trade; bleared, smeared with toil;
> And wears man's smudge and shares man's smell: the soil
> Is bare now, nor can foot feel, being shod.
> And for all this, nature is never spent;
> There lives the dearest freshness deep down things;
> And though the last lights off the black West went
> Oh, morning, at the brown brink eastward, springs –
> Because the Holy Ghost over the bent
> World broods with warm breast and with ah! bright wings.

CHAPTER 3

Kingdom of God

Christians believe that in and through Jesus Christ, humans are reunited to God, healed from sinfulness, and empowered for life in a community of forgiveness, reformation, and solidarity. Salvation transforms individual persons and personal relationships, but it is also always a corporate reality, with social and political dimensions.

The fact about Jesus' mission that is most clearly attested by his own remembered words, least subject to scholarly dispute, and most fundamental to his historical role is that he was the prophet of God's kingdom or reign. As the earliest gospel announces, "After John had been handed over, Jesus came into Galilee proclaiming the gospel of God, and saying, 'The time has been fulfilled, and the kingdom of God has drawn near: repent and believe in the gospel' " (Mark 1:14–15). Matthew and Luke summarize Jesus' message similarly (Matt. 4:23, 9:35; Luke 4:43, 8:1).

The kingdom or reign of God (Mark 1:14–15) is a corporate and political metaphor. The title Jesus is most likely to have used for himself, "Son of Man" (Mark 2:10, 14:62; Matt. 26:63–4), indicates a role in the corporate redemption of Israel, that is, in the divine defeat of oppressive evil powers (see Dan. 7:8–29). When early Christians proclaimed Jesus himself as the bringer of salvation, they drew primarily on Jewish appellations that referred to roles with and for God's *covenant* people. Preeminent among them are "Christ," one anointed for consecration to a sacred role, as David was anointed king (1 Sam. 16:13); "Son of God," a title also applied to King David (2 Sam. 7:14); and "High Priest," a representative of the people in corporate sacrifice, particularly on the Day of Atonement (cf.

Parts of this chapter are based on the following works: "Jesus, Christ, and Ethics," in David R. Bauer and Mark Allan Powell (eds.), *Who Do You Say That I Am? Biblical Witnesses to Christ in Theological and Pastoral Perspective* (Louisville, KY: Westminster John Knox Press, 1999), pp. 228–45; "Christ and Kingdom: The Identity of Jesus and Christian Politics," in Stephen J. Pope (ed.), *Hope and Solidarity: Jon Sobrino's Challenge to Christian Theology* (Maryknoll, NY: Orbis Books, 2008), pp. 242–54.

Lev. 6:6–19). When these titles are appropriated by Jesus' followers, their meaning is transformed, insofar as Jesus himself is confessed as the one in whom salvation arrives. This process will be discussed further in the next two chapters.

But is salvation beginning now, in history and in human communities? This is an essential question for Christian social ethics and politics, especially if they are to reply meaningfully to the persistent reality of evil laid out in Chapter 2. The narrative of an originally good creation is a religious response to evil realities. But that response is ethically and politically incomplete until it shows how and why evil can be resisted successfully. I am convinced that Jesus understood God's kingdom to be a future reality that is nonetheless accessible in a practical way within the limits of history. This becomes more evident when we contrast Jesus' preaching of the kingdom with the understanding of God's kingdom in Jewish apocalyptic. In addition, Jesus' exorcisms and healings are signs of God's power overcoming evil and changing the present world.

The purpose of the present chapter is to emphasize that Jesus' ministry of the kingdom gives *content* to salvation; that Jesus saw salvation as *corporate* and *political*; and that Jesus understood God's kingdom to be presently *effective* in transforming social and political life. It will emphasize the inclusiveness of Jesus' kingdom and consider its openness to sinners, the poor, women, and "outsiders" (Gentiles). Yet it will not go unremarked that Jesus' open table fellowship and his preaching of an inclusive kingdom of salvation were already before the end of the New Testament era being turned into the foundation of a polemic against the Jews.

BIBLICAL SOURCES AND THEIR INTERPRETATION FOR THEOLOGY AND ETHICS

The primary focus of study will be the synoptic gospels, since it is there that the symbol "kingdom of God" is central. Historical-critical research and social history are useful for elucidating the practical meaning of this symbol. The social history of Jesus' time and place gives the known facts dimension and vitality, and social history alerts us to aspects of the narratives that were much more obvious to the biblical writers as first-century Mediterranean people than to "outsiders" like ourselves.[1] In particular, Jesus' preaching of the kingdom will be placed in the context of his

[1] Sean Freyne, *Jesus, a Jewish Galilean: A New Reading of the Jesus-Story* (London: T & T Clark, 2004), p. 6.

Jewish faith and of Jewish apocalyptic. While Jesus' message is in striking
ways very similar to Jewish apocalyptic, it is also different in important
respects. The differences help highlight elements that are distinctive of
and important in Jesus' own mission and ministry. Jesus' Jewishness and
his mission to Israel can be further contextualized by recalling that he
lived in Jewish Galilee, a place outside Jerusalem where in different eras
alternating Gentile and Jewish populations had been settled.

As we turn to the Christian New Testament, we do so as "readers" who
are already situated in communities and practices that are shaping our
identities, our horizons, our options, and our interpretive lenses. In fact,
the New Testament itself, with its four gospels and multiple epistles, is
already a community document, reflecting a lively pluralism of religious
experience, belief, and practice.[2] Even within the New Testament, traditions are inherited, contested, renegotiated, and reconceived in relation to
the practical needs of the authors' communities. There is no such thing as
a pure "world of the text" to which the modern interpreter can resort.[3]

Reading the scriptures, preaching the scriptures, celebrating liturgies
around the scriptures, and aspiring to a scripturally informed morality
and politics always assume a community and its ongoing process of formation. The ongoing Christian tradition provides a practical-doctrinal
"rule of faith" (Irenaeus).[4] With good reason, one biblical scholar entitled
a work *The Bible as the Church's Book*.[5] In every era, Christians tend to
read the bible selectively, sometimes confirming biases but sometimes also
challenging their own historical and political situations, as well as bringing current political values back to their critical readings of the text.[6]

[2] Roger Haight, "Scripture: A Pluralistic Norm for Understanding Our Salvation in Jesus Christ," in Andrés Torres Queiruga, Lisa Sowle Cahill, Maria Clara Bingemer, and Erik Borgman (eds.), *Jesus as Christ: What Is at Stake in Christology* (London: SCM Press, 2008), pp. 13–23, at 20–3.
[3] This kind of approach takes its lead from Hans W. Frei, *The Eclipse of Biblical Narrative: A Study in Eighteenth and Nineteenth Century Hermeneutics* (New Haven, CT: Yale University Press, 1974); and *The Identity of Jesus Christ: The Hermeneutical Bases of Dogmatic Theology* (Minneapolis: Fortress Press, 1975). Frei does not deny that the bible is read in a community, but I want to heighten caution about whether the bible can reorder that community and "ordinary experience" without the biblical narrative itself being reordered in the process. See Kwok Pui-lan, *Postcolonial Imagination and Feminist Theology* (Louisville, KY: Westminster John Knox Press, 2005), p. 182, on "hybridized" understandings of Jesus Christ.
[4] This is a point frequently made by theological ethicist James M. Gustafson. See "Moral Discernment in the Christian Life" and "The Place of Scripture in Christian Ethics: A Methodological Study," in James M. Gustafson, *Theology and Christian Ethics* (Philadelphia: Pilgrim Press, 1974), pp. 99–120 and 121–45, respectively.
[5] Phyllis A. Bird, *The Bible as the Church's Book* (Philadelphia: Westminster John Knox Press, 1982).
[6] Elisabeth Schüssler Fiorenza, *Bread Not Stone: The Challenge of Feminist Biblical Interpretation* (Boston: Beacon Press, 1984), pp. xi, xvi–xvii.

Allen Verhey insists on a "communal hermeneutic" of scripture, in which scripture is both an inherited text with an "original" genesis and meaning and a source of performative reappropriations that sustain and adapt "the life and politics of the community."[7] Each interpreting community, including the communities "behind" the canonical scriptures, is subject to critical evaluation (for which we see a biblical model in Paul's critique of the Corinthians' eucharist [1 Cor. 11:17–18, 20–2]). The New Testament is "authoritative" or "revelatory" for Christians today *when and because* engagement with it mediates "transformative encounter with the living God,"[8] enabling life within God's reign, as inaugurated in the ministry of Jesus. The key issue for Christian politics is what ways of life the scriptures reflect and enable, and what ways of life they decisively negate. The reign of God replaces exclusionary boundaries with the embrace of outcasts, the reconciliation of enemies, and the bonding of a new community of brothers and sisters in Christ.

JESUS REMEMBERED AND PREACHED IN THE GOSPELS

The normative content of Christian practices is defined primarily by the fact that Jesus proclaimed and actively embodied the kingdom of God, remembered in the gospels to be the center of his ministry. One can appreciate the meaning of Jesus' preaching of the kingdom by connecting it to the contours of his life, understood within the larger context of first-century Judaism under Roman rule (late Second Temple Judaism).

Historically verifiable information about the life, career, and death of Jesus of Nazareth as a figure in history is notoriously scant. Nevertheless, prominent biblical scholars are in consensus that, while not intended to be detailed historical records, the canonical gospels do go back to memories of Jesus during his lifetime, which were preserved and transmitted both in oral tradition and in distinctive Christian practices.[9] It is at least

---

[7] Allen Verhey, "Scripture and Ethics: Practices, Performances, and Prescriptions," in Lisa Sowle Cahill and James F. Childress (eds.), *Christian Ethics: Problems and Prospects* (Cleveland: Pilgrim Press, 1996), p. 27. Verhey traces this hermeneutic back to "a work too much neglected" (James M. Gustafson, *Treasure in Earthen Vessels: The Church as a Human Community* [New York: Harper & Brothers, 1961]).

[8] Sandra M. Schneiders, *The Revelatory Text: Interpreting the New Testament as Sacred Scripture* (San Francisco: HarperCollins, 1991), p. 197.

[9] Sean Freyne places the gospels in "the biographic encomium genre of Greco-Roman antiquity" (*Jesus, a Jewish Galilean*, p. 5). Thus, although due allowance must be made for the interpretive and propagandistic aspects of such biographies, the gospel writers do have "historicizing" tendencies and give leads as to the specifics of Jesus' life. Moreover, they are acutely sensitive to the political conditions of their own day, including sources of ethnic, racial, or urban/rural division.

possible to give a minimal historical outline of Jesus' biography.[10] These facts already begin to communicate his message and convey his effect.

Among the certain or virtually certain historical facts of the life of Jesus are that he was born around the time of the death of Herod the Great in 4 BCE; spent his childhood and early adulthood in Nazareth, a Galilean village; was baptized by John the Baptist; called disciples; taught in the villages, towns, and countryside of Galilee, though apparently not in cities; preached "the kingdom of God"; aimed his message to other Jews, as one of many reform movements in Judaism; went to Jerusalem for Passover about 30 CE; created a disturbance in the Temple area; had a final meal with his disciples; was arrested and interrogated by Jewish authorities; and was executed on the orders of Pontius Pilate, the Roman prefect.[11]

If one assumes that the gospels are a performative retelling of the story of Jesus, a retelling that is in substantial continuity with the historical shape of Jesus' life – if not with each and every factual detail of his speech and actions – an even fuller portrayal emerges. In addition to the facts just given, we might add that Jesus was a healer especially famed for exorcisms; taught in parables and aphorisms; had many followers, including several women who supported him financially and were loyal to the end; had a special circle of twelve close associates; was a prophet who challenged Temple authorities; and was crucified outside the walls of Jerusalem by the Roman prefect on the charge of being a messianic pretender.[12]

After Jesus' death, his disciples fled, soon claimed to have seen him, and subsequently believed that he would return within their lifetimes to establish God's reign. They formed a community to prepare and to convert others to faith in Jesus as God's Messiah.[13] In this community they confessed Jesus as present and alive to them, an experience they

James Dunn sees the New Testament as grounded in historical memories of Jesus, mediated over a generation or more by oral traditions (containing the basics of Jesus' life, death, and resurrection), that go back to eyewitnesses and are cited explicitly by Paul (1 Cor. 11:2; 2 Thess. 2:5) (James D. G. Dunn, *Christianity in the Making*, vol. 1: *Jesus Remembered* [Grand Rapids, MI: Eerdmans, 2003], pp. 335–6). On distinctive practices, see Terrence W. Tilley, *The Disciples' Jesus: Christology as Reconciling Practice* (Maryknoll, NY: Orbis Books, 2008); and "Remembering the Historic Jesus: A New Research Program?" *Theological Studies*, 68/1 (2007), pp. 3–35.

[10] The groundbreaking and probably most frequently cited version is E. P. Sanders, *The Historical Figure of Jesus* (London: Penguin Books, 1995), pp. 10–14. See also Dunn, *Jesus Remembered*, pp. 312–24; and Gerd Theissen and Annette Merz, *The Historical Jesus: A Comprehensive Guide*, trans. John Bowden (Minneapolis: Fortress Press, 1998), pp. 569–72.

[11] Sanders, *Historical Figure of Jesus*, pp. 10–11; Theissen and Merz, *Historical Jesus*, pp. 569–72.

[12] Dunn, *Jesus Remembered*, p. 334.

[13] Sanders, *Historical Figure of Jesus*, p. 11.

attributed to the sending of the Spirit. Very shortly after Jesus' death, they were already proclaiming him as Messiah or Christ. This and other titles, such as Son of God, were recast from Jewish tradition to express a new experience. Early on, the followers of Jesus Christ were worshipping him as divine.[14] It is through this confessional and liturgical lens – with its community-forming and moral repercussions – that the biblical writers and their communities recall and retell the story of Jesus.

When we move to the content and veracity of claims about the resurrection, the presence of the Spirit in the church, or the divinity of Christ, we are no longer in the realm of "history" in the sense of facts that can be known apart from communal participation in their reality. They are not accessible to the historian but to the church and to the believer. These claims concern "the real Jesus," the post-resurrection Jesus who is still present to the church.[15] Evidence for (not proof of) Christian claims in this realm involves intellectual coherence with other Christian claims, but also affective-imaginative power and moral-political attestation. To accept such evidence and live against the horizon of the worldview it generates constitutes conversion.

The post-resurrection memory of Jesus is encapsulated in a speech made by Peter to a Gentile audience under the Roman administration, at a gathering that includes some of Peter's Jewish companions.

I truly understand that God shows no partiality, but in every nation anyone who fears him and does what is right is acceptable to him. You know the message he sent to the people of Israel, preaching peace [*shalom*] by Jesus Christ – he is Lord of all. That message spread throughout Judea, beginning in Galilee after the baptism that John announced: how God anointed Jesus of Nazareth with the Holy Spirit and with power; how he went about doing good and healing all who were oppressed by the devil, for God was with him. We are witnesses to all that he did both in Judea and in Jerusalem. They put him to death by hanging on a tree; but God raised him on the third day and allowed him to appear, not to all the people but to us, who were chosen by God as witnesses, and who ate and

[14] This is one-half of the basic thesis of Larry W. Hurtado, *How on Earth Did Jesus Become a God? Historical Questions About Earliest Devotion to Jesus* (Grand Rapids, MI: Eerdmans, 2005); the other half is that by "divinity" the New Testament authors had in mind "binitarian subordinationism." See also Larry W. Hurtado, *At the Origins of Christian Worship: The Context and Character of Earliest Christian Devotion* (Grand Rapids, MI: Eerdmans, 2000), and Richard N. Longenecker, *Studies in Hermeneutics, Christology and Discipleship* (Sheffield: Sheffield Phoenix Press, 2006), which stress the confessional and liturgical grounding of biblical christology.

[15] Sandra Marie Schneiders, *The Revelatory Text: Interpreting the New Testament as Sacred Scripture*, 2nd edn. (Collegeville, MN: Liturgical Press, 1999), p. xii; Luke Timothy Johnson, *The Real Jesus: The Misguided Quest for the Historical Jesus and the Truth of the Traditional Gospels* (San Francisco: HarperCollins, 1996).

drank with him after he rose from the dead. He commanded us to preach to the people and to testify that he is the one ordained by God as judge of the living and the dead. All the prophets testify about him that everyone who believes in him receives forgiveness of sins through his name.

While Peter was still speaking, the Holy Spirit fell upon all who heard the word [Gentile and Jew alike] (Acts 10: 34–44).

Several items in this speech are of ethical and political, and not only religious, interest. First of all, the basis of the evangelization is a memory of key events in the life of a man who was from Nazareth, was baptized by John, preached in Galilee, and went to Jerusalem, where he was executed. Second, however, the framework in which this memory is presented is oriented first and foremost to the formulation of a persuasive message about divine action that empowered and raised Jesus and ordained him eschatological judge, and that *even now* is reconciling and empowering all who believe. The text's proclamation and evangelization arise within and come out of a present experience of God in reordered identities and relations, and this present experience is linked back to Jesus' identity and his relations to those around him. The heart of Jesus' ministry "in Judea and Jerusalem" was generous beneficence and service: he "went about doing good and healing all who were oppressed by the devil" (v. 38). The mission of the disciples expands this inclusiveness, reaching to Jew and Gentile, "for God shows no partiality" (v. 34). Originally "sent to the people of Israel," the risen Jesus is now "Lord of all" (v. 36). Although the Gentile hearers are subsequently baptized (v. 48), the narrative presents the Holy Spirit as a divine gift to Gentiles even before baptism, and without circumcision.

In the mission of the disciples, Jesus has a status that goes beyond the events of his life to encompass the experience of him as raised and exalted by God. Peter's speech does not directly assert that Jesus is "God" or "divine." But for the community to whom Luke writes, it is now clearly apparent that God's Spirit gave Jesus power during his lifetime (v. 38), that he is now "Lord" of all (v. 36), that sins are forgiven in his name (v. 43), and that God not only raised him (v. 40) but has appointed him judge of living and dead (v. 43). The Holy Spirit is from God, in Jesus, and present to those who hear and believe (vv. 38, 44).

HISTORICAL RESEARCH ON JESUS

Historical study of Jesus of Nazareth and of the political, cultural, and religious matrices of his life has interested theologians and biblical scholars since at least the eighteenth century. As with any other historical figure it is impossible to return to Jesus' lifetime and regain the perspective of his personal acquaintances, friends, family, followers, and adversaries, much less of his own feelings and consciousness. Historical research does not aim to recapture Jesus "as he really was" in his own day or to validate (or invalidate) the present reality of Jesus Christ as risen and present to the church. Instead, it employs critical historical tools to learn what can be known with certainty or probability about Jesus as a real individual who lived in the past, accessible to the methods of the historian, and about the first-century Palestinian environment in which he lived, taught, and was killed ("social history").[16] Besides supporting certain basic biographical facts about Jesus, history, social history, and social science are important

the impact of Jesus in his own time. Historical
the circumstances in which the New Testament was
ters and suggests directions; helps us imagine what
eant to those who encountered him in the first cen-
how he might have been responding to their needs
orical understanding helps eliminate faulty readings
reflect how Jesus was received in his own era and
analogies from his time to ours.
an that the findings of the social sciences about Jesus
vater-tight. Various phases, schools of thought, and
ced different pictures of Jesus, depending, for example,
give to his similarity to his Jewish context, the influ-
nan culture and religion, the reliability with which
historical information within their overriding theo-
e historical ordering of and influences on the gospels
of Jesus, the correspondence of details in the gospels
ilable from contemporaneous non-Christian authors,
of noncanonical gospels to understanding Jesus (e.g.,
Gospel of Thomas).

For example, Jesus has been compared to a Mediterranean Jewish peasant (John Dominic Crossan, Sean Freyne),[17] a Hellenistic sage (Burton

---

[16] For an overview of these issues and of major contributions in the field of historical Jesus research, see Mark Allan Powell, *Jesus as a Figure in History: How Modern Historians View the Man from Galilee* (Louisville, KY: Westminster John Knox Press, 1998). For a brief and centrist summary of basic findings, see Daniel J. Harrington, S.J., *Jesus: A Historical Portrait* (Cincinnati, OH: St. Anthony Messenger Press, 2007).

[17] Amy-Jill Levine, Dale C. Allison, Jr., and John Dominic Crossan (eds.), *The Historical Jesus in Context* (Princeton University Press, 2006); Freyne, *Jesus, a Jewish Galilean*.

Mack),[18] a prophet of Wisdom personified as Sophia (Elisabeth Schüssler Fiorenza)[19], a Jewish miracle worker and eschatological prophet (John P. Meier),[20] a Jewish eschatological prophet who claimed a unique role (E. P. Sanders),[21] and a charismatic but noneschatological Jewish healer and social reformer (Marcus Borg).[22] There is variation in terms of both the strength and importance of Jesus' Jewish identity and his relation to a divine power. Yet all agree that "kingdom of God" was central to the teaching of Jesus, that he saw himself in relation to God's momentous action to establish a new order, and that his ministry was marked by an iconoclastic willingness to share table with offensive social "rejects" and unrepentant sinners.[23]

One important area of research from the last quarter of the twentieth century onward has been the Jewishness of Jesus, his resemblance to his Jewish environment, and the Jewish origins of titles such as "Messiah," "Son of Man," and "Son of God." Needless to say Jesus is not similar in every respect to his religious context, and the Judaism of the period was itself diverse in outlook. For example, a Jesus who was more like a Greek philosopher than a Jewish teacher or a Jesus who was not fully Jewish but an ethnic hybrid or a proto-Christian cannot be validated by current knowledge of life in first-century Galilee. In the words of Daniel Harrington:

Most of Jesus' teachings about God, creation, covenant, obedience to God's will, righteousness, and eschatology are consistent with his Jewish theological heritage. Furthermore, the early Christian beliefs about Jesus – his relationship to God as Father, his identity, the significance of his life, the movement he began, his teachings about the coming kingdom of God, and his instructions about human attitudes and actions – use the language and concepts of Judaism. To say the same thing in other terms Christian theology, Christology, soteriology, ecclesiology, eschatology, and ethics are rooted in Judaism.[24]

[18] Burton L. Mack, *The Lost Gospel: The Book of Q & Christian Origins* (New York: HarperCollins, 1993).

[19] Elisabeth Schüssler Fiorenza, *Jesus, Miriam's Child, Sophia's Prophet: Critical Issues in Feminist Christology* (New York: Continuum, 1994).

[20] John P. Meier, *A Marginal Jew: Rethinking the Historical Jesus*, vol. 1: *The Roots of the Problem and the Person* (New York: Doubleday, 1991).

[21] Sanders, *Historical Figure of Jesus*.

[22] Marcus J. Borg, *Jesus: Uncovering the Life, Teachings, and Relevance of a Religious Revolutionary* (San Francisco: HarperSanFrancisco, 2006).

[23] See Powell, *Jesus as a Figure in History*, pp. 174–6.

[24] Daniel J. Harrington, S.J., "Retrieving the Jewishness of Jesus: Recent Developments," in Bryan F. LeBeau, Leonard Greenspoon, and Dennis Hamm, S.J. (eds.), *The Historical Jesus through Catholic and Jewish Eyes* (Harrisburg, PA: Trinity Press International, 2000), pp. 67–84, at 68.

This point is important both theologically and politically, for Christians have often developed the distinctiveness of Jesus at the expense of respect for Jews and Judaism, contrasting Jesus to a supposedly negative religious environment out of which he arose and which he transcended or even negated.[25] Historical critics have often played into this tendency, by identifying "dissimilarity" to his Jewish environment as one criterion of the authenticity of sayings or actions attributed to Jesus by the gospel narrators. On the contrary, each of the gospel authors in his own way reaffirms the Jewish identity of Jesus.[26] Credible proposals about Jesus have to be credible within first-century Judaism, and also credible as a bridge to early Christianity, not in total discontinuity with either.[27]

PALESTINE UNDER ROMAN RULE

The infancy narratives in Matthew and Luke place Jesus' birth in Bethlehem, perhaps a device to make a theological connection between Jesus and King David.[28] More historically plausible is the information that Jesus was raised in Nazareth in Galilee, a town in the northern part of Palestine with an undistinguished reputation (John 1:46). Following his father, Joseph, Jesus worked as a skilled construction worker or craftsman (*tekton*) in wood or stone (Mark 6:2–3; Matt. 13:55). He was brought up in the Jewish faith – circumcised and named on the eighth day after his birth, presented in the Temple at forty days, and taken by his parents on a Passover pilgrimage to the Temple at the age of twelve.

Jerusalem, the capital of Judea in southern Palestine, was the center of Jewish religious practice, which was focused for all Jews of the time on the Jerusalem Temple. In Jesus' time, Jews were united not by a body of doctrine, but by the fundamental beliefs that there is one true God, who had created a covenant with Israel, and that transgressions would bring retribution, while repentance would bring forgiveness. Jews were also

[25] See Judith Plaskow, "Feminist Anti-Judaism and the Christian God," *Journal of Feminist Studies in Religion*, 7 (1991), pp. 99–108; and Amy-Jill Levine, *The Misunderstood Jew: The Church and the Scandal of the Jewish Jesus* (New York: HarperCollins, 2006).

[26] The principle of dissimilarity from both his Jewish context and early Christianity was formulated in 1954 by the German scholar Ernst Käsemann. See Sean Freyne, "Jesus the Jew," in Queiruga et al. (eds.), *Jesus as Christ: What Is at Stake in Christology?* pp. 29–31. On how Jesus fits into the Jewish narrative of salvation, see Sanders, *Historical Figure of Jesus*, pp. 80–91.

[27] N. T. Wright, *Jesus and the Victory of God, Christian Origins and the Question of God*, vol. 2 (Minneapolis: Fortress Press, 1996), pp. 90–3.

[28] The anointing of David took place in Bethlehem (1 Sam. 16), which was also the birthplace of his grandfather (Ruth 4). Micah 5 states that the Messiah should be born in Bethlehem.

[29] Sanders, *Historical Figure of Jesus*, pp. 80–1; Dunn, *Jesus Remembered*, pp. 286–92.

united by a way of life centered on the land of Israel, the law of Moses, and the Temple, for all of which the Torah was the defining source. As a Galilean, Jesus worshipped at the synagogue in his hometown, since the Temple in Jerusalem was too far away for frequent visits. As a young man, he was a follower of John the Baptist, who led an ascetic life, preached repentance and reform, and baptized followers as a sign of renewal. After the death of John, Jesus began his own ministry in Galilee, settling in the town of Capernaum but traveling to the Galilean border areas.

Though outside the cultic center of Jewish life, in contact with Greco-Roman culture, and subject to the Roman imperial order, Galilean Jews were not engaged in a special struggle to resist Gentile culture, because "Galilee was without a doubt a land with a Jewish stamp."[30] The institutions in Galilee, including numerous synagogues and schools, were Jewish, and Jewish magistrates judged cases according to Jewish law. Archeological excavations in Palestine have yielded widespread evidence of Jewish burial sites, stone vessels used for ritual washing, ritual baths, and aniconic coinage.[31] Such finds attest that "the largely village culture within which Jesus' ministry was conducted ... was thoroughly Jewish in ethos, affiliation and practice."[32] This does not mean that there were no tensions between Jews and Gentiles, since Galilee was surrounded by Hellenistic cities. In Galilee itself, the proportion of Jews to Gentiles had shifted under various conquerors, and in different eras, the majority at the time had persecuted the minority, Jews and Gentiles alike.[33]

Nor was Galilee a particularly depressed region economically. Traditions about God as Creator, about divine care for the creation, and about the promise of a plentiful land for the descendants of Abraham found lush illustration in Galilee. According to the description of the Jewish historian Josephus:

The land is everywhere so rich in soil and pasturage and produces such a variety of trees that even the most indolent are tempted by these facilities to engage in

[30] Theissen and Merz, *Historical Jesus*, p. 169.
[31] Eric M. Meyers, "Sanders's 'Common Judaism' and the Common Judaism of Material Culture," in Fabian E. Udoh (ed.), with Susannah Heschel, Mark Chancey, and Gregory Tatum, *Redefining First-Century Jewish and Christian Identities: Essays in Honor of Ed Parish Sanders* (Notre Dame, IN: University of Notre Dame Press, 2008), pp. 153–74.
[32] Sean Freyne, "The Galilean Jesus and a Contemporary Christology," in *Theological Studies*, 70/2 (2009), p. 291. See also Sean Freyne, "Archaeology and the Historical Jesus," in John R. Bartlett (ed.), *Archaeology and Biblical Interpretation* (New York: Routledge, 1997), pp. 117–44; and Mark A. Chancey, *The Myth of a Gentile Galilee*, Society for New Testament Studies Monograph Series 118 (New York: Cambridge University Press, 2002).
[33] Theissen and Merz, *Historical Jesus*, pp. 169–70.

agriculture ... The cities too are plentiful and because of the richness of the soil the villages everywhere are so densely populated that even the smallest of them has a population of over fifteen thousand inhabitants.[34]

Nazareth was a farming village in the Roman period, while the lakefront town of Capernaum was a center for the region's thriving trade in salted fish. The fact that women were probably involved in the preparation and preservation of this product may have made it easier for Jesus to attract women to his retinue, possible for them to contribute to his support, and more acceptable for them to travel with him and the male disciples.[35]

Despite the relatively comfortable lifestyle possible in Galilee, the situation of the peasant class in any agrarian society diverges widely from that of elites. Wealth and social status were connected to ownership of land. Peasants had to deal with a lack of assets by exploiting networks of family, friends, and better-situated "patrons," who demanded loyalty, personal service, honor, and political support in return for favors.[36] Nor were Galilee's inhabitants immune to the effects of changeable weather patterns; to the demands of absent rulers, both Roman and Jewish, who demanded tribute; or to those of expanding urban centers like Sepphoris and Tiberias. As demands from city centers grew, larger estates developed, while small landowners, leaseholders, and hired laborers became more economically marginal and more susceptible to others' greed and exploitation. Jesus' predictions of beatitude for the poor, hungry, and weeping invited struggling villagers and peasants to envision that their lot would be reversed and the ancestral promise of a bountiful land fulfilled.[37]

During Jesus' lifetime, Jewish Palestine was relatively independent of immediate Roman control. A line of local client rulers represented Roman interests, collected tribute, and were responsible for keeping the peace and public order. The Jewish ruler of Galilee was Herod Antipas; his counterpart in Jerusalem was Herod Archelaus; both were sons of Herod the Great. It is not hard to imagine that there were in Galilee persistent structural tensions, if not frequent or widespread violence, on several levels – "tensions between Jews and Gentiles, town and country, rich and poor, rulers and ruled. When Jesus proclaimed here a turning point in everything, one which was beginning in the present, he found an audience

---

[34] JW 3.41–43, as cited in Freyne, *Jesus, a Jewish Galilean*, pp. 38–9.

[35] Freyne, *Jesus, a Jewish Galilean*, pp. 44, 48–52.

[36] K. C. Hanson and Douglas E. Oakman, *Palestine in the Time of Jesus: Social Structures and Social Conflicts*, 2nd edn. (Minneapolis: Fortress Press, 1998), pp. 70–1.

[37] Freyne, *Jesus, a Jewish Galilean*, pp. 46–7; Theissen and Merz, *Historical Jesus*, pp. 171–3.

which had reasons to long for a change."[38] He must also have reached an audience with reason to fear that change might really happen. Josephus says Herod Antipas executed John the Baptist because of the threat that John's protests against Herod's marriage to his half-niece, Herodias, could engender widespread revolt.

Although taxes imposed by Romans and local administrations, and for upkeep of the Temple system, could be oppressive to peasants and small farmers, the Roman government preferred to operate at a distance and to confer relative autonomy on local officials and ways of life. It was only due to his ineffectiveness at suppressing dissent that Herod Archelaus in Jerusalem was deposed as king and put under the authority of a Roman governor (prefect), who from CE 26 to 36 was Pontius Pilate. Local Jewish rule reverted to the high priest and his council. The high priest commanded the guards who policed the Temple.

During his reign, Herod Archelaus appointed the high priest, but when Rome imposed a prefect it took over this prerogative. The high priest at the time of Jesus, Joseph Caiaphas, was an intermediary between the people and Rome, and responsible to Rome. The Roman prefect, accompanied by Roman troops, came to Jerusalem during the three major religious feasts, especially Passover, to ensure crowd control; armed uprisings were not infrequent, though no major insurrection threatened at the time of Jesus' execution. As high priest, Caiaphas would have been responsible for making sure that no troublemakers disrupted festivals, a sufficient reason to arrest Jesus. Jesus had a following, even if not remarkably large. Moreover, he had alarmed some by his attack on the Temple, perhaps even predicting its destruction.[39] The gospels, as confirmed by Josephus, report that Caiaphas had Jesus arrested and sent him to Pilate. Only the Roman prefect had the authority to impose the death sentence.[40]

Many Jews hoped for liberation from Rome's control, looked and longed for divine vindication and help, and entertained a variety of expectations about how this might occur. Messianism in ancient Israel focused on the restoration of the Davidic kingship: the house of David is ensured forever (2 Sam. 7). The Messiah would be a descendant of David,

---

[38] Theissen and Merz, *Historical Jesus*, p. 175. Sean Freyne maintains that first-century Galilee was relatively prosperous and peaceful, while others, like Bruce Malina, Richard Horsley, and John Dominic Crossan construe deep-seated oppression, peasant unrest, and spiraling violence.

[39] Mark 13:1–2, Matt. 24:1–2, and Luke 21:5–6 portray Jesus as predicting the destruction of the Temple. The historical nature of this report is, however, uncertain, because the gospels were written retrospectively after the actual destruction of the Temple by the Romans in 70 CE.

[40] Sanders, *Historical Figure of Jesus*, p. 269.

who is "the one anointed" ("Messiah" in Hebrew, "Christ" in Greek) by God to resume David's role. But the Davidic line was broken by the Babylonian exile, and messianic expectation had diminished by the time of Jesus. Moreover, the figure of King David had always been ambiguous, representing both God's protection of the nation and the danger of trusting Israel's covenant, governance, and future to a fallible human king, instead of placing confidence solely in the leadership of God. After the exile, hope for the Messiah took different forms:

Relatively few people expected a Davidic Messiah who would liberate the Jews by defeating the Roman army. Some people expected a very grand sign that the time of liberation had arrived (such as the collapse of Jerusalem's walls), while others probably expected no more than that God would strengthen the hands of the righteous and strike terror into the hearts of Rome's soldiers.[41]

Jesus led one of a number of reform movements within Judaism, all of which represented distinctive ways of interpreting Jewish tradition to contend with first-century Jewish experience. Jesus is frequently portrayed by the gospels in argument with the Pharisees, especially in the Gospel of Matthew. In reality the Pharisees and Jesus probably had much in common. The pronounced conflicts of the gospels owe more to struggles within Jewish Christianity after the destruction of the Temple by the Romans in 70 CE than to Jesus' probable attitudes. The Pharisees sought to bring all Jews into connection with the Temple by extending opportunities for purity observance to homes and villages in a sort of "democratizing" move. They also emphasized common meals with religious discussion. The Pharisees may have originated as an apocalyptic group, not only reinterpreting Jewish law, but also resisting imperial oppression. Yet, at least by the time of Jesus, the Pharisees were not militants. They worked within the Roman order to effect change.[42] The Sadducees were more conservative, with more influence over the Temple and its priesthood. The Essenes at Qumran, whose beliefs and sectarian way of life are portrayed in the Dead Sea Scrolls, stressed ascetic community and coming divine intervention. The Zealots, in contrast, took up armed resistance against the Roman occupiers and the Jews who collaborated with them.[43]

---

[41] Ibid., p. 32. For a historical overview, see ibid., pp. 18–32; and Harrington, *Jesus: A Historical Portrait*, pp. 13–17, 70–3.
[42] Freyne, *Jesus, a Jewish Galilean*, pp. 132–3.
[43] Harrington, *Jesus: A Historical Portrait*, p. 16.

Jesus certainly did not advocate violent revolt and, as against the Sadducees, was involved in a controversy over the Temple that evidently earned him the hostility of Temple officials (Mark 11:15–19). His reaching out to Jews in the diaspora and to those who had infringed the requirements of purity give him significant affinity with the Pharisees, and, like the Pharisees, Jesus still observed Jewish law. He shared their interest in the topics of resurrection, Sabbath observance, and the application of purity norms.[44]

Jesus also bears some resemblance to the Essenes, perhaps as a result of his association with John the Baptist. An important connection among the Essenes, John, and Jesus is to be found in apocalyptic, though their appropriation of apocalyptic themes is certainly not identical. In other words, although Jesus interprets Jewish life and beliefs in his own distinctive way, he casts his vision from elements available in his religious milieu. John Meier calls Jesus a "marginal Jew" because, unlike other prophets, he works miracles (healings and exorcisms) that confirm his authority.[45] Yet even miracles are not altogether exceptional; "like other ancient peoples, Jews believed in miracles but did not think that the ability to perform them proved exalted status."[46] The function of Jesus' miracles in underlining his message about the kingdom will be treated later in the chapter.

APOCALYPTIC

Jewish apocalyptic dates from the late sixth century BCE and is a genre in which historical events are interpreted in light of a transcendent world of angels; the prospect of eschatological judgment and divine action; and revelations to a seer by means of heavenly journeys, visions, and angels. The constant element in apocalyptic is that tribulations and traumas in this world are placed in the perspective of an otherworldly realm that envisages salvation and retribution.[47] Some apocalyptic movements expect that the present order will be overturned as a result of events within history; others hope that a world to come will judge and reject the historical

[44] Ibid., p. 17. See also Anthony J. Saldarini, *Pharisees, Scribes and Sadducees in Palestinian Society: A Sociological Approach*, 2nd edn. (Grand Rapids, MI: Eerdmans, 2001).
[45] John P. Meier, *A Marginal Jew: Rethinking the Historical Jesus*, vol. 2: *Mentor, Message, and Miracles* (New York: Doubleday, 1994).
[46] Sanders, *Historical Figure of Jesus*, p. 133.
[47] John J. Collins, *The Apocalyptic Imagination: An Introduction to Jewish Apocalyptic Literature*, 2nd edn. (Grand Rapids, MI: Eerdmans, 1998), pp. 5, 11, 280.

order instead of transforming it. But by definition, apocalyptic projects a radical intervention of supernatural origin that suddenly supervenes upon the world as we know it. God is in control of all human destiny, no matter what current adversity seems to say. Humans cannot shape their destiny, but God will be victorious.

This framework could be utilized by various groups to fit their situations. Apocalypse could provide exhortation or reassurance in the face of persecution, or consolation for the suffering of this life and the inevitability of death. Motifs like "Son of Man" are transferred among apocalyptic contexts but reinterpreted. The designation "Son of Man" is possibly of Canaanite origin, referring to Baal; it is reconstrued for Jewish use in Daniel 7 (the only example of full apocalyptic in the Hebrew Bible), then picked up in Mark 13:26 (and later gospels), where it reverberates with cumulative associations.[48] For example, according to John Collins, Baal is the "rider of clouds" and a divine figure, but subordinated to El, the father of gods and human beings.

El is the prototype for the Ancient of Days in Daniel. In Daniel (7:13), the "one like a son of man" comes on the clouds but is subordinate to the Ancient of Days – although the one who usually rides the clouds is Yahweh. So here we have a figure that shares some divine activities but is still subject to a father god. "One like a son of man" can also be used to refer to an angelic or human being; Daniel uses similar expressions to refer both to Gabriel and to the seer "Daniel" (e.g., 8:15, 17). So to the divinely acting but still subordinate apocalyptic figure, there is conjoined the ambiguous possibility of human or angelic nature. In the New Testament, the phrase "son of man" is still sometimes used to refer to angels (Rev. 14:14),[49] and its use by the Jesus of the gospels is ambiguous and multivalent. In the hands of the gospel authors, this title is a vehicle for associating Jesus, his role, and his work with an end time of historical tribulation and divine intervention through a special agent.

Despite its otherworldly focus, apocalyptic deliberately creates a worldview for the sake of actions that follow, though the response expected is more typically not armed revolution (as was taken up by the Maccabees), but patient waiting in a countercultural society (Daniel, Essenes), sometimes accepting and even cooperating with the interim status quo. The apocalypses powerfully denounce the evils of this world and offer an alternative vision of another world, but seldom provide "a program for effective action."[50]

---

[48] Ibid., p. 19.　　[49] Ibid., pp. 101–3.　　[50] Ibid., p. 283.

The book of Daniel, the last book in the canonical Hebrew scriptures, is an apocalyptic writing inspired by the imposition of Hellenistic "reforms" on Jewish life and worship under the reign of Antiochus Epiphanes, in the mid–second century BCE.[51] Sacrifice in the Temple had been forcibly replaced by a pagan cult. Daniel 7 anticipates the imminent overthrow of Antiochus, who will be replaced by "one like a human being" ("son of man"), whose rule is subsequently equated with "the kingdom of the holy ones of the Most High" (vv. 26–7). Daniel replies to the idea that Jews could serve Gentile kings and still maintain religious purity and holiness. The time for accommodation to Gentile rule is over. The Jews no longer aspire to the Gentile court. There is no compatibility between the kingdom of God and Gentile kingdoms. Since some have had to lay down their lives out of loyalty to their religion, they are supported by the promise of resurrection at the end of historical time (Dan. 12). The focus is on the higher world and a destiny in the world of angels.[52] The seers of apocalypses have despaired of the usefulness of human efforts and his torical action. (The author of Daniel did not foresee that, within about a year, the Maccabees were actually to solve the problem for the next one hundred years by capturing the Temple area, throwing off Roman rule, and restoring traditional Jewish worship.)

The only other apocalypse in the bible, Revelation, is written in similar circumstances. Christians in Asia Minor (Turkey) were forced to participate in rituals of emperor worship. The narrator describes his vision of the risen Jesus, which gives him confidence that present tribulations will soon be brought to an end. The Lamb of God will vanquish God's enemies, cast aside those who have not been faithful, and reign victorious from the New Jerusalem. Revelation is replete with violent rhetoric depicting the fate of the unrighteous. But their fate will be enacted through divine agency, not by human hands. There will be "a new heaven and a new earth," but not until the old heaven and earth have passed away (Rev. 21:1).

Sean Freyne notes the links between Daniel and the prophetic message of Isaiah, who constructs his interpretation of the present and his hopes for the future around the image of Zion, the restored city of the Lord. The memory of Davidic kingship no longer carried as much power for the post-exilic Jewish community as did Jerusalem, now lifted up and healed of divisions as Zion, the new bride of Yahweh (still a theme in

---

[51] Sean Freyne, *Jesus, a Jewish Galilean*, p. 126.
[52] Collins, *Apocalyptic Imagination*, pp. 113–14.

Revelation). Isaiah envisions that in Zion "the servants of Yahweh" will enjoy his favor (Isa. 65:8–15, 66:14), while those who have betrayed him for other religions and oppressed the needy will be punished in an eschatological reversal (65:1–7, 11–12). The individual figure "servant of the Lord" (chs. 40–55) seems also to refer to the collective Jacob/Israel; and the "suffering servant" (chs. 52–3) is ultimately vindicated for suffering and rejection borne on behalf of others and becomes a model for imitation. Echoes of this earlier prophetic voice are heard both in the Jewish documents from Qumran and in early (Jewish) Christianity.[53]

The figure of a warrior messiah who would liberate Israel and drive out the Gentiles reappears in the first century BCE in the Psalms of Solomon and the Dead Sea Scrolls. But the messianism of the Essene community at Qumran is distinctive in that the royal messiah is paired with and subordinate to a priestly messiah. Both are human messiahs and the focus is on the community of which they are a part, not their roles as such. The eschatological age will be brought by divine action, and the messiahs will fulfill their roles only within that age. The Dead Sea Scrolls of Qumran show God, not a human messiah, preaching "good news to the poor," "releasing captives," and so on, quoting from Isaiah 61:1 (where the speaker is not God but a prophet). The scrolls also mention a community meal, featuring bread and wine, and an anticipated messianic banquet with bread and wine blessed by the priestly messiah in the eschatological age. Unlike Jesus' open meals and his imagery of feasts where insider and outsider status are reversed (Matt. 22:2–14; Luke 14:16–24), the Essene meal is limited to observant community members. In fact, the Qumran Community Rule styles community members as Sons of Light, opposed to Sons of Darkness, whom the former "may hate" because God does.[54]

Yet also displayed in the Qumran documents is a sort of "realized eschatology," in which the righteous enjoy fellowship with the angels that was promised to the dead in the apocalypses of Daniel and Enoch. This hint of the present dimension of the kingdom, later to be developed in the gospels, is a most distinctive feature of the Dead Sea Scrolls: "they were already living the risen life with the angels."[55] Even so, the primary

---

[53] Freyne, *Jesus, a Jewish Galilean*, pp. 103–8. On similar uses of Isaiah by Daniel, the Qumran documents, and early Christian writings (especially Matthew), see also Joseph Blenkinsopp, *Opening the Sealed Book: Interpretations of the Book of Isaiah in Late Antiquity* (Grand Rapids, MI: Eerdmans, 2006).

[54] Collins, *Apocalyptic Imagination*, pp. 157–65; Harrington, *Jesus: A Historical Portrait*, pp. 106–7, 110.

[55] Ibid., p. 174.

orientation of the Essenes at Qumran was otherworldly. The Essene community was not socially or politically engaged, but sectarian, an elite group that went into the wilderness to prepare for definitive divine action, not to gauge how to begin transforming the world to better reflect God's design.

Certainly there are parallels between the message of the Jesus movement, Isaiah, Daniel, and the Qumran documents, but in what way was the worldview of Jesus himself apocalyptic? Was his expectation so otherworldly? Did he expect cataclysmic final events to occur soon? John Collins identifies Jesus' purported apocalypticism as one of the most debated issues since the rise of historical-critical approaches to the bible.[56] (Some, such as Albert Schweitzer and Rudolf Bultmann, have seen Jesus' apocalypticism as a reason to discredit any significant relevance of his teaching to Christian faith at all.) Given the now incontrovertible Jewish identity of Jesus, it must be agreed that his preaching of the kingdom of God is set in an apocalyptic framework. But to what extent did Jesus share or modify the typical features of this worldview? What effect might this have had on his ethical and political outlook? And what difference does that make for Christian ethics today?

KINGDOM PRESENT AND FUTURE

The phrase "kingdom of God" (from the Greek *basilea*, which may also be translated less patriarchally as "reign") appears sixty-two times in the synoptics. John the Baptist baptized people as a mark of "repentance for the forgiveness of sins" and as a sign of commitment to begin a new life in preparation for the full coming of God's kingdom and judgment (Mark 1:4; Luke 3:3). John's future focus, desert habitat, ascetic lifestyle, and call for repentance resemble Jewish apocalyptic reform movements. Though John likely served as a mentor to Jesus and though the first followers of Jesus may have been disciples of John, Jesus ultimately carved his own path. In typical Jewish usage, "kingdom of God" had an especially strong connection with eschatological or apocalyptic beliefs, expressing hope in God's definitive salvation, vindication, and restoration of Israel in the future, a hope that Jesus retains.[57] Yet, "whereas John emphasized the future coming of God's kingdom, Jesus also stressed its present dimensions."[58]

---

[56] Ibid., p. 257.
[57] Meier, *Marginal Jew*, vol. 2: *Rethinking the Historical Jesus*, pp. 269–70.
[58] Harrington, *Jesus: A Historical Portrait*, p. 18.

What the kingdom represents is illustrated repeatedly by means of another characteristic feature of Jesus' teaching, the parables. Mediated by provocative stories about characters such as the Prodigal Son, Good Samaritan, workers in the vineyard, dishonest steward, and woman with a lost coin, "kingdom of God" is a complex symbol that suggests a plurality of meanings and draws on a number of elements in the experience of hearers. It is rightly and often noted that the parables have to do with reversals of expectation, mercy and beneficence shown in unanticipated ways, and favor bestowed on those who appear undeserving or insignificant. However, there has been and still is less agreement on whether the parables of the kingdom should be heard as applying to spiritual and religious realities or also to social and political ones; whether the kingdom is a gift or comes with entrance criteria; and whether the kingdom is a future state or a present reality.

Understanding what Jesus meant by the kingdom is supported by information about the original context of his teaching and its likely meaning to its first hearers. Important for that context are Israel's memory of the kingship of David, its first-century subjection to foreign rule, and its hope for God's reign in the future.[59] Some of the diverse motifs of Jewish expectation that played into Jesus' kingdom preaching were a climactic period of tribulation, the defeat of Satan, the return of Yahweh to Zion/Jerusalem, the building of a new temple, the meek inheriting the land, the imagery of a great feast, abundance and prosperity, the removal of disabilities and defects, an eschatological pilgrimage of other nations to Israel, a final judgment and vindication of the faithful, and (in the latter half of the Second Temple period) the general resurrection of the dead. These motifs did not constitute one comprehensive narrative, nor were they all operative in the outlook of any given group. However, it is fair to say that they affected the worldview of Jesus and other Jews by constituting a framework spanning past, present, and age to come. Israel is called to be faithful, prepare, persevere in difficulty, and maintain hope for God's future display of righteous power, the revelation of his kingly rule over all creation (see the opening verses of Pss. 93, 96, 97, 99). A variation of special importance for early Christianity, and perhaps for Jesus' own self-understanding, is the involvement of a special agent in realizing God's designs.[60]

---

59 Dunn, *Jesus Remembered*, p. 390. See 1 Samuel 13:14 (where the kingdom of God is promised to David), 1 Chronicles 29:10–12, and Daniel 4:3 for examples.
60 Dunn, *Jesus Remembered*, pp. 390–6, 475.

Jesus' use of the symbol "kingdom of God" does not present vindication and transformation as future acts of God in the sense that they are now only to be anticipated and not enjoyed. For Jesus, God's kingdom does exist as a transcendent realm that will come to earth in the future (as the Lord's Prayer petitions; Matt. 6:10; Luke 11:2), perhaps through a cosmic event (Mark 13:24–7). But Jesus' distinctive message, as compared with most apocalyptic, is that "kingdom of God" also designates God's future *as* present now, in and through Jesus' ministry. In reply to a question about the nature of his role, Jesus says, "The blind receive their sight, the lame walk, the lepers are cleansed, the deaf hear, the dead are raised, and the poor have the good news brought to them. And blessed is anyone who takes no offense at me" (Matt. 11:2–6). He exhorts hearers to get ready, prepare, and to hope, but also to lay hold of what is available now. The kingdom "is among you" (Luke 17:20).[61]

The kingdom now seems insignificant, like a mustard seed or yeast (Matt. 13:31–3). To find the kingdom requires discernment and perseverance, illustrated by the parables of the hidden treasure and the precious pearl (Matt. 13:44–6). Finding the kingdom will not be easy, and many will fall by the wayside. When the kingdom is present in fullness, God's judgment will separate and reward appropriately the good and the bad, just as wheat is harvested and weeds thrown into the furnace (Matt. 13:30) or good fish kept and bad fish thrown away (Matt. 13:47–50). The completion and full manifestation of God's reign are future events.[62]

But Jesus' disciples are also to live out of the kingdom in their daily lives and relationships. God's anticipated reign is even now changing the status quo. Jesus brought together in table fellowship people who scandalized many (Mark 2:15–16; Matt. 11:19; Luke 7:34, 15:1–2, 19:10). God's action brings a "revolution" to the present world. Jesus proclaimed the "loving forgiveness of God the Father, a prodigal father who freely bestows his forgiveness on sinners who have no strict claim on God's mercy."[63]

In fact, the kingdom is so real that it has already faced violent opposition and "suffered violence" (Matt. 11:12; Luke 16:16). Opposition is to be expected, given Jesus' signature idea of reversal, of insiders becoming outsiders, and outsiders becoming insiders at the final banquet (Matt. 8:11–12; Luke 13:28–29). Key to the kingdom are love, reconciliation, and forgiveness, particularly in the form of the Torah injunction to love one's

[61] See Sanders, *Historical Figure of Jesus*, pp. 169–88, for an overview of different senses of "kingdom" in the gospels, in relation to Jewish thought.
[62] Harrington, *Jesus: A Historical Portrait*, pp. 24–5.
[63] Dunn, *Jesus Remembered*, p. 331.

neighbor as oneself as the counterpart of love of God (Lev. 19:18; Matt. 22:35–40; Mark 12:28–31; Luke 10:25–28). Beyond one's neighbor, disciples also extend love to enemies, a radically different basis for a community ethic (Matt. 5:43–48; Luke 6:27–28, 32–36).

The Gospel of Luke draws a connection between Isaiah and the programmatic message of Jesus, with its iconoclastic overtones (Luke 4:16–21). Recall that Daniel invokes Isaiah's image of Jerusalem/Zion as the place of divine renewal. Freyne suggests that "as a Jewish Galilean prophet with deeply held convictions, Jesus had shown continuing and real concern for the central role that Jerusalem was expected to play within the perspective of restoration hopes, especially as these had been articulated by Isaiah."[64] This helps explain why Jesus was impelled to make the fatal final journey to Jerusalem and to confront practices regarding the Temple; why his radical social message is part of a collective religious vision; how that message and that vision are practical, political, and "this-worldly" as well as spiritual and ecclesial; and why their consequences were and still are threatening to many religious, social, and political authority structures. The apocalyptic worldview tends to be quietist, despairing of hope for changing the evil world, defeating or converting oppressors. But Jesus' kingdom worldview reorders all relationships and exercises of power. He proclaims that God's promise of liberty for captives and freedom for the oppressed "is now fulfilled in your hearing" (Luke 4: 21). The kingdom of Jesus is both politically potent and extremely dangerous.

Jesus' teaching embodies a tensive view of the eschatological time, with divine action expected in the future, yet incorporating anticipatory transformation in the present. Sayings about the inbreaking dynamic of the kingdom "are widely regarded as expressing the 'voice' of the historical Jesus about the kingdom of God."[65] The Jesus of the gospels does not withdraw permanently into the desert or forswear engagement with the structures, oppressions, and possibilities of everyday life. He preaches in the villages of Galilee, engaging ordinary experience and the activities of local people. God's reign is active in these places. The "modified apocalyptic dualism" with which Daniel Harrington characterizes Paul may also be hypothesized of Jesus.[66] Jesus does not see the world in extreme

---

[64] Freyne, *Jesus, a Jewish Galilean*, p. 109.

[65] Harrington, *Jesus: A Historical Portrait*, p. 26.

[66] Daniel J. Harrington, S.J., and James F. Keenan, S.J., *Paul and Virtue Ethics: Building Bridges Between New Testament Studies and Moral Theology* (New York: Rowman & Littlefield, 2010), p. 114. Each chapter is single-authored.

dualisms, as does most apocalyptic; nor does he emphasize rejection, hatred, and violence toward sinners, outsiders, and oppressors, another common feature of apocalyptic. Paul believes that although this world is under the dominion of sin, death, and the law, the life, death, and resurrection of Jesus have introduced a new age, the age of Christ and the Holy Spirit, that already turns back the opposing powers and reveals God's power.

The communities that produced the New Testament proclaim that God's decisive action to inaugurate a new age has already begun, since the Messiah has already come and the first fruits of the resurrection have been given. Among Jesus' Jewish contemporaries, the resurrection was expected to be a collective event at the end of time. Individuals were not raised immediately upon dying. The resurrection of Jesus changes this timing. In Paul's framework the resurrection of Jesus implies that all others are in fact also already raised, since resurrection is collective. Through Jesus' resurrection, "it became possible for all humans – Gentiles and Jews alike – to become the children of light and to do the deeds of light insofar as they followed the leadership of Christ and his Holy Spirit" (see Rom. 1:16–17).[67]

Paul writes to the Colossians, "Live in a manner worthy of the Lord, so as to be fully pleasing, in every good work bearing fruit and growing in the knowledge of God, strengthened with every power, in accord with His glorious might.... He delivered us from the power of darkness and transferred us to the kingdom of his beloved Son, in whom we have redemption, the forgiveness of sins" (Col. 1:10–11, 13).

Yet the realized eschatology of Christian texts does not negate the value of endurance under suffering and hope for God's future. God has "made us alive with Christ" and "raised us up with him and seated us with him in the heavenly places in Christ" (Eph. 2:5–6). Nevertheless, all creation still groans and waits; "and not only that, but we ourselves, who have the firstfruits of the Spirit," still await the fullness of redemption (Rom. 8:22–3).

The New Testament illumines Jesus' ministry with the resurrection's glow. The gospels were written decades or a generation after Jesus' death and portray the life of Jesus and the politics of the church on the basis of their conviction that Jesus is raised and now present and empowering the faithful through the Spirit. The resurrection-oriented "kingdom-present" accent of the gospels is key for Christian politics and for liberation

---

[67] Ibid., p. 26.

theology. But did Jesus himself share this emphasis? And what difference does it make whether he did? In Christian understanding, the Jesus of history cannot be separated from the later church and its theologies, as though the messages of the latter were self-sufficient and normative on their own terms, whether or not the Jesus of history resembles them.

Therefore, we must ask whether the "modified apocalyptic dualism" of the Jesus of the gospels is in reality just the eschatology of the gospel authors, more specifically of Matthew and Luke, and not that of Jesus himself, who may have shared the more radical apocalyptic hopes of his Jewish contemporaries. Frank Matera makes the case that Mark, the earliest gospel, is closer to traditional apocalyptic, from which it might be inferred that so was Jesus' "historical" message. If so, a transformative Christian politics of the kingdom can trace its pedigree to the New Testament (and perhaps to the risen Jesus), but not to Jesus of Nazareth as a historical figure. To Matera, the question is whether the author of Mark expected the *parousia* (second coming) of Jesus to arrive through some future decisive event during the lifetime of the disciples (i.e., late first century) or whether it had already arrived in the resurrection of Jesus. Either way, he implies, kingdom life would not have been a realized possibility during Jesus' own lifetime (except "in a hidden way accessible only through faith," presumably without concrete social signs).[68] If so, the Jesus of history does not license an activist social stance, though the resurrection option in the later canonical materials does provide an alternative basis for a theology and politics of present effective action for the church.

There is undeniably some ethical-political value to the dualistically apocalyptic slant discerned by Matera in early gospel materials and clearly retained in Revelation. It consists in the hope that "God's decisive action" will change what human action cannot, evil in the face of which historical action seems completely impotent. Today such conditions would include intransigent forms of misery like wars, genocides, torture, rape, grinding poverty, tsunamis, and famines.[69] At the same time, the downside of a view of salvation that is almost entirely future-focused is that it leads to political disengagement or passivity, not likely to have been the stance of Jesus. And theologically and religiously, it amounts to a denial

[68] Frank J. Matera, *New Testament Theology: Exploring Diversity and Unity* (Louisville, KY: Westminster John Knox Press, 2007), pp. 23–4.
[69] On the merits of apocalyptic for Christian politics, see J. Matthew Ashley, "The Turn to Apocalyptic and the Option for the Poor in Christian Theology," in Daniel G. Groody (ed.), *The Option for the Poor in Christian Theology* (Notre Dame, IN: University of Notre Dame Press, 2007), pp. 132–54; and David Rhoads (ed.), *From Every People and Nation: The Book of Revelation in Intercultural Perspective* (Minneapolis: Augsburg Fortress, 2005).

that salvation really arrived in the earthly Jesus, who throughout his lifetime, and not only after the resurrection, Christians proclaim to be God incarnate.

Moreover, apocalyptic is not the entirety of the tradition even of Israel, for whom the covenant and covenantal existence were certainly possible historically, albeit at divine initiative. The Temple cult, and especially purity and dietary laws, though subject to distortion and abuse, have their highest meaning as ways of sanctifying ordinary life. (Israel and Jewish theology have no doctrine of original sin.) Apocalyptic plays a role within the tradition as a corrective to versions of the Davidic kingship model that put too much faith in strong human leaders who make Israel a nation like the other nations. Apocalyptic in Jewish tradition is a counterweight to eschatologies in danger of placing excessive confidence in human messiahs. But Israel as a whole certainly never abandoned the idea that the covenant has social and political dimensions that should govern historical existence. The "salvation-present" thread of Jewish faith and tradition lends weight to the likelihood that Jesus' own eschatology builds on that and is reflected in – not overcome by – the gospel portrayals.

It is not possible to conclude decisively how Jesus in his historical ministry balanced the tension of "present" and "not yet," in contrast to the early church that read the possibilities through the lens of the risen Christ. Nevertheless, to take away entirely from Jesus himself the present emphasis (with its political repercussions) would not be acceptable for three reasons. First, it leaves the interpreter unable to account for Jesus' scandalous authority, manifest in his healings and provoking controversies that led to the cross (to be discussed later). Second, it reinstates the Bultmannian gap between Jesus and the early church, conceding in effect that Jesus himself, as a figure in history, is not the source and norm of later theologies. Third, the resulting perspective regresses back beyond Jesus to a pre-Christian worldview, a one-sided neo-apocalypticism that is inadequate not only to the gospels, but to the complexity of Jewish expectations.

For Christian ethics and politics, the present dimension of the kingdom is essential to validate action and transformation. This validation comes both from the historical memory of Jesus conveyed by the gospels and from the gospel proclamation of Jesus as the Christ. The tension between the present and the future is, however, crucial to make sense of the continuing brokenness, suffering, and failure that afflict not only "the world" but the church itself. The gospel solution is not the Essene alternative of withdrawal to the desert for a resurrection experience in an elite enclave. It is courageous and hopeful engagement with the real conditions of human life in a prophetic attempt to make a difference.

From earliest times, Christians have understood that their ultimate hope is "the presence of our Lord Jesus Christ at his coming" (1 Thess. 2:19; cf. 4:15, 5:2). They have always prayed for the return of Christ to complete what began in his ministry of the kingdom (1 Cor. 16:22; Rev. 22:20). The symbol of the second coming of Christ represents the confidence that sins, failures, and limits on what is begun now will be compensated by divine power in the future. The second coming is the christological "not yet" of the kingdom; the resurrection is the "now."

What practical content does Jesus' ministry of the inbreaking reign of God signify for Christian politics?

THE KINGDOM AND THE POOR

The prophecy of Isaiah forms Jesus' apparent self-understanding, his mission, and the content of his kingdom preaching: "Behold the Spirit of the Lord God is upon me, because the Lord has anointed me: he has sent me to bring good news to the poor" (Isa. 61:1). Jesus is portrayed claiming this text as his keynote (Luke 4:16–21; see Mark 6:1–6). The Hebrew terms behind the English translations (especially *'aniyyim*) denote material poverty, that is, lack of economic security due to factors like poor harvests, enemy invasion, bad management, exploitation by neighbors, or entrapment in a cycle of debt. Widows, orphans, and strangers or aliens were in a particularly vulnerable position and were therefore singled out as the special responsibility of the Israelite community to protect (Deut. 15:7–11; 19:22; 24:10–15). Brought up as a "blue collar worker" in a small village in Galilee, Jesus would have had plenty of opportunities to observe how people could labor under tax burdens, be caught up in unending debt, lose property and become day laborers, and even be reduced to the point of destitution.[70]

Jesus is especially critical of those who exploit the vulnerable in order to amass excessive wealth while others go in want of basic necessities. Wealth is dangerous. It breeds inhuman and irreligious values, gives a false sense of security, and interferes with devotion to God and compassion for one's neighbor. The poor, like the widow who donated her scant resources to the Temple, are often more generous than the rich (Mark 12:41–4). "You cannot serve God and wealth" (Matt. 6:24). "How hard

---

[70] Dunn, *Jesus Remembered*, pp. 516–26.

it is for those who have wealth to enter the kingdom of God!" (Mark 10:23), even more difficult than passing a camel through the eye of a needle (10:25). Jesus tells an earnest seeker to first give his money to the poor if he wants to enter the kingdom of heaven (Mark 10:21).

But Jesus also encourages those who have plenty to share with the poor, as illustrated in the parables of the Good Samaritan (Luke 10:29–37) and of the rich man and Lazarus (Luke 16:19–31). The Samaritan apparently did not give away all his possessions, for he travels on his way, presumably fulfills the purpose of his trip, and returns with enough money to pay the bills of the man he rescued.[71] The point is that he reacted with compassion even to a Jew, with whom a Samaritan would have shared a mutual feeling of hostility. As the parable of judgment in Matthew brings home, the kingdom requires compassionate action toward others' suffering: "Whatever you did for the least of these brothers of mine, you did for me" (Matt. 25:40).[72] Jesus was not a political or economic reformer in today's sense. He was not a "community organizer," he did not make global proposals about a just economic system, and he did not preach universal community of property or complete economic equality. He did call people to relate with active compassion to human deprivation, a stance that if taken seriously would change the economic and political institutions standard in most societies. Jesus also backed his position with reference to the traditional Israelite idea that the poor are a part of God's covenant people and are entitled to share in the nation's prosperity.

"The new note he brought was the renewed assurance that God's kingdom is precisely for the poor, and not just as a future hope. The poor could even now experience the good news."[73] God's presence to the poor precedes financial security and is not dependent on it; but if the privileged want to share in the kingdom with the poor, their attitudes and actions must change in ways that will necessarily have far-reaching social effects. Sincere conviction and consistent action would produce quite a different politics of inclusion and redistribution. Jesus' specific teachings and practices were obviously subversive enough to attract the hostility of both the Jewish political and religious leadership and the Roman imperial officials. Since enacting the good news of the kingdom for and with

[71] Jeanne Stevenson-Moessner, "The Road to Perfection: An Interpretation of Suffering in Hebrews," *Interpretation*, 57 (2003), p. 286.
[72] On the original context and addressees of this text, see John R. Donahue, S.J., "The 'Parable' of the Sheep and the Goats: A Challenge to Christian Ethics," *Theological Studies*, 47/1 (1986), pp. 3–31.
[73] Dunn, *Jesus Remembered*, p. 526.

the poor obviously figured high on his agenda, it is logical to surmise that it posed a substantial threat to those with wealth and power.

WOMEN AND THE KINGDOM

Another area in which Jesus' ministry arguably was and is iconoclastic is the status of women, both in his religious community and in Greco-Roman society. The past half-century has produced an enormous literature in feminist biblical interpretation.[74] Feminist scholars have argued that Jesus himself treated women with uncommon respect and that the early Christian movement constituted a "discipleship of equals" in which patriarchy was decisively challenged.[75] Unfortunately, some scholars have defended Jesus' affirmation of women by drawing him in contrast to Jewish religion and culture that he supposedly rejects.[76] I think this problem can be countered simply by acknowledging that virtually every culture known to the human race has been or is patriarchal to some degree, usually to a significant one. Jesus' target is not Judaism per se but patriarchal distortions in his environment.

In the Mediterranean cultures of Jesus' era, the norms structuring gender reflected the unequal dynamics of an "honor–shame" system, in which male honor, status, and power were closely tied to men's ability to assert dominance, provide for and protect the family, and control kin women. Public political, economic, and cultic roles were generally reserved for men. Women were defined by their sexual and reproductive roles in family and society. Women's purity reflected on male honor, requiring firm constraints on women's demeanor and conduct. Women were expected to keep the family from shame by their modesty, sexual exclusivity, and submission to male authority. Women perceived to have violated these norms could be put to death (honor killings), even if the

---

[74] Among feminist biblical critics, Elisabeth Schüssler Fiorenza has been perhaps the most groundbreaking, prophetic, and radical. See especially *In Memory of Her: A Feminist Theological Reconstruction of Christian Origins* (New York: Herder and Herder, 1983), as well as *Bread Not Stone* and *Journal of Feminist Studies in Religion*, 25/1 (2009), Special Issue in Honor of Elisabeth Schüssler Fiorenza, which includes an assessment of the state and future of feminist theology.

[75] This is the phrase of Elisabeth Schüssler Fiorenza (e.g., *In Memory of Her*, pp. 135, 152; and *Discipleship of Equals: Critical Feminist Ekklesia-logy of Religion* [London: SCM Press, 1993]). However, she also calls the bible and its models a "prototype" rather than an "archetype," meaning that every new *ekklesia* must innovate, not just replicate (pp. 33–4). Hence the "discipleship of equals" was not a lost "golden age" of the early church. It was a critical ideal or vision inspired by Jesus, one still awaiting full realization, or at least different actualizations in different sociocultural environments.

[76] For examples and criticism of this tendency, see Levine, *The Misunderstood Jew*.

violation was unintentional or coerced. Due to the assumed inferiority of women and to their valence as closely controlled tokens of male power, women lacked access to formal education and had very limited economic or social independence from father, elder male relative, husband, or in the case of a widow, son.[77]

This does not mean that there were no exceptions or that these supposed norms were never subject to local adaptation. Undoubtedly, some women acted as advisers to male family members, exercised political clout due to the status of their natal family, or engaged with husbands or independently in economic activity. Jewish women may have enjoyed legal protection of rights like inheritance and ownership of property.[78] Greater sequestration may have been the lot of elite women rather than poor or peasant women, who out of economic necessity worked alongside men in the fields or market and who prepared food in common areas or courtyards. Nevertheless, it is safe to assume that women in general were regarded as having less status, authority, and freedom of movement than men and that not a few women were the victims of poverty, exploitation even within the family, and violence.

It therefore is no great detraction from the general worth of Jewish religion and culture to say that in the first century it suffered from gender hierarchy – so did Greco-Roman culture, other world cultures, and the emerging Christian culture ("wives be submissive"; Col. 3:18; Eph. 5:22; cf. 1 Pet. 3:1–6; 1 Tim. 2:11–12), in which the problem only worsened with time. Twenty-one centuries later, the same problem besets women studying the bible in a rural village in Chiapas: "So many things ... were being challenged as they were learning to read the Bible through the mind, eyes and heart of a woman. Had God really decreed that wives need to be submissive to their husbands in all things? Or was that a culturally conditioned value that now needed to be reexamined?"[79]

To the extent that Jesus supports women's equality he is doing so as a Jewish prophet and teacher targeting a pervasive form of human oppression, embodied in his own culture and almost everywhere else. In addition, one need not identify as unique to Jesus whatever gender-inclusive

[77] See Hanson and Oakman, *Palestine*, pp. 23–6.
[78] Richard H. Hiers, *Women's Rights and the Bible: Implications for Christian Ethics and Social Policy* (Eugene, OR: Pickwick, 2012).
[79] Barbara E. Reid, O.P., *Taking Up the Cross: New Testament Interpretations Through Latina and Feminist Eyes* (Minneapolis: Augsburg Fortress, 2007), pp. 9–11, 74–6.

message his teaching implies.[80] He can be seen as drawing on a feminist impulse already present in Judaism.[81] What is important for Christian feminists is whether gender equality is essential to Jesus' vision of the reign of God, not whether Jesus is the first, only, or loudest voice to have spoken up for gender equality.

A bigger problem for feminist biblical interpretation is whether claims about the egalitarianism of Jesus can really be verified on the basis of the New Testament (assumed to embody a true memory of what Jesus essentially stood for). Some defenders of male precedence in society, family, or church assert that women cannot be fully equal because Jesus chose only male apostles or because "the twelve" were men. (The twelve, not necessarily to be identified with the apostles, are sent out on mission by Jesus in Mark 6; the number represents the twelve tribes of Israel.) Some may even grant that respect for women in the New Testament is notable and exemplary, with the caveat that this respect still assumes (and promotes) a scheme of gender differentiation in which women, though "respected," are still subject to male "headship" and/or assigned to distinctive feminine roles. Some feminists argue from the other side that the New Testament and the communities that produced it, including the association of Jesus and his first followers, are no gender-equal utopia and hence of little use for feminists today. It is arguable (and has been argued by feminist critics) that the gospel narratives in fact suppress women's voices and some roles that may have existed historically.[82]

Jesus did resist exploitative hierarchies of power, and he had little tolerance for those who use positions of authority to "lord it over" other people. Yet Jesus does not seem to have made the equality of women as much a

[80] For developments toward greater equality for women in the first century more generally, see Ross Shepard Kraemer, *Her Share of the Blessings: Women's Religions among Pagans, Jews, and Christians in the Greco-Roman World* (New York: Oxford University Press, 1994); and Amy-Jill Levine, *Women Like This: New Perspectives on Jewish Women in the Greco-Roman World* (ACLS Humanities E-Book, January 1, 2009). For a study of women's religious practices in ancient Israel, as concerned with reproduction and maternity, see Carol Meyers, *Households and Holiness: The Religious Culture of Israelite Women* (Minneapolis: Fortress Press, 2005).

[81] Elisabeth Schüssler Fiorenza: "The issue is not whether or not Jesus overturned patriarchy but whether Judaism had elements of a critical feminist impulse that came to the fore in the vision and ministry of Jesus. The reconstruction of the Jesus movement as the discipleship of equals is historically plausible only insofar as such critical elements are thinkable within the context of Jewish life and faith. The praxis and vision of Jesus and his movement [are] best understood as an inner-Jewish renewal movement that presented an alternative option to the dominant patriarchal structures rather than an oppositional formation rejecting the values and praxis of Judaism" (*In Memory of Her*, p. 107).

[82] See Karen L. King, *The Gospel of Mary of Magdala: Jesus and the First Woman Apostle* (Santa Rosa, CA: Polebridge Press, 2003).

signature of his movement as he did justice for the poor and the inclusion in table fellowship of people considered offensive by the "righteous." In his world, it was simply taken for granted that the husband is the head of the household and that there was a clear division between women's and men's roles and tasks.[83] It seems quite unlikely that even among Jesus' first disciples, the men would have regarded the women as their equals in every respect. The later gospel authors are, if anything, less interested in equality for women. Feminist biblical interpretation is thus an endeavor in which normative readings of the texts are undertaken in communities of faith and practice that provide interpretive lenses and an ongoing experience of Jesus Christ present in Spirit.[84] As Gloria Kehilwe Plaatjie notes of South African nonacademic and academic women reading the prophetess Anna (Luke 2:36–38) as a role model, contextual readings can subvert both "Western" and African imperial and patriarchal discourses. However, neither particular women's experiences and viewpoints nor the biblical text itself are alone adequate authorities. Both must be evaluated critically in terms of wider criteria of political, economic, and social justice.[85]

The viability of today's feminism does not stand or fall with the possibility of demonstrating that Jesus, during his historical lifetime, endorsed all its concerns. Insight into the meaning of the Christian life in this and other areas continues to emerge historically, under the guidance of the "Spirit of God" (1 Cor. 7:40). "A feminist critical hermeneutics has to explore and assess whether and how Scripture can become an enabling, motivating resource and empowering authority in women's struggle for justice, liberation and solidarity."[86] Even within androcentric biblical stories, a feminist hermeneutic of suspicion, remembrance, and reclamation can lead to an inclusive reading in which "women together with men stand at the heart of the gospel story."[87]

Contemporary feminism assumes a culture in which movements for human rights, women's rights, and participatory democracy are global, highly visible, and politically powerful. From such a standpoint,

---

[83] Harrington, *Jesus: A Historical Portrait*, p. 53.

[84] Schneiders, *Revelatory Text*, pp. 75–6.

[85] Gloria Kehilwe Plaatjie, "Toward a Post-apartheid Black Feminist Reading of the Bible: A Case of Luke 2:36–38," in Musa W. Dube (ed.), *Other Ways of Reading: African Women and the Bible* (Atlanta and Geneva: Society of Biblical Literature and WCC Publications, 2001).

[86] Schüssler Fiorenza, *Bread Not Stone*, p. xxiii.

[87] Elaine M. Wainwright, *Towards a Feminist Critical Reading of the Gospel According to Matthew* (Berlin: De Gruyter, 1991), p. 152. See also Elaine M. Wainwright, "Feminist Criticism and the Gospel of Matthew," in Mark Allan Powell (ed.), *Methods for Matthew* (Cambridge University Press, 2009), pp. 83–117.

an open-minded re-reading of scripture quickly elucidates the degree to which subsequent tradition has submerged, distorted, and denied even those gender-egalitarian implications of the ministries of Jesus (and Paul) that are in fact still visible in the canonical accounts.[88] These accounts may not overcome patriarchy entirely, and in some instances capitulate to and advance it. Yet Elisabeth Schüssler Fiorenza asks, "My vision of Christian life, responsibility, and community compelled me to reject the culturally imposed role of women and not vice versa. What was this liberating vision that came through to me despite all the patriarchal pious packaging and sexist theological systematization?"[89] The sources of this vision are multiple, not simple.

Jesus and Paul obviously valued women as assets in their ministries and as sources of strength. There were several women who traveled with Jesus and the disciples, providing financial support (Mark 15:41; Luke 8:1–3). There are many women whom Paul mentions as leaders in the house churches, even calling Junia "outstanding among the apostles" (Rom. 16:7). Among the others exercising ministries in his churches are Phoebe, a deacon (Rom. 16: 1–2), and Prisca, host of a house church with her husband Aquila (Rom. 16:3–5; Acts 18). Female religious leadership was not unprecedented in the cultures of the era, particularly toward the end of the first century, when the early Christian movement developed and the gospels were written.[90] During Jesus' lifetime, Galilean women traveling around with male itinerant preachers, unaccompanied by male family members, may have been more unusual.

It is evident that Jesus interacted with women in a way that was atypical for a man of his place and time. The fact that his recorded interactions with women must be viewed partly as products of later community experience makes it more rather than less likely that his own practice was culturally challenging. Women were frequently the beneficiaries of Jesus' healing miracles.[91] They appear in his parables, and women's work is the

---

[88] For an overview of women in the New Testament, see Bonnie B. Thurston, *Women in the New Testament: Questions and Commentary* (Eugene, OR: Wipf & Stock, 2004). For a critical feminist treatment, see Elisabeth Schüssler Fiorenza (ed.), *Searching the Scriptures: A Feminist Commentary*, 2 vols. (New York: Crossroad, 1995, 1997); and Carol A. Newsom and Sharon H. Ringe (eds.), *Women's Bible Commentary*, expanded edn. with Apocrypha (Louisville, KY: Westminster John Knox Press, 1998).

[89] Schüssler Fiorenza, *Discipleship of Equals*, p. 92.

[90] See Kraemer, *Her Share of the Blessings*.

[91] For a nuanced, critical view that considers whether the memory of women healers is suppressed, see Elaine M. Wainwright, *Women Healing / Healing Women: The Genderization of Healing in Early Christianity* (London: Equinox, 2006).

subject of stories Jesus tells and the images he uses. Women such as Martha and Mary of Bethany, the sisters of Lazarus, and Mary Magdalene were among his friends. It is women, including his mother, Mary, whom the gospels remember as remaining near the cross after the male disciples had fled. Women are also reported to have been among the first witnesses to the resurrection, in all four gospels. This record is remarkable because it reflects badly on the "heroes" of the story, the male apostles, and because the testimony of women was not regarded equally in Jewish courts.

Feminist biblical interpreters have repeatedly drawn attention to the fact that the most important woman in the New Testament is Mary of Magdala, from a town near the Sea of Galilee noted in Roman times for its export of salted fish.[92] Long defamed, stereotyped, and theologically marginalized as a prostitute, then "rehabilitated" as Jesus' lover, the biblical Mary is quite different. She is described as someone who had been exorcised of "seven demons" and who subsequently became one of the financial supporters of Jesus (Luke 8:1–3; cf. Mark 15:41; Matt. 27:55).[93] It may even be that the label "demon-possessed" was an attempt by some to discredit her in the Christian movement after Jesus' death.[94] In later tradition, she is unfairly (deliberately?) confused with the sinful woman who anoints Jesus' feet with ointment during a dinner at a Pharisee's house (Luke 7:36–50).

In reality, biblical depictions always name Mary Magdalene first in the lists of women disciples, indicating her priority in the minds of those who composed and passed on the traditions. She is remembered as first among the witnesses to the resurrection (Mark 16:1, 6–7, 9–11; Matt. 28:1, 7–10; Luke 23:55–24:1 ,6–10). In John, she not only is the first to see Jesus risen, but is also sent by him to "announce" the gospel, qualifying her as an apostle by the same criteria as Paul (John 20:11–18; see also Matt. 28:10; Mark 16:9).

Reviewing the long history of misinterpretation of this Mary, as well as her equally stereotypical depiction in icons of popular culture such as the rock opera *Jesus Christ Superstar*, Nikos Kazantzakis's book and film *Last Temptation of Christ*, and Dan Brown's book *The Da Vinci Code*, Pamela Thimmes reflects with evident exasperation:

Reading Mary Magdalene through these disparate lenses is reading her character through a long theological tradition that is at base a long socio-cultural,

[92] Reid, *Taking Up the Cross*, p. 147.
[93] For an extensive overview, see Pamela Thimmes, OSF, "Memory and Re-Vision: Mary Magdalene Research since 1975," *Currents in Research: Biblical Studies*, 6 (1998), pp. 193–226.
[94] Reid, *Taking Up the Cross*, p. 148. See also Jane Schaberg, *The Resurrection of Mary Magdalene: Legends, Apocrypha, and the Christian Testament* (New York: Crossroad, 2002).

socio-sexual and socio-political tradition. As a result, she is usually drawn as a composite figure who is understood sexually, a character configured by men in a male-dominated church and culture. She conforms to the demands of the institution: she is ravaged in word and in art, she is a flexible, pliable figure to which everything that is valued and abhorrent sticks.[95]

The "sticking" process is not random. Mary is confined to "traditional" female sexual categories and roles, relegated to the place of "sinner." Her only acceptable stance becomes penitence and remorse. She is valued for self-abnegation and for recognizing the gratuity of her place in Jesus' circle. Even in modern "recoveries," her status depends on her sexual or romantic affiliation with the male protagonist. Mary Magdalene is thereby undermined and excluded as a model for women's active leadership in the community of disciples who follow Christ.[96] This serves the androcentric trajectory of texts and tradition, but it contradicts and betrays the essential relation of Mary to Jesus and his mission, a relationship of special faithfulness that is displayed in all four gospels. Apparently already in the early written testimony there is "a mighty struggle over the authority of Mary's prophetic witness."[97] In the gospels of Mark and Luke, Mary and the other women do not encounter Jesus himself, but rather special "angelic" messengers who tell them what has happened. In Mark, they fail to spread the word as commanded; in Luke, their report is dismissed as "nonsense" (24:11). Yet both Matthew and John, using independent sources, attest that the resurrected Christ appeared directly to Mary Magdalene and sent her to spread the good news. She faithfully announces to the disciples, "I have seen the Lord!" (John 10:18), and her message is favorably received. Magdalene is the exemplary disciple of Jesus, a faithful co-sufferer at the hour of his death, and the evangelical witness to the risen Christ, a witness one evangelist remembers the risen Jesus to have called by name (John 20:16).

JESUS AND GENTILES

Just one other specific New Testament woman will enter into discussion here, because her story is unusual and provocative. It urges us to probe the ambiguous nature of gospel portrayals of women, the difficulty of

[95] Thimmes, "Memory and Re-Vision," 195.
[96] Karen L. King, "Canonization and Marginalization: Mary of Magdala," in Kwok Pui-Lan and Elisabeth Schüssler Fiorenza (eds.), *Women's Sacred Scriptures* (London and New York: SCM and Orbis Books, 1998), pp. 29–36, 31.
[97] Reid, *Taking Up the Cross*, p. 114.

ascertaining how well they reflect Jesus' own perspective, and the need
to engage such stories in a continuing community of interpretation that
is formed and tested by practices. The story also communicates the possibility and credibility of expanding the meaning of the kingdom beyond
what Jesus explicitly taught, regarding both women and "outsiders."[98]

This is the story of the "Canaanite" (Matt. 15:21) or "Syrophoenician"
(Mark 7:26) woman, a Gentile who has come to plead with Jesus, a Jewish
prophet, to heal her daughter. She grants and affirms his special status in
relation to Israelite expectation when she exclaims, "Have pity on me,
Lord, Son of David. My daughter is tormented by a demon!" (Matt.
15:21). She crosses the boundary of presumed religious hostility to get his
attention and refuses to give up when Jesus ignores her and moves on in
silence, while the disciples advise him to send her away (Matt. 23). Jesus
does not at first seem open-minded. He defends limiting his concern to
fellow Jews ("I was sent only to the lost sheep of the house of Israel";
Matt. 15:24; cf. 10:5–6) and, even worse, compares her and her daughter
to "dogs" who do not deserve to eat the "children's" food (Matt. 15:26;
Mark 7:28). When she reminds him that even dogs are allowed to eat
table scraps, Jesus relents (Matt. 15:28; Mark 7:29–30): he tells the woman
her daughter is already healed and, in Matthew's version, praises her great
faith (Matt. 15:28).

Few admirers of Jesus' compassion, his commendation of love of
neighbor, and his inclusive kingdom message can fail to be disturbed
by this story. Even given that Jesus was immersed in Jewish culture and
did not come into contact with many Gentiles, how could he have failed
to relate with more empathy to this mother's desperation? When a man
approaches him in a Jewish crowd and asks for "compassion" and a similar healing for his son, Jesus demonstrates to the disciples the power of
faith and prayer by healing the boy immediately (Matt. 17:14–20; Mark
9:23–25; cf. Luke 9:37–43). True, Jesus finally gives the Gentile woman
what she wants. But it seems that she must first accept his brusque attitude, his comparison to dogs, and his relegation of non-Jews to marginal status in his mission and even in God's eyes. Must we concede that
Jesus looks down on her because she is a "woman without a man" and a
"foreigner"?[99]

[98] See also Tatha Wiley, *Paul and the Gentile Women: Reframing Galatians* (New York: Continuum, 2005).
[99] Tat-siong Benny Liew, "Re-Mark-Able Masculinities," in Stephen D. Moore and Janice Capel Anderson (eds.), *New Testament Masculinities* (Leiden: Brill, 2004), p. 121.

Another possible reading is that the canonical texts represent struggles going on in late-first-century Christianity over the Gentile mission, especially in Matthew's predominantly Jewish Christian community. Jesus is remembered as fulfilling Isaiah's prophecy that justice will be proclaimed to the Gentiles, who will now hope in the name of Jesus (12:18–21). This message was undoubtedly hard to hear for a Jewish audience, and some of the story's redactors may have felt it acceptable and true to their perception of Jesus only after toning it down so that the primacy of Israel is retained and the basic objectionability of Canaanites acknowledged.[100] Certainly we know from the letters of Paul and the Acts of the Apostles that not everyone in the church was quick to accept Gentiles on the same footing as Jews.

A more radical reading traces the struggle or at least development back to the history of Jesus himself. The Gentile woman challenges Jesus' perception of his own mission, which was undoubtedly first and foremost a reform of Second Temple Judaism, which he intended to bring closer to the Mosaic covenant and the prophets. At first resistant, Jesus learns that even a Gentile, and a female Gentile at that, can have great faith and be the object of divine favor.[101] In fact, "the greatest surprise is that through dialogue Jesus seems to change his mind and comes to display great openness to the faith of this non-Jewish woman." Through her, Jesus may even "understand better that his mission includes not only his own people, Israel, but also outsiders like the Canaanite woman and her daughter."[102]

After his death, followers of Jesus would worship him as a god. Three centuries later, the Council of Nicaea declared him an incarnation of the divine Son or Word of God, fully divine – but Chalcedon stresses that he is equally human and, as human, "like us in all things but sin." This surely requires that the child, youth, and man Jesus developed his self-understanding and his orientation in the world as a result of a learning process. Jesus of Nazareth required an education in his own Jewish traditions, rituals, and scriptures. He learned to how to hone the skills of a craftsman, how to make preparations for travel or the weather, and how to get from Nazareth to Galilee. He also learned what his religious

---

[100] Elaine M. Wainwright, *Shall We Look for Another? A Feminist Rereading of the Matthean Jesus* (Maryknoll, NY: Orbis Books, 1998), pp. 44–5, 48.

[101] Joanna Dewey, "The Gospel of Mark," in Elisabeth Schüssler Fiorenza (ed.), *Searching the Scriptures*, vol. 2: *A Feminist Commentary* (New York: Crossroad, 1994), pp. 485–6. See also Joanna Dewey, "Jesus' Healings of Women: Conformity and Non-Conformity to Dominant Cultural Values as Clues for Historical Reconstruction," *Biblical Theology Bulletin*, 24/3 (1994), pp. 122–31.

[102] Daniel J. Harrington, S.J., "Interreligious Dialogue?" *America* (August 4–11, 2008), p. 39.

traditions and his sense of mission demanded in relation to others, including Israel's traditional enemies. It is at least conceivable that Jesus of Nazareth expanded his sense of the kingdom he proclaimed through interactions with unexpected people like tax collectors, prostitutes, "sinners," Samaritans, and Gentiles. As a Galilean, Jesus kept his hopes for Jewish restoration focused on Jerusalem (accounting for his final journey and confrontation there). But he also ventured into Galilee's border areas, for example Tyre (where he met the "Syrophoenician woman") and the villages around Caesaria Philippi. Though viewed as part of "greater Israel," these areas would have brought increased contact with non-Jews.

Here Jesus might have gained a new perspective on the prophecies from Isaiah and entertained a new sense of freedom in dealing with Israel's traditional enemies.[103] What he learned, then embodied in his other stories and interactions with outsiders (e.g., dialogue with the Samaritan woman at the well [John 4:1–42], parable of the Good Samaritan [Luke 10], and the healed Samaritan leper who thanked Jesus [Luke 17]), was understandably unpalatable to some disciples and contentious in the next generation's churches.[104] After all, the "mission to the Gentiles" did not really take hold until the activity of Barnabas and Paul more than a decade after Jesus' death (Acts 11:19–26).

Many Jews already thought that "the nations" would recognize Jerusalem in the end time and participate in the coming kingdom.[105] The biblical hint of a gradual expansion of Jesus' mission during his lifetime, perhaps through an adjustment in his own horizon, validates later attempts to link "the Galilean Jesus" with the cause of those who are aliens in a majority culture or who have mixed ethnic identities and to bridge the gaps between different kinds of religious belonging through mutual learning rather than persecution or conversion.[106] Historically speaking, Jesus may not have made these social and interreligious programs his own, at least not as defining features of his mission. Yet they are valid extensions of his preaching of the kingdom of God and are set by its trajectory.

JESUS' LIFE AS AGENT OF THE KINGDOM

Jesus teaches his disciples to pray for the coming of the kingdom and to appeal to God as "Father" – "Abba" in Hebrew – in whose beneficence

[103] Freyne, *Jesus, a Jewish Galilean*, pp. 109–10.
[104] Wainwright, *Shall We Look for Another?* p. 98.
[105] Sanders, *Historical Figure of Jesus*, p. 192.
[106] For examples of these directions of research, see *Theological Studies*, 70/2 (2009).

they can trust (Luke 11:2; Matt. 6:9). Contrary to some proposals,[107] Abba is a more formal term than "Daddy" and is not unique to Jesus as an appellation for God, but was already familiar within Judaism.[108] Its importance is not only that it expresses Jesus' intimate relationship to and confidence in God, but that it communicates to "the poor" and to all the disciples that God is the only patron to whom they owe allegiance and the only one whose favor is assured. Elisabeth Schüssler Fiorenza believes that the instruction to Christians to address God and only God as "Father" (Matt. 23:9) implicitly rejects the power and status of human fathers in a patriarchal system, "and thus claims that in the messianic community all patriarchal structures are abolished."[109] Jesus' prayer for the coming of the kingdom is a prayer for a renewal of the relationship to God promised for Israel. His teaching about prayer is directed to his disciples to encourage them to live in trust before God as their Father and caring provider and with one another in solidarity.[110]

That for which they pray includes physical sustenance, forgiveness of sins, and protection in the trials to accompany the arrival of the kingdom at God's hand. In turn, certain responses are required, especially forgiveness of the sins of others. Humility in prayer and persistence in asking God to meet our needs are key themes in Luke, the gospel most devoted to prayer.[111] Jesus himself exhibits these virtues and prays frequently, especially in times of trial – his prayer at Gethsemane and the variously reported final cries on the cross are familiar in Christian piety and art. Moreover, for Jesus, prayer is not merely an individual spiritual activity. At Gethsemane, it was part of his suffering that he prayed alone, the desired company of friends having failed him (Matt. 26:39; Mark 14:35–6; Luke 22:41–2; John 12:27; Heb. 5:7–8). He endured a loneliness in prayer that was heightened at his death ("My God, my God, why have you forsaken me?" Mark 15:34).

In Judaism, collective worship and sacrifice are essential. The individual discovers a relation to God within a people before God. It is significant, then, that Luke frames Jesus' infancy and childhood with Temple rituals and presents the opening of his ministry as the reading of a text from Isaiah in his hometown synagogue (Luke 2–4). It is appropriate that Jesus' final meal with his disciples becomes the central liturgical prayer of

[107] Joachim Jeremias, *The Prayers of Jesus* (Minneapolis: Fortress Press, 1978), ch. 1.
[108] Dunn, *Jesus Remembered*, p. 548; see pp. 711–18 for discussion.
[109] Schüssler Fiorenza, *In Memory of Her*, p. 147.
[110] Dunn, *Jesus Remembered*, p. 551.
[111] Harrington, *Jesus: A Historical Portrait*, pp. 48–51.

his followers and of the church, and that the risen Jesus is recognized in the collective breaking of the bread (Luke 24:30–1).

Prayer, then, is a conduit of God's favor and constitutes the identity of the believer not only in relation to God but also in relation to a community formed around God's presence. Jesus teaches his disciples to pray that the kingdom will come, a collective event for Israel. His prayer must be seen in the light of his total representation of the kingdom – as corporate, religious, political, and presently transformative. To pray is to place oneself in the presence of God – a personal, spiritual exercise that is also thoroughly interrelational, both with God and with "neighbor." The presence of God invoked by prayer is the basis of, the interior quality of, and the cohering power of the life of the covenant community and of the *ekklesia* gathered around Jesus. Prayerful attitudes and actions define the kingdom, and for this very reason prayer for Jesus does not lead to long-term withdrawal from social intercourse. To the contrary, the life of prayer, piety, or "spirituality" is the kingdom existence in which male, female, rich, poor, Gentile, Jew, righteous, and sinner are incorporated in a new reality. Piety and holiness are not excluding but including forces, enacted in Jesus' own practice of the open communal meal.[112] The *presence* of the kingdom (and hence its accessibility in the eucharist and necessary effect on all social hierarchies), though still incomplete and awaited in hope, is realized in Jesus. This is what leads to the most startling and offensive claims that the gospel authors make about Jesus, claims that trace back to aspects of his historical ministry, the way he was perceived by others, and his probable self-perception. Jesus' healings and exorcisms were to his contemporaries the deeds of an eschatological prophet who enacts the kingdom of God.[113] Not only is the kingdom real and effective for Jesus, it is present in and through Jesus. His authority not only to preach the kingdom and to pray for its arrival, but also to perform it through his deeds, evokes devotion from some, questioning and rejection from others. This authority is underwritten by Jesus' healings and exorcisms, which testify in visible form that God acts in Jesus' acts.

The healing miracles define Jesus as mediating divine power to those who believe in God.[114] Isaiah's prophecies of the end time are realized: "The blind see, the lame walk, lepers are cleansed, the deaf hear, the dead

[112] Dunn, *Jesus Remembered*, p. 603.
[113] Eric Eve, *The Healer from Nazareth: Jesus' Miracles in Historical Context* (London: SPCK, 2009), p. 144.
[114] Ibid., p. 502.

are raised" (Matt. 11:5; Luke 7:22; Isa. 35:5–6). The exorcisms are a sign that even now, even for those incapable of a personal confession of faith, Satan's power over the world is being broken. Jesus claims that by casting out demons "by the finger of God," he confirms that "the kingdom of God has come to you" (Matt. 12:28; Luke 11:20).

It is important to realize that both healings and exorcisms are about more than impressing an audience with Jesus' special gifts, or even relieving an individual of a terrible affliction. These miracles restore the afflicted person to his or her social place within the community, healing the community itself from alienating forms of suffering. Those who are mentally or physically impaired obviously lose function and suffer a diminished role in family and community. Beyond that, they might be blamed for having brought on suffering by sin, like the man born blind (John 9:1–10:21), or categorized as unclean and ostracized, like the woman who had hemorrhaged (menstrual) blood for twelve years (Luke 8: 43–48). The Gerasene demoniac is wild and tormented, living among tombs, repeatedly breaking his chains and shackles (Luke 8:26–31). Jesus frees him so that he becomes once again "clothed and in his right mind" (Luke 8:35). The healings and exorcisms restore persons within transformed relationships often attributed to "faith." Jesus does not just prophesy the future fruits of faith; he himself acts as the one who accomplishes what other prophets have foretold (Matt. 13:16–17; Luke 10:23–4).[115]

Jesus "both challenged the existing social order and advocated an alternative"[116] – a present and immediate alternative. He scandalized patrons of the social order and all their "clients" by reaching out to people ground down by economic exploitation or by class- and gender-biased interpretations of purity, and even to those who had violated legitimate expectations (no adultery, prostitution, or collusion with the Roman oppressors). In the tradition of the Jewish prophets, there can be no breach between covenant faithfulness to God and responsibility for the way social norms affect the most vulnerable, whether those norms are in themselves defensible or not. This kingdom is *God's* kingdom. So designated, it would be recognizable to all Jews as "a radical reorientation of values and power."[117] This was the basis of Jesus' challenge to Jewish religious authorities, which was also a reaffirmation of the covenant between God and Israel.

---

[115] Meier, *Marginal Jew, Volume II: Rethinking the Historical Jesus*, p. 1043.

[116] Marcus J. Borg, *Jesus in Contemporary Scholarship* (Valley Forge, PA: Trinity Press International, 1994), p. 98.

[117] Sanders, *Historical Figure of Jesus*, p. 169.

An incident in the Jerusalem Temple, as reported variously in the gospels (Matt. 21:12–13; Mark 11:15–17; Luke 19:45–6; John 2:13–16), was the immediate precipitating event that led to Jesus' execution by the Romans, with the apparent collusion of the Jewish chief priests and elders.[118] It is likely that Jesus spoke of the Temple's destruction and rebuilding in accordance with some contemporary apocalyptic ideas (Matt. 26:61; Mark 14:58; John 2:19; Acts 6:14). This constituted decisive evidence against him in the hearing before Caiaphas (Matt. 26:61, 62) and was a very politically sensitive threat not only to Jews but also to the Romans. In the bigger picture, it is not unlikely that the socially challenging and disruptive effects of his practices and teachings were also contributory to his imprisonment, trial, and death at the hands of Pilate. For this outcome, the Roman government bore the main responsibility.

As one moves chronologically through the gospels from Mark to Matthew and Luke to John (who terms all Jesus' adversaries "the Jews"), it is easy to receive the opposite impression: Pilate was manipulated by the Jewish leaders, or was even bowing to the wishes of the entire Jewish people (e.g., Matt. 27:25). As Daniel Harrington advises:

Such passages need to be read in their late first-century historical context: Jerusalem had been destroyed and Christians were accommodating themselves to life within the Roman Empire. When removed from that historical context, these texts can contribute to anti-Semitism and obscure the Jewishness of Jesus as well as the Jewish character of early Christianity.[119]

The polemics of John's gospel reflect late-first-century (90–100 CE) conflict between Jewish Christians and the Jewish author over claims being made about Christ, which may have led to the expulsion of members of John's community from their synagogues, which John retrojects as a conflict between "the Jews" and Jesus himself.[120] These texts illustrate the ability of religious in-group exclusivism and violence to penetrate even those religious movements that began as a protest against such dynamics. When Christianity opened to Gentiles but defined itself over against "the Jews," as not included in God's salvation, it betrayed Jesus' eschatological kingdom in favor of apocalyptic dualism. Jesus came to reform Israel,

---

[118] As a general resource, see Raymond E. Brown, *The Death of the Messiah: From Gethsemane to the Grave*, 2 vols. (New York: Doubleday, 1994).
[119] Harrington, *Jesus: A Historical Portrait*, p. 74.
[120] Hurtado, *How on Earth?* pp. 152–3.

to recall Israel to a covenant including the poor and the stranger. Jesus opened his table to all who want to share in God's feast. Jesus even is remembered to have been receptive to Gentile and Samaritan "outsiders" and to have envisioned that God's kingdom might extend further than he originally imagined. An inclusive rather than an exclusive view of salvation is a distinctive note of Jesus' ministry.

How did Jesus see his own role, and with what Jewish symbols did he interpret it? Did he anticipate his death, and what meaning did he give to it? These are difficult questions, to which there are no certain "historical" answers. Some indications can be gathered from the use of what later came to be called "christological" titles in the New Testament, interpreted in light of historical and theological hypotheses about their possible use by Jesus himself or their function in connecting later construals of Jesus' significance with the historical activity of Jesus of Nazareth. To interpret Jesus' death and mission in the light of such titles begins to raise large and foundational issues for Christian theology that will be addressed further in Chapters 4 and 6.

The significance of these titles in the immediate context is that they are defining elements of the New Testament milieu within which Jesus' ministry of the reign of God is presented. The gospel biographies are composed to show continuity between Jesus of Nazareth and Jesus Christ risen and exalted, to show there was something about the man Jesus who lived in Galilee that connects with later experiences and helps make Christian claims credible. In turn, the power and reality of the kingdom as inaugurated by Jesus in history are underwritten by titles that connect his life with his divine source and his ultimate destiny. When gospel authors make use of titles such as "Son of God" in describing Jesus' life, they "emphasize that Jesus was always God's Son and during his lifetime his disciples understood something of his unique relationship to God, though there was more to learn from his death and resurrection."[121] Among the most important titles that serve this function are "Son of God," "Messiah," "Lord," and "Son of Man."

These titles are relevant to the sociopolitical significance of Jesus in several ways. They indicate a relation to God that gives Jesus' words and actions exceptional authority and shows why Jesus' disciples are empowered to live differently. As mentioned earlier in the chapter, most biblical scholars agree that Jesus likely used "Son of Man" self-referentially, apparently invoking his own authority: "the Son of Man has authority on

---

[121] Matera, *New Testament Theology*, p. 41.

earth to forgive sins."¹²² Jesus' projection of authority was adequate to pro-
voke the outrage of religious leaders. "He regarded himself as having full
authority to speak and act on behalf of God. Sinners who followed him,
but who may or may not have returned to the Mosaic law, would have a
place in God's kingdom."¹²³ In reply to a question from Peter about what
Jesus' followers would receive, he replies that they would inherit eternal
life and that "the twelve" would judge the twelve tribes of Israel (see Matt.
19:27–9). This makes Jesus God's delegate at the judgment, second only to
God himself. Not only that, but Jesus claims an unmediated relation to
God, as commissioned to express God's will.¹²⁴ Jesus may have used "Son
of Man" to indicate an awareness of his unprecedented role, even if the
exact nature of that role was not yet clear.

The synoptics, especially Matthew, use the designation "Son of Man"
for the one who will come from heaven in the end time and usher in the
kingdom of God: "the Son of Man is to come with his angels in the glory
of his Father" (Matt. 16:27); all on earth will see "the Son of Man coming on the clouds of heaven with power and great glory. And he will send
out his angels with a great blast, and they will gather his elect" (Matt.
24:30–2). The gospels also portray Jesus as using the phrase to speak of
his own impending death: "He began to teach them that the Son of Man
must suffer greatly and be rejected by the elders … and be killed, and rise
again after three days" (Mark 8:31). John also uses this phrase to refer to
the earthly activity of the Son of Man, to his future suffering, and to his
future judgment and glory. However, in contrast to the synoptic gospels,
John's uses "lack strong apocalyptic trappings, the element of realized
eschatology dominates; and only in John does the Son of man descend.
That descent means that during his ministry he can offer life to those
who believe in him."¹²⁵

Jesus at least used "Son of Man" as a circumlocution for "a person,"
"one," or "I, the speaker" as was common: "the Son of Man has nowhere
to lay his head" (Matt. 8:20; Luke 9:58). Whether he referred to himself as
Son of Man in anticipation of the likely results of his antagonism toward
the authorities is difficult to settle with certainty. It is historically plausible, given the accumulating events and forces against him, that Jesus did
anticipate rejection in Jerusalem and that he sought to frame both his
purpose there and his final destiny in religious symbols that expressed his

---

¹²² Dunn, *Jesus Remembered*, pp. 724–5.
¹²³ Sanders, *Historical Figure of Jesus*, p. 238.   ¹²⁴ Ibid., p. 239.
¹²⁵ Raymond E. Brown, *An Introduction to the Gospel of John*, ed. Francis J. Moloney (New York:
     Doubleday, 2003), p. 255.

experience of God; his commitment to God's reign; and the restoration of
Israel, its Temple, and its covenant. (The historical likelihood that Jesus
predicted not only that he would be killed, but that he would rise in three
days, is questionable.) As Sanders concludes, "It is not possible to come
to a firm conclusion about Jesus' use of the phrase 'Son of Man.' He used
it; sometimes he used it of himself; he expected the Son of Man to come
from heaven, but it is not certain that he identified himself as the future
Son of Man."[126]

Dunn speculates that Jesus may have seen in the designation "Son of
Man" a Danielic overtone of vindication of righteous suffering (Dan.
7:13), "a signal which gives him hope of vindication, whatever happened
to him."[127] In any event, this title resonates with many Jewish expectations
about the salvation of Israel in the end time. It suggests that God's intervention might involve a human agent or one with "more" than human
status (a lower divinity or an angel). And certainly it is credible that Jesus
appealed to all of these, especially the hope of vindication after the trials
that certainly lay ahead.

Another candidate for Jesus' self-description is "Messiah." He was executed on the charge of pretending to the kingship of Israel. Caiaphas follows up testimony that Jesus has threatened the Temple with the demand
that he swear under oath whether or not he is "the Messiah, the Son of
God" (Matt. 26:63). Israel's ideal of Davidic kingship was based in the
promise of the prophet Nathan to David that he would have a son who
would build (now rebuild) the Temple and who would also be regarded
as God's son (2 Sam. 7:12–14).[128] It is not unlikely that some called Jesus
Messiah during his lifetime, hoping that he would liberate them from
Roman rule. However, Jesus rejected royal power and privilege as a model
for discipleship (Mark 10:35–45) and, through many words and deeds, can-
celed the idea that God's Messiah would bring royal and military power.

It is possible that Jesus might have accepted other current meanings or
connotations of messiahship. There were several variants in play during his
lifetime, such as the two human messiahs of the Dead Sea community, for
whom the priestly messiah is the most important, not the kingly or royal
messiah. Yet Jesus is never remembered as using the title "Messiah" to
refer to himself or as unambiguously accepting its application to him by
others (with the possible exception of Mark 14:62).[129] Most significantly,

[126] Ibid., p. 248.   [127] Dunn, *Jesus Remembered*, p. 760.
[128] Ibid., pp. 628–34.   [129] Ibid., p. 653.

suffering – which Jesus accepted as part of his own role and went on to endure – was never associated in Jewish traditions with messiahship.

It is much more likely that Jesus considered himself an eschatological prophet, one with special agency in the drama of God's decisive victory. "For in terms of eschatological expectation, the role of prophet was almost as prominent as that of royal Messiah and more widespread than the hope of an anointed priest."[130] Certainly Jesus was considered a prophet, though perceived by many (including his enemies) to have broken the old prophetic categories. The suffering that Jesus underwent was proper to the role of a prophet, resonated with the suffering servant of Isaiah 53 and the righteous suffering of the Maccabean martyrs, and could be linked with the apocalyptic Son of Man imagery of Daniel and Qumran, as well as with the ideal of suffering on behalf of Israel and for the renewal of the covenant. Jesus would suffer as a result of faithfulness to his call, as others had done before him, but may also have seen his and the disciples' suffering as part of the eschatological tribulation, in which he had a special role, perhaps as a covenant sacrifice.[131]

After Jesus' death and resurrection, his followers reworked traditional categories such as Son of Man, Son of God, and Messiah so that they carried extraordinary new meanings. Though Jesus was a Jewish prophet, Christian Jewish proclamations were to stretch if not break the mold. Post-resurrection confessions of Jesus' significance also invoked titles that were less likely than Son of Man, prophet, or even Messiah to have been used by Jesus himself or by others during his lifetime. The basis of this expansion was a radical experience of Jesus as the Christ, in continuity with the remembered Jesus of history, but locating that life against a greatly changed horizon. The post-resurrection church reinforced the idea that the presence of Christ in the community empowers a new reality consistent with Jesus' preaching of the kingdom of God, God's future work yet a present possibility. "In the resurrection of Christ creation is restored and the kingdom of God dawns."[132] This possibility, salvation, is attested in already occurring relationships and practices, practices out of which Jesus is confessed as Christ.

---

[130] Ibid., p. 655. See also Meier, *Marginal Jew*, vol. 2: *Rethinking the Historical Jesus*, p. 1044.

[131] Dunn, *Jesus Remembered*, p. 818. .

[132] Oliver O'Donovan, *Resurrection and Moral Order: An Outline for Evangelical Ethics* (Leicester and Grand Rapids, MI: Inter-Varsity Press and Eerdmans, 1986), p. 15.

Chapter 4 will probe the practical and theological question, Who is the Christ, the one who has "authority" and brings salvation? Chapter 5 will consider, How is the Spirit of Christ present to the church and believers, converting and sanctifying persons and communities? Chapter 6 will ask, What does Jesus Christ do that is salvific, enabling sinful humans to reorder practices and begin life in God's kingdom?

CHAPTER 4

Christ

Soon after Jesus' death, his followers were already coming together in his memory, inspired by their experiences of the resurrection (1 Cor. 15:3–8). "They devoted themselves to the apostles' teaching and fellowship, to the breaking of bread and the prayers" (Acts 2:42). They shared common meals in their homes (Acts 2:46), celebrated liturgies in the name of Jesus as Lord (Phil. 2:11), and aspired to practices embodying God's reign. These included forming communities that crossed boundaries of gender, class, ethnicity, and tradition (Gal. 3:28); treating one another with charity, humility, and forbearance (1 Cor. 13); sharing goods with other community members (Acts 2:44–5, 4:32–5); and observing truthfulness, promise-keeping, honesty, and marital fidelity in their conduct in general (see the letter from Pliny quoted later). These earliest groups of Christ followers in Jerusalem and Galilee were Jewish, a sect within the broader movement of Jewish apocalyptic. They were unique in proclaiming Jesus as God's Messiah, as the one in whom God's reign had already begun, and as one whom God had especially exalted. They expected the risen Jesus to return soon with divine power to establish the eschatological kingdom (*parousia*).

Sometime before Paul wrote his first preserved letter (1 Thess.) in 51 CE, these Christian Jews began to reach out to and accept Gentiles as members of their group. Some of the latter may already have been "God fearers," that is, adherents of other cults who were attracted to the morality or the monotheism of Judaism and who had become proselytes or "fellow travelers," without yet converting. Their inclusion provoked a major and divisive controversy over circumcision as an entrance requirement for new Christ followers. The issue was resolved in favor of Paul's position, against circumcision, at a council in Jerusalem in 47 or 48 CE (Gal. 2:1–14; Acts 15).

An even larger issue for the emerging Jesus movement was fidelity to Jewish monotheism, in view of the apparently contradictory fact that

Christian Jews (and later Christian Gentiles) regarded Jesus as sharing attributes and activities that belonged to the one God of Israel. New Testament christologies grow out of liturgical practices, like baptism, hymns of praise and proclamation, celebrating the eucharistic meal, and repetition of basics of the faith.[1] To express their experience of salvation from God in and through the risen and exalted Christ, early Christian confessions reworked traditions, imagery, and vocabulary available in their religious and cultural milieus. As indicated in the preceding chapter, titles for Jesus were many. They included Son of Man, prophet, Messiah, second Adam, Son of God, Word or Wisdom, and Lord.

Early Christian usage went far beyond previous Jewish usage in suggesting that Jesus himself was divine. This claim was the consequence of believers' corporate experience of salvation, in which Jesus had a unique role and presence. The divinity of Jesus Christ is important for Christian ethics and politics (the politics of salvation) because it guarantees that Jesus embodies and communicates the decisive transformation of violence, suffering, and death. The gospels and the epistles offer more than one way to understand what is meant by claiming Christ's divinity. In any version, this claim is radical. It scandalized and antagonized both fellow Jews and defenders of the Roman cult. Hence Paul reports that he had persecuted Christian Jews, who had obviously done something extremely objectionable (Gal. 1:13–14).[2]

Extra-biblical corroboration of early devotion to Jesus "as a god" can be found in a letter to the Emperor Trajan from Pliny, the Roman governor of a province in what is modern-day Turkey. The letter is dated about 112 CE, which would be at or toward the end of the composition of the New Testament materials. It offers accounts of Christian activities going back twenty years. Pliny writes to Trajan for advice about how to handle people who are accused of being Christian, thus undermining the unifying worship of common gods in the Roman Empire. Pliny reports the following information as having been obtained from former Christians:

They were wont, on a stated day, to meet together before it was light, and to sing a hymn to Christ, as to a god, alternately [antiphonally[3]]; and to oblige

---

[1] See Richard N. Longenecker, *New Wine into Fresh Wineskins: Contextualizing the Early Christian Confessions* (Peabody, MA: Hendrickson, 1999); and Larry W. Hurtado, *Lord Jesus Christ: Devotion to Jesus in Earliest Christianity* (Grand Rapids, MI: Eerdmans, 2003), pp. 134–53.

[2] Larry W. Hurtado, *How on Earth Did Jesus Become a God? Historical Questions about Earliest Devotion to Jesus* (Grand Rapids, MI: Eerdmans, 2005), pp. 32–8, 168–73.

[3] An alternative translation is "chant antiphonally a hymn to Christ as to a god." Pliny (the Younger), "Epistles," 10.96, in J. Stevenson (ed.), *A New Eusebius: Documents Illustrative of the*

themselves by a sacrament [or oath], not to do anything that was ill: but that they would commit no theft, or pilfering, or adultery; that they would not break their promises, or deny what was deposited with them, when it was required back again; after which it was their custom to depart, and to meet again at a common but innocent meal.[4]

Pliny expresses indignation at such impiety but seems to view the reported activities as fairly harmless. He thus has scruples about how tough to be with supposed Christians who are mere youths, who deny the accusation, who repent of Christian membership, who were Christians some time in the past, or who have really done nothing wrong other than professing loyalty to Christ. His decision, approved by the emperor, is to execute those who will not give up this rapidly spreading new "superstition" and release those who recant or against whom the charge is not proved. Trajan instructs Pliny not to seek out offenders actively or to accept anonymous accusations.

CHRISTOLOGICAL PLURALISM AND ITS PRACTICAL ORIGINS

Though Christians may have been singing to Christ "as to a god," they did not all mean the same thing by it, or so the New Testament record indicates. For example, Paul and Luke preserve "two-stage" christologies dating from the first two decades after Jesus' death. These christologies seem to attribute full redemptive or "christological" identity to Jesus only after his resurrection (Acts 2:32, 36) or not until the second coming (Rom. 1:3–4; Acts 3:19–21, 5:31, 13:32–3).[5] In the gospels, these earlier christologies are subsumed within later christologies that present a Jesus who was Messiah, Son of Man, and Son of God at least from the time of his public ministry. The gospels recount that at his baptism, God speaks from heaven and declares Jesus to be "My beloved Son" (Mark 1:11; Matt. 3:17; Luke 3:22). Both of these types could be regarded as two-stage or "adoptionist," in that they allow for a view of Jesus as a human being who was elevated to a new status by God at some specific time (baptism,

---

History of the Church to A.D. 337 (London: SPCK, 1974), as cited in Hurtado, *How on Earth?* p. 13.

[4] "Letters of Pliny the Younger and the Emperor Trajan," in *The Works of Josephus*, trans. William Whiston (Peabody, MA: Hendrickson, 1987); accessed July 26, 2009, on the website of "From Jesus to Christ," a four-part television series for Frontline, WGBH Educational Foundation (1998), www.pbs.org/wgbh/pages/frontline/shows/religion/maps/primary/pliny.html.

[5] Raymond E. Brown, *An Introduction to New Testament Christology* (New York: Paulist Press, 1994), pp. 110–14.

resurrection, second coming). Certainly the gospels do not present the special status of Jesus as "divine" (which is a later, nonbiblical characterization) to be obvious during his lifetime, even after his baptism. In Mark no one acknowledges Jesus as "Son of God" until after the crucifixion. Similarly, Matthew and Luke use the transfiguration story to remind us that Jesus' glory is only rarely glimpsed. Yet notwithstanding its apparent obscurity to his associates during his life, the gospel authors push Jesus' christological identity back to his infancy and boyhood (Luke 1–2; Matt. 2:15), and ultimately to his conception (Luke 1:26–38; Matt. 1:21, 23).[6] This is an identity that they now view from the standpoint of the resurrection.

Some New Testament materials affirm Jesus' identity as God's Son by associating him with a being that existed even prior to his conception, thus producing "preexistence" christologies. Prominent among these is the Gospel of John, though hints may be found as early as the Pauline letters (Phil. 2:3–6).[7] According to John 1, "In the beginning was the Word, and the Word was with God, and the Word was God" (1:1). John has Jesus assert, "I and the Father are one" (10:30), designate himself with the title "God's Son" (10:36), and appeal to the Father to be glorified "with the glory that I had in your presence before the world existed" (17:5). However, no passage in the New Testament states explicitly that the Father and Son are "one" in divinity, that the Son coexisted eternally with the Father, or that Jesus is the incarnation of a being equal in divinity to the Father.[8] In fact the prologue to John's gospel (1:1) states that the Word existed "in the beginning," without claiming either that the Word is equal to the Creator or that Jesus of Nazareth is the incarnation of the Word (though this can be inferred from the placement of this claim at the beginning of a gospel about Jesus of Nazareth as the Christ). For this very reason, Arius was able in the fourth century to interpret John 1:1 as meaning that Jesus as Son of God is the incarnation of the Word and is divine – but not eternal or equal to the Father and Creator.[9] Larry Hurtado concludes that, although worship of Christ started very early, the New Testament as a

---

[6] Ibid., pp. 126–32.

[7] Larry Hurtado sees the Philippians hymn (Jesus "being in the form of a God," 2:6) as presuming Jesus' preexistent (if unequal) divinity (*How on Earth?* pp. 97–102). However, other scholars propose that "in the form of a God" refers to being created "in the image of God" and refers to Jesus' role as the "Second Adam." See Brown, *Introduction to New Testament Christology*, p. 134; James D. G. Dunn, *Christology in the Making: A New Testament Inquiry into the Origins of the Doctrine of the Incarnation*, 2nd edn. (Grand Rapids, MI: Eerdmans, 1996; 2nd edn. first published London: SCM Press, 1989).

[8] Brown, *Introduction to New Testament Christology*, pp. 133–41, 143.

[9] Ibid., p. 143.

whole presents a "binitarian" form of monotheism, in which the Spirit is not divine and the Father and Son are not equal. Rather, the Son is subordinate to the Father and Creator.[10]

New Testament pluralism on how best to express Jesus' special status as the bringer of God's salvation provides an important norm. James Dunn's judgment applies equally well to subsequent theologies: "Christology should not be narrowly confined to one particular assessment of Christ, nor should it play one off against another," for "from the first the significance of Christ could only be apprehended by a diversity of formulations which though not always strictly compatible with each other were not regarded as rendering each other invalid."[11] This point is instructive for ethicists who want to affirm the divinity of Christ as the guarantor of salvation and of transformative politics. This affirmation can be achieved in many ways – for example, along lines coherent with the multiple liberationist theologies and christologies of non-Western origin that express Christ's significance in culturally specific terms. Innovation and diversity also flourish in christologies and christologically based politics aimed at Western, "postmodern" audiences for whom past formulas have lost their disclosive power.

I do not suggest that contemporary theology and ethics should retrench on the eventual consensus of the bible, that Jesus was Son of God for his entire existence; or on the traditional doctrinal consensus that he is an incarnation of God and so divine; or on the corollary that Jesus incarnates God, and God preexists Jesus of Nazareth. The point, rather, is the propriety of contemporary flexibility in articulating exactly what is meant by these claims, flexibility found not only in the diversity in the bible, but in that of the tradition. Flexibility is necessary not only to provide credibility to audiences today, but also to accommodate all the affirmations about God in Christ that are important for Christian social ethics. Historical and theological studies of Nicaea and Chalcedon confirm that the ensuing doctrines are responses not only to biblical and liturgical expressions of faith, but also to social conditions and challenges that shape Christian concerns and help define acceptable and unacceptable responses.[12] Conciliar

---

[10] Hurtado, *How on Earth?* pp. 48–9.

[11] Dunn, *Christology in the Making*, pp. 266–7. See also Roger Haight, "Scripture: A Pluralistic Norm for Understanding Our Salvation in Jesus Christ," in Andrés Torres Queiruga, Lisa Sowle Cahill, Maria Clara Bingemer, and Erik Borgman (eds.), *Jesus as Christ: What Is at Stake in Christology?* (London: SCM Press, 2008), pp. 13–32.

[12] See Lewis Ayres, *Nicaea and Its Legacy: An Approach to Fourth-Century Trinitarian Theology* (Oxford: Oxford University Press, 2004); and Stephen T. Davis, Daniel Kendall, S.J., and Gerald O'Collins, S.J. (eds.), *The Incarnation: An Interdisciplinary Symposium on the Incarnation*

formulas set parameters for talking about God and Christ without specifying exactly what should be said. Pluralism has been even more rampant
in soteriological theories than in christological ones; there has never been a
definitive doctrinal consensus concerning how exactly Jesus saves us (to be
explored in Chapter 6).

A feminist, Asian, postcolonial theologian engages five different images
of Jesus today: "the Black Christ in the works of black and womanist
theologians; Jesus as Corn Mother; Jesus as the Feminine Shakti in India;
Jesus as the theological transvestite; and Jesus as the Bi/Christ."[13] A collection on African christology considers Jesus as priest, prophet, and poten-
tate; Jesus as the nurturer of life and friend of women; Jesus, master of
initiation; Christ as chief; Christ as ancestor and elder brother; Jesus as
healer; Christ the liberator; and Christ the risen and victorious vindicator
of the rejected.[14] Are these experimental images really so radical? Just as
in biblical times and throughout the centuries, Christians today express
divine presence, salvation, and resurrection in ways that are meaningful to their own communities and can challenge and change their own
contexts. All christology is political. This is not inherently a liability; it
is part of the mission of theology. We are hardly dispensed in our own
day from "making sense of the mystery of God's presence in our lives,"
a responsibility from which the classical formulations cannot provide an
easy escape.[15]

The preface to a collection of essays on christology observes "questions of Christ's significance for us, the meaning of his divinity, and his
relevance for the world come up again and again, not because others
failed to answer them but because contexts, worldviews, and horizons
change."[16] These contexts and horizons both prompt and test theological
responses. Theologies gain authority to the extent that they can explain
the practical crises and conflicts faced by Christians, and form Christian
identity to address and ameliorate these crises in a way that is coherent
with God's reign.

of the Son of God (New York: Oxford University Press, 2002); also published on Oxford
Scholarship Online (November 2003), dx.doi.org/10.1093/0199248451.001.0001 (accessed
January 10, 2005).

[13] Kwok Pui-lan, *Postcolonial Imagination and Feminist Theology* (Louisville, KY: Westminster John
Knox Press, 2005), p. 174.
[14] Robert J. Schreiter (ed.), *Faces of Jesus in Africa* (Maryknoll, NY: Orbis Books, 1995).
[15] Dennis J. Billy, C.Ss.R., "The Person of the Holy Spirit as the Source of the Christian Moral
Life," *Studia Moralia*, 36 (1998), pp. 325–59, at 332.
[16] Tatha Wiley, Preface to Tatha Wiley (ed.), *Thinking of Christ: Proclamation, Explanation,
Meaning* (New York: Continuum, 2003), pp. 9, 7–8.

To recall that the earliest Christian confessions were sited liturgically is to envision them as the vocalizations of specific, historical people who gathered to celebrate the new identity they shared, while still remaining part of other communities that continued to form them and to whose spaces they would return. Diversity among christologies corresponds to diversity in the social and political contexts of the church. Diversity is consistent with a recognizable similarity among authentic portraits of Jesus Christ (as among the four gospels) and a similarity in authentic embodiments of God's kingdom. In what do this similarity and authenticity consist?

The distinctive practices of Jesus and his disciples, the Jesus-movement, are *reconciling practices, practices that can heal* the fractured persons and communities that we are. To engage in these practices reflectively is to do christology in and through practice.[17]

Then as now, being a consistently virtuous or "reconciling" Christian or Christian community is sometimes more, sometimes less successful. Even though the kingdom calls for the reversal of status hierarchies, the fact is that even in the New Testament house churches, some people were still the patrons, some the guests, beneficiaries, or "clients." Not all had equal resources or authority.[18] This is what permitted the eventual incorporation of Greek norms of household order into Christian communal behavior and why Paul rebuked the Corinthians for preserving society's status divisions at the common meal (1 Cor. 11). Christians in all their various memberships should be challenging, not inscribing, the exclusionary values of household and society. They should take care of people that others have forgotten (Matt. 25), not honoring those who enjoy the preponderance of power. Yet this central gospel message requires intellectual and practical adaptation in different settings. True theological statements connect our understanding to our reality and our practices (Chapter 1), but those statements never capture the whole of reality. That is uniquely true of statements about God. The advice to the Thessalonians still holds: "Do not quench the Spirit … test everything; hold fast to what is good" (1 Thess. 5:19, 21).

---

17 Terrence W. Tilley, *The Disciples' Jesus: Christology as Reconciling Practice* (Maryknoll, NY: Orbis Books, 2008), p. 2; emphasis added.

18 New Testament scholars David Balch and Carolyn Osiek, for example, argue that archaeological research on the early Christian house churches suggests that status divisions persisted at Christian meals, even though the eucharist was supposedly enacting the new reality of communities that are "one" in Jesus Christ (Gal. 3:28); see Carolyn Osiek and David L. Balch, *Families in the New Testament World: Households and House Churches* (Louisville, KY: Westminster John Knox Press, 1997).

One might even say that there is in Christian theology both a valuable systematic impulse and an ultimate antisystematic norm. The impetus to create theological systems to explain the Christian experience of God derives from humanity's intellectual capacity, drive toward understanding, and need for and satisfaction in "reflective equilibrium" (a phrase of John Rawls).[19] Reflective equilibrium is a state in which judgments have been tested, coherence in beliefs is achieved, and beliefs have been made consistent and comprehensive enough to serve as guides for action. Intellectual analysis helps achieve this, and so does theological systematization. Intellect and understanding are distinctive of human nature, constituents of human happiness, and necessary to further on a wide scale the kinds of relationships the gospels commend.

On the other side, no theological system can (or should attempt to) achieve a reflective equilibrium that can completely account for all the intellectually paradoxical dimensions of the reality of God in Christ. As Reinhold Niebuhr warns, theological systems and formulas will inevitably wind up in "metaphysical absurdities" due to the unconditioned character of the divine, and the conditioned and contingent character of the human mind. Though paradoxical theological assertions have been necessary to refute heresies, they have also, perhaps inevitably, produced another "long series of heresies in which either the human or the divine quality of the life of Christ was denied or obscured."[20] Theological systematization is an important step, phase, or dimension of the experience and knowledge of God, but it requires the virtue of humility, or what Jon Sobrino has called "chastity of intelligence."[21] The most complete and authentic knowledge of God appears at the point where intellectual insight, moral and liturgical practices, and affective and imaginative conversion join.

TWO CHRISTOLOGICAL PARADIGMS

It is possible to distinguish at least two different types of christology that attempt to account theoretically for the reality of salvation, the experience of God, the priority of the biblical witness, and the sociopolitical contexts of the church. These are Word christology and Spirit christology. Word

[19] John Rawls, *A Theory of Justice* (Cambridge, MA: Harvard University, 1971), pp. 48–51.
[20] Reinhold Niebuhr, *The Nature and Destiny of Man: A Christian Interpretation*, vol. 2: *Human Destiny* (Louisville, KY: Westminster John Knox Press, 1996; originally published New York: Charles Scribner's Sons, 1943), p. 70.
[21] Jon Sobrino, *Christ the Liberator: A View from the Victims*, trans. Paul Burns (Maryknoll, NY: Orbis Books, 2001), p. 53.

christology has been dominant historically, but Spirit christology is gaining ground as a biblically prevalent alternative that speaks just as effectively to the needs of our time.

Word christology, derived from the prologue to John's gospel, provides
the basis of a strong affirmation of the divinity of the second person of
the Trinity and of Jesus Christ as Word incarnate; it has been in posses-
sion from Nicaea onward. Especially as developed in Eastern theology
(the Cappadocians), Word christology furnishes a theology and spirituality of human participation in the divine life ("divinization").[22] The roots
of Cappadocian theology are in Plato's vision of the ascent of the soul
toward and into union with the divine, a vision mediated through the
theology and spirituality of Origen, for whom human desire is fulfilled
in contemplation of the Word.[23] For the Cappadocian fathers as well as
Augustine, redemption and sanctification are understood as union with
the person of Christ, the Word incarnate. Salvation is participation in
the life of God (see 2 Pet. 1:4), a share in which Christ cannot communicate to us unless he is fully God. Through Christ, one is united with the
Father.[24]

Word christology has a lasting hold on the Christian imagination
because it expresses and mediates *participation* in God, a share in divine plenitude. As Nicaea's primary defender and promoter, Athanasius,
writes, "He became man that we might be divinized."[25] In her contemporary Word Christology, Kathryn Tanner explains, "By way of the incarnation humanity is united to, bound up with, the Word," so that Trinitarian
relationships "thereby come to include the human."[26] Word christology
also supports the idea that, sin aside, authentic humanity is possible only
in union with Jesus Christ, the perfecter of human nature.

Spirit christology, rooted in Luke–Acts and some Pauline letters,
is an alternative (not an opposite) that stresses the reality or presence

---

[22] See Norman Russell, *The Doctrine of Deification in the Greek Patristic Tradition* (New York:
Oxford University Press, 2004); Anthony Meredith, *The Cappadocians* (Crestwood, NY: St.
Vladimir's Seminary Press, 2000), pp. 47–9, on Gregory of Nazianzus; and Ayres, *Nicaea*,
pp. 304–8, on Gregory of Nyssa. It must be remembered that not all Word christologies easily accommodate the idea that through Christ, Christians participate in the divine life. The
Protestant Reformers emphasized the distance between humanity and God, even after salvation.
Recent modifications of this viewpoint will be considered in Chapter 5.
[23] Anthony Meredith, *Cappadocians*, pp. 16–17.
[24] Ayres, *Nicaea*, pp. 304–12.
[25] Athanasius, *De Incarn.* 54 (*Patrologia Graeca*, ed. Migne, 25, 192b), as cited by John P. Galvin,
"Jesus Christ," in Francis Schüssler Fiorenza and John P. Galvin (eds.), *Systematic Theology:
Roman Catholic Perspectives*, vol. 1 (Minneapolis: Augsburg Fortress Press, 1991), p. 264.
[26] Kathryn Tanner, *Christ the Key* (Cambridge University Press, 2010), p. 143.

of God not only in Jesus Christ, but also in the church, through the
risen Christ who sends his Spirit.[27] Because of the historical dominance of a Word christology based on John's gospel, the Spirit christology that is more visible in the synoptics has been called one of "the
'forgotten truths' of Christianity."[28] A growing literature attempts to
correct that problem, without necessarily displacing Word christology
from the shared center of the tradition. The Spirit paradigm gathered
momentum in the modern and postmodern periods, though it does find
precedents in figures like Ignatius of Antioch, Cyril of Alexandria, and
Augustine. Representative authors include Friedrich Schleiermacher,
Shailer Mathews, D. M. Baillie, Geoffrey Lampe, Piet Schoonenberg,
Jürgen Moltmann, Michael Welker, David Coffey, Ralph Del Colle,
Roger Haight, James Dunn, Elizabeth Johnson, and Elisabeth Schüssler
Fiorenza. On the issue of how Jesus Christ's divine status is joined with
or communicated to humans in a saving way, Spirit christology works
salvation through Christian community as inbreaking kingdom of God
and body of Christ, whereas Logos or Word christology highlights salvation as self-transcendence and contemplation, toward union with the
divine.

Today Spirit christology enables a spirituality and ethics of Christian
unity in countercultural communities that include the excluded and take
up the cross in pursuit of the reign of God. Among its strong points are
concrete models of discipleship and church derived from Jesus' life, death,
and resurrection and from the practical ideals of the early churches. Spirit
christology's appeal lies in its connection to the Jesus of the gospels and
to the radical social implications of the kingdom of God he preached. Its
potential to portray the inclusive presence and work of the Spirit in history and creation also makes it amenable to ecological concerns and to
interreligious respect and dialogue.

---

[27] For a discussion of the personhood of the Spirit and the place of the Spirit in the Trinity, see
Ralph Del Colle, *Christ and the Spirit: Spirit-Christology in Trinitarian Perspective* (New York:
Oxford University Press, 1994); Bernd Jochen Hilberath, "Identity through Self-Transcendence";
Kilian McDonnell, "A Response to Bernd Jochen Hilberath"; Jürgen Moltmann, "The
Trinitarian Personhood of the Holy Spirit"; David Coffey, "Spirit Christology and Trinity";
and Ralph Del Colle, "A Response to Jürgen Moltmann and David Coffey": all in Bradford E.
Hinze and D. Lyle Dabney (eds.), *Advents of the Spirit: An Introduction to the Current Study of
Pneumatology* (Milwaukee, WI: Marquette University Press, 2001), pp. 263–92, 293–9, 300–12,
313–36, and 337–436, respectively; and David Coffey, *"Did you Receive the Holy Spirit When You
Believed?" Some Basic Questions for Pneumatology* (Milwaukee, WI: Marquette University Press,
2005), pp. 42–74.
[28] Edward Schillebeeckx, *Jesus: An Experiment in Christology*, trans. Hubert Hoskins (New York:
Seabury Press, 1979), p. 570.

Critics of Word christology identify its potential abstraction from history, its downplaying of the humanity of Jesus, and its presentation via seemingly arid and obsolete creedal formulations as reasons to move to a different model. But critics of Spirit christology see it as undermining traditional faith in the divinity of Jesus Christ as Son of God and as abandoning doctrinal parameters essential to Christian orthodoxy.

My purpose is to bring these two approaches together, showing their essential connection and validation in the practical Christian life, especially Christian ethics. From the standpoint of Christian ethics, the evolving language of God as Spirit offers unparalleled resources for responding to the practical challenges facing today's Christians. This is true both because references to the concrete life, death, and resurrection of Jesus Christ are integral to Spirit christology and because Spirit christology comprehends the church as a dynamic mediator of salvation in and for the world and all creation.[29] Yet a Word christology carries forward a crucial reason for Christian theology and theological ethics to foster hope that salvation brings real historical transformations: human participation in the divine life through the incarnation of God in Jesus Christ.

An adequate Spirit christology can protect the idea of human participation in the divine or "divinization" either by expressly bridging to a Word or Wisdom christology, or by proposing a parallel concept via the language of God as Spirit.[30] On the other hand, Word christologies need to incorporate an orientation to Jesus' inauguration of the reign of God and its historical relevance for the poor. These values are readily visible in the synoptic gospels, Acts, and Paul's letters to particular churches.

The controversial nature of new Spirit christologies is evident in the reactions provoked by the proposal of Roger Haight. Haight's book, *Jesus: Symbol of God*, was written to make theology more adequate to

---

[29] See Bradford E. Hinze, "Releasing the Power of the Spirit in a Trinitarian Ecclesiology," in Hinze and Dabney (eds.), *Advents of the Spirit*, pp. 347–81; and Mary Elsbernd, "Toward a Theology of Spirit That Builds Up the Just Community," in Bradford E. Hinze (ed.), *The Spirit in the Church and the World*, College Theology Society Annual Volume 49, 2003 (Maryknoll, NY: Orbis Books, 2004), pp. 152–66.

[30] Some proponents of a Spirit Christology maintain that it is more adequate and comprehensive than a Word Christology, because the former can include the insights of the latter, while going beyond them. In the view of David Coffey, "Logos Christology understands the mystery of Christ simply and solely in terms of the hypostatic union between the Logos and the humanity of Christ," to which the work of the Spirit in Christ can then only be subsequent ("Spirit Christology and the Trinity," in Hinze and Dabney [eds.], *Advents of the Spirit*, p. 317). Roger Haight also endorses the superiority of a Spirit Christology, though in relative rather than absolute terms, as more adequate to postmodern sensibilities (*Jesus: Symbol of God* [Maryknoll, NY: Orbis Books, 1999], pp. 451, 465–6).

the situation of Christians at the turn of the twenty-first century, more intelligible, persuasive, and inspiring to faith seekers today. Haight eloquently retrieves scriptural traditions associating Jesus with the Spirit of God and depicts the risen Jesus as sending the Spirit of Christ. Yet his book has been a flashpoint for defenders of a more traditional "high christology." These claim – also out of practical concerns – that Haight's revisions cannot sustain authentic Christian belief and spirituality. In my view authentic Christianity can be sustained *only* by a christological pluralism that includes several approaches, including but not limited to Spirit christology.

A reconsideration of Word christology and Spirit christology in relation to biblical and conciliar sources will show that the terms of any "orthodox" christology are inherently interdependent with the life of the church, and hence also necessarily dynamic and paradoxical. The councils of Nicaea and Chalcedon do not settle all that clearly what full "divinity" means, much less how it can be reconciled in one person with full humanity. The potential to combine aspects of both paradigms, Word and Spirit, and the benefits of so doing for the justice commitments of global Christianity will be developed at the end of Chapter 5 via the theologies of Jürgen Moltmann, Elizabeth Johnson, and Anselm Min.[31]

WORD, OR LOGOS, CHRISTOLOGY

The centerpiece of classical Word christology is the affirmation that a pre-existent divine being became incarnate in Jesus. Word christology is the preeminent model in Christian history for symbolizing, explaining, and expressing liturgically the divine status of Jesus Christ. Virtually every significant Christian theologian assumes this model as a point of departure; some of its more notable proponents are Cyril of Alexandria, Athanasius, the Cappadocian fathers, Augustine, Aquinas, and Karl Rahner. Though it finds considerable support in Paul (1 Cor. 8:6; Phil. 2:6–8; Col. 1:15–17; Heb 1:1–3, 6, 9:26, 10:5–10), the primary biblical source of a Word christology is the prologue to John's gospel (which the First Epistle of John closely resembles and which is echoed in 2 John 7).

---

[31] A theologian who engages a similar project, oriented primarily by trinitarian theology and Word christology, is Kathryn Tanner. Her theology is not as centrally concerned with Christian ethics and global justice as the theologies of Moltmann, Johnson, and Min, but it does take account of a politics of the kingdom of God in union with the Spirit. Both the present chapter and Chapter 7 make reference to Tanner's *Christ the Key*.

John 1 is the cornerstone text. "In the beginning was the Word, and the Word was with God, and the Word was God. He was in the beginning with God. All things came into being through him, and without him not one thing came into being" (John 1:1–3, NRSV). John 1:1–18 encapsulates John's view of Jesus Christ as a divine being, God's Word (1:1, 14), who is also the light (1:5, 9) and God's only Son (1:14, 18). This being becomes flesh and comes into the world, suffers rejection, but empowers all who accept him "to become God's children, so that they share in God's fullness – a gift reflecting God's enduring love."[32] In fact, John's gospel goes much further than the others in presenting Jesus "as an incarnate revelation descended from on high, indeed from another world, to offer people light and truth."[33] Yet John 1, taken alone, does not assert the divinity of Jesus Christ, much less of "Jesus of Nazareth," as clearly as some would have it. Neither is mentioned in the text, and the Word itself is asserted both to have been *with* God and to have *been* God – an equivocal depiction, to be sure.

If Jesus Christ is the incarnation of the Word of God, then is Jesus Christ somehow "preexistent" to his historical existence as Jesus of Nazareth? Those wishing to defend the divinity of Christ in biblical and conciliar terms sometimes assert the simple identity of Jesus and God, without clarifying how the eternal Word of God and the man Jesus are or are not the same, or at least acknowledging that the very attempt to do so is necessarily full of conundrums. Frequently, modern authors use the terms or names "Jesus," "Jesus of Nazareth," "Jesus Christ," "Lord," and "Son of God" interchangeably while addressing the divinity of Jesus Christ. Relying on the later para- or neo-Chalcedonian view (to be discussed later in this chapter) that the divine Word is the "person" of Jesus Christ, so that Jesus has or is no human person, these authors can obscure that the man Jesus of Nazareth is fully human and not simply to be equated with a descending divinity.

For example, even though John Wright accepts that "the man Jesus did not exist as a human being before he was born," he takes Roger Haight to task because "he will not speak of the preexistence of Jesus."[34] Larry Hurtado argues for "a sort of view of Jesus" that sees him as existing in

[32] Raymond E. Brown, *An Introduction to the New Testament* (New York: Doubleday, 1997), pp. 337–8.
[33] Raymond E. Brown, *An Introduction to the Gospel of John*, ed. Francis J. Moloney (New York: Doubleday, 2003), p. 259.
[34] John Wright, "Roger Haight's Spirit Christology," *Theological Studies*, 53 (1992), pp. 729–35, at 731, 730.

some divine status or mode before becoming a human being by referring to John 1:1–18[35] and asserts flatly that "the term 'god' is applied to Jesus ... unambiguously" in John 1:1[36] (which mentions neither Jesus nor Jesus Christ by name). Gerald O'Collins states clearly that Jesus' humanity or human nature cannot be viewed as preexistent. Yet he rebukes Haight for not seeing that "the person who came to be known historically as Jesus" is preexistent[37] and asserts that "Orthodox Christian faith believes that Jesus of Nazareth was personally identical with the eternally pre-existent Son of God or Logos."[38]

New Testament authors do not yet raise the technical question of the relation between Jesus' humanity and divinity, nor specify the precise relation between Jesus Christ and the Logos. Their general purpose is to publicize their belief that the Jesus they remember is truly the Christ or Messiah, so it is this latter identity, formulated by appellations such as "Jesus Christ," "Lord," and "Son of God," that is their overriding focus. New Testament texts that associate preexistence, the Word, or Logos with Jesus Christ cannot be read to define the precise terms of this relationship, that of his humanity and divinity, or that of the Word to the one creator God.

"Jesus of Nazareth" is a designation found rarely, if at all, in ancient Christian authors, but it is familiar and important to modern ones because it connotes for the Christian imagination a specific cultural and geographical scenario that lends interest and texture to the Jesus of the gospels. Concrete, contextual images enhance our appreciation of his significance in our own lives and circumstances. Although we customarily use "Jesus of Nazareth" and "Jesus Christ" as interchangeable names, the two designations can be distinguished as referring to different aspects of Jesus' identity and role. "Jesus of Nazareth" refers to his concrete historical life, ministry, and death; "Jesus Christ" refers to his salvific role, which is contingent on his divine nature, his resurrection and exaltation, and his presence to believers through the Spirit in community.

---

[35] Ibid.

[36] Hurtado, *Lord Jesus Christ*, p. 637. Hurtado is on firmer ground in citing John 17:5, where before his death Jesus prays for "the glory that I had in [God's] presence before the world existed" (p. 101). In a discussion of the Christological hymn in Philippians 2:6–11, Hurtado argues further that for its original audience, "Jesus' preexistence had become a part of Christian belief" (Hurtado, *How on Earth?* p. 101). But the hymn makes the explicit connection to "being in the form of a God" (v. 5) to "Christ Jesus" (v. 6), not simply "Jesus," and proclaims that the name "Jesus" should occasion the confession that "Jesus Christ is Lord" (v. 11).

[37] Gerald O'Collins, *Christology: A Biblical, Historical and Systematic Study of Jesus* (Oxford University Press, 1995), p. 243.

[38] Ibid., p. 237.

The key point of contact between Word and Spirit christologies is the affirmation that it is in reality God who is incarnate or embodied in Jesus, now seen in light of the resurrection as the Christ. True unity of the human and divine is essential to traditional Christian faith, to trust in our salvation, and to Christian social commitment. Nicaea and Chalcedon furnish structures and parameters for understanding this unity theologically. Yet Christians and theologians always require nourishing recourse to the rich, polyvalent biblical imagery that remains the best access to the mysteries behind the conciliar formulas.

JEWISH BACKGROUND

The dialectical, dynamic, allusive, and "unclosed" character of John's affirmation of the divinity of Christ is in continuity with its Jewish background. The depiction of a Word who was with God at the creation of the world and who descends into the world recalls the figure Wisdom of the Hebrew scriptures (Sir. 24, Wisd. 9, Prov. 8). However, in Jewish tradition, Wisdom was always a personification of the one God, never a distinct divine being. John does not employ the specific term "Wisdom" (Sophia) in speaking of Jesus, possibly because Jesus is a male. Instead, he uses the Greek "Logos," or "Word," already in use in Hellenistic Judaism. John attributes to "the Son of Man" (Jesus) characteristics that Wisdom shares. Both preexist with God, come into the world from heaven, communicate divine knowledge, offer spiritual food, and produce division among those who accept and those who refuse. Like Wisdom, Jesus is the manifestation of God's glory, is the light of God in the world, and will ultimately return to heaven.[39]

Unlike the apocalyptic Son of Man, Jesus as Word has already descended and is already active in history, as is divine Wisdom.[40] The realized eschatology of John's gospel is laid out in terms of the community of the Beloved Disciple (19:26, 35; 20:35; 21:24). The inner life of this community is idealized in Jesus' "farewell discourses" (11–17): "The glory that you have given me I have given them, so that they may be one, as we are one, I in them and you in me, so that they may become completely one."[41]

---

[39] Brown, *Introduction to the Gospel of John*, p. 259.
[40] Ibid., pp. 261–3.
[41] See Frank J. Matera, "Christ in the Theologies of Paul and John: Diverse Unity of New Testament Theology," *Theological Studies*, 67/2 (2006), pp. 247–51.

In early Christian usage, the identification of Jesus Christ with the divine Word or Wisdom is one way of maintaining a creative tension between
the core Jewish affirmation that there is but one God and the practice of
early Christian Jews, who honored Jesus Christ as divine. Imagery already
established in the Jewish scriptures is renegotiated in relation to Christ;
that imagery permits ambiguous assertions about the divine status of the
Word ("In the beginning was the Word, and the Word was with God and
the Word was God"; 1:1) to be predicated indirectly of Christ; and the
relation of the Son to the Father is elevated without being precisely specified ("It is God the only Son, who is close to the Father's heart, who has
made him known"; 1:18).

Another merit of this terminology or imagery for emerging Christianity
is its ability to span and unite Christianity's Jewish heritage and its new
Hellenistic constituents. In Greek philosophy and culture, the Logos
(Word or Reason) was conceived as an immanent divine principle of
rationality in the world. The Jewish writer Philo had already adapted the
Greek concept of Logos for a Jewish theology of the transcendent creator
God.[42]

Scholars agree that the Word, Wisdom, and Logos are ways of speaking about divine immanence in the world, and God's action in the world
and with God's people. However, in the Hebrew Bible, these figures are
never placed in competition with God or attain the status of independent
divine beings.[43] Recent work on Jewish antecedents of a Logos christology, in the form of a heavenly eschatological figure who is preexistent
but not God, lends credence to the thesis that, to the extent that early
Christ worship developed within Christian Jewish communities on the
basis of familiar traditions and within communities that were strongly
opposed to threats to Jewish monotheism, their preexistence christologies
were subordinationist.[44]

As we saw in Chapter 3, the Jewish precedent is to honor quasi-divine
angelic and eschatological figures ("the Son of Man" in Dan. 7; 1; En.
48:5), not placed on a par with God.[45] Pheme Perkins shows that, compared with Gnostic Christian christologies, which borrowed from Jewish

[42] John J. Collins, *Encounters with Biblical Theology* (Minneapolis: Fortress Press, 2005), p. 185.
[43] Dunn, *Christology in the Making*, pp. 251–3.
[44] Hurtado, *How on Earth?* pp. 111–33; Thomas H. Tobin, "The Prologue of John and Hellenistic
Jewish Speculation," *Catholic Biblical Quarterly*, 52/2 (2004), pp. 252–69; and Paul A. Rainbow,
"Jewish Monotheism as the Matrix for New Testament Christology: A Review Article," *Novum
Testamentum*, 33/1 (1991), pp. 78–91.
[45] Collins, *Encounters with Biblical Theology*, pp. 180–6.

apocalyptic traditions, "orthodox" or canonical christologies may even maintain a firmer distance between the Logos who becomes incarnate and God the Creator.[46] Though Jesus' followers acclaimed him as "the Christ" (Messiah) and honored him as divine, the relation between God and Jesus Christ was not settled soon. Indeed, most if not all early christologies were subordinationist. Subordinationism is compatible both with early Word christologies that see a being less than the creator God as having become incarnate in Christ and with early christologies that interpret Jesus' divinity as a "two-stage" process inspired by the Spirit. Lewis Ayres maintains that strands of subordinationism continued to exist even in "pro-Nicene" theology after the council.[47]

CLARIFICATION WITH INDETERMINACY: THE COUNCILS

Christology deals in paradoxes. Christ has to be divine to *save*, human to save *us*.[48] Yet, "in holding one and the same individual to be both fully divine and fully human, we seem to claim something that is logically inconceivable: an individual who has mutually exclusive sets of characteristics, being simultaneously eternal, incorruptible, immutable, and a-spatial on the one hand, and temporal, corruptible, changeable, and spatially determined on the other."[49] "One cannot say undialectically that Jesus is God, nor that he is merely a human being, because the doctrine is that Jesus is both truly human and divine."[50]

Nicaea was convened to combat theories and symbol systems that protected monotheism and explained the relation of Jesus Christ to the creator God by positing between the two a lesser divinity or creature that became incarnate in Jesus. The Nicene Creed was a consensus document, geared to exclude Arius. The teaching of Nicaea is that "the Lord Jesus Christ the Son of God" is "true God from true God, begotten not made, consubstantial (*homoousios*) with the Father," not derivative and unequal to the Father.

---

[46] Pheme Perkins, "Gnostic Christologies and the New Testament," *Catholic Biblical Quarterly*, 43/4 (2004), p. 605.
[47] Ayres, *Nicaea*, pp. 134–66.
[48] This is the way Colin Gunton puts it in "Historical and Systematic Theology," in Colin Gunton (ed.), *Cambridge Companion to Christian Doctrine* (Cambridge University Press, 2006), p. 3.
[49] Gerald O'Collins, "The Incarnation: The Critical Issues," in Davis, Kendall, and O'Collins (eds.), *The Incarnation*, pp. 6–7.
[50] Roger Haight, "The Case for Spirit Christology," *Theological Studies*, 53 (1992), pp. 257–87, at 275.

Entangled with the theological reasons were political reasons for calling the council. The Emperor Constantine had recently reunited the Roman Empire through military ventures ostensibly conducted under the aegis of Christ. According to both Lactantius and Eusebius, Constantine's decisive victory in 312 at the Milvian Bridge was due to his embracing the cross and entrusting his success to Christ's intervention. The vindication of "Constantine's victory and kingship as an achievement of Christ the Victor and King" was to become "a full-blown theology of history and an apologia for the idea of a Christian Roman empire."[51] Ecclesial disunity threatened Constantine's ideology and his hold on his winnings. It was Constantine who convened the Council of Nicaea in 323 and demanded that controversies be solved in the interests of imperial peace, law, and order. From this perspective, diversity and theological ferment are neither productive nor tolerable. Uniformity is the theo-political desideratum.[52]

This set of pressures may call into question the credibility of the Nicene resolution, but that resolution still deserves consideration in its own right, as a strategy among competing theological factions or interpretations and in terms of its "effective history" – its positive or negative effects on the churches. No doubt many readings are possible and no definitive one shall be ventured here. The Nicene preference for unity, transcendence, mono-theism, and "incarnation" as "descent" had weaknesses and introduced problems that have been mentioned. Chief among these are a central-ized and hierarchical theological norm, neglect of the humanity of Jesus Christ, and the marginalization of historical transformation in favor of trust in eternal life. Possible strengths are not missing, however. Among these are the power of a theology and piety of incarnation of the Word to transmute Jewish monotheism without splitting it apart, to offer a com-pelling alternative to Greco-Roman polytheism, to have cultural appeal via metaphors of Logos and Word, to bring home the truly divine status of someone who had only too obviously at that point been a real man who was executed, and to offer low-status believers the hope of transcend-ing historical traumas even though their political power was nil.

Theologically, Nicaea was an attempt to resolve the obvious conun-drum of worshipping a historical figure in the context of a monotheistic faith and to exclude "explanations" that might be dangerous to the lived possibility of salvation as truly available and yet also proleptic. Nicaea had

---

[51] Jaroslav Pelikan, *Jesus through the Centuries* (New Haven, CT: Yale University Press, 1999), p. 51.
[52] Elisabeth Schüssler Fiorenza, *Jesus: Miriam's Child, Sophia's Prophet: Critical Issues in Feminist Christology* (New York: Continuum, 1995), p. 20.

somehow to bring together different scriptural vocabularies, and scripture remained the context and ultimate referent of its creed.[53] This strategy should remain as much a norm of subsequent theology as the creed that resulted.

The creed itself neither stipulated a clear, coherent, and uniform theological explication of scripture's meaning nor assumed that adherents were in agreement on what that explication would be. Some signatories (like Eusebius of Caesarea) viewed the Son as coeternal with the Father in that he existed potentially in the Father's will.[54] Some stressed unity, some difference, avoiding modalism and subordinationism only because the creed kept both poles in tension. Some were willing to accept only one divine hypostasis, not three, and saw the Son as the "image," "reflection," and so on, of the Father, deemphasizing the Son's distinct being.[55] Hence the careful wording of Nicaea: "We believe in ... one Lord Jesus Christ the Son of God, begotten as only begotten of the Father, that is of the being of the Father, God of God, Light of Light, true God of true God, begotten not made ... who ... was incarnate and became man."[56] Some Eastern theologians thought Nicaea was "dangerously modalist" because it did not uphold clearly enough the distinction between the Father and the Son.[57] The creed skirted some sensitive issues, like whether "begotten" connotes inequality, whether the Son is begotten eternally,[58] the meaning of *ousia*,[59] and what a divine "hypostasis" is.[60]

Nicaea's definition of three persons (*hypostases*) in one divine nature (*ousia*) became the preeminent norm for subsequent theological explanations of the fact of Christ worship. Nevertheless, this norm was and remains a moving target for theology. The precedent Nicaea established was not substantive clarity about what constitutes the divinity of Jesus Christ. What Nicaea made normative was the accountability of theology to general parameters within a "dynamic tradition," referring to scripture, and constituted by a "shifting community" of thinkers.[61]

Athanasius was to make acceptance of the creed the test, without specifying what it meant.[62] Unity was maintained by letters and contacts, not by a single formula. Its supporters kept reaffirming that it was really impossible to know the Father–Son relation.[63] As Ayres sums it up, the signers of the creed agreed that the relation between Father and Son

---

[53] Ayres, *Nicaea*, pp. 141, 277.   [54] Ibid., pp. 90–1.   [55] Ibid., p. 59.
[56] Nicene Creed, as quoted in Ayres, *Nicaea*, p. 19.
[57] Ayres, *Nicaea*, pp. 431–2.
[58] Ibid., p. 91.   [59] Ibid., p. 97.   [60] Ibid., p. 295.
[61] Ibid., p. 82.   [62] Ibid., p. 99.   [63] Ibid., p. 432.

is ultimately mysterious. What they insisted upon was that there is an "ineffable closeness" between the Father and the Son and that the Son's being is from the Father "in some indescribable sense."[64] The Nicene formulations regarding the three persons in God do not entirely eliminate the theological pluralism that existed before and during the council; the fact of different theological interpretations of Nicaea follows necessarily from the mysterious nature of that to which it points. Augustine's caveats on Trinitarian language still hold. "The super-eminence of the Godhead surpasses the power of customary speech." Therefore, the term "person" is used in communicating the mystery of the Trinity, not to completely explain God, but so that what might be understood "might not be left [wholly] unspoken."[65]

Much the same analysis can be made of Chalcedon, the debates that produced it, and the theologies that followed.[66] This council was convened by the Emperor Marcian in 451 to alleviate rifts in the church that were undermining his Christian support base. The emperor also mandated that the "two natures" language of Cyril of Alexandria and Pope Leo I provide the framework of consensus.

Nicaea had established that the Son is equal in divinity to the Father, of one "substance" (*homoousias*), and that the Son is incarnate in Jesus Christ. What Nicaea left unspecified was how divinity and humanity are then related in Jesus Christ. While a Logos christology purports to guarantee that God is truly present in Jesus Christ, it can encounter difficulty in expressing how it is that Jesus Christ retains his true and full humanity. The intractable nature of this problem, and its persistence despite the Nicene formulations, provided the major impetus for Chalcedon. From the standpoint of the politics of salvation, it is absolutely essential to affirm that through his complete identity with the human condition (save sin) Jesus Christ unites our reality with that of God. It is equally essential

[64] Ibid.

[65] Augustine, *On the Trinity*, trans. Arthur West Haddan, in *Nicene and Post-Nicene Fathers*, First Series, ed. Philip Schaff, vol. 3 (Buffalo, NY: Christian Literature Publishing Co., 1887), book 5.9. Revised and edited for New Advent by Kevin Knight, www.newadvent.org/fathers/1301.htm (accessed July 30, 2009). See Elizabeth Johnson, "Trinity: To Let the Symbol Sing Again," *Theology Today*, 54/3 (1997), pp. 304–6.

[66] See Jaroslav Pelikan, *The Christian Tradition: A History of the Development of Doctrine*, vol. 1: *The Emergence of the Catholic Tradition (100–600)* (University of Chicago Press, 1971), pp. 256–69. Khaled Anatolios makes the case that debates about the relation of Christ, as divine, to the Father resulted in a pluralism of theologies of the Trinity that persisted through Chalcedon and provide still-valuable elements for productive theological diversity today (*Retrieving Nicaea: The Development and Meaning of Trinitarian Doctrine* [Grand Rapids, MI: Baker Academic, 2011]).

to affirm that through his complete sharing in the divine reality, Jesus Christ has or is the power that really transforms us.

In the fifth century as now, it was tempting to minimize the full humanity of Christ, out of fear of compromising his divinity. It was divinity (and hence unique access to God through Jesus) that seemed to require a stronger defense, given that those outside the fold were more than willing to grant that Jesus was a mere man. Many Christians held that the divine nature completely overwhelmed and subsumed the human nature, so that Christ has one nature, not two; or that the Word/Son replaces the human mind, will, soul, and/or reason of Jesus.

An immediate cause of Chalcedon was a 449 synod at Ephesus, which upheld the view of Eutyches that Christ has only one, divine nature. The parties to the debate engaged in mutual anathematization and violence, resulting in the beating and death of one of Eutyches' opponents. Using "two natures" and "one person" language, Chalcedon affirms the full humanity of Christ, especially as over against the view of Apollinaris that the incarnate Word took on a human body without a soul, substituting the divine Word for the human spiritual soul.[67] This kind of thinking is dangerous to the reality of salvation: whatever is not assumed in Christ is also not healed of sin and death.

On the contrary, asserted Chalcedon, Jesus Christ is fully human as well as divine – "consubstantial" with both God and humanity. It remained and remains a matter of debate how this can be explained theologically. In fact, the wording of Chalcedon preserves the paradox rather than resolves it:

consubstantial with the Father as regards his divinity, and the same consubstantial with us as regards his humanity ... begotten before the ages from the Father as regards his divinity and ... from Mary, the virgin God-bearer ... as regards his humanity; one and the same Christ, Son, Lord, only-begotten, acknowledged in two natures which undergo no confusion, no change, no division, no separation; at no point was the difference between the two natures taken away through the union.[68]

Sarah Coakley argues that the bishops at Chalcedon rejected the emperor's demand for greater precision in their conclusions and did not aim at a fully systematic christology or at a precise metaphysic of the

[67] William P. Loewe, "Classical Christology," in Wiley (ed.), *Thinking of Christ*, pp. 49–65, at 56. Christ was viewed to have a single intellect, will, and consciousness, that of the divine Word.
[68] Ibid., p. 60, citing Norman J. Tanner (English edn.), *Decrees of the Ecumenical Councils*, vol. I (Nicaea I–Lateran V) (London and Washington, DC: Sheed and Ward and Georgetown University Press, 1990), p. 86.

being of Christ. Their definition rules out certain aberrant interpretations and provides "an abstract rule of language (*physis* and *hypostasis*) for distinguishing duality and unity in Christ." Christ has a fully human nature (*physis*) and a fully divine nature (*physis*), in one person (*hypostasis*). Two full natures, human and divine, are united in "one and the same Son and only-begotten God, Logos, Lord Jesus Christ."[69]

Yet there is no "supposition that this linguistic regulation thereby *explains* or *grasps* the reality towards which it points."[70] Although the language of Chalcedon does make direct and substantive affirmations about Christ, they are not univocal, empirical, or "literally" true. Instead they constitute an open-ended horizon that sets boundaries while remaining "apophatic" about the mystery of Christ's person.[71]

Among the unresolved issues of Chalcedon are what constitutes the divine and human natures of Christ, whether the meaning of person is the same whether one is speaking of Christ or the Trinity, whether the person of Christ is identical with the preexistent Logos, how the one person is related to the two natures, how the two natures relate to one another, and whether the risen Christ is male.[72] Necessarily, then, Chalcedon represents a crucial moment in what is still an ongoing process, carried forward, especially in the East, not only by theologies but by liturgy.[73] As Coakley concludes, the apophatic horizon of Chalcedon "could shelter many more alternatives than later official clarifications, East and West, would appear to allow."[74]

In fact, christologies go off the rails when their ostensible precision and clarity surpass the bounds of Chalcedonian propriety. One example may be a "neo-Chalcedonian" solution (tracing back to Tertullian, Ambrose, and Augustine)[75] to a fundamental christological question: How can a divine and a human nature can be united in one person? Any satisfactory answer must avoid implying either that two natures in Christ require two persons or that if there is one person there can be only one nature (divine). Eutyches, for example, was condemned in the run-up to Chalcedon for holding that the humanity of Jesus is in the incarnation absorbed by his

---

[69] Loewe, "Classsical Christology," p. 60, citing Chalcedon.
[70] Sarah Coakley, "What Does Chalcedon Solve and What Does It Not? Some Reflections on the Status and Meaning of the Chalcedonian 'Definition,' " in Davis, Kendall, and O'Collins (eds.), *The Incarnation*, p. 161.
[71] Ibid., pp. 160, 163.   [72] Ibid., p. 162.   [73] Ibid.
[74] Ibid., p. 163. For agreement on this point in relation to Chalcedon, see also John P. Galvin, "Jesus Christ," in Francis Schüssler Fiorenza and John P. Galvin (eds.), *Systematic Theology: Roman Catholic Perspectives*, vol. 1 (Minneapolis: Augsburg Fortress Press, 1991), pp. 271, 274.
[75] J. N. D. Kelly, *Early Christian Doctrines*, 2nd edn. (New York: Harper & Row, 1960), pp. 334–8.

divine nature.[76] The alternative that won the day after Chalcedon maintained that the two natures are united in the person of the divine Word. This theology, by making room for two natures within a strong emphasis on Christ's divinity, played prominently as a strategy against those who persisted in maintaining that Christ has only one nature (divine). While not explicitly defined at Chalcedon, this view governed supporting and consequent theological interpretations of Chalcedon's definition of Jesus Christ as one person in two natures.

Related to the theology of the Word as the person of Jesus Christ, and increasing in status with it, is the concept of the "communication of properties" (*communicatio idiomatum*). This formula holds that although the Word is the subject of both natures, different powers and experiences are predicated properly of each. In Christ, the Word does what is appropriate to the divine nature, while the "flesh" does what is appropriate to the human nature.[77] The purpose of the *communicatio idiomatum* is to reconcile biblical portrayals of the emotions, ignorance, and suffering of Jesus with his impassible divinity, accommodating the belief that in Christ "God suffers," while avoiding the inference that God changes.[78] Because of the union of the two natures in the Logos, what may strictly be said only of one nature may be attributed by extension or metaphorically to the other, without any objectionable "mixing" of the two.

The theology of the Word as the person of Jesus Christ and the formula of the communication of properties drew on language in the *Tome* of Leo (449), which slightly antedates Chalcedon, and was read and acclaimed at that council, without, however, being explicitly incorporated into its final definition. The *Tome* was a rebuttal to the condemned "one nature" theology of Eutyches. Commentators who interpret Chalcedon as holding "the divine Word" to be "the unique subject of the Incarnate" cite

---

[76] Ibid., 331–2. Kelly points out that what Eutyches actually held is not easy to figure out and has probably been misunderstood.

[77] Gillian R. Evans, *The First Christian Theologians: An Introduction to Theology in the Early Church* (Malden, MA: Wiley-Blackwell, 2004), p. 246.

[78] See "Neo-Chalcedonianism," *Concise Oxford Dictionary of the Christian Church*, ed. E. A. Livingstone (Oxford University Press, 2006), Oxford Reference Online, Boston College Libraries, July 30, 2009, www.oxfordreference.com/views/ENTRY.html?subview=Main&entry=t95.e400; "Neo-chalcedonism," *The Oxford Dictionary of Byzantium*, ed. Alexander P. Kazhdan (Oxford University Press, 1991), Boston College Libraries, August 6, 2009, www.oxfordreference.com/views/ENTRY.html?subview=Main&entry=t174.e3748; and "Communicatio idiomatum," in *The Concise Oxford Dictionary of World Religions*, ed. John Bowker (Oxford University Press, 2000), Oxford Reference Online, Boston College Libraries, July 30, 2009, www.oxfordreference.com/views/ENTRY.html?subview=Main&entry=t101.e1630.

Leo's *Tome* as confirmatory. [79] Yet Leo's most emphatic point is that Jesus Christ is *both* truly divine and truly human; he does not assert that the person or subject of Christ is divine only; and he presents the divine and human capacities, experiences, and natures in fairly dialectical terms. On the one hand, "it is not part of the same nature" to weep at the death of a friend and to raise that friend to life; yet on the other, Christ's "unity of person … is to be understood in both natures," and the properties of the two natures are "inseparable."[80]

In the same vein, Chalcedon's main concern is the full humanity and divinity of Christ, and the unity of his person: "the property of both natures is preserved and comes together into a single person and a single subsistent being; he is not parted or divided into two persons but is one the same only-begotten Son, God, Word, Lord Jesus Christ."[81] Chalcedon affirms that Jesus Christ, one person, is Son and Word without specifically denying that the person of Christ is in a mysterious and paradoxical way also human. The latter might seem to be required by Chalcedon's premise that Jesus Christ is "consubstantial with the Father as regards his divinity, and the same consubstantial with us as regards his humanity; like us in all respects except for sin."

Whatever its theological and conciliar pedigree or lack thereof, the theology of the Word as the sole person of Christ, and the *communicatio idiomatum* as the explanation of the relation between the two natures, grew in influence, garnered reinforcement at the Second Council of Constantinople in 553,[82] and attained functional authority almost equivalent to Chalcedon. For this reason alone, the approach deserves respect. This theology and formula do have the virtue of asserting that it is truly God who approaches us in Jesus Christ, and of preserving the unity of the person of Christ and the character of the impassibility (*aseity*) inherent in divine status. After all, unless God is beyond and infinitely superior to all forms of affliction, evil, and disintegration, then God not only is not truly God, but also cannot save human beings.

[79] See, e.g., Kelly, *Early Christian Doctrines*, pp. 341, 334–8.
[80] Leo the Great, *Letter 128: To Flavian – "The Tome,"* in Church Fathers, www.newadvent.org/fathers/3604028.htm (accessed June 21, 2012), IV and V.
[81] Evans, *First Christian Theologians*, p. 246; citing Tanner, *Decrees of the Ecumenical Councils*, p. 86.
[82] The Anathemas of II Constantinople assert that there is only one person in Christ, not two (V), and lend credence to the theology of one divine person in Christ by insisting that no one may reject that "there is only one person, the Lord Jesus Christ *one of the holy Trinity*" (IV; emphasis added). Consistently with Chalcedon, II Constantinople affirms that the one person "is composed of the two natures," adding that "the two are in one" in an "ineffable union" (VII); www.iclnet.org/pub/resources/text/history/council.2constan.txt (accessed June 21, 2012).

On the other side, this solution seems to create as many problems as it resolves. God's capacity to be affected by and respond to human suffering is supported by biblical narratives, while in a different cultural and philosophical context, changelessness can appear less essential to divine goodness than divine compassion. While there is truth to a model of the incarnation that proclaims Christ's sovereign saving power as the Word, there may also be room for a model that celebrates God's total solidarity with suffering creation. The idea that the Word or Logos is Christ's person seems to preserve Christ's unity, divinity, and divine impassibility at the expense of his full humanity, and hence at the expense of the incarnation. William Loewe warns, "In ordinary, nontechnical language it has become unintelligible to speak of Christ as someone who is fully human but not a human person."[83] "One divine person" christology skirts dangerously near the Apollinarian heresy, that in Christ there is only a divine mind, soul, or reason, and not a human one, and the Monothelite heresy (condemned in 680 at III Constantinople), that there is only one will in Christ, a divine one. In fact, this theology seems to contradict one of Chalcedon's most distinctive claims: Jesus Christ is "like us in all things but sin."

In regard to theological penetration of the incarnation, Karl Rahner cautions, "What is in question is ... formulations intended to maintain and defend more clearly and effectively the simple statement that this Jesus is God and man in the face of misunderstandings and theories which explain it away"[84] – perhaps a danger in "divine person only" theologies. As Rahner notes, the Chalcedonian definition merely provides that "the centre of unity in which the two realities [divine and human] meet and are therefore realities of the same subject, is called ... *persona.*" "These terms," however, "are not given further philosophical explanation." Therefore, the provision of Chalcedon that the two natures are "unmixed and undivided" must necessarily be and remain "dialectical," pointing to a "mystery."[85]

Ill at ease with the paradox of two full, unmixed, and unseparated natures in Christ – which is really the "scandal" of the incarnation – the theory that Jesus Christ is not a human "person" seeks intellectual control over the way divine and human natures coexist in Christ. Chalcedon was more modest in its analysis because it was more courageous in its

[83] Loewe, "Classical Christology," p. 62.
[84] Karl Rahner, "Jesus Christ," in Karl Rahner (ed.), *Encyclopedia of Theology: The Concise Sacramentum Mundi* (New York: Crossroad, 1975), p. 761.
[85] Ibid., 762.

affirmation: the infinite really is united with the finite, the eternal with the mortal, the unchangeable with the changing, the divine with the human, the Son and Word with the man Jesus of Nazareth.

Assertions like "Mary is the Mother of God (*theotokos*)" and "One of the Trinity suffers" are and should remain mysterious, analogical, and allusive. Cyril of Alexandria was willing to use the phrase "the impassible suffering of the Son"[86] and considered his opponents' fear of attributing suffering to God exaggerated.[87] Intellectual clarity on such matters is beyond our grasp. The truth of theologies of the incarnation can still be tested for coherence with biblical narratives and in light of the reality of salvation expressed in liturgical and moral practices. Christian ethics and politics, as arenas of salvation, demand both Jesus' full divinity *and* his full, uncompromised humanity. Theologies envisioning Christ as a divine person may be only partly to blame for the historical yet unbiblical tendency of Word christologies to minimize a concrete politics of salvation as key to Christian identity and as essential participation in Jesus' ministry of God's reign.

Nicaea and Chalcedon set the bar for contemporary christologies in that they accept the fact of intellectual paradox, prioritize practical unity in the church over the coherence of theological systems, and leave plenty of room for substantially different approaches. The quest for greater doctrinal rigor in determining the orthodoxy of derivative proposals runs up against the fact that the bar-setting conciliar formulations are not all that doctrinally rigorous. In fact, they gained much of their authority by uniting and inspiring ongoing communities of discourse, liturgy, and pastoral practice. Christologies today likewise interact with theological, ecclesial, ethical, and social problems and disputes. They would do well to put more emphasis on orthopraxis, both liturgical and moral, as a criterion of truth and validity alongside doctrinal continuity.

Certainly there are necessary parameters to diversity, both theological and practical. Christologies must affirm the full humanity and divinity of Jesus Christ, in a Trinitarian framework; affirm the eschatological reality of salvation; and serve the inauguration of God's reign in personal conversion and spirituality, and in an ecclesial and political "option for the poor."

---

[86] John J. O'Keefe, "Impassible Suffering? Divine Passion and Fifth-Century Christology," *Theological Studies*, 58 (1997), p. 45, citing Cyril, *Quod unus sit Christus*; and *Scholia on the Incarnation*.

[87] Ibid., see 50.

Word christologies have been very successful in affirming the divine origin of Jesus Christ and salvation, of ensuring hope in eternal life, and in conforming the spirituality of believers to the possibility of an elevating and transforming relation to God – ineffable, impassable, and infinite. Where Word christologies have not been as successful is in affirming the character of salvation as historical conformity to the inbreaking reign of God. Salvation as kingdom life inaugurates love of neighbor as a concomitant of love of God and as breaking out into reordered familial, ecclesial, communal, and political relationships.

The revival of Spirit christology is a response both to overly supernaturalistic interpretations of the Christian life and to a new awareness of the Christian mission as including an option for the global poor. Before turning more extensively to those christologies, it is important to emphasize that the Word paradigm itself does offer potential resources for a this-worldly spirituality and an activist Christian political ethic. These were not fully mined in the premodern era, when Word christology gained dominance, and hierarchical, nonparticipatory, and apparently immovable social systems were also hegemonic. The political potential of Word christologies lies primarily in their emphasis on the incarnation as an event in which *God* is truly one with humanity. In the humanity of Christ united with his divine nature, other human beings are also united with God.

This union is developed metaphysically or ontologically by later theologies of the Word, but the Gospel of John displays the process or reality of unification of disciples with Jesus Christ in terms of concrete communal relationships. This takes place through the Spirit sent by the risen Christ (7:39, 20:2) and by the Paraclete ("Comforter," "Advocate," "Helper"), also identified as the "Holy Spirit," and the "spirit of truth" (14:15–17, 25–6; 15:22–5; 16:7–11, 12–15).[88] This process begins in the relation of Jesus to his Father, expands to include the disciples, and contains a mission to "the world" (see especially John 14–17). Jesus prays, "As you Father are in me and I am in you, may they also be in us, so that the world may believe that you have sent me. The glory that you have given me, I have given them, so that they may be one, as we are one" (17:21–2). The community

---

[88] See Frank J. Matera, *New Testament Theology: Exploring Diversity and Unity* (Louisville, KY: Westminster John Knox Press, 2007), pp. 302–7.

formed in Jesus' name embodies his ideal of sacrificing love. "If you love me you will keep my commandments" (John 14:15).[89]

Obviously Johannine christology contains potential for a Spirit approach. Nevertheless, the developing tradition overall read the Word christology of John in terms of the two natures of Christ, that of a human being and that of the divine Word. Through the incarnation, God shares in human nature, and humans share in the divine nature. Along similar lines, 2 Peter claims that by "divine power" we "may become participants of the divine nature" (1:3–4) and urges the faithful to support faith with goodness, mutual affection, and love (2 Pet. 1:5–7), though 2 Peter envisions this more as a path to the "eternal kingdom" than as a beginning of the kingdom now (1:11).

In his study of the Council of Nicaea and its surrounding and supporting (diverse) theologies, Lewis Ayres contends that "pro-Nicenes treat the Word present in Christ as the ultimate agent in the process of redemption."[90] Redemption means that our bodies and our lives in the world are transformed through unity in Christ with the divine Word.

The closeness of the Word to the Father means that our union with Christ is a real union with the one life of God. Because Father and Son share eternally in the one power of God, Christ's body (and hence our bodies) are directly affected by the life of God.[91]

The intimate union of the Word and the Father, and the presence of the Word in Christ to believers united in the body of Christ, have a dramatic transformative effect on the Christian life: identity, spirituality, community, and practice.

This transformation is played out theologically in the Eastern idea of "divinization" (*theosis*). This was a concept familiar in Greek and Roman religions. It was appropriated early by Christian authors such as Ignatius of Antioch, Justin Martyr, Clement of Alexandria, Origen, Athanasius, and the Cappadocians, especially Gregory Nazianzus.[92] Norman Russell points out that this term was often intended metaphorically or figuratively, not literally and ontologically, to refer to and encourage the ascent of the soul to God through baptism, participation in the church as body

[89] Daniel J. Harrington, S.J., "Love and the Holy Spirit," *America* (April 21, 2008), p. 31.
[90] Ayres, *Nicaea*, p. 305.   [91] Ibid.
[92] The theme of union with the Word as a union with the life of the Father can be seen in Gregory of Nazianzus's account of "divinization," or *theosis*. See Meredith, *Cappadocians*, p. 48. However, it is Cyril of Alexandria who really develops participation in the divine as a real and specifiable change in being for the believer, as discussed later in the chapter.

of Christ, and imitation of Christ. In the fifth century, Cyril of Alexandria takes the idea to a new level. Cyril understands deification as a recovery of the created divine likeness and develops the idea in terms of the moral life, the sacraments, sanctification and filiation, and ultimate attainment of incorruptibility.[93]

In Cyril's vision, the Word became human so that humans might become divine. Just as Christ's humanity is transformed by union with his divinity, so we are transformed by union with Christ, elevated "to a dignity that transcends our nature." He is divine by nature; we are so by adoption.[94] Union with Christ restores humanity's created likeness to God. Then, through a dynamic process beginning at baptism, humans advance toward transcendence. Together, the divine Spirit and the divine Son bring about sanctification and filiation. Morality is an important part of this process; when humans choose good, they participate in the divine, "for 'the divine ... is in everything that is beautiful, and is the source, root and origin of all virtue.'"[95] Participation in God implies beautiful and virtuous moral relationships; to do the good and live virtuously is to advance in likeness to God and to participate in the divine life.

The strengths of the Word model for christological politics are its strong portrayal of the salvific nature of the incarnation and its emphasis in Christian conversion on prayer, contemplation, the transcendence of alienation and suffering, and the practice of uniting and reconciling love in community. Its foundation is divine immanence in history in a personal and saving way in the person of Jesus Christ, whose very being entails an elevation of human possibilities through union with God. The incarnation means that "the human is already elevated in union with Christ above itself to enjoy the very life of God."[96]

Yet Word christologies can tend to abstractness or ethereality regarding the specific demands of "love" and have a proclivity at the ethical level to invoke transcendence, rather than resistant engagement, in the face of the suffering and conflicts of history. Ayres's compelling and quite

[93] Russell, *Deification*, pp. 11–13; 196, citing Cyril, *In Jo.* 1.991a–93b.
[94] Ibid., p. 191, citing Cyril, *In Jo.* 1.9.91c. See also Daniel A. Keating, "Divinization in Cyril: The Appropriation of Divine Life," in Thomas G. Weinandy and Daniel A. Keating (eds.), *The Theology of St. Cyril of Alexandria* (London: T & T Clark, 2003); and John A. McGuckin, *St. Cyril of Alexandria: The Christological Controversy: Its History, Theology, and Texts* (Leiden: Brill, 1995).
[95] Russell, *Deification*, pp. 00–00, citing *Res. Tib.* 14.
[96] Tanner, *Christ the Key*, p. 258. Tanner underscores the incarnation of the Word and the divinity of Christ as the guarantor of human transformation. Reflecting a christology in which the Word is the person of Jesus Christ, she asserts that "Jesus' ... very humanity takes its shape from the second person of the Trinity that he is" (p. 185).

inspirational rendering of the beauty of the Nicene approach to God is strikingly void of references to the Jesus of the synoptics and his "preferential option for the poor," the kingdom of God and its inbreaking through radical social practices, or the cross and the sacrifices it suggests for Christian living.

To have content and practical force, Christian ethics needs such references. Liberation theologian Jon Sobrino laments the fact that "by the time of the fourth-century conciliar debates, it is clear that the kingdom of God plays no role whatsoever in christology." Instead, faith in Christ took theoretical form by way of reference "to the *person of God* (which is better expressed in the titles of Son, Lord, Word) ... and not – in addition – to the *Kingdom of God*."[97] As a consequence, even though Jesus was called the Messiah ("Christ"), the title ceased to refer to the hope of the poor. Cyril's thesis that deification in Christ requires moral transformation and engagement did not take a strong hold in the Word christologies of Latin Christianity. The need for a corrective recommends the complementarity of Word and Spirit approaches to christology. The reinvigoration of the Spirit paradigm sustains in theology the flexibility, polyvalence, and imaginative power of biblical ways of proclaiming salvation from God in Jesus Christ.

SPIRIT CHRISTOLOGIES

Word christologies emphasize unity with God in the divine Word, transcendence, and hope for a share in the glory of Christ's Sonship. Spirit christologies bring us back to history, the humanity of Christ, the concrete ecclesial texture of the experience of God, and empowerment for God's reign. Contemporary Spirit christologies also have ecumenical and interreligious appeal.

Spirit christologies encourage greater attention than Word christologies to social suffering and social change and to the gospels' renderings of events in the life and ministry of Jesus, as well as to the practical challenges facing the first Christian churches. The latter touchstones connect faith in Jesus as the Christ with a historical memory of Jesus of Nazareth, of the experience of salvation from God mediated through specific aspects of his life and death, and through equally specific experiences of the first believers and their communities.

---

[97] Jon Sobrino, "The Kingdom of God and the Theologal Dimension of the Poor: The Jesuanic Principle," in John C. Cavadini and Laura Holt (eds.), *Who Do You Say That I Am? Confessing the Mystery of Christ* (Notre Dame, IN: University of Notre Dame Press, 2004), p. 113.

The Gospel of Luke and the letters of Paul are key sources for Spirit christology. In Luke's gospel and Acts, the Spirit is the uniting force that drives salvation history. Luke's theology of the Spirit is deeply rooted in Jewish sources, but moves beyond Judaism by speaking of the Spirit as the Spirit of Christ or Jesus (Acts 16:6–7).[98] For Luke–Acts, God's Spirit enables Mary to conceive Jesus and is active and present in Jesus from the start. With the descent of the Holy Spirit at Christ's baptism, he is designated "beloved Son" and anointed for his ministry with God's power (Luke 3:22; cf. Acts 10:38). Jesus is "full of the Holy Spirit" (Luke 4:1) and conducts his ministry "in the power of the Spirit" (4:14). The Spirit is behind Jesus' healings and exorcisms. Luke narrates Jesus' last breath with the words, "Father into your hands I commend my spirit" (23:46; quoting Ps. 31:6).

According to Roger Haight, the "fundamental metaphor" of Spirit christology is "empowerment." "God as Spirit, the principle of life and dynamic energy, is present and active in Jesus in a special way."[99] Haight notes that the later conciliar affirmations of the Spirit as in principle "not less divine than the Logos" serve as confirmations of the canonical validity and orthodoxy of Spirit christologies. If "Spirit too is affirmed to represent true God," then "whatever can be said of Jesus' divinity by using Logos language can also be expressed in terms of Spirit."[100]

Luke's "second volume," the Acts of the Apostles, carries the inspiration of the Spirit into the early church. The Spirit of God incarnate in Jesus becomes, or extends to, the Spirit of Christ embodied ecclesially. The risen Jesus instructs his apostles "through the Holy Spirit" (Acts 1:2), promises that they will be baptized with the Holy Spirit (Acts 1:3), and assures them that they will receive power to witness to the gospel "when the Holy Spirit has come upon you" (Acts 1:8). After Jesus' ascension this promise is fulfilled at Pentecost, when, with signs of wind and tongues of fire, "all of them were filled with the Holy Spirit and began to speak in other languages, as the Spirit gave them ability" (Acts 2:4). The Spirit empowers the church for prophecy and for mission. Peter confirms the role of the risen Jesus Christ in the sending of the Spirit to the church: "Being therefore exalted at the right hand of God, and having received

---

[98] Max Turner, "The Spirit and Salvation in Luke-Acts," in Graham N. Stanton, Bruce W. Longenecker, and Stephen C. Barton (eds.), *The Holy Spirit and Christian Origins: Essays in Honor of James D. G. Dunn* (Grand Rapids, MI: Eerdmans, 2004), pp. 103–16, 105.

[99] Roger Haight, S.J., *The Future of Christology* (New York: Continuum, 2005), p. 175.

[100] Ibid., p. 177.

from the Father the promise of the Holy Spirit, he has poured out this which you see and hear" (Acts 2:33).

For Luke, the Spirit of God sent by Christ brings all categories of needy people into a reconciling community, whose ideal is to embody holiness, goodness, generosity, and service. New variations on Christian community are progressively established, in the Spirit, throughout the world.[101] The gifts of the Spirit among believers both unite them to God in a saving way and enable the church's prophetic, witnessing, and missionary roles, expanded geographically and temporally in Acts.

The Spirit is also absolutely essential to the proclamation of salvation from God in Christ as presented in the earliest New Testament writings, the letters of Paul. The Spirit is a crucial aspect of Paul's faith in Jesus Christ as Messiah, Lord, and Savior. The Spirit is also crucial to the eschatological framework within which believers live out salvation in the church, where they are conformed to Christ's image (Rom. 8:29) and live as Christ's body (Eph. 2:16; 1 Cor. 10:16–17, 11:29, 12:12–26) in worship, in relationships within the community, and in their life in the world.[102]

In Paul, Spirit language is as complex as it is pervasive. Although terminology referring to the Spirit is of key significance to Paul, it carries a "semantic indeterminacy" that enables it to be "deployed richly, and variously, in later Christianity," but is also impossible to pin down.[103] The relations between the Spirit and Christ, and between the divine Spirit and the human spirit, remain "inchoate" and "tantalizing." This guarantees that the Spirit of God and of Christ will remain a "mysterious and elusive" reality.[104] Spirit christologies thus balance the drive for intellectual cogency seen in many Word christologies with a symbolic and narrative confession of the mystery yet proximity of God.

For Paul, the Spirit is God's personal presence indwelling in the community and instituting God's new covenant with his people, just as the God of the Hebrew Bible dwells in the midst of his people (1 Cor. 14:24–5; 2 Cor. 6:16).[105] Paul thinks primarily of the Spirit in relationship to God the Father or Creator, naming the "Spirit of God" more frequently than the "Spirit of Christ." Paul refers the sending of the Spirit of Christ back

---

[101] Turner, "The Spirit and Salvation," p. 101.
[102] Gordon D. Fee, *Paul, the Spirit, and the People of God* (Peabody, MA: Hendrickson, 1996), p. 7.
[103] John M. G. Barclay, "*Pneumatikos* in the Social Dialectic of Pauline Christianity," in Stanton et al. (eds.), *Holy Spirit and Christian Origins*, pp. 157–67, at 166.
[104] Alexander J. M. Wedderburn, "Pauline Pneumatology and Pauline Theology," in Stanton et al. (eds.), *Holy Spirit and Christian Origins*, pp. 144–56, at 156.
[105] Fee, *Paul, the Spirit*, pp. 15–20.

to God's agency (Gal. 4:6) and depicts a most intimate relationship of closeness and knowledge between the Spirit and God (1 Cor. 2:7, 10–12; Rom. 8:26–7).[106] That Paul, then, can also speak of the Spirit as the "Spirit of Christ" (Gal. 4:6; Rom. 8:9–11; Phil. 1:19) can be read as evidence of a "high Christology" in Paul.[107]

Christ's sending of the Spirit is invariably associated with his resurrection, giving rise to later debates over whether the risen Christ should in some sense be equated with the Spirit.[108] In communities of faith, worship, and practice, Christ and the Spirit are inevitably experienced together, so there is a natural convergence and overlap in the ways the two are named and proclaimed. Pauline churches are articulating the reality of God, Christ, and Spirit in their communities, not a theology of the Trinity.[109] Though Paul does not simply identify Christ and the Spirit, they are very closely associated, even inseparable.

Paul's imagery of Christ as the "Second Adam" reinforces Christ's decisive role in defining transformed Christian existence in the Spirit. In 1 Corinthians (21–2, 42–9) Paul reverses Philo's sequence in which the "heavenly man" is the paradigm for other human creatures and makes Christ the "Second Adam," who rectifies the sin of the first Adam.[110] Jesus Christ shares the effects of human fallennness, "following through Adam's plight to the end (death) and thus becoming a new Adam in resurrection beyond death."[111] Paul's switch in sequence permits him to depict two qualitatively different stages of human life and identity: that of the first Adam who sinned and died, and that of the Second Adam in whose defeat of sin and death we share in the

---

[106] Ibid., p. 29.   [107] Ibid., p. 30.

[108] James Dunn is sometimes understood to give a positive answer to this question (*Christology in the Making*, pp. 145–7), whereas Gordon Fee argues the negative case (Gordon D. Fee, *God's Empowering Presence: The Holy Spirit in the Letters of Paul* [Peabody, MA: Hendrickson, 1994], pp. 548–9). However, the matter is complex, as Robert Jewett points out ("The Question of the 'Apportioned Spirit' in Paul's Letters: Romans as a Case Study," in Stanton et al. [eds.], *Holy Spirit and Christian Origins*, pp. 193–206, at 197), and as Dunn actually recognizes in his treatment, which avoids any simple equation of Christ and Spirit. Rather, "the exalted Christ and the Spirit of God are one and the same as far as the believer's experience is concerned" (*Christology in the Making*, p. 146); "the equivalence between Spirit and Christ is only a function of the believer's limited perception" (ibid., p. 147); and there is an "overlap" between the categories "Spirit of God" and "exalted Christ" in Paul's categories or symbolism (ibid.).

[109] James D. G. Dunn, *Jesus and the Spirit* (London: SCM, 1975), p. 326; Anthony C. Thiselton, "The Holy Spirit in 1 Corinthians: Exegesis and Reception Theory in the Patristic Era," in Stanton et al. (eds.), *Holy Spirit and Christian Origins*, pp. 207–28, at 223.

[110] Elisabeth Schüssler Fiorenza, "1 Corinthians," in James L. Mays (ed.), *Harper's Bible Commentary* (San Francisco: Harper & Row, 1988), p. 1188; Dunn, *Christology in the Making*, pp. 98–128.

[111] Dunn, *Christology in the Making*, p. 113.

"life-giving Spirit."[112] Through our shared humanity with Adam we fall heir to the penalties for his sin. Through Christ's perfect reenactment of the original human destiny of faithfulness, obedience, gratitude, and love, we share in Christ's resurrection to new life with and in God.

Second Adam christology does not stipulate the preexistence of Christ as divine Logos as a vehicle for expressing his divinity,[113] though the preexistence theme is not entirely absent either (see Phil. 2:6–7).[114] Paul does draw on a descending "heavenly man" figure indebted to Jewish biblical and philosophical sources. These sources portray an intermediate divine reality that enables the soul to become a child of God and to be transformed by contemplation of the divine.[115] However, this figure does not enjoy equality with God the Father Creator.

Paul recognizes a higher, "fully divine" status of Jesus Christ but communicates this status most centrally by means of Spirit language. God's Spirit is in Christ, and the risen Christ sends the Spirit. The Spirit effects the salvation of human beings through participation in Christ, a human being, yet Son of God and Lord. The comprehensive model in Paul for union with God in Christ is union with the risen Christ through the action of the Spirit in the Christian community.

SPIRIT AND THE POLITICS OF SALVATION

Since, in Christ, God is "reconciling the world to himself" (2 Cor. 5:19), God gives the anticipatory, eschatological gift of divine life to those in whom the Spirit dwells (Rom. 8:11, 15, 23). In the grace of Jesus Christ and the fellowship of the Spirit, "it is no longer I who live, but Christ who lives in me" (Gal. 2:20). Paul puts resurrection life in a "modified" apocalyptic perspective that, according to Daniel Harrington, includes the present influence of Jesus Christ and the Spirit on the course of history.[116] Pheme Perkins adds that Paul's apocalyptic perspective includes the resurrection as an event with power for the present. "Believers are not aliens in a hostile world, but persons in whom the transforming power of

---

[112] Schüssler Fiorenza, "1 Corinthians," p. 118.
[113] Ibid., p. 119.
[114] On the idea of preexistence in Paul, see Gordon D. Fee, *Pauline Christology: An Exegetical-Theological Study* (Peabody, MA: Hendrickson, 2007).
[115] Tobin, "Prologue of John," p. 260.
[116] Daniel Harrington, S.J. and James Keenan, S.J., *Paul and Virtue Ethics: Building Bridges Between New Testament Studies and Moral Theology* (New York: Rowman & Littlefield, 2010), p. 114. Harrington and Keenan are the authors of alternate chapters.

the Spirit unleashed by the Messiah's death and resurrection is already at work."[117]

The Spirit indwells children of God and their community (Rom. 8:9). "As the Son and Spirit, with the Father, constitute a community of love, so they are sent by the Father to establish and nurture ... participation in relations that are divine."[118] "When we cry, 'Abba! Father!' It is that very Spirit bearing witness with our spirit that we are children of God ... and joint heirs with Christ" (Rom. 8:15–17). The Spirit is discovered in the "ceaseless outgoing and return of the desiring God." The Spirit is inherent in the relation of Father and Son, in the incarnation, in the church as body of Christ, and in the believer's participation in redemption. To share in Christ's community is to share in divine life.[119]

Spirit christologies thus provide an opportunity to portray the incorporation of believers into Christ and into the divine life in relational terms, which is important for the concrete historical reality of Christian ethics. A relational and communal model of incorporation into divine life is found in the "farewell discourse" of John's gospel (14–17), and Cyril refers divinization to ecclesial life. Yet Word christologies have tended historically to treat "nature" as an ontological category, focusing attention away from salvation's historical theatre. The union of divine and human in Christ, and derivative unity of humans with God, are treated as states of being given immediately with the fact of the incarnation, not portrayed as consisting in diachronic relationships. But in Spirit christologies, Christ's status is narrated as a relation of sonship and fatherhood. Believers come to share in the relation of sonship through communal membership; what they share is not the "nature" of God, but the relation of Son and Father, through the mediation of the Spirit. Hence salvation can be connected with and given practical definition by the particularities of community life as biblically depicted.

Christ is the criterion for activity filled with the Spirit (1 Cor. 12:3). The "fellowship of the Spirit" (2 Cor. 13:13) is a shared experience of the Spirit, out of which communal life grows.[120] The politics of salvation is a politics

[117] Pheme Perkins, "Resurrection and Christology: Are They Related?" in David B. Capes et al. (eds.), *Israel's God and Rebecca's Children: Christology and Community in Early Judaism and Christianity* (Waco, TX: Baylor University Press, 2008), p. 74.

[118] Charles Hefling, "Gratia: Grace and Gratitude – Fifty Unmodern Theses as Prolegomena to Pneumatology," *Anglican Theological Review*, 83/3 (2001), p. 484.

[119] Sarah Coakley, "Is there a Future for Gender and Theology? On Gender, Contemplation, and the Systematic Task," *Criterion*, 47/1 (2009), p. 10.

[120] James D. G. Dunn, *The Christ and the Spirit*, vol. 2: *Pneumatology* (Grand Rapids, MI: Eerdmans, 1998), pp. 345–6.

of "Spirit-empowered obedience to Christ" (Gal. 5:6, 13–26),[121] a politics of identification and solidarity with "this crucified yet risen Lord (2 Cor. 5:15)."[122] Those in whom the Spirit lives take on the sufferings of Christ (8:17), but God's love will sustain and overcome difficulty (8:31–39). The Spirit of Christ makes disciples one with Christ in the body of Christ, establishing a real relation to the Father and enabling love of others as well as love of God.[123] The moral life is a practice of worship, carried out within the community of faith but carrying into roles and obligations in the larger world.[124]

In the churches, the eucharist is the ritual that most of all effects the real union of Christians with Christ's resurrected body and, in the community, as the body of Christ (1 Cor. 6, 11). Other liturgical practices, as well as ascetic, aesthetic, and moral practices, rituals, and daily customs, also image for Christians the concretely transformative effects of their faith in Christ and serve as unifying emblems of shared existence in a real social and material world, a life in which "divinization" is already being enacted.[125]

Similarly to Luke, Paul believes that life in Christ changes the life of the believer and the church at the liturgical, ethical, and social levels. The community as a whole is "God's temple," in which "God's Spirit dwells" (1 Cor. 3:16), for the encounter with Christ in the Spirit is a corporate event.[126] Though Paul does not take the "biographical" approach of the gospel, he is certainly working against a basic background of assumptions or traditions about the story of Jesus' life, including and especially his ministry of the kingdom of God and perseverance to the cross.[127]

The "fruits" of the Spirit – love, joy, peace, forbearance, kindness, goodness, fidelity, gentleness, self-control (Gal. 5:22–3) – affect every aspect of Christian living, particularly in terms of the corporate life of the community. The Holy Spirit is the continuing agent of sanctification, individually

[121] Hurtado, *Lord Jesus Christ*, p. 97.
[122] Anselm Min, *The Solidarity of Others in a Divided World: A Postmodern Theology after Postmodernism* (London: T & T Clark, 2005), p. 97.
[123] John R. Meyer, "Coordinating the Immanent and Economic Trinity," *Gregorianum*, 86/2 (2005), pp. 252–3.
[124] Matera, *New Testament Theology*, pp. 196–7.
[125] Stephen J. Davis, "Fashioning a Divine Body: Coptic Christology and Ritualized Dress," *Harvard Theological Review*, 98:3 (2005), pp. 335–62.
[126] Dunn, *Pneumatology*, p. 344.
[127] Richard A. Burridge, *Imitating Jesus: An Inclusive Approach to New Testament Ethics* (Grand Rapids, MI: Eerdmans, 2007), p. 143.

and corporately (1 Thess. 4:3–8).[128] The Spirit, making salvation effective, enables the community to overcome strife, division, adversity, weakness, and suffering (1 Cor. 12–14; Rom. 8: 23, 26–7).[129] The Spirit empowers disciples to persevere and embody redemption in and for a broken world.

Luke's gospel fills out the political impact of salvation with a Jesus who begins his ministry by reading from the book of Isaiah: "The Spirit of the Lord is upon me, because he has anointed me to bring good news to the poor" (4:18). Luke's gospel is often identified as the gospel most aligned with the "option for the poor" as characterizing Jesus' ministry of the reign of God. "The poor" usually connotes economic poverty, but its fundamental sense is any type of marginalization of those lacking access to the goods or roles valued in a given culture. In Luke's gospel, the empowering of Jesus by the Spirit is good news for all those despised within the system of honor and shame of first-century Greco-Roman societies. This includes the economically poor, those suffering from illness and physical disabilities, those possessed by evil spirits, those engaging in despised professions, and even those in need of forgiveness.[130]

The Spirit even crosses boundaries of ethnicity, nationality, and religion, breaking down divisions between Jew and Gentile (John 4:21–4). While Peter is preaching to Cornelius and other Gentiles, the Spirit falls upon them, and Peter acclaims them as accepted into God's people (Acts 10:44–8). Paul maintains that the blessing of Abraham promised by God to the Gentiles is fulfilled by the power of the Spirit (Gal. 3:14). In the Spirit both Jew and Gentile have access to the Father (Eph. 2:18). The renewing and transforming work of the Spirit is inherently communal, practical, and expansive.

The conclusion of Luke's gospel illustrates narratively that recognition of Christ and authentic celebration of his presence in the eucharist already implies or requires reformed communal relationship of hospitality and generosity. In the Gospel of Luke, no one actually sees the risen Jesus in the events surrounding the discovery of the empty tomb. In fact, "the apostles" do not believe the message of the women who, on the testimony of "two men in dazzling clothes" whom they met at the tomb when they

---

[128] Victor Paul Furnish, "The Spirit in 2 Thessalonians," in Stanton et al. (eds.), *Holy Spirit and Christian Origins*, pp. 229–40, at 239.

[129] On Paul's view that believers are sustained by the ongoing intercession of the Spirit in their weakness, expressed in charismatic experiences, see Jewett, "'Apportioned Spirit,'" pp. 200–2.

[130] Bruce W. Longenecker, "Rome's Victory and God's Honour: The Jerusalem Temple and the Spirit of God in Lukan Theodicy," in Stanton et al. (eds.), *Holy Spirit and Christian Origins*, pp. 90–102, at 100–1.

went to anoint Jesus' body, returned to tell the others that Jesus had risen (24:1–12).

The first narrated appearance[131] of the risen Jesus happens later in the day, when an anonymous and unrecognized Jesus meets and walks with two disciples who are journeying along a road to the nearby village of Emmaus (24:13–16). They are discussing the life of Jesus, how he met his death, the disappointment of their hopes, and the astounding message of the women (vv. 18–24). Although the stranger assures the disciples that this is all in accord with the scriptures, they neither seem convinced nor recognize the speaker's true identity (vv. 25–7). Obviously this story will resonate and carry appeal for Luke's community or any later community that finds the presence of the risen Jesus hard to discern in daily life or in times of dismay and confusion, when religious beliefs have been shaken.

Despite their unsettled emotions and concerns about their future, the disciples, having reached their destination, have the presence of mind to stop the stranger from going on his way alone at nightfall. Instead, they prevail upon him to "stay with us, because it is almost evening." Their new friend agrees to an overnight delay, and together they share a meal. While they are at table, Jesus "took bread, blessed and broke it, and gave it to them. Then their eyes were opened, and they recognized him; and he vanished from their sight" (vv. 30–1). The evident eucharistic message is that although Jesus risen may be difficult to recognize and only fleetingly held in view, it is in the community's eucharistic celebration that he is really present and understood.

Yet the message is not confined to the sacramental significance of the "breaking of the bread." Jesus is not known in or by the simple performance of a liturgy or rite, even one faithfully reenacting the remembered words and deeds of Jesus himself at his last meal. There are at least two further conditions of the eucharistic "real presence" of Christ: a community of companions who in Jesus' memory accompany one another on their religious journey, in solidarity with one another despite uncertainty and doubt; and a communal practice of hospitality to strangers, in which disciples rise above their own troubles to consider others' needs, offering shelter, sustenance, and fellowship (Matt. 25).

---

[131] Later in Jerusalem it is reported that Jesus has also appeared to "Simon" – time sequence unspecified – possibly to uphold the priority of Peter among the apostles (Luke 24:34). Back in Jerusalem, Jesus appears finally to a gathering of disciples, proving to them that he is not "a ghost" by eating "a piece of broiled fish" (24:36–43). The risen Jesus is a real bodily presence, but evidently not one that is of an ordinary nature or easy to recognize.

Community, in other words, is not created by performing liturgy in a certain way; nor does it consist in liturgical performance alone. Rather, authentic liturgy arises from the "performance" of community identity, an ongoing process, not secure from ambiguity but always and necessarily involving Jesus' kingdom practices. The risen Jesus is present and recognized truly when and only when kingdom relationships to God and neighbor are enacted concretely, in the whole of life.

Catholic theology since the Second Vatican Council has further developed the idea that the sacraments are the work of the Spirit and that their communication of grace involves community belonging and practices. According to Louis-Marie Chauvet, the Spirit is the powerful relation of the Son of God to human beings, mysteriously enacted and made visible in the sacraments,[132] which, for Chauvet, also entail an ethical dimension. In line with Luke's Emmaus story, social ethicist David Hollenbach sees the sacraments as enactments of communal life. The sacraments engage the ultimate reality in which Christians exist with their particular life in community, touching the heart and imagination, and inspiring and enabling faithful and prophetic social action.[133] Conversely, ethical and political failure on the part of the community is also a symptom that the celebration of sacraments does not adequately mediate Christ and calls into question the ongoing identity of the community as Christian. Susan Ross points out, for example, that sacramental practice marred by "clerical domination" is not unconnected to Christian inattention to world hunger, the need for reconciliation, the failures of communal living, and sexism.[134]

CONCLUSION

In sum, then, for the gospels, Acts, and Paul, the Spirit provides the vital connection between Jesus and the Father, between the risen Christ and

[132] Louis-Marie Chauvet, *Symbol and Sacrament: A Sacramental Reinterpretation of Christian Existence*, trans. Patrick Madigan, S.J., and Madeline Beaumont (Collegeville, MN: Liturgical Press, 1995), p. 520. See also Philippe Bordeyne and Bruce T. Morrill (eds.), *Sacraments: Revelation of the Humanity of God: Engaging the Fundamental Theology of Louis-Marie Chauvet* (Collegeville, MN: Liturgical Press, 2008); and Kilian McDonnell, *The Other Hand of God: The Holy Spirit as the Universal Touch and Goal* (Collegeville, MN: Liturgical Press, 2003). A useful review of literature and issues, as well as an argument that a Spirit christology and a Spirit-focused sacramental theology contend best with religious pluralism, is Glenn Ambrose, "Religious Diversity, Sacramental Encounters, and the Spirit of God," *Horizons*, 37/2 (2010), pp. 271–91.
[133] David Hollenbach, *Justice, Peace and Human Rights: American Catholic Social Ethics in a Pluralistic World* (New York: Crossroad, 1988), pp. 193–5.
[134] Susan A. Ross, *Extravagant Affections: A Feminist Sacramental Theology* (New York: Continuum, 1998), p. 173.

the church, and between the church and the world. The "Spirit of God" is sent by the risen Jesus, as "the Spirit of Christ" for the church and its mission. The developing Spirit christologies of the gospels take Jesus' Spirit-inspired Sonship to the beginning of his existence. In that the identity and function of the Word in John's gospel resonate with that of Wisdom/Sophia in the Hebrew Bible, the association of Christ and Spirit is even taken into the realm of "preexistence" (as later Trinitarian theology makes more explicit). All four gospels and especially Acts portray the Spirit as just as essential and original in the inspiration of Christian community as in the Sonship of Jesus. In Acts, the Holy Spirit is given by the risen Christ to guide the church. The inspiration of the Spirit assures the Christian community that the mission to the Gentiles, the expansion of the church from Jerusalem to Rome, and the development of church structures (as well as their modification) are all part of the divine plan of salvation.[135] Early Christians worship and are baptized in the name of Father, Son, and Spirit. Later theological interpretations have even extended the presence of God in Spirit globally, interreligiously, and ecologically.[136]

In the New Testament itself, there is ambiguity as to whether the Spirit is of God or of Christ or both and whether the Spirit is a mode or manifestation of divine presence or a distinct personal entity. My emphasis has been on God's Spirit as empowering Christ and on the Spirit of the risen Christ, since my central subject matter has been Jesus as the Christ. In the chapter to follow, the central concern will be to show how Christians are united to Christ in the church as a community of life, belief, and practice, through the power of the Spirit, considered primarily as the Spirit of Christ. For example, Luke's Jesus promises the Spirit to those who pray to God for this gift (11:13). And as we have just seen, Paul portrays the Spirit (either of God or of Christ) as operative at every level of community life.

However, the New Testament also portrays the Spirit in more properly personal terms, particularly in the farewell discourses of John's gospel, lending support to the later conciliar affirmation of the personhood of the Spirit (at I Constantinople in 381, as described later). On the one hand,

---

[135] Brown, *Introduction to the New Testament*, pp. 281–3, 295.
[136] See Veli-Matti Kärkkäinen (ed.), *Holy Spirit and Salvation: The Sources of Christian Theology* (Louisville, KY: Westminster John Knox Press, 2010); David H. Jensen (ed.), *The Lord and Giver of Life: Perspectives on Constructive Pneumatology* (Louisvlle, KY: Westminster John Knox Press; 2008); Veli-Matti Kärkkäinen (ed.), *The Spirit in the World: Emerging Pentecostal Theologies in Global Contexts* (Grand Rapids, MI: Eerdmans, 2009); and Paul D. Murray, Diego Irarrázaval, and Maria Clara Bingemer (eds.), *Lord and Life-Giver: Spirit Today* (London: SCM Press, 2011).

John's usage does at points resemble that of Paul, as when the risen Jesus breathes on his disciples, saying, "Receive the Holy Spirit," presumably his own (John 20:22–3). Yet Jesus also promises his disciples to ask the Father to "give you another Advocate, to be with you forever. This is the Spirit of truth, whom the world cannot receive, because it neither sees him nor knows him. You know him, because he abides with you, and he will be in you" (14:16–18). Jesus promises that "the Holy Spirit, whom the Father will send in my name" will teach the disciples (14:26). And the Spirit will witness to Jesus. "When the Advocate comes, whom I will send to you from the Father, the Spirit of truth who comes from the Father, he will testify on my behalf" (15:26).

Among the questions that are not resolved in the New Testament are whether a Spirit christology can account as well as a Word christology for the divine status of Jesus Christ (or whether Spirit christologies are essentially "adoptionist"); whether the Holy Spirit is not only "of God" and hence "divine," but a divine being distinct from the Father and Son and their functions (whether the Spirit is another name for their powers of love, reconciliation, and salvation, or is a divine "person"); and whether, more particularly, the roles or "missions" of the risen Christ and the Spirit are really different (whether both reconcile sinners to God and neighbor, empower new life, and make God present in the church).

In 325, the first ecumenical council at Nicaea confessed the Son and Father to be equal. The creed of Nicaea, which focused on the equal divinity of the Father or Creator and the Son or Word, affirmed simply belief "in the Holy Spirit." Nicaea did not clarify the distinct personhood or the divinity of the Holy Spirit, which continued to be denied by some. The First Council of Constantinople (381) expanded the wording of the Nicene Creed to proclaim the Holy Spirit, "the Lord, the Giver of Life, who proceeds from the Father, with the Father and the Son he is worshipped and glorified." The affirmation that the Spirit "proceeds from" the Father implies that, like the Son, the Spirit is of the same "substance" (*ousia*) as the Father and is equally divine, hence to be worshipped with the Father and Son.[137]

Geoffrey Wainwright interprets the Nicene–Constantinopolitan Creed to establish that "the Spirit's holiness belongs to the defining and originating holiness of God," that the Spirit can make Christ known to humans "because he has his eternal being from the Father," and that "he" shares

[137] The Western church was later to add to this creed the infamous "*filioque* clause," which has been for centuries a bone of contention between the Eastern and Western churches because it appears to make the Spirit subordinate to the Son ("proceeds from the Father and from the Son").

God's self-giving character. Like the Father and the Son, the Holy Spirit may be called "Lord" and has a "life-giving" role.[138]

The Spirit is the ecstatic, uniting, and returning power of God that makes both the incarnation and salvation possible, reconciling relationships here and now. The communication of the Spirit as "Giver of Life" is simultaneously the communication of the Father and the Son. This is the experiential or ecclesial basis for affirming the equal divinity and authentic personhood of the Spirit.[139] The Holy Spirit "presents the divine reality to creatures by gathering the community and the individual into the divine presence."[140] When individuals and community are gathered to God and reconciled, they experience the Spirit in the Spirit's own right as "God in person."[141]

The precise identity of the Spirit is as complicated a question as it is theologically important. The present treatment, as concerned primarily with Christ, salvation, and Christian politics, in no way pretends to resolve this issue, or even address all of its aspects.[142] In the next chapter, on the Spirit, my focus will not be on the Holy Spirit in its own right (as a distinct divine "person" in the Trinity) or on "ontological" claims about the divinity of the Spirit. I am interested mainly in the contributions Spirit christologies can make to theologies of salvation in Christ as empowering Christians personally, ecclesially, and politically. This empowerment assumes the presence of the risen Jesus in the church by the power of the Spirit. I see the contributions of Spirit christologies as complementary to those of Word christologies, though it is valid for any given theologian to prefer and write from either of these perspectives.

[138] Geoffrey Wainwright, "The Holy Spirit," in Colin Gunton (ed.), *Cambridge Companion to Christian Doctrine* (Cambridge University Press, 1997), pp. 280, 282.

[139] Ralph Del Colle, "A Response to Jürgen Moltmann and David Coffey," in Hinze and Dabney (eds.), *Advents of the Spirit*, p. 346. Del Colle also maintains that this requires the personhood of the Spirit and the procession of the Spirit from the father and the Son (*filioque*).

[140] Ralph Del Colle, "The Holy Spirit: Presence, Power, Person," *Theological Studies*, 62/2 (2001), p. 326.

[141] Jürgen Moltmann, *The Source of Life: The Holy Spirit and the Theology of Life*, trans. Margaret Kohl (Minneapolis: Augsburg Fortress, 1997), p. 45.

[142] For more in-depth introductions to these issues, see Del Colle, *Christ and the Spirit*; Wainwright, "Holy Spirit," pp. 272–96; Barbara Finan, "The Holy Spirit: An Issue in Theology," *Spirituality Today*, 38 (1986), pp. 9–18, www.spiritualitytoday.org/spir2day/863812finan.html (accessed July 22, 2009); Hinze and Dabney (eds.), *Advents of the Spirit*; Coffey, *"Did You Receive the Holy Spirit?"*; Michael Welker, *God the Spirit*, trans. John F. Hoffmeyer (Minneapolis: Fortress Press, 1994); Jensen (ed.), *The Lord and Giver of Life*; Veli-Matti Kärkkäinen, *Pneumatology: The Holy Spirit in Ecumenical, International and Contextual Perspective* (Grand Rapids, MI: Baker Academic, 2002); and Hinze (ed.), *The Spirit in the Church and the World*.

In the chapter to follow I will explore resources for a Spirit-oriented interpretation of Christ, salvation, and church in two major figures from the tradition, Thomas Aquinas and Martin Luther. The value of aspects of both the Word and the Spirit paradigms for Christian ethics will then be traced in the work of three contemporary theologians, each of whom advocates a Christian politics with relevance and power for the challenges of global justice. The important addition made by these three is a theology of the transforming Spirit at work not only in Christians and the church, but in the world, in interreligious work for justice, and in creation.

CHAPTER 5

Spirit

As clarified at the conclusion of Chapter 4. the present chapter will focus on the Spirit of Christ in the church as the power that draws Christians together and unites them to Christ in practice, belief, and hope. The power of the Spirit is essential for Christian ethics as enabling ongoing personal conversion, community solidarity, and the practical enactment of the kingdom of God – the reconciling politics of salvation. Shawn Copeland, considering racism, makes the point eloquently:

> The gift of God's loving Spirit creates a new basis for community. Women and men experience themselves as transformed persons who are called to live out this gift of love concretely through transformed human relations and who are knit together and empowered by that same Spirit to witness to a new reality.[1]

Jesus was the prophet of God's inbreaking reign, and he embodied it in his own life and ministry. As oriented by the corporate metaphor "kingdom of God," the salvation from evil that Jesus inaugurates brings personal liberation and has social and political results. Because the Jesus of the gospels sees God's eschatological action as beginning now and because the risen Jesus is present to and in the church, Christian ethics and politics trust that it can begin to change evil hearts and social structures.

When the later church proclaims Jesus as truly human and divine, it testifies that in Jesus and the communities founded in his name, sin and suffering are overcome by God's healing presence and power. As we saw in the preceding chapter, Word christologies emphasize that, in Jesus Christ, God enters history personally. Spirit christologies, more than Word christologies, typically make visible the remembered events of Jesus' life and death, and draw in dynamic, relational terms the connections among God the Creator, Jesus, and Jesus' followers. In Luke, the Spirit is the power behind Jesus' conception and birth, empowers Jesus at his baptism,

---

[1] M. Shawn Copeland, "Knit Together by the Spirit as Church," in Colleen M. Griffith (ed.), *Prophetic Witness: Catholic Women's Strategies for Reform* (New York: Crossroad, 2009), p. 16.

and enables Jesus to cast out demons and heal the sick. Christ sends the Spirit to the church at his resurrection. According to Paul, the Spirit enables believers to live as Christ's body in Christian community, in worship and liturgies, in personal relationships, and in life in the larger world.

Not only is a Spirit christology "about" the relation of Jesus Christ to God; it is also integrally "about" the presence of God in Christ to believers, to the church, and for the world. Biblically, the Spirit is related to Jesus not only as divine creative power to or in the man Jesus, but also as enabling the empowering presence of the risen Christ in the community gathered in his name. The existence of the church as a community of salvation and liberation reveals the Spirit's unity with Jesus Christ (and also, from the standpoint of Trinitarian theology, the Spirit's equality with Christ: the divinity of the Spirit). "In both the Christ-event and in the Church the Word and the Spirit do God's work together."[2]

For Christian ethics and politics, biblical Spirit imagery and the theology of the Holy Spirit offer indispensable ways to express how it is that the incarnation actually comes to change the lives of people and communities that live at great historical and geographical distances from Jesus of Nazareth and his disciples. According to Christian creeds, Jesus Christ unites full humanity and full divinity in his unique existence; the church as Christ's body filled with his Spirit is the historical place where human beings actually experience the union of our own humanity with his, and hence with his divinity and resurrection. Authentic Christian communities actually do embody God's inbreaking reign, just as Christ does. There the Spirit is at work.

Contemporary theologians (and ethicists) find Spirit christology attractive because it offers a way to understand the humanity of Christ in concrete terms, to see the risen Christ as historically present in a dynamic way, to explain practically how we participate in Christ, and to enliven hope, solidarity, and commitment.

SPIRIT, ETHICS, AND EMPOWERMENT

There is no experience of Christ in history that is not mediated by the Spirit.[3] From a christological standpoint, the Spirit is considered

---

[2] Denis Edwards, "Sketching an Ecological Theology of the Holy Spirit and the Word of God," in Paul D. Murray, Diego Irarrázaval, and Maria Clara Bingemer (eds.), *Lord and Life-Giver: Spirit Today* (London: SCM Press, 2011), p. 14.

[3] Barbara Finan, "Holy Spirit: An Issue in Theology," *Spirituality Today*, 38 (1986), 9–18, www.spiritualitytoday.org/spir2day/863812finan.htm (accessed March 28, 2011; unpaginated).

the one who makes the risen Christ existentially present and active to Christians. To experience the Spirit is to experience God's reign through the risen Christ, and thus to live as though the reign of God has been inaugurated. Kirsteen Kim says quite rightly, on the basis of her youthful experiences of the charismatic movement, that the first thing to understand about the theology of the Holy Spirit is that "when God calls us to follow Jesus, we are not simply expected to emulate the behavior of a distant historical figure by 'being good,' but we are offered the power to become like Jesus."[4] Kathryn Tanner connects this insight to a Word theology: "if the Spirit of God is secure in the Word of God, it is also secure, irrevocable, in the humanity united to that Word."[5]

Spirit christology, drawing on the synoptics and Paul, gives content to human sanctification or regeneration by referring the Christian life to the example of Jesus' ministry. To neglect the historical particularities of Jesus' life and subjectivity not only threatens his full humanity, but deprives Christians of concrete normative reference points for their own lives.[6] Christian ethics and politics are interested in the particulars of Jesus' humanity, both because his full humanity is necessary to mediate divine life to us and because those particulars illustrate concretely what "divinized" life in the world is like.

The presence and work of the Spirit liberate believers for service to others, carrying the sanctification of persons and of Christian congregations into public realms.[7] The gifts of the Spirit draw people into "public force fields." In fact, according to Michael Welker, the charisms constitute "forms of participation and of inclusion in public powers."[8] The gifts of the Spirit affect human beings existentially, bringing them into a "domain of resonance, extending beyond particular times and cultures," even aiming toward "universal communication" and "universal community."[9] In Trinitarian perspective, the action of the Spirit can yield a norm and theology of social justice. The Spirit builds communities that

---

[4] Kirsteen Kim, *The Holy Spirit in the World: A Global Conversation* (Maryknoll, NY: Orbis Books, 2007), p. v.

[5] Kathryn Tanner, *Christ the Key* (Cambridge: Cambridge University Press, 2010), pp. 35–36.

[6] Jon Sobrino, *Christ the Liberator: A View From the Victims*, trans. Paul Burns (Maryknoll, NY: Orbis Books, 2001), pp. 135–7.

[7] Ralph Del Colle, "The Holy Spirit: Presence, Power, Person," *Theological Studies*, 62 (2001), p. 332. See also Michael Welker, *God the Spirit*, trans. John F. Hoffmeyer (Minneapolis: Fortress Press, 1994), pp. 239–64.

[8] Welker, *God the Spirit*, p. 242.

[9] Ibid., p. 243, 244, 248.

reflect "diversity, fundamental equality in originality, and the primacy of relationships."[10]

Writing from Latin America, José Comblin finds the action of the Spirit in the experience of the poor, as they become agents in the struggle against unbalanced political power. In communities of the poor, the experience of the Spirit is an experience of something new, of something that reverses their situation, an experience of rebirth.[11] "The Spirit is the strength of those who have no strength. It leads the struggle for the emancipation and fulfillment of the people of the oppressed."[12] According to Jürgen Moltmann (citing Rom. 8 and Col. 1), God's Spirit renews all creation, not only healing suffering, but overcoming "the mortality of created being itself."[13] Elizabeth Johnson sees the indwelling Spirit as empowering humans "to live as sisters and brothers, friends and lovers, priests and prophets, co-creators and children of the natural world which God so loves."[14]

For a theology, soteriology, and politics of the kingdom of God, a renewed theology and christology of *God's* empowering presence in community is key. The Holy Spirit is this presence. If it is God who not only is present in creation, not only incarnate in Jesus Christ, but also here and now incarnate in human hearts, relationships, and communities, then inconceivable possibilities lie within reach.

EMPOWERMENT BY THE SPIRIT IN THE THEOLOGICAL TRADITION

To treat theologies of the Spirit and their relation to Christ and salvation in the entire Christian theological tradition would be a vast undertaking. My more limited purpose here is to explore – and only quite briefly – some ways in which a couple of the theological "greats," Thomas Aquinas and Martin Luther, might offer unexpected resources for a Spirit-inspired ethics and politics. These two thinkers provide anchors in the Roman

[10] Mary Elsbernd, "Toward a Theology of Spirit That Builds Up the Just Community," in Bradford E. Hinze (ed.), *The Spirit in the Church and the World*, College Theology Society Annual Volume 49, 2003 (Maryknoll, NY: Orbis Books, 2004), pp. 152–66, at 162.
[11] José Comblin, *The Holy Spirit and Liberation*, trans. Paul Burns (Maryknoll, NY: Orbis Books, 1989), pp. 21, 54.
[12] Ibid., p. 185.
[13] Jürgen Moltmann, *The Source of Life: The Holy Spirit and the Theology of Life*, trans. Margaret Kohl (Minneapolis: Fortress Press, 1997), p. 122.
[14] Elizabeth A. Johnson, "Creator Spirit and Ecological Ethics: An Ancient Frontier," in Irarrázaval and Bingemer (eds.), *Lord and Life-Giver*, p. 31.

Catholic and the Protestant strands of Christian ethics. Interpretation of their thought also can illustrate how new concerns about global solidarity and justice provide new lenses with which to read and reenvision the Christian theological heritage.

Thomas Aquinas is usually considered to develop a Word over a Spirit christology and to see the theological virtue of charity as a participation in the divine nature, united to human nature through the incarnation, in a way that is reminiscent of the "divinization" theologies of the early church.[15] While, for Aquinas, the theological virtues orient all human conduct to friendship with God as its final end, Aquinas is typically understood to have a substantive ethics and politics based more on natural law than on the theological virtues. Yet the idea of the theological virtues as a participation in God establishes a view of sanctification as actual and reliable progress in the moral life, even if the content of moral action is furnished mostly by reason. This, in turn, is important for a Christian politics of dedication to the global common good, especially a politics that is committed to produce concrete, tangible political changes that serve justice.

In addition, however, I will suggest in Chapter 7 that there is a synergy in Aquinas's ethics between the natural and theological virtues and, in the present chapter, that the work of the Spirit constantly infuses the moral life with new energy and direction. (Natural law, the natural virtues, and the theological virtues will be taken up further in Chapter 7, in relation to the content of Christian politics.)

Martin Luther famously rejected any hint of the "works righteousness" he discerned in the Catholic piety of his time and urged believers to trust for their salvation solely in the promises of God in Christ. In order to avoid overconfidence in human powers and to give glory to the mercy of God, he insisted, against medieval Scholastic theology, that grace does not create any ontological change. For Luther, we are viewed as righteous in God's eyes because we share in the benefits of Christ's sacrifice, not because our inherent nature or being is different. We have an "imputed righteousness" and remain *simul justus et peccator*. Faith should be active in love, but practical moral results are not guaranteed. Instead, God imputes to those who trust in him the merits of Christ, who died for our sins. Salvation is by faith alone.

---

[15] See Norman Russell, *Fellow Workers With God: Orthodox Thinking on Theosis* (Yonkers, NY: St. Vladimir's Seminary Press, 2009).

Yet the stereotypical portrait of Luther as having a doctrine of "forensic" justification by faith that excludes any real doctrine of sanctification, much less an energetic Christian politics, may be too one-sided. Drawing on some new Luther research, I will present the case that Luther may have seen the union of Christ with believers, through the Holy Spirit, as endowing them with a reliable power actually to mend lives and relationships. If true, this reading may provide a point of contact with Aquinas's theology of the work and gifts of the Holy Spirit, and may even imply practical moral consequences that resemble those of Aquinas's theology of the infused theological virtues as bringing lasting and visible transformation. Recent work on Luther's theology of union with Christ in the Spirit brings additional resources for global political action from the thought of this great Reformer and creates a theological opening for ecumenical convergence on the politics of salvation. Similar directions in research on John Calvin are not as extensively developed but are under investigation.[16]

AQUINAS

For Aquinas, we are saved by the incarnation of the Word (*ST* III.34. a3; 48.a1.r.ad.2).[17] Through the union of his divine and human natures, Christ makes us " 'partakers of the Divine Nature' " (II.22.a1.r.ad.3; citing 2 Pet. 1:4; I–II.62.a1). However, the passion and death of Christ contribute to his saving work, as out of love he produces a superabundance of merit (III.48.a6; 50.a1, a6).[18] At the existential level of conversion and sanctification, the cross inspires in us an appreciation of God's love, mercy, and forgiveness (III.46.3). Our confrontation with the suffering and death of Christ conforms our affections in gratitude and love, creating practical dispositions to imitate in our own lives Christ's

---

[16] See J. Todd Billings, "United to God through Christ: Assessing Calvin on the Question of Deification," *Harvard Theological Review*, 98 (2005), pp. 315–34; and Paul S. Chung, *The Spirit of God Transforming Life: The Reformation and Theology of the Holy Spirit* (New York: Palgrave Macmillan, 2009).

[17] In the present discussion, citations of the *Summa Theologiae* will be given in the text. The translation used is by Fathers of the English Dominican Province (New York: Benziger Brothers, 1947).

[18] Although Aquinas says, "From the beginning of his conception Christ merited our eternal salvation" (III.48.5.r.ad.2), he also says that Christ's passion is the "satisfaction" by which we are "delivered from sin" (III.48.5.r.ad.1) and that Christ's passion "merited salvation" (III.48.1). Aquinas seems to have combined (but not completely distinguished or aligned) the soteriological strategies of incarnation and cross. He simply says that Christ out of love gave "more" compensation for sin than was required (III.2.2).

"obedience, humility, constancy, justice, and the other virtues" (III.46.3; cf. 48.1.r.ad.2).

The incarnation takes human capacities and human destiny beyond the natural limits of creation. Humans are created with the capacity to know the goods that constitute their natural happiness. These goods include knowledge and love of God (I-II.3.a4, a8; I-II.109.3.r.ad.3), though not personal friendship with God, as well as basic human goods such as life, family, and political society (I-II.94.a2). Although human being is always sustained by God's grace, in our present state of sin, grace is necessary for salvation (I.23.a5), as both healing from sin and elevation to the new possibilities of loving friendship with God. Like Luther, Aquinas rejects any idea that human initiative or works cause salvation (I-II.62.a1; I-II.51.4). Through the grace of God in Christ, humans are restored from the sin that impedes the enjoyment of natural goods and are enabled to attain the "supernatural" happiness of union with God in friendship (II-II.23.a1; 26.a2). The theological virtues are dispositions to, and principles of union with, an end that would otherwise exceed human capacity (I-II.62.a1–3). Charity, as a participation in the divine essence, gives our souls a new form and end (23.2), a new "nature."

To be friends with God would be impossible were it not for likeness of nature, since true friendship presupposes basic equality (here Aquinas follows Aristotle).[19] Since friendship with God surpasses human nature, grace elevates nature with the theological virtues, "a kind of participation in the Godhead" (I-II.62.a1). Grace enfolds the entire moral life within the desire for and possibility of friendship with God. This possibility exists only because grace gives humans a nature beyond the "natural," a share in the divine.

Aquinas thus calls charity the "friendship of man for God" and a "fellowship of everlasting happiness." This friendship comes "by the infusion of the Holy Ghost, Who is the love of the Father and the Son, and the participation of Whom in us is created charity" (II-II.23.2; cf. 23.2.r.ad.1; 23.3). Faith, hope, and charity are all infused, the "mother and root of all" being charity (I-II.62.4).

The language of infusion serves to distinguish the origin of the theological virtues from that of the natural ones, since the latter are acquired through habituation by education and practice (I-II.51.a2). To say that the theological virtues are "infused" signifies primarily that they are divine

---

[19] Aristotle, *Nicomachean Ethics*, trans. Terence Irwin (Indianapolis: Hackett, 1985), book viii, chs. 4–8.

gifts, totally reliant on God, not the result of human processes of formation. Yet this expression may give the erroneous impression that the theological virtues not only have an immediate and total effect, but also that they arrive independently of any contingent historical mediations. The notion of "infusion" seems to connote a sort of miraculous and sudden transformation of individual interiority, quite apart from a person's relationships and context.

Yet such a conception of grace does not sit well with the biblical narratives of salvation, particularly Jesus' preaching of the reign of God and Paul's model of conformity to Christ in a community marked by transformed practices (1 Cor. 13). It also does not cohere well with the existential experience of believers, as requiring and receiving divine support for Christian living, support that is highly dependent on membership in the Christian community. It is even at odds with Aquinas's own idea that the biblical passion narratives that inform personal prayer and liturgical celebrations gracefully transform the affections and dispositions of believers.

Therefore, it is important to clarify that, for Aquinas, God always interacts dynamically in Christian existence, constantly inspiring and enabling Christians to persevere and to act. Sanctifying grace is not just a change in our "nature," but the presence of the Spirit "indwelling in us" (*ST* I-II.109.r.ad.1). After all, dynamic interaction is characteristic of what we know humanly of "friendship," the relationship to which Aquinas analogizes union with God. Aquinas himself sees that union as intimate, active, and reciprocal (I-II.65.5).

This dynamic interaction occurs on at least four planes: the original gift of the theological virtues; divine aid to specific human actions; the continuing influence of the Spirit, who bestows the grace of wisdom and the gifts of the Spirit; and the continuing presence of the Spirit to the Christian through the community of the church.

First, when Aquinas affirms that the theological virtues come from God and that we are helped by divine grace to persevere and to act, the stress appears to lie on individual conversion. Yet Aquinas does not eliminate human relationships and communities as spheres of grace. Is it not possible, indeed probable and truer to scripture and experience, to say that the church is the place of habituation to the theological virtues through the power of the Holy Spirit?[20] Do we not come to participate

---

[20] Arguably, this is not what Aquinas himself explicitly states. Perhaps the best evidence for a communal and practical understanding of grace in Aquinas is his theology of the sacraments, to be discussed later. For a concise but more technical discussion of the types and occasions of grace

in the divine nature, enjoy friendship with God, and exhibit the virtues of charity, faith, and hope, as we are joined to the body of Christ, in the community gathered in his name? If we are "infused" with charity, this may happen, not in the moment, but as our hearts, minds, bodies, and spirits become more and more permeable to the Spirit of Christ enlivening his body, the church community.

Pamela Hall makes a similar suggestion, drawing an analogy to Christian formation from the "narrative" character of the moral life, moral knowledge, and moral reasoning:

> Perhaps, too, men and women grow in the love of God, and in an understanding of what God is, by an acquaintance with other friends of God. ... We appropriate, and learn to enact, the New Law in part by the influence and example of others engaged in the same project.[21]

Aquinas cites Jeremiah's testimony that the Lord writes the divine laws on human hearts (Jer. 31:31, in *ST* I-II.106.1) to make the point that grace is infused, not learned or habituated. Yet the text he cites from Jeremiah actually sets knowledge and observance of the laws in the context of God's covenant with Israel, which is a covenant with a historical people, for whom the laws not only guide, but emerge from, ongoing practices. The covenant and laws come from God as a call to form a new community of liberation by and gratitude to God, a call issued not to the individual heart, but to the whole people gathered around Moses on Sinai. Becoming a covenant people involves relational events among God, Moses, representatives of the people, and the people as a whole (Exod. 19). The laws bind individuals in a corporate identity dedicated to God, of which a distinctive way of life is the visible and historical manifestation. To be a people means to be a community whose daily existence will be centered on God's commandments. There is reciprocity of inner personal devotion and corporate worship and action; but, if anything, the latter is the prior and primary arena of God's gracious work.

Aquinas himself uses St. Paul's corporate metaphor of the body of Christ to hint that humanity's union with Christ and salvation do not occur individualistically, with an ontological change in individuals on a one-by-one basis. "For, just as the natural body is one, though made up of diverse members, so the whole Church, Christ's mystic body, is reckoned

---

in Aquinas, see Joseph P. Wawrykow, "Grace," *The Westminster Handbook to Thomas Aquinas* (Louisville, KY: Westminster John Knox Press, 2005), pp. 63–9.

[21] Pamela M. Hall, *Narrative and the Natural Law: An Interpretation of Thomistic Ethics* (Notre Dame, IN: University of Notre Dame Press, 1994), p. 87.

as one person with its head, which is Christ." Thus Christ redeems all members through his action, just as if a man who sinned with his feet were to redeem himself by the work of his hands (III.49.1). It is through the scriptures, prayers, and liturgies of the church that we learn of the passion and cross of Christ, as well as his resurrection; through participation in the church we are inspired by the love of charity that brings pardon of sins and redemption (III.49.1).[22]

Second, in addition to habitual grace (the infused virtues or habits of faith, hope, and charity), there is a kind of "helping" grace that "bespeaks God's active involvement in human acting."[23] Even after the gift of charity, we still need "the help of grace in order to be moved by God to act" and to do so "righteously" (I-II.109.9). This is because "grace is to some extent imperfect, inasmuch as it does not completely heal," at least in this world (I-II.109.9.r.ad.2). We can still sin and need further grace to persevere (109.10). "The graced person is still a work in progress, as the person strives to grow in conformity to God's will."[24] "The special divine presence – Aquinas called it 'a friendly and intimate conversation' of God with us (I-II, 65, 5) – leads men and women to act. Thus daily life summons forth and realizes grace."[25] The actions of daily life, of course, involve participation with other people in decisions, acts, practices, and structures, all of which shape our identities and virtues. These are the realms of "God's active involvement in human acting."

Third, the Holy Spirit inspires individual persons with the gift of wisdom (II-II.45.5; 177.1) and the gifts of the Spirit (I-II.68) for the good of the church. The grace of wisdom is given to women as well as men, according to Aquinas, though women may teach only "privately, to one

---

[22] My main point here is that, even for Aquinas, grace reaches us historically and communally. One inference that could be drawn from this is that "there is no salvation outside the church." With other contemporary theologians, I would reject that, on the basis that God can work through multiple communities and traditions, not only Christian churches. According to Thomas O'Meara, Aquinas also thinks that God redeemingly approaches people who have no exposure to Christianity, but Aquinas's example of a person raised alone in the wild by animals would not support the idea that salvation is always humanly social and communal. For an intriguing discussion, see Thomas F. O'Meara, O.P., "The Presence of Grace outside Evangelization, Baptism and Church in Thomas Aquinas's Theology," in Michael F. Cusato, O.F.M., and Michael F. Coughlin, O.F.M. (eds.), *That Others May Know and Love: Essays in Honor of Zachary Hayes, O.F.M.* (St. Bonaventure, NY: St. Bonaventure University Press, 1997), pp. 97–100. O'Meara explains that the problem of the "wild child" (*nutritus in silva*) was a common medieval topos and was cited several times by Aquinas, prior to his writing of the *Summa Theologiae*, by which time he might have become more aware of entire cultures of "infidels."

[23] Wawrykow, "Grace," p. 64.

[24] Thomas F. O'Meara, O.P., *Thomas Aquinas: Theologian* (Notre Dame, IN: University of Notre Dame Press, 1997), p. 65.

[25] Ibid., p. 120.

or a few, in familiar conversation," and not by publicly addressing "the whole church" (II-II.177.2). The Holy Spirit also works in all the faithful through the gifts – wisdom, understanding, counsel, courage, knowledge, piety, and fear of the Lord (I-II.68). Each of these touches and helps one of the virtues – understanding and knowledge support faith (II-II.8, 9); fear of the Lord supports hope (19), wisdom supports charity (45), counsel supports prudence, a virtue of the practical reason (52), whereas the speculative reason is supported by understanding (I-II.57.2; II-II.8), piety supports justice (II-II.121), and the gift of fortitude supports the virtue of fortitude (140). The gifts bring interior transformations in the individual, as Servais Pinckaers has it, working to "give our acts a higher vitality and perfection."[26]

According to Aquinas, the gifts are not exactly like the cardinal and theological virtues or habits. The gifts differ from the virtues in that the latter modify nature, creating an enduring change, and hence are steady and reliable. The gifts, in contrast, are experienced as "inner promptings" that result from initiatives of divine inspiration (I-II.68.1). Nevertheless, Aquinas still terms the gifts "habits" (68.3, 4). Like habits, the Holy Spirit's gifts "abide in" us, making us always readier to follow the Spirit's lead (68.3), "as moved by God" (68.1.r.ad.1). The gifts do not change our natures. Instead, they testify that God is always actively present in the course of human lives. Here is a bridge to Martin Luther, who sees salvation as a dynamic union of the soul with Christ, by the power of the Holy Spirit.

From the standpoint of Christian spirituality, the emphasis on the interior working of the Holy Spirit, and on the person's total reliance on divine grace, can contribute to the renewal of Christian morality as the joyous living-out of what has been generously given. Developed in the writings of the Catholic author Servais Pinckaers,[27] this was also the specific aim of Martin Luther, rendered perhaps most eloquently in his small early work, *On Christian Liberty* (1520). In the words of Pinckaers:

The work of the Holy Spirit is to enter within us by touching the two deepest cords of our hearts, the affinity for truth and the yearning for goodness and

---

[26] Servais Pinckaers, O.P., *Morality: The Catholic View*, trans. Michael Sherwin, O.P. (South Bend, IN: St. Augustine's Press, 2001), p. 88.

[27] See Servais Pinckaers, O.P., *The Sources of Christian Ethics*, 3rd ed., trans. Mary T. Noble (Edinburgh: T & T Clark, 1995); and *Morality: The Catholic View*. For a discussion of Pinckaers on the Holy Spirit, see Dennis J. Billy, C.Ss.R., "The Person of the Holy Spirit as the Source of the Christian Moral Life," *Studia Moralia*, 36 (1998), pp. 325–59, at 332–7.

happiness. The Spirit acts through a quiet light and a gentle motion that produce in our souls wisdom and love.[28]

As Charles Bouchard argues, it is essential to see the gifts as enabling the Christian life and Christian moral discernment holistically. The gifts go beyond intellectual and rational knowledge to confer or enhance knowing that is "connatural" or instinctive.[29] The gifts of the Spirit help us in a mode that is "intuitive, prompt, supra-deliberative," lending to action "a 'fluid mobility,'" and even attraction, ease, and delight.[30] The gifts involve the emotions and affections; their effects can be best expressed in a mix of images of sight, sound, taste, and touch. Sometimes "the prompting of reason is not sufficient, and there is need for the prompting of the Holy Ghost" (I-II.68.2). The gifts of the Spirit come into play "when logic cannot take us any further."[31] This happens often in our relationships with other people, in discerning the moral dimensions of social bonds, and in grappling with their requirements and effects.

Spirit-inspired actions may be termed "fruits of the Holy Spirit" (I-II.70.1). Aquinas enumerates twelve, following Galatians 5:22–3 – charity, joy, peace, patience, long-suffering, goodness, benignity, meekness, faith or fidelity, modesty, continence, and chastity (70.3). These terms seem to denote further dispositions of character or attitudes rather than concrete types of action, which may be a good reason they have not enjoyed much development in Thomistic theology or moral theology. But at least they help Aquinas make the point that the dynamic, continual presence of the Spirit in the moral life results in specific, observable, practical consequences.

Fourth, though Aquinas refers to the Holy Spirit as working interiorly in the believer (I-II.108.r.ad.2), he also finds the Holy Spirit at work in the discernment of the community and in the gospel, of course transmitted and interpreted communally (I-II.106.1.r.ad.1).[32] It is generally agreed that Aquinas does not have a well-developed ecclesiology; however, he does see the life of the church as comprising a historical extension of the

---

[28] Pinckaers, *Morality: The Catholic View*, p. 85.

[29] Charles E. Bouchard, O.P., "Recovering the Gifts of the Holy Spirit in Moral Theology," *Theological Studies*, 63 (2002), pp. 539–58. On the affective character of practical moral knowledge, Bouchard commends Daniel C. Maguire, "Ratio Practica and the Intellectualistic Fallacy," *Journal of Religious Ethics*, 10 (1982), pp. 22–39.

[30] Ibid., citing Walter Farrell, O.P., and Dominic Hughes, O.P., *Swift Victory: Essays on the Gifts of the Holy Spirit* (New York: Sheed & Ward, 1955), p. 181.

[31] Bouchard, "Recovering the Gifts," 554.

[32] See John Mahoney, *Seeking the Spirit: Essays in Moral and Pastoral Theology* (London: Sheed & Ward, 1981), especially ch. 8, pp. 97–117.

incarnation.[33] The Holy Spirit is the "soul" and "heart" of the church (III.8.1.r.ad.3). The Spirit is present in the activities of the church, and hence to and in church members as they carry out those activities. "The Holy Spirit giving life to the church is 'the soul' of the Body of Christ, while the virtues, gifts, charisms, and ministries give to grace concrete forms and voices.... Touched by the depths of the life of the Trinity, men and women, images of Christ, form a collective Christ the church."[34] For example, liturgical rites such as baptism should conform to the tradition or wisdom of the church, since the church is governed by the Holy Spirit (III.72.12). The selection of individuals for ecclesiastical office should be carried out by consultative deliberation, which will be guided by the Holy Spirit, not just by casting lots (I-II.95.a8).

The most theologically important and practically salient way in which the church continues the incarnation is through its sacramental liturgies. For Aquinas, "the moments of liturgy are the historical actions of Christ present today in this world."[35] The sacraments are effective signs of a sanctifying reality, and that reality is Christ.[36] All the sacraments convey to recipients the saving effects of Christ's passion and death for the remission of human sin. Aquinas tends to envision sacramental grace as internally affecting the soul. For instance, baptism is seen as taking away the guilt of sin and the "debt of punishment," thus removing barriers to eternal life ("the heavenly kingdom"), rather than as incorporating people into a new community actually engaged in kingdom practices (Gal. 3:28) (III.69.7).

Still, the celebration of a sacrament is necessarily a material and not only a spiritual process, in which the elements, relationships, and transitions of ordinary life take on extraordinary significance and power (III.60.4). Christ or the Spirit may work inwardly by leading one's will to desire the good; but in the sacraments Christ also works through the outward actions of human ministers (III.68.4; 69.5.1) and does so in a communal setting. Through the visible actions of the sacraments, Christ instructs and converts human beings through the senses, as is appropriate to their embodied and spiritual nature (III.79.1).[37] The eucharist above all is Christ's bodily presence to us, in friendship and as a sign of his enduring love (III.75.1).[38]

[33] O'Meara, *Thomas Aquinas*, p. 137.
[34] Ibid., pp. 138–9; citing *The Sermon-Conferences of St. Thomas Aquinas on the Apostles' Creed*, p. 125.
[35] Ibid., 147.
[36] Wawrykow, *Westminster Handbook to Thomas Aquinas*, p. 128.
[37] O'Meara, *Thomas Aquinas*, pp. 141, 143.
[38] For a discussion of Aquinas's treatment of the eucharist, see ibid., 144–8.

In the sacraments, sanctifying grace is given for the remission of sins, according to Aquinas. Yet the grace of the sacraments also has moral and practical consequences, in that it leads to "growth and stability in righteousness." This is especially true of the sacrament of confirmation, in which the baptized receive the Holy Spirit (III.72.7). By comparison, Aquinas's description of the grace of the eucharist seems more spiritual than practical and communal. Explicitly contrasting the eucharist to confirmation, Aquinas says of the former that, by it, "a man procures grace whereby he is enabled to lead the spiritual life" and "stand perfect in himself by union with God" (III.79.2.r.ad.1). Even so, Aquinas does not neglect to add that the virtue of charity bestowed in the eucharist presses the recipient on to action and just works (79.2.r.ad.2).

In summary, then, Aquinas conceives of grace primarily as conferring a new nature, a participation in the divine that makes human beings capable of enjoying friendship with God. In his discussion of the sacraments, his focus shifts somewhat from the incarnation, a more visible premise of his treatment of the theological virtues, to the saving effects of the death of Christ. In Aquinas's discussions of the gifts of the Spirit, of the presence of the Spirit in the church, and of the sacraments, the historical, processive, and corporate character of salvation comes to the surface. Although the infused virtues lend a certain stability and reliability to the life of faith and to faithful action, the discussions of Spirit and sacraments reveal Aquinas's appreciation of the dynamic, personal, and communal character of God's saving relation to us.

Although for Christians, reasonableness remains the essential guide to moral decision making, charity and the Spirit convert all human capacities. Current scholarship on Aquinas's ethics has put to rest any idea that Christian identity is simply frosting on a natural law cake. Aquinas "was a teacher and preacher of theology: this was his vocation and ministry."[39] "The core of Thomistic ethics is not the natural law, but the virtues ... strategies of love whereby those devoted to God are transformed in God's goodness."[40] Questions about our ultimate happiness in God "constitute the backbone of the entire Thomistic moral theology."[41]

All human powers of discernment and action are captivated by one's gracious opportunity to befriend God and to welcome the Spirit

[39] Ibid., p. xx.

[40] Paul J. Wadell, C.P., *The Primacy of Love: An Introduction to the Ethics of Thomas Aquinas* (New York: Paulist Press, 1992), p. 1.

[41] Servais Pinckaers, "The Sources of the Ethics of St. Thomas Aquinas," in Stephen J. Pope (ed.), *The Ethics of Aquinas* (Washington, DC: Georgetown University Press, 2002), pp. 17–29, at 23.

as constant companion. Christians see their relationships to others in a new perspective, against the horizon of reconciliation in Christ – not just for themselves or all Christians, but for all human beings and creation. Christians act on the basis of a vision of all reality as inherently related to God and destined for God as the universal common good (III.46.4; I-II.2.8).[42]

One shortcoming of Aquinas's theology of the Spirit as conforming believers to Christ in the church is that, while he envisions sacramental grace to have social and practical origins and efficacy, he does not consider (as far as I am aware) whether the social and practical relationships surrounding sacramental celebrations can enhance or undermine the mediation of graced friendship with God in Christ.[43] This lacuna will be ameliorated somewhat by Luther. The main point of the discussion thus far, however, has been to show that, contrary to stereotypes, Aquinas does not have a static or individualist view of the "infused" virtues. Instead, love of God and neighbor requires a dynamic engagement with and reliance on the Holy Spirit in continuous relationship and in community.

A further important contemporary question is whether Christians' transformed identity and action begin to transform other communities, inasmuch as individuals are members of many at once. Do grace and the Holy Spirit enable Christian communities, as well as individuals, to act in a new way? And what about the interactions of the church as a whole or of individual churches with multiple other communities? What social and political changes might result from those dynamic relationships? Although Thomas Aquinas the ethical and political thinker is also a Christian, a spiritual writer, and a theologian, it is important for the church's commitment to global justice not to let his morality of natural law become ecclesially isolated or to make of the church simply a contrast society and not a catalyst for political action.

We will return to some of these considerations at the end of this chapter, as well as in Chapters 7 and 8. Next, we turn to the theology of Martin Luther as an alternative yet possibly complementary approach to the work of the Spirit in Christian morality and politics.

[42] See William C. Mattison III, *Introducing Moral Theology: True Happiness and the Virtues* (Grand Rapids, MI: Brazos Press, 2008), p. 301.
[43] Theologians since the thirteenth century have used the term *ex opere operato* – officially adopted at Trent – to stipulate that the sacraments produce grace in and of themselves, apart from the character or the intentions of the celebrant. However, the character and intentions of the celebrating community may be another matter, at least in contemporary perspective. The possibility that distorted Christian practices lead to distorted sacramental celebrations and theologies will come up again in a discussion of Good Friday liturgies in the next chapter.

LUTHER

In his outlook on society and politics, Luther is much more Augustinian than Thomistic. Aquinas trusts that there is a significant capacity to realize the human good and the common good despite the fact of sin. Moreover, grace restores humanity's moral capacity, even as it transforms it into something substantially different. Therefore, as we shall see in Chapter 7, Aquinas is unafraid to talk about the right ordering of human relationships and societies as goals that are proximately attainable. Augustine, on the other hand, has an acute awareness of the reality of sin in the world, of the irrepressible nature of the *libido dominandi*.[44] He draws a sharp contrast between the eternal city and the earthly city.[45]

Scholars of Augustine are not of one mind about the optimism or pessimism with which he viewed Christian participation in the public and political spheres.[46] Robert Markus sees civil government and politics as neutral in themselves.[47] Others, like Peter Burnell,[48] Eugene TeSelle,[49] and David Hollenbach,[50] are convinced that Augustine sees human republics as serving good though limited natural virtues and ways of life. Christian virtue can support and supplement natural justice. Jean Bethke Elshtain puts a stronger emphasis on the "limits of politics" and of what politics can accomplish, though still stressing that Augustine delighted in and cared for temporal existence.[51] Still others, like Phillip Cary[52] and possibly Peter Brown,[53] hold that for Augustine there is no such thing as a good albeit limited natural society, since every society not united by love of God is vicious at its heart.

[44] Augustine, *The City of God*, trans. Marcus Dods (New York: Random House, 1950), I, preface and I.30.
[45] Ibid., XIV.28.
[46] For a useful overview see Peter J. Burnell, "The Status of Politics in St. Augustine's City of God," *History of Political Thought*, 31 (1992), pp. 13–29.
[47] Robert A. Markus, *Saeculum: History and Society in the Theology of St. Augustine* (Cambridge: Cambridge University Press, 1970).
[48] Burnell, "Status of Politics," 28–9.
[49] Eugene TeSelle, *Living in Two Cities: Augustinian Trajectories in Political Thought* (Scranton, PA: University of Scranton Press, 1998).
[50] David Hollenbach, S.J., *The Common Good and Christian Ethics* (Cambridge University Press, 2002), pp. 121–3.
[51] Jean Bethke Elshtain, *Augustine and the Limits of Politics* (University of Notre Dame Press, 1995).
[52] Phillip Cary, "United Inwardly by Love: Augustine's Social Ontology," in John Doody, Kevin L. Hughes, and Kim Paffenroth (eds.), *Augustine and Politics* (Lanham, MD: Lexington Books, 2005), pp. 3–33.
[53] Peter Brown, *Augustine of Hippo: A Biography* (London: Faber & Faber, 1967), pp. 308–9, 338.

Recently some Augustinian ethicists in a new generation have argued that Augustine provides theological warrants for wholehearted Christian investment in politics, specifically the politics of modern liberal democracies. Eric Gregory and Charles Mathewes argue, for example, not that Augustine held political positions identical to their own, but that elements in his theology permit the development of new forms of "Augustinian" politics, which are more sanguine than earlier generations of Augustinians (at least Protestant Augustinians) about the reformatory potential of Christian social ethics.[54]

Eric Gregory counters Augustine's ostensible insistence that Christians fix their hearts not on the social order, but on God alone, the only truly worthy object of our love. Taking book X of *The City of God* as his key, Gregory maintains that this notion is undermined by Augustine's theology of the incarnation,[55] according to which the Word inheres in every creature.[56] In a similar vein, Charles Mathewes not only sees Augustine as "world-affirming," but as suggestive of the "sacramentality of created reality as a whole."[57] Political action, while not ultimate, can still mediate proleptically the eschatological community of the kingdom of God.[58]

Christian social ethicists working against racism, sexism, militarism, and poverty in local, national, and global contexts have good cause to take another look at Augustinian pessimism and its premises of the ultimate viciousness of "pagan" civic virtues and the limited scope of grace. These reinterpretations can help shape a new Lutheran trajectory as well, as will be indicated later. Augustine's own politics, however, reflects a fourth-century context; the realities of Roman rule, even under Christian emperors; and the threat of the Germanic invaders who took control of Rome in 410 CE.

[54] See Eric Gregory, *Politics and the Order of Love: An Augustinian Ethic of Democratic Citizenship* (University of Chicago Press, 2008); and Charles T. Mathewes, *A Theology of Public Life* (Cambridge University Press, 2007). For a critical overview of some of these authors, see Peter Iver Kaufman, "Christian Realism and Augustinian (?) Liberalism," *Journal of Religious Ethics*, 38 (2010), pp. 690–724. Kaufman maintains (and I agree) that not only was Augustine no liberal progressivist, but once his views on coercion of religious dissidents, torture, and means in war are taken into account "his tough love no longer looks much like love" (p. 712). However, the worth of these new interpretations does not stand or fall with their strict adherence to Augustine's political views. Rather, as is often done with the "greats" of theological tradition, some revisionist Augustinians are playing on tensions within Augustine's views to arrive at innovative possibilities for the extension of his thought.

[55] Gregory, *Politics and the Order of Love*; see pp. 8–9 for an opening statement of the thesis. See Augustine, *City of God*, I.22.20.

[56] Gregory, *Politics and the Order of Love*, p. 286; citing Augustine, *City of God*, X.3.

[57] Mathewes, *Theology of Public Life*, pp. 87, 100.

[58] Ibid., pp. 285, 305.

For Augustine, although peace of a sort can be had as "the well-ordered concord of civic obedience and rule," the civic order does not participate in the virtue or true peace that come from charity. "The heavenly city … makes use of this peace only because it must,"[59] not because it has an integral connection with God's redeeming presence. In fact, although a temporal republic may agree on and peacefully sustain a common way of life, it can never attain true justice or true virtue if love of God is not its uniting core.[60]

True worship (*latreia*),[61] an authentic connection to God, is available only through Christ. Augustine, of course, does admire many of the "pagan" virtues of the Romans that led to their military and political successes. Moreover, he sees the hand of God in the conquests of the Christian emperors Constantine and Theodosius.[62] Yet, even though Augustine exhorts Christian officials and generals to enter the fray of worldly life,[63] in order to better earthly peace with an intention of love, they must be prepared to accept its necessary miseries.[64] Augustine's critics could legitimately object that he compromises too readily with those presumed necessities, as in the notorious example of judicial torture,[65] his failure to set clear limits on means in war,[66] and his call for the government to curtail the Donatists with armed force.[67] And a similar critique could be leveled against Luther's call for violent repression of the so-called Peasants' War.[68]

Nevertheless, Augustine does exhort Christians to improve matters where they can, regarding Christianity as having "little, though a little reformatory power"[69] toward greater political justice. This seems to assume that Christians at least are morally changed by charity, since once God is truly recognized and desired as the *summum bonum*, all other goods fall into their rightful places as objects of moral and political action. In addition to writing letters to public figures like Marcellinus and Boniface, Augustine was involved personally with other African bishops in trying

[59] Augustine, *City of God*, XIX.17.
[60] Ibid., XIX.24–.26.   [61] Ibid., X.1.   [62] Ibid., V.
[63] Augustine, Letter l38, "To Marcellinus"; Letters 189 and 220, "To Boniface."
[64] Augustine, *City of God*, XIX.4, 7, 27.
[65] Ibid., XIX.6.
[66] Augustine, *Letter to Faustus the Manichean*, book XXII.74, 76. The "real evil in war" is not killing but the lack of an "inward disposition" of love.
[67] Augustine, *A Treatise on the Correction of the Donatists* (c. 417), Christian Classics Ethereal Library, www.ccel.org/ccel/schaff/npnf104.v.vi.i.html (accessed May 4, 2012).
[68] Martin Luther, *Against the Robbing and Murdering Hordes of Peasants* (1525), Scroll Publishing online, www.scrollpublishing.com/store/Luther-Peasants.html (accessed May 4, 2012).
[69] Burnell, "Status of Politics," 29.

to change Roman institutions and policies, as Robert Dodaro has shown from letters and sermons. Augustine advocated for the poor, for condemned criminals, and for the right of sanctuary, and against slavery, torture, and capital punishment.[70] Christians are not only capable of rectitude in politics; they ought to and can be personally committed to political justice, and they can make aspects of the political order more just. Resonances of these expectations can also be found in Luther.

Yet neither Augustine nor Luther would ever envision the church as the seed of general social reform toward just structures that reflect heavenly goals. Augustine, like other premodern figures, does not envision the possibility of broad democratic participation or global movements for equality, rights, and political self-determination. Luther works against a similar horizon of perceived political possibilities.

Luther, too, draws a strong distinction between the heavenly kingdom and the temporal kingdom. He even depicts civil law and government as existing simply to counter sin[71] – as necessary because a human being is essentially no more than a "savage wild beast."[72] Luther seems ambivalent about whether the grace given to Christians will do much to change this situation at the practical level. On the one hand, once the faithful know they are promised salvation in Christ, and hence freed from trying to gain God's favor through works of the law, they become "Christs to one another."[73]

Here faith is truly active through love (Gal. 5:6), that is, it finds expression in works of the freest service, cheerfully and lovingly done, with which a man willingly serves another without hope of reward; and for himself he is satisfied with the fullness and wealth of his faith.[74]

---

[70] Robert Dodaro, O.S.A., "Between the Two Cities: Political Action in Augustine of Hippo," in Doody et al. (eds.), *Augustine and Politics*, pp. 99–115.

[71] In his 1522 treatise, *Temporal Authority: To What Extent It Should Be Obeyed?*, Luther says that the law of the temporal sword has existed from the beginning of the world; it is not just a result of sin, although it may have been given in anticipation of sin (in *Luther's Works*, vol. 45: *The Christian in Society II*, ed. Walther I. Brandt [Philadelphia: Fortress Press, 1962], p. 86). Some interpret this text as saying that government and law are natural and part of the creation, but there is ambiguity in Luther's writing on this point. Later, in the *Lectures on Genesis*, written about 1544–54, Luther asserts that there was no need of government before sin; government and laws were instituted to rule corrupt human beings (in *Luther's Works*, vol. 1: *Lectures on Genesis, Chapters 1–5*, ed. Jaroslav Pelikan [Saint Louis: Concordia, 1955], pp. 104, 115).

[72] Luther uses this simile in *Temporal Authority*, pp. 90–1; in his *Lectures on Galatians*, he uses the comparable image of a "furious and untamed beast" (in *Luther's Works*, vol. 26: *Lectures on Galatians 1535, Chapters 1–4*, ed. Jaroslav Pelikan [Saint Louis: Concordia, 1963], p. 308).

[73] Martin Luther, *A Treatise on Christian Liberty* (1520), trans. W. A. Lambert (Philadelphia: Fortress Press, 1957), p. 29.

[74] Ibid., p. 28.

On the other hand, Luther is so impressed by the depth of human sin, and so committed to protect the absolute gratuity of salvation, that he keeps very clear of any suggestion that, even after grace, there is anything inherent in human beings to make them worthy in God's eyes. Luther emphasizes more firmly than Augustine – perhaps even against Augustine – that salvation in Jesus Christ does not bring moral sanctification.

In the first place, actually living the Christian life is always a struggle, for "the flesh" (worldly desires and ambitions) is ever at war with the spirit converted to Christ. Obedience to the law and subjection of the body are necessary, not to earn salvation, but to purify the body of evil lusts, a process never completed.[75] Once a Christian has accepted forgiveness and become "righteous by faith," "he should not become so smug, as though he were pure of all sins." He (or she) must "face the constant battle with the remnants of sin."[76]

In the second place, Luther takes human unworthiness to an even deeper level than the daily moral struggle. Nothing we can ever be or do can make us deserving of the mercy we have been shown. The Christian "is righteous and holy by an alien or foreign holiness," which is "a pure gift of God."[77] In God's eyes (*coram Deo*), we are regarded as righteous; in ourselves we remain corrupt and worthy of damnation (*simul justus et peccator*). Luther's theological and pastoral priority is to underline the absoluteness and gratuity of grace. To serve this point, he downplays if not rejects any hint that humans can "possess" grace's effects.

Luther's *Lectures on Galatians* (particularly 2:15–21) are generally considered the key to his views on this point. There he argues that Christian righteousness or the righteousness of faith is a wholly "passive righteousness," by which God confers on us an acceptance that we do not deserve.[78] "A Christian is not someone who has no sin or feels no sin; he is someone to whom, because of his faith in Christ, God does not impute his sin."[79] This does not change, even after the reception of justifying grace and its consequence, the ability to trust God rather than ourselves, that is, to have faith. Faith unites Christ to the soul as bride to bridegroom, each claiming as his or her own what belongs to the other, but with no essential change in the identity or worthiness of the two partners. Christ takes

[75] Ibid., pp. 22.
[76] *Luther's Works*, vol. 12: *Selected Psalms I*, pp. 328–9, as cited by Carter Lindberg, "Do Lutherans Shout Justification but Whisper Sanctification?" *Lutheran Quarterly*, 13 (1999), p. 2.
[77] Ibid.
[78] Luther, *Lectures on Galatians*, pp. 4–9. [79] Ibid., p. 133.

on the soul's sin, death, and damnation; upon the soul, Christ bestows his righteousness, life, and salvation.[80]

Luther objected vehemently to all the contrary positions he found in medieval scholastic theologies. Obviously totally unacceptable was the Pelagian view that because of our efforts, God rewards us with charity. But almost equally objectionable to Luther were the ideas that faith requires the "form" of charity to be perfected and that, once grace is given, human beings then have the power to earn "merits" toward salvation.[81] A substantial passage from his *Lectures on Galatians* can illustrate this position of Luther and lead into questions and revisions gaining currency in Lutheran theology. These have to do with the integrity and consistency of divine grace and faith as reorienting the whole of life. In *Galatians*, Luther says, against the scholastics' "dreams":

Where they speak of love, we speak of faith … if it is true faith, it is a sure trust and firm acceptance in the heart. It takes hold of Christ in such a way that Christ is … the One who is present in the faith itself … But how He is present; this is beyond our thought, for there is darkness … Where the confidence of the heart is present, therefore, there Christ is present, in that very cloud and faith. This is the formal righteousness on account of which a man is justified; it is not on account of love, as the sophists say.[82]

True faith alone justifies; and in faith Christ is present, in some mode that remains hidden, dark, and clouded. No further addition of "love" is required. Luther envisions love not as an immediate content or effect of justifying grace, but as a subsequent movement toward sanctification and moral regeneration, expressed as love of neighbor. It is clear from this passage that, for Luther, neighbor love follows after and can have no part in the justification of sinners. God's mercy, to which the believer clings in faith, is alone necessary and sufficient.

Yet if, in faith, Christ is actually present in and to the believer, what are the effects of this presence? True, Christ is present in a manner that surpasses understanding. But if he is truly present, and constantly so, does not this constitute a relationship out of which the believer not only may but must live? Rather surprisingly, in support of this latter possibility, Luther does claim:

---

[80] Luther, *On Christian Liberty*, pp. 14–15. This metaphor is repeated in *Lectures on Galatians*, p. 168.
[81] *Lectures on Galatians*, pp. 127–31.
[82] Ibid., p. 130.

It is well known that the new obedience in the justified brings with it the daily growth of the heart in the Spirit who sanctifies us, namely, that after the battle against the remnants of false opinions about God and against doubt the Spirit goes on to govern the actions of the body so that lust is cast out and the mind becomes accustomed to patience and other moral virtues.[83]

In the 1970s, some theologians of the Evangelical Lutheran Church of Finland began dialogue with Russian Orthodox partners, and hence explored supportive resources in the thought of Martin Luther. A first and seemingly obvious point of division between the two traditions is the difference between the Orthodox theology of grace as divinization, enabling progressive sanctification, and the Lutheran view that grace consists in God's "forensic" determination to "impute" righteousness to people who will always remain sinners, both in terms of basic status and in most of their activities.

But when the Finnish theologians went back to the writings of the master with an eye to common ground with the Orthodox, they discovered the unexpected possibility that Luther may have brought justification and sanctification more closely together than Lutheran orthodoxy has assumed. In fact, ambiguities and new directions were found most especially in his *Lectures on Galatians*, the flagship document of the theology of "justification by faith alone." While Luther there repudiates any idea of an "ontological change" in the natures of persons of faith, he does seem to see Christ as constantly present to and even in the believer, conforming the identity of the latter to his own in a relation of "participation" or "indwelling." Here Luther's language converges with that of Aquinas (*ST* I-II.109.r.ad.1).

The theological leader of the new Finnish interpretation of Luther is Tuomo Mannermaa of the University of Helsinki, whose 1980 proposal was translated into English almost two decades later.[84] Mannermaa holds that the theology of Luther himself was distorted by later Lutheranism, instigated by the theology of Melancthon and the Formula of Concord of 1577. The target of the latter was the doctrine of Osiander, and not, as might be assumed, objectionable "Catholic" doctrines of sanctification

[83] *Lectures on Galations*, 381, as cited by Lindberg, "Do Lutherans Shout Justification?" 2.
[84] See Tuomo Mannermaa, *Christ Present in Faith: Luther's View of Justification*, ed. Kirsi Stjerna (Minneapolis: Fortress Press, 1998); for history of publication, see "Editor's Foreword," p. vii. See also Carl E. Braaten and Robert W. Jenson (eds.), *Union with Christ: The New Finnish Interpretation of Luther* (Grand Rapids, MI: Eerdmans, 1998), which contains a chapter by Mannermaa, "Why Is Luther So Fascinating? Modern Finnish Luther Interpretation"; and Veli-Matti Kärkkäinen, *One with God: Salvation as Deification and Justification* (Collegeville, MN: Liturgical Press, 2004).

premised on an essential change in human nature. Osiander agreed with Luther that God dwells in the believer (rather than changing human nature in itself), but he separated the divine and human natures of Christ and emphasized the indwelling of the divine nature alone. In its response, the Formula of Concord asserts that the fullness of God dwells in the believer but adds that this indwelling "follows the antecedent justification by faith," to the effect that God is not yet present in the believer when he or she is declared "righteous through faith for Christ's sake." As a consequence, in later Lutheran theology, "grace and gift are separated and emphasis has been laid on the forensic aspect."[85]

But in contrast to this theology, as noted by the Finnish school, Luther announces God's promise that

we are to become participants of the divine nature and be exalted so high in nobility that we are not only to become loved by God through Christ, and have His favor and grace as the highest and mot precious shrine, but also to have him, the Lord Himself, dwelling in us in His fullness.[86]

According to the Finnish Lutherans, both grace and gift are given in Christian righteousness, through the indwelling and real presence of Christ, which is simultaneous with justification. American theologian Robert Jenson agrees with this assessment: "At least for the initial great Protester himself, God's declaring us holy and his making us actually holy are the same act done by the same means."[87] Righteousness is never just forensic, but is always effective in the lives of those upon whom it is bestowed. "Christ himself, both his person and his work is the Christian righteousness, that is, the 'righteousness of faith.' Christ – and therefore also his entire person and work – is really and truly present in the faith itself."[88] Faith means precisely "participation in the person of Christ,"[89] and even participation in the divine being, essence or nature.[90] "In other words," in Luther's own words (echoing Athanasius), "God becomes man so that man may become God."[91]

[85] Kärkkäinen, *One with God*, p. 56; see Mannermaa, *Christ Present*, pp. 3–6.
[86] Mannermaa, "Justification and Theosis," in Braaten and Jenson (eds.), *Union with Christ*, p. 34, citing "Crucigers Sommerpostille (1544), WA [*Weimarer Ausgabe*] 21, 458: 11–22."
[87] "God's Time, Our Time: An Interview with Robert W. Jenson," *Christian Century*, (May 2, 2006), 31–5, www.religion-online.org/showarticle.asp?titles=3405 (accessed July 14, 2010). See also Robert W. Jenson, "Luther's Contemporary Theological Significance," in Donald K. McKim (ed.), *The Cambridge Companion to Martin Luther* (Cambridge University Press, 2003), pp. 272–88.
[88] Mannermaa, *Christ Present*, p. 5.   [89] Ibid., p. 8.
[90] Mannermaa, "Justification and Theosis," p. 33.
[91] Ibid., citing an early Christmas sermon, *WA 1*, 28, 25–32.

For Jenson, it is better and more true to Luther, as well as to the formative fourteenth-century Byzantine theologian, Gregory Palamas, to avoid language of "essences" and "natures," and instead to focus on the "energies" or activities of the Trinitarian persons' mutual life. Through union with Christ, the believer participates in the mutual love of the Trinity.[92] To hear the gospel preached and participate in the sacraments is to apprehend Christ himself; to apprehend something is to be shaped by it. In the church we apprehend and are conformed to Christ. Luther's use of the word "imputation" (occurring not least of all in *Galatians*) should be understood in the sense of a judgment of fact about the changed reality of our existence, given our new relation to Christ (not a new "nature").[93]

This claim need not undermine the idea that our righteousness is always from Christ, but it does signify that the person's own existence changes because of Christ's presence within it. The characteristics of God that are present in Christ – albeit not without continuing struggle against sin[94] – are "righteousness, wisdom, power, holiness, joy, peace, eternal life – and especially love."[95] Hence the Christian is capable of and will do good works, whose true agent is Christ.[96] The Christian becomes a "Christ" to the neighbor, identifying with his or her suffering, loving without consideration of worthiness, and willingly taking up Christ's cross.[97]

Luther is often recognized for his stress on the faith, conscience, and even "priesthood" of the individual believer, and the Finnish Lutherans likewise tend to envision participation in Christ in terms of individual justification and sanctification. Yet it should be evident from the importance to Luther of the preaching and hearing of the Word in the Spirit, as defining true Christianity, that the church is also central. It is biblically well attested that it is through the sensible media of sight, sound, and touch that Christ is recognized and embraced.[98] "Now wherever you hear or see this Word preached, believed, professed, and lived, do not doubt that the true catholic church: 'a Christian holy people' must be

---

[92] Robert W. Jenson, "Response to Mark Seifrid, Paul Metzger, and Carl Trueman on Finnish Luther Research," *Westminster Theological Journal*, 65 (2003), pp. 246–7.

[93] Ibid., p. 248.

[94] Mannerma, *Christ Present in Faith*, pp. 20, 63–71; citing, e.g., *Lectures on Galatians*, *LW* 26: 134; 27: 72–3.

[95] Mannermaa, "Justification and Theosis," p. 35.

[96] Ibid., p. 50.

[97] Kärrkäinen, *One with God*, pp. 58–61.

[98] Paul Helm, "Senses, Intellect and Spirit," *American Theological Inquiry*, 3 (2010), pp. 4–7.

there, even though their number is small."⁹⁹ Luther also retained great significance for the sacraments of baptism and eucharist.

The priesthood of all is bestowed through faith and baptism, but ministerial offices are necessary to guarantee faithful preaching of the Word and administration of the sacraments,¹⁰⁰ implying the social life of the church as the premise of the bestowal of grace. The sacraments are external signs through which the Holy Spirit brings forgiveness; the inward experience is effected by the outward.¹⁰¹ The experience of the Holy Spirit in the church through word and sacraments is the experience of union with Christ. In turn, the quality of personal and ecclesial life is renewed. Especially in Luther's later work, he develops an appreciation for incremental growth in righteousness and the agency it requires.¹⁰²

Simo Peura, a scholar of the Finnish school, turns to Luther's *Large Catechism* to illustrate that Christians undergo existential change in a communal process of conversion and formation. The *Large Catechism* includes an exposition of the Ten Commandments, followed by an explanation of the Nicene Creed. The creed professes that the Holy Spirit produces faith in Christ and enables us to receive Christ and all his gifts. To this end, the Spirit first leads us into the community of the church, then reveals Christ's work to us through the preaching of the word, effecting faith and bestowing salvation.¹⁰³

The effects of the Spirit's work go beyond the individual to changed relations among fellow Christians; it also motivates and enables activism of the church in the form of service, as well as on behalf of social and structural changes. Here we see in Luther, at the practical level, a move that is similar to Augustine's exhortations to political action in letters and homilies and his own efforts to change Roman social policies. For Luther similarly, Christian *diakonia* entails a responsibility to distribute aid to

⁹⁹ Martin Luther, *On the Councils and the Church* (1539), *LW* 41: 150, as cited by Dennis Ngien, "Theology of Preaching in Martin Luther," *Themelios*, 28 (Spring 2003), pp. 28–48, at 28.
¹⁰⁰ Paul S. Chung, *The Spirit of God Transforming Life: The Reformation and Theology of the Holy Spirit* (New York: Palgrave Macmillan, 2009), p. 125. See also Fred W. Meuser, "Luther as Preacher of the Word of God," in McKim (ed.), *Cambridge Companion to Martin Luther*, pp. 136–48.
¹⁰¹ Scott Hendrix, "Luther," in David Bagchi and David C. Steinmetz (eds.), *Cambridge Companion to Reformation Theology* (Cambridge University Press, 2006), pp. 39–56, at 54, 51; Cambridge Collections Online, cco.cambridge.org/uid=1925/extract?id=ccol0521816483_CCOL0521816483A003 (accessed July 14, 2010).
¹⁰² Mary Gaebler, "Luther on the Self," *Journal of the Society of Christian Ethics*, 22 (Fall 2002), p. 116.
¹⁰³ Simo Peura, "What God Gives Man Receives: Luther on Salvation," in Braaten and Jenson (eds.), *Union with Christ*, pp. 76–95, at 90.

the poor. To this end, parishes should choose a pastor and found a common chest. Through this fund, the people of the parish can have access to resources for basic needs; pool assets in times of scarcity; facilitate purchases, loans, and grants; and encourage education and the building of schools. The common chest offers a local economic alternative to serfdom and the exploitation of the poor.[104]

Although Luther betrayed his own social principles by urging the violent repression of the Peasants' War (a revolt against socioeconomic oppression), he was otherwise a tireless foe of the greed and financial monopolies that characterized early capitalism. He railed against unfair trade practices and usury, calling for more government control. In *Trade and Usury* (1524) and other works, Luther argues for change toward structural justice, and urges state and church to work together to limit the scope and effects of avaricious practices that ruin small businesses and turn traders into "a dangerous class."[105]

There is abundant evidence, then, not only that for Luther justification signals an incipient process of transformation of the believer in the Spirit, but that this process is communal and ecclesial in nature and produces social-structural results. Conversely, Luther is not unmindful of the fact that communal, ecclesial conditions affect the quality of worship and the true proclamation of the gospel. It is certainly well known that Luther's insistence on "justification by faith alone" was in great part a response to what he regarded as unfaithful Catholic practices such as the sale of indulgences, clerical unchastity, and the multiplication of ecclesial rules and regulations (and of dispensations from same). All of these undermined the authenticity of the gospel message and produced a false theology of works righteousness, while placing institutional control of the life of faith over the personal conviction of believers. Luther sees, as Aquinas seems not to, that corrupt social-ethical and ecclesial relations can interfere with the authentic preaching of the word and celebration of the sacraments, and hence with the life of faith. One of Luther's opening salvos was against "the Babylonian captivity of the church" on the grounds that it prevents the faithful's appreciation of "the glory of baptism and the blessedness of Christian liberty."[106] Luther rejected the

---

[104] Chung, *Spirit of God Transforming Life*, pp. 124–8, citing *The Preface to the Leisnig Ordinance of a Common Chest* (1523), *LW* 45: 161–46, 191.

[105] Ibid., p. 129, citing *LW* 45: 171–2, 245.

[106] Martin Luther, *The Babylonian Captivity of the Church*, in *Three Treatises* (Minneapolis: Fortress Press, 1970), p. 196.

Catholic theology of the "sacrifice" of the mass, on the grounds that the eucharist does not consist in human, propitiatory action, but in "the work of God who stoops down to give us gifts that we cannot obtain for ourselves."[107] Even for Luther, God's gift of grace sanctifies, producing (rather than produced by) sacrifices: "sacrifices are rendered in the bodily life of the believer as his or her life is a channel of God's love and care for the neighbor in need."[108]

Such rereadings of Luther are supported by revisionist work on the letters of Paul.[109] Paul should not simply be read through the lens of later perspectives, including Luther's, that put an almost exclusive emphasis on "justification by faith," understood as an inward personal conversion of the individual. For Paul, Luther's most important biblical mentor, the community of the church as body of Christ is essential to salvation, and not only as a collection of individuals whose interiority has been similarly changed. In contrast to traditional theologies of forensic justification via imputation of righteousness to individual sinners, Paul's model of justification is strongly communal and even apocalyptic, in the gospel sense outlined in Chapter 3. It is important not to read what may have been Luther's concern with personal conscience and salvation back into Paul, who, as a Jew, was above all concerned about God's covenant people and the terms of its expansion to include Gentiles. Furthermore, a socially attuned reading of Paul's theology of justification can become a new lens through which to appreciate similar undercurrents in Luther.

If the communal dimension of Paul's view of salvation in Christ is brought back to Luther, that can help contemporary interpreters to expand the social investment and effect of a Lutheran social ethics. Douglas Harink makes this recommendation to the Finnish theologians. Harink takes the potential of a Lutheran ethics beyond individual sanctification to worldwide social impact, in much the manner of Gregory and Mathewes interpreting Augustine. Harink reminds us that for Paul, salvation is a community affair, and one that brings practical consequences. "God's *apokalypsis* is not only a showing, but also a doing which effects

[107] John T. Pless, "Vocation: Where Liturgy and Ethics Meet," *Journal of Lutheran Ethics* (May 2002), para. 9, www.elca.org/What-We-Believe/Social-Issues/Journal-of-Lutheran-Ethics/Issues/May-2002/Vocation-Where-Liturgy-and-Ethics-Meet.aspx (accessed April 9, 2012).

[108] Ibid., para. 19.

[109] For a concise introduction to some of the debates, see N. T. Wright, "New Perspectives on Paul," *10th Edinburgh Dogmatics Conference* (August 25–8, 2003), www.ntwrightpage.com/Wright_New_Perspectives.htm (accessed April 9, 2012). See also N. T. Wright, *Justification: God's Plan and Paul's Vision* (London: SPCK, 2009).

what is shown."[110] God's act of justification inaugurates a new creation, one that "is always cultural, corporate and political in nature."[111] Hence human struggles for social and structural justice can claim as their warrant and power the prior action of God.[112]

On the whole, then, original research on Luther's theology makes a credible case that sanctification or regeneration already begins with justification. In the very act of faith that grace makes possible, existential change is worked, experienced, and manifest.[113] There are good reasons to take Luther's soteriology beyond the personal to the ecclesial and political realms. Conformity to Christ in the Spirit requires the liturgy of the Word; it is expressed as relations of love and care among church members, in a more Christ-like fulfillment of one's worldly vocation, and in Christian advocacy for more just social practices and institutions.

Yet given the undeniably Augustinian tenor of Luther's political ethics, it is necessary to add a caveat: a realistic appraisal of human sinfulness has always been and remains a distinctive and necessary contribution of the Augustinian trajectory in Christian social thought. Luther's own theology and ethics are dialectical and paradoxical. Even if we are newly created by the indwelling of Christ, Luther's idea of "imputation" conveys that human nature is at some level incorrigible. Expressing his difficulty with the Finnish Lutherans, Mark Seifrid confesses, "I cannot help but affirm that there is an irreducible minimum of content in the Gospel where the human being guilty of sin and condemned meets God the justifier and savior of sinners."[114]

Alongside gratitude to Christ, celebration of the Spirit, and hope that Christians become Christs to others, Luther gives his theology of the cross a central place. To participate in Christ's saving work is to be conformed to Christ's cross as well as his resurrection. A genuine Christian or theologian "is one who can see God at work in suffering and in the cross, just as

---

[110] Douglas Harink, *Paul among the Postliberals: Pauline Theology beyond Christendom and Modernity* (Grand Rapids, MI: Brazos Press, 2003), pp. 68, 69.

[111] Douglas Harink, "Setting It Right: Doing Justice to Justification," *Christian Century*, 122 (June 14, 2005), p. 25.

[112] See also Philip G. Ziegler, "Justification and Justice: The Promising *Problematique* of Protestant Ethics in the Work of Paul L. Lehmann," in Mark Husbands and Daniel J. Treier (eds.), *Justification: What's at Stake in the Current Debates* (Downers Grove, IL: InterVarsity Press, 2004), pp. 118–33.

[113] See Bruce L. McCormack, "What's at Stake in Current Debates over Justification? The Crisis of Protestantism in the West," in Husbands and Treier (eds.), *Justification: What's at Stake*, pp. 81–117, at 94.

[114] Mark A. Seifrid, "Paul, Luther, and Justification in Gal. 2:15–21," *Westminster Theological Journal*, 65 (2003), p. 228.

God was condemning sin and saving humanity through the suffering and death of Christ."[115] Luther follows Augustine in affirming that all humans remain sinners always. Living the Christian life entails suffering, as we contend with the evil in our own hearts, the evil afflicting our neighbor, and the evil that always finds its way into the most "just" institutions.

Next we turn to three contemporary theologians who bring together elements of Word and Spirit Christologies to form distinctive versions of a Christian politics of liberation throughout the world.

WORD AND SPIRIT: RECONCILED IN PRACTICE

The irreducible variety of confessions and claims about Christ is validated, tested, reconciled, and played out in liturgy, prayer, and practical discipleship as well as in theological inquiry. "Pro-Nicene" theology in general understood the participation of creatures in the Creator to be mysterious and incomprehensible.[116] Progress toward it requires a discipline and practice that reshape the imagination and one's way of being in the world.[117]

The interdependence of Word and Spirit Christologies is visible in the work of three contemporary theologians: Jürgen Moltmann, Elizabeth Johnson, and Anselm Kyongsuk Min. All are concerned with the global political responsibilities of Christian discipleship and theology. Similar in that they write from "first world" cultures in the North Atlantic context, they are different in being male, European, and Protestant; female, North American, and Roman Catholic; and male, first-generation Korean American, and Roman Catholic with explicitly interreligious concerns.

Moltmann's primary ethical focus is creation and ecology; Johnson's focus is the liberation of women; and Min's focus is the need for a "post-modern" theology of liberation that can create justice and solidarity across ethnic, racial, cultural, and religious differences. Each addresses oppression and suffering in the global environment. For each, a theology of the Spirit is an integral part of christology and serves specifically as a link to moral concerns, in conjunction with gospel indications of a "politics" of Jesus to be developed for a contemporary audience. Each also incorporates strengths of a traditional Word christology, especially the divinity of Jesus Christ as a premise of participation in the life of God and of broad social transformation.

---

[115] See Hendrix, "Luther," p. 45.
[116] Lewis Ayres, *Nicaea and Its Legacy: An Approach to Fourth-Century Trinitarian Theology* (Oxford: Oxford University Press, 2004), p. 319.
[117] Ibid., p. 434.

The emphases are different. The Spirit has become increasingly integral to Moltmann's originally christocentric work, as the one who realizes for us the presence and future of God.[118] Johnson's christology develops around a paradigm of God's Word or Wisdom or "Sophia" that is embodied in Jesus, as well as energetically present as Spirit throughout a world in need of hope and healing.[119] Min proposes a theological paradigm of "solidarity of others in the body of Christ," which allows the Spirit to be front and center in his presentation of Christ. By the power of the Spirit, Christian communities and their praxis are sustained by Christ's risen body, "eschatologically transformed."[120]

All three identify an experience of evil and human suffering that becomes the occasion for a liberative theology of salvation in Jesus Christ, grounded not in abstractions but in the powerful experience of God's presence. Moltmann poignantly and repeatedly recounts his own history as a young German prisoner of war, consumed by his belated grasp of his country's role in the destruction of Jews and crushed by shame, guilt and despair.[121] His christology speaks existentially to the sin of oppressors as well as the innocence of victims, the "hell of guilt" as well as the "hell of suffering."[122] Johnson, on the other hand, is most accountable to the "radical suffering" of women and other victims of violence and degradation who are virtually destroyed by the evil of immense injustices that grip them in a personal and soul-destroying way.[123] Yet the christologies of both are ultimately joyful and celebratory, full of hope in the love and power of God.

Min's tone is more sober in expectation and more attentive to the continuing power of sin in the world, though he also has the widest possible expectations of the presence of the Spirit in history. He dedicates his first book "to all the anonymous sisters and brothers struggling on the liberation front throughout the world, often languishing and dying in jails."[124]

---

[118] Jürgen Moltmann, *The Spirit of Life: A Universal Affirmation*, trans. Margaret Kohl (Minneapolis: Fortress Press, 2001); and Moltmann, *The Source of Life*.

[119] Elizabeth A. Johnson, *She Who Is: The Mystery of God in Feminist Theological Discourse* (New York: Crossroad, 1994), p. 135.

[120] Anselm Kyongsuk Min, *The Solidarity of Others in a Divided World: A Postmodern Theology after Postmodernism* (New York: T & T Clark, 2004), p. 146; see p. 148 on the Spirit and the body of Christ.

[121] For example, Moltmann, *The Source of Life*, pp. 1–9; Jürgen Moltmann, *Jesus Christ for Today's World*, trans. Margaret Kohl (Minneapolis: Fortress Press, 1994), pp. 2–3.

[122] Moltmann, *Jesus Christ for Today's World*, p. 143.

[123] Johnson, *She Who Is*, p. 249.

[124] Anselm Kyongsuk Min, *Dialectic of Salvation: Issues in Theology of Liberation* (Albany: State University of New York Press, 1989), p. x.

In his second book, he criticizes Moltmann for ignoring "conflict and negation" and lacking a "political praxis."[125] While this in my view is not a fair criticism of Moltmann, it does reveal Min's first priority: solidarity in an ongoing "emancipatory quest for structures of justice" that does not shrink from or minimize the difficulty of the challenge.[126]

MOLTMANN

Moltmann's theology is Trinitarian, eschatological, and hopeful of salvation as initiating liberation in this world. God is a living and dynamic community, one that is immanent in creation and history, drawing into God all of creation, through God's life-creating Spirit.[127] Building on his own experience of "forsakenness," Moltmann proposes a "solidarity christology" in which God takes on and thus heals "our vulnerable and mortal existence," including guilt and despair.[128] Politics and ethics are essential to Moltmann, grounded in the life, death, and resurrection of Jesus Christ, referred to Jesus' ministry to "the poor" and focused through the kingdom of God.[129] Christ's presence is experienced in the Spirit, the giver of life,[130] who is also a distinct divine person. Moltmann rejects the disputed *filioque* clause of the Nicene Creed as suggesting a questionable subordination of the Spirit to the Son and as in any event redundant and unnecessarily provocative, since the Spirit and the Son are always reciprocal and co-defining.[131]

Noting (like Johnson) the compatibility and sometimes interchangeability of biblical uses of "Word," "Wisdom," and "Spirit" in relation to creation, Moltmann affirms the agency of both Spirit and Christ in creation and in its renewal.[132] "Everything has its genesis in a fundamental underlying unity, which is called God's Wisdom, Spirit or

---

[125] Min, *Solidarity of Others*, pp. 210–11.

[126] Ibid., p. 219.

[127] For an excellent critical overview, see M. Douglas Meeks, "Jürgen Moltmann's Systematic Contributions to Theology," *Religious Studies Review*, 22 (1996), pp. 95–102; and Jürgen Moltmann's response, "The Adventure of Theological Ideas," same issue, pp. 102–5.

[128] Moltmann, *The Spirit of Life*, p. 8.

[129] Moltmann, *Jesus Christ for Today's World*, pp. 7–29; Moltmann, "The Adventure of Theological Ideas," pp. 102–3; and Jürgen Moltmann, *The Way of Jesus Christ: Christology in Messianic Dimensions*, trans. Margaret Kohl (Minneapolis: Fortress Press, 1993), pp. 42–3.

[130] Moltmann, *The Way of Jesus Christ*, p. 41. See also Moltmann, "The Trinitarian Personhood of the Holy Spirit," in Bradford E. Hinze and D. Lyle Dabney (eds.), *Advents of the Spirit: An Introduction to the Current Critical Study of Pneumatology* (Milwaukee, WI: Marquette University, 2001), p. 304.

[131] Moltmann, *The Spirit of Life*, pp. 306–9; Moltmann, *The Source of Life*, pp. 17, 37.

[132] Moltmann, *Jesus Christ for Today's World*, pp. 286–90.

Word."[133] "The mediators of creation – the Spirit and the Word – wait and strive in everything for the liberation of all things."[134] Creation, redemption, and renewal are a unity.[135]

Moltmann relies on Spirit imagery to communicate the participation in the life of God that underlies the hopeful, anticipatory transformation of human relations in history, to one another and to "nature." Since the Spirit exists in fellowship with the Father and the Son, the fellowship of the Holy Spirit with us (2 Cor. 13:13) "corresponds to his eternal divine fellowship," and in fact "*is* that very fellowship itself."[136] "Our limited human lives participate in the eternal circular movement of the divine life."[137] From the church "gathered" for worship, Christians are sent out for vocations in society,[138] envisioning and practicing "the new creation of all things" (Rev. 1:1–6).[139] God's indwelling sanctifies all creation according to the norm of the kingdom of God, through the Spirit.

JOHNSON

The point of departure of Elizabeth Johnson is the suffering of women and the realization that symbols and metaphors used to communicate the mystery of God also endorse certain patterns of human being and relationship. She believes that to retrieve and create feminine imagery for God will dislodge patriarchy. Her Word christology is built around the feminine imagery for God latent in the personification of God as Lady Wisdom in the Hebrew Bible and in New Testament texts that suggest a connection between Jesus and Wisdom. Johnson may even be said to have a "descending" and "preexistence" Christology insofar as Jesus is the embodiment of divine Wisdom, or Sophia. The ethical content of her theology is set forth in close conjunction with Jesus' life, death, and resurrection.

Following Elisabeth Schüssler Fiorenza and others,[140] Johnson maintains that some Pauline letters, as well as texts in the gospels of Matthew

---

[133] Ibid., p. 95.   [134] Ibid., p. 99.
[135] Moltmann, *The Spirit of Life*, p. 9.
[136] Ibid., p. 90.   [137] Ibid., p. 91.   [138] Ibid., p. 95.   [139] Ibid., pp. 93, 117.
[140] Johnson, *She Who Is*, p. 95. Johnson cites Elisabeth Schüssler Fiorenza, *In Memory of Her: A Feminist Reconstruction of Christian Origins* (New York: Crossroad, 1983), p. 133, as well as James Dunn, M. Jack Suggs, and Raymond Brown. A more recent and very relevant work is Elisabeth Schüssler Fiorenza, *Jesus: Miriam's child, Sophia's Prophet: Critical Issues in Feminist Christology* (New York: Continuum, 1994). Another feminist theologian with a similar and complementary argument is Gloria L. Schaab, "The Power of Divine Presence: Toward a *Shekhinah* Christology," in Anne M. Clifford and Anthony Godzieba (eds.), *Christology: Memory, Inquiry, Practice*, College Theology Society Annual Volume, 48 (2002), pp. 92–115.

and John, portray Jesus in terms of the feminine Sophia (Lady Wisdom) of the Hebrew Bible (particularly Prov. 8 and Wis. 7). 1 Corinthians refers explicitly to Jesus as "the wisdom of God" (1:24), while other letters attribute roles or qualities shared with Sophia, such as being the image of God, instrumental in creation (Col. 1:15; 1 Cor. 8:6), and the light of God's glory (Heb. 1:3). Matthew has Jesus defend his characteristic kingdom behavior, befriending "tax collectors and sinners," with the rejoinder "wisdom is vindicated by her deeds" (Matt. 11:19).

In relation to John's prologue, which prefers the language of Word or Logos to Wisdom to suggest the divine status of Jesus Christ, Johnson notes that the book of Wisdom had involved Sophia in the act of creation (9:1–2). The New Testament substitution of "Word" ("Logos") for "Sophia" would have arisen from Jewish thought, especially Philo, and tacitly avoided feminine imagery for Jesus or God.[141] Yet "Jesus Christ is the human being Sophia became."[142] Sophia is linked to the Spirit partly by functions of Wisdom as the Spirit of God and partly by New Testament associations of the Spirit and Jesus Christ (who is Sophia incarnate).

For Johnson the retrieval of a Wisdom christology does not distance Christian faith and practice from the example of Jesus or from the concrete instances of human suffering that salvation heals. The works of Sophia are correlated with the "option for the poor" indicated by Jesus' ministry and his suffering and death, and are especially applied to the liberation of women, an end to which feminine names and roles for the divine lead.[143]

The ability to image Jesus as Sophia or Wisdom provides an important corrective to the tendency to emphasize the wrong historical characteristics of Jesus of Nazareth when defining christology and its implications for Christian practices. In Johnson's feminist christology, the maleness of Jesus of Nazareth is an important part of his historical identity, but not constitutive of his role as the Christ. Johnson repeats the maxim of Gregory Nazianzus, "What is not assumed is not redeemed." The salvific role of Jesus Christ is contingent on his having a human nature, not a specifically male one.[144] Here, the abstraction of Word christology from historical particularity is an asset, as long as it is complemented by integral

---

[141] Johnson, *She Who Is*, p. 98.

[142] Ibid., p. 99. A point that should perhaps be noted more explicitly by Johnson is that, in the Hebrew Bible, Wisdom, while imaged as a woman, is a personification of the divine rather than a distinct divine person. Wisdom, Word, or Logos is a divine being in his or her own right only in Christian tradition.

[143] Ibid., pp. 156–61, 246–73.   [144] Ibid., p. 153.

references to dimensions of the gospels that depict the Christian life with reference to the concrete realities of Jesus' life and of early Christianity.

The tone and tenor of *She Who Is* are full of light and delight. Johnson's aim is to question traditional language about God in order to recover submerged biblical images and metaphors that can communicate with new beauty and power what the liberating and healing presence of God means for all people. "Light dawns, courage is renewed, tears are wiped away, a new moment of life arises."[145] Nevertheless, the crucial point of departure for this quest is human suffering, especially the suffering of women to whom God's compassion is hidden. To speak of the powerful love of Sophia-God "serves as an ally of resistance and a wellspring of hope. But it does so under the rule of darkness and broken words ."[146]

MIN

Min insists that the conditions of the contemporary world demand a renewal of the doctrine of the Holy Spirit. The fact and unacceptability of human suffering mandate practices of resistance and change among the peoples, cultures, and religions of the world.[147]

Min is a Korean immigrant to the United States, and his theology borrows from Korean analogues, particularly those within Minjung theology, an indigenous Christian theology of liberation.[148] Minjung theology discerns the action of the Spirit in the voice of oppressed and marginalized Korean peoples, who suffer the impact of regional struggles for power and who experience high levels of domestic inequality.[149] A culturally specific response to oppression is *han. Han* is "the feeling of outrage at blatant injustice, the sense of helplessness to vindicate oneself, the awareness, however indeterminate, of the moral contradictions and inequities of the existing social structure, and the tenacious hope, often suppressed into resignation, in the ultimate triumph of justice." Theology

[145] Ibid., p. 272.   [146] Ibid.
[147] Min, *Solidarity of Others*, pp. 91–5.
[148] Anselm Kyongsuk Min, "From the Theology of Minjoong to the Theology of the Citizen: Reflections on Minjoong Theology in 21st Century Korea," *Journal of Asian and Asian American Theology*, 5 (Spring 2002), pp. 17–25; and "Asian Theologians," in Donald W. Musser and Joseph L. Price (eds.), *A New Handbook of Christian Theologians* (Nashville: Abingdon, 1996), pp. 22–48.
[149] See James T. Bretzke, S.J., "Cracking the Code: Minjung Theology as an Expression of the Holy Spirit in Korea," *Pacifica*, 10 (1997), pp. 319–30; and "Minjung Theology and Inculturation in the Context of the History of Christianity in Korea," *East Asian Pastoral Review*, 28 (1991), pp. 108–30.

must resolve the *han* of the Minjung without dulling consciousness of injustice, perpetrating masochism, or feeding into cycles of revenge and violence.

The disciple's vocation is to channel "suppressed anger and indignation" into transformative practices of liberation by living "in" and putting "on" Christ (2 Cor. 5:15). [150] This vocation assumes both the incarnational union of the disciple with Christ and the work of the Spirit in the church as the place where that union is realized. The risen body of Christ, experienced socially as the Christian community, concretizes the union of Jesus' humanity with the divine Word.[151] The Spirit calls us to "the solidarity of others in the solidarity of the Son" and forbids Christians "to abdicate the whole realm of politics in the name of human impotence."[152]

Min has a powerful view of the participation of Christians in the divine life and underwrites this participation in both Word and Spirit images. He develops the content of participation beyond personal transformation and spiritual ascent to God, emphasizing the economic and political ramifications of conversion. Gospel memories of Jesus do not establish specific political programs, yet some basic dimensions are clear. Jesus of Nazareth preached the *basileia* (kingdom or reign) of his Father, and its eschatological demand for conversion and a new way of living. This way is characterized by imitation of God's love and mercy, self-sacrifice for others, trust in God's care, freedom from the bonds of wealth and power, and a preferential warning to the rich, as well as preferential action for the poor. Jesus embodied all these values in his own life and death, and is vindicated by being raised from the dead and exalted as Lord, Messiah, and Son of God.[153]

Min raises an important issue for Christian ethics under contemporary conditions of globalization: the *universality* of incorporation into Christ. Is the transformative presence of the Spirit wide enough to make changes in sinful social structures across all cultures and religions? Min is clear that the Spirit acts in the world to "incorporate" all humanity and creation into the Sonship of Christ and reconciliation with God. "The Spirit of divine sonship is also and always the Spirit of universal human solidarity as sisters and brothers in the one family of God the Father."[154] The Spirit, as the Spirit of the risen Lord, seeks to actualize universally what Jesus of Nazareth accomplished in the particularity of his historical life.

---

[150] Min, "Asian Theologians," 28. [151] Min, *Solidarity of Others*, p. 145.
[152] Ibid., pp. 128, 129. [153] Ibid., pp. 96–7. [154] Ibid., p. 99.

Pauline indications for this universalizing solidarity are that the Gentiles are "fellow heirs" of the promise in Christ (Eph. 3:6), that both Jews and Gentiles have access to the Father (Eph. 2:18), and that there is "one Spirit," "one God and Father of us all, who is above all and through all and all" (Eph. 4:4–6).[155] Min links Jesus' preaching and example of the kingdom of God with a universal critique of violations of human dignity that cry out for resistant practices, eschatologically grounded practices that can be shared throughout the religions and cultures of the world.[156] The body of Christ and its action are expansive, because Christ is expansive, "universal," and "eschatological."

Despite differences in ethical accent and symbolic usage, these three theologians support the general point that christologies are motivated by particular experiences of Christian faith and life. Salvation from God in Jesus Christ is salvation from specific kinds of sin and suffering, and is constituted by different concretizations of a renewing relation to God made possible in Christ. Biblical authors and their narratives reflect such differences and provide an inexhaustible resource for mediating and expressing this relationship.

Metaphors of God in Christ as Word and Spirit are among the most powerful of these resources, yet cannot be contained by any one doctrinal formulation. The inspiration and proving ground of Word and Spirit christologies, and especially of their necessary interdependence, is the practical life of the church, including its eucharistic fellowship, personal relationships, communal practices, clarifying discourse, and political engagement. This is as true today as it was for the first believers who brought Jesus Christ within the ambit of their worship of the one true God.

As global experiences of Christianity read and test the scriptures and formulate contextual appropriations of Christ, christology becomes ever more performative, less theoretical and "metaphysical," and less defined by models influential in the past. A challenge that is larger than before, even if not entirely new, is the need for christology to proclaim and understand Christ in a way that relates to other religious traditions appreciatively rather than defensively or antagonistically. In a book on Aquinas, Anselm Min entertains the possibility that, just as in different

---

[155] Ibid.
[156] Min proposes a "confessionalist pluralism of praxis," respecting the integrity of various religions (Ibid., p. 170) but calling them to a "dialogical rationality" (p. 86), and especially to a praxis of liberation on behalf of a common humanity and dignity that has been violated (p. 137).

eras, different "sacraments" suited the Israelites and the Christian church, so different "totalities" of religious symbols and practices might mediate salvation "precisely with their irreducibly particular, historically differentiated contents."[157]

Another point of consideration is the cross-fertilization among traditions in today's global cultures of mass communication, migration, and composite identities. The Indian theologian Felix Wilfred advises, "The question today is: Can Jesus Christ be interpreted in such a way that people who have been sustained by their religious traditions – Hinduism, Buddhism, Taoism, etc. – need not break their spiritual journey to encounter Jesus Christ, but can meet him on their spiritual journey and interpret him as they experience him?"[158]

Such questions cannot be answered theoretically, that is, by deducing answers from doctrines already held about Christ. Divine providence and the mysteries of Word, Christ, and Spirit have a dynamic and inclusive character that cannot be captured in doctrine, within the confines of institutional Christianity, or even within specifically "Christian experience." Wilfred cites "the dark night of suffering of the black people, the humiliations of the 'Untouchables' of India, the experience of marginalization by the indigenous peoples, the anguish of the innocent HIV/AIDS patients and the agonies of the terminally ill" as places where experiences of Jesus Christ and of salvation bring new illuminations, sometimes shattering old certainties.[159] Rather than domesticating christology, we must valorize the appropriation of Christ in other faiths and by the global poor. Wilfred calls for "apophatic Christology" and "contemplative pluralism" that do not deny the unity of God, but refuse to see it as something already given and available to our understanding. Rather, it is "something hidden and forming the object of our continuous quest that is refreshing and transforming."[160]

This and the preceding chapter have traced the ways early Christians began to proclaim Christ as "divine" on the basis of their experiences of him as risen and present in their communities of worship and in their outreach to "the poor," sinners, and Gentiles. I have considered two biblical

[157] Anselm K. Min, *Paths to the Triune God: An Encounter Between Aquinas and Recent Theologies* (University of Notre Dame Press, 2005), p. 106.
[158] Felix Wilfred, "Christological Pluralism: Some Reflections," in Andrés Torres Queiruga, Lisa Sowle Cahill, Maria Clara Bingemer, and Erik Borgman (eds.), *Jesus as Christ: What Is at Stake in Christology?* (London: SCM Press, 2008), p. 86.
[159] Ibid., p. 90.   [160] Ibid., p. 93.

paradigms for maintaining the humanity and divinity of Christ: Jesus Christ as incarnate Word and Jesus Christ as filled with God's Spirit, raised, and exalted. Arguing for renewed attention to Spirit christologies as an asset to contemporary theologies of Christ and to the politics of salvation, the present chapter has uncovered resources for a Spirit-inspired Christian politics in Aquinas and Luther and concluded with a discussion of three theologians who unite elements of Word and Spirit christologies for a global vision of justice.

Christological reflection on salvation in Jesus Christ continues in different social and global locations. The New Testament presents a variety of views of the identity of Jesus Christ, and this pluralism continues in the tradition. Both the bible and the creedal statements of Nicaea and Chalcedon affirm that Jesus Christ is fully human and fully divine, and that humans are saved from evil and sin by God through Jesus Christ. These remain the fundamental norms for subsequent theology. Within those parameters, a variety of approaches and explications are both possible and necessary. No single formulation will ever be adequate to the reality that it indicates. In fact, any single christology will always to some degree misrepresent the mystery of Jesus Christ.

In addition to seeing Christ as human and divine, and as bringing salvation, there are two practical and political norms of christology. Theologies of Christ must cohere with a vision of the reign of God as including an "option for the poor"; and they must actually advance God's reign as making a difference for those who suffer evil and injustice.

Chapter 3 presented Jesus' ministry of the reign of God as establishing the content or the specific practices of the life of salvation and its politics, and also argued that Jesus himself saw God's reign as inbreaking historically. Chapters 4 and 5 showed the value of a theology of the Spirit and a Spirit christology in establishing the power of the church and its members to live in a redeemed way and to promote a global politics of God's reign. At the same time, Word christologies also support a necessary dimension of Christian politics of liberation: we are empowered because the incarnation of God in Jesus Christ gives us a share in God's own life.

Chapter 6 will probe further the question of what specifically Jesus Christ does or has done to enable new life. Perhaps the most biblically prominent answer is that Jesus Christ, as risen and exalted, sends his Spirit to the church. We are united to the body of Christ, in the church, through the power of the Holy Spirit. Another answer, made more explicit and developed by the early councils, is that, as God incarnate, Jesus Christ unites our human nature with its divine source. Chapter 6 will take up the answer that has perhaps been most salient in Christian piety through the ages, yet has become the most problematic today: Jesus Christ saves us from sin by his death on a cross. The question before us is, How can Jesus' death on a cross be related to the reconciliation of human beings to God and neighbor, and to liberation for practices of the kingdom, by the power of the Spirit?

CHAPTER 6

Cross

"Was it not necessary that the Christ should suffer these things?" (Luke 24:26). This tormenting question has bedeviled Christians down to the present day. Multiple answers have been given, no one of which is fully satisfying. This is one reason the key plank of Christian faith, salvation in Jesus Christ, has never been explained definitively by any creed or council. *That* we are saved is clear; *how* we are saved is not. What is particularly elusive is the precise relation between Jesus' suffering death and human salvation from God.

We saw in the preceding two chapters that there are at least two central biblical models for understanding Christ, incarnation of the Word and embodiment of God's Spirit, and that present salvation is the consequence of the unity of God with our humanity. Through the incarnation, we are "divinized" by a share in the divine nature. Or, through the sending of the Spirit by the risen Jesus, we too taste resurrection and are empowered to live a Spirit-filled existence in a filial relation to God. Is the cross even necessary for our salvation? Is salvation despite, and not because of, the cross?

Until the mid–twentieth century, the reigning Western paradigm of Christian salvation was the Anselmian theory of Christ's death as atoning for sinful humanity by paying a debt to God. Recent liberationist, feminist, and antimilitarist theologies strongly critique personal and structural violence, leading many to reject the atonement paradigm as sacralizing violence. Robert J. Daly insists that the "assumption of the necessity of Christ's suffering resulted in and/or went along with false ideas about God. Such false ideas about God and a consequent false morality

Parts of this chapter are based on the following works: "The Atonement Paradigm: Does It Still Have Explanatory Value?" *Theological Studies*, 68 (2007), pp. 418–32; "Celebrate the Mystery You Imitate," in Martin Stuflesser and Stephan Winter (eds.), *'Ahme nach, was du vollziehst …': Positionsbestimmungen zum Verhaltnis von Liturgie und Ethik* (Regensburg: Friedrich Pustet, 2009), pp. 137–49.

are inevitable if the scapegoating death of Jesus is a necessary, divinely planned, transactional sacrificial event that God brings about like a puppet master manipulating human events."[1]

Feminist and womanist theologians give voice to what is now a frequent and justified complaint: "The disciple's role is to suffer in the place of others, as Jesus suffered for us all. But this glorification of suffering as salvific, held before us daily in the image of Jesus hanging from the cross, encourages women who are being abused to be more concerned about their victimizer than about themselves."[2] Roger Haight speaks for many when he expresses doubt about atonement theories that make salvation available through the cross, "indirectly make Jesus' death something good,"[3] and engender a spirituality that is fascinated by suffering. He objects to theologies that portray God as willing that Jesus suffer and that make the cross metaphysically "necessary," "according to a concept of the transcendent order of justice."[4]

Indeed, a chorus of voices objects that the atonement paradigm sanctifies violence (Denny Weaver, Stephen Finlan); worships a divine sadist (Dorothee Soelle); turns God into an omnipotent child abuser (Rita Nakashima Brock); encourages women to be scapegoats (Mary Daly); depoliticizes and spiritualizes the cross, obscuring its real cause, Jesus' praxis (Elisabeth Schüssler Fiorenza); speaks no word of salvation to African American women and others resisting oppression (Delores Williams); and provides murderous fanatics, fascists, and torturers with validating symbols (Jürgen Moltmann, Mark Taylor).[5]

---

[1] Robert J. Daly, S.J., "Images of God and the Imitation of God: Problems with Atonement," *Theological Studies*, 68 (2007), pp. 48–9.

[2] Joanne C. Brown and Rebecca Parker, "For God So Loved the World?" in Joanne C. Brown and Carole R. Bohn (eds.), *Christianity, Patriarchy, and Abuse* (New York: Pilgrim Press, 1989), p. 8.

[3] Roger Haight, S.J., *The Future of Christology* (New York: Continuum, 2005), p. 78.

[4] Ibid., p. 80.

[5] J. Denny Weaver, *The Nonviolent Atonement* (Grand Rapids, MI: Eerdmans, 2001); Stephen Finlan, *Problems with Atonement: The Origins of, and Controversy About, the Atonement* (Collegeville, MN: Liturgical Press, 2005); Dorothee Sölle, *Leiden* (Stuttgart: Kreuz, 1973), p. 38; and Elga Sorge, *Religion und Frau: Weibliche Spiritualität im Christentum* (Stuttgart: Kohlhammer, 1985), p. 43, as cited by Jürgen Moltmann, *The Way of Jesus Christ: Christology in Messianic Dimensions* (Minneapolis: Fortress Press, 1993), pp. 175–6; Rita Nakashima Brock, "And a Little Child Shall Lead Us: Christology and Child Abuse," in Brown and Bohn (eds.), *Christianity, Patriarchy and Abuse*, pp. 42–61; Mary Daly, *Beyond God the Father: Toward a Philosophy of Women's Liberation* (Boston: Beacon Press, 1973), p. 77; Elisabeth Schüssler Fiorenza, *Jesus: Miriam's Child, Sophia's Prophet: Critical Issues in Feminist Christology* (New York: Continuum, 1994), pp. 98–107; Delores S. Williams, *Sisters in the Wilderness: The Challenge of Womanist God-Talk* (Maryknoll, NY: Orbis Press, 1993); Jürgen Moltmann, "The Cross as Military Symbol for Sacrifice," in Marit Trelstad (ed.), *Cross Examinations: Readings on the Meaning of the Cross Today* (Minneapolis: Augsburg Fortress, 2006), pp. 259–63; Mark Lewis Taylor, "American Torture and the Body of Christ: Making and Remaking Worlds," in the same volume, pp. 264–77.

Christians today often respond to the fact of the cross by explaining it as a historical consequence of Jesus' life and ministry rather than as a divine or theological necessity. Many also explain cross-centered Christian piety by interpreting the cross as a symbol of God's solidarity with the innocent victims of injustice. These strategies are valid in themselves. But are they adequate? One problem is that they fail to account for the role of the cross in the conversion and transformation of sinners and oppressors. Yet this effect is central in biblical sources, especially the letters of Paul. Another problem is that they fail to explain the appeal to oppressed people themselves of the cross not only as God's accompaniment of suffering, but also as taking away sin. This piety needs to be engaged receptively as well as interrogated before its value is assessed by academic theologians.

Legitimate moral objections to some uses of sacrifice and atonement will be discussed in this chapter. Yet I will argue that these symbolic matrices can be reconstrued and validated in theologies of salvation that address both the hope of human liberation and the facts of human guilt and despair. They follow complex biblical narratives of salvation that in turn reflect the real multivocity of human experiences of sin, suffering, and salvation, as well as the mysterious character of God's healing presence in Christ.

I believe that, like christologies, soteriologies should remain pluralistic. The plurality of metaphors for redemption in the bible and tradition are more than an indicator of the cultural diversity of authors and audiences, and more than accommodation to the limits of human understanding. This plurality, Trevor Hart suggests, "points to the multi-faceted nature of the redemptive activity of God itself," of "the fullness of God's saving activity in Christ and the spirit." We risk losing sight of this full and multidimensional activity of the divine in human life unless we continually refer to a dialectical array of metaphors, narratives, and concepts of salvation.[6] Looking at the cross from the experience of poor, rural Latina women, Barbara Reid notes that metaphors for the cross can lead in both dangerous and positive directions. She concludes that from the perspective of resurrection faith, the complex and varied meanings of the cross can come together in a "journey in relationship with the One whose love is not extinguished even by death."[7]

---

[6] Trevor Hart, "Redemption and Fall," in Colin E. Gunton (ed.), *The Cambridge Companion to Christian Doctrine* (New York: Cambridge University, 1997), pp. 189–206, at 190. See also Matthew M. Boulton, "Cross Purposes," *Harvard Divinity Bulletin*, 34 (2006), pp. 101–7. Boulton reviews several recent works on atonement, emphasizing the coexistence of diverse models in the bible, tradition, and contemporary theology.

[7] Barbara E. Reid, O.P., *Taking Up the Cross: New Testament Interpretations through Latina and Feminist Eyes* (Minneapolis: Fortress Press, 2007), p. 183.

The cross is never salvific alone, as a human, historical event of unjust accusation, state torture, and capital punishment. The human, historical event of the cross is a humanly caused evil, suffered by a human person, Jesus of Nazareth, and his friends and loved ones, as well as by the human, historical perpetrators. Nevertheless, as an African American theologian insists, there is "power in the blood,"[8] spiritually, liturgically, theologically, and politically. A model of salvation through sacrificial love, embodied on the cross, can and does have transformative moral and political value if (and only if) linked with a vibrant belief in the incarnation and resurrection.

The present reappropriation of the cross as atonement will begin with New Testament soteriologies, showing the interpenetration and complementarity of incarnational and sacrificial themes. Next, following Richard Southern, I will try to recover Anselm from the "Anselmians." Anselm himself focused not on the death of Christ or on divine appeasement but on Jesus' unbreakable relationship with God as restoring the harmony of creation. Anselm's soteriology will be complemented by that of Julian of Norwich, for whom the cross represents God's persistent love. Then five criteria for atonement soteriologies will be offered and developed in relation to contemporary theologians of liberation and justice. The basic argument will be that the cross as atonement must speak both to victims and to perpetrators and must be kept together with incarnation and resurrection.

In the end, the meaning of the cross cannot be grasped fully through conceptual analysis and systematic theology. Instead, salvation and the cross must be appropriated, tested, and integrated through the kinds of Christian practices (liturgy and ethics) within which New Testament metaphors for salvation were generated in the first place.[9] The practical liturgical and social significance of atonement theologies will be demonstrated by recent revisions of the Catholic Good Friday rite.

BIBLICAL PERSPECTIVES ON CROSS AND SALVATION

The first Jewish Christians found explanatory models of Jesus' suffering and death close at hand in their martyrological traditions, in temple sacrifice, and in the liturgy of the Day of Atonement, lending to

[8] JoAnne Marie Terrell, "Our Mothers' Gardens: Rethinking Sacrifice," in Trelstad (ed.), *Cross-Examinations*, p. 37.
[9] See Richard N. Longenecker, *New Wine into Fresh Wineskins: Contextualizing the Early Christian Confessions* (Peabody, MA: Hendrickson, 1999).

interpretations of Christ's suffering death as expiation for sin.[10] One of
the most prolific and imaginative of early theologians of Christ's death,
the apostle Paul, created a rich yet hardly coherent matrix of interpretive
metaphors, among which atoning sacrifice is prominent. Sinners are saved
by Jesus Christ, "whom God put forward as a sacrifice of atonement by
his blood" (Rom. 3:25). "God proves his love for us in that while we were
still sinners Christ died for us. Much more surely then, now that we have
been justified by his blood, will we be saved through him from the wrath
of God" (Rom. 5:8–9).

Paul's view of Christ and salvation, as well as his apostolic role, are
inspired by the revelation to him of the risen Christ, who calls him to
cease opposition to the Christian movement and bring the gospel to the
Gentiles (Gal. 1:15–16; 1 Cor. 9:1). According to Frank Matera, the notion
of a crucified messiah could only have been a contradiction in terms to
Paul before this point, since the Jewish law and scriptures held that "God's
curse rests on him who hangs on a tree" (Deut. 21, 23; cf. Gal. 3:13). While
this "curse" had once referred to exposed corpses of capital criminals, in
the first century it was taken to mean crucifixion as the method of execution.[11] In Paul's eyes originally, Jesus had died a shameful death, possibly
as a penalty for violating God's law.

After his conversion experience, Paul was forced to ask what the meaning of Christ's death could have been, if he had met such an end yet was
the one whom God had "established as Son of God in power" (Rom. 1:4).
Paul answers this question in a complex way, utilizing multiple sources in
Jewish and biblical tradition, as well as early Christian formulas and confessions, weaving them together around the shocking and enigmatic fact
of the crucifixion. "For I handed on to you as of first importance what I
in turn had received: that Christ died for our sins in accordance with the
scriptures, and that he was buried, and that he was raised on the third
day in accordance with the scriptures" (1 Cor. 15:3–4). The cause of the
original problem – Jesus' ignominious execution – is seen in light of resurrection and salvation. It then becomes the focus of the kerygmatic and

[10] See, e.g., Gerard S. Sloyan, *Why Jesus Died* (Minneapolis: Fortress Press, 2004), pp. 80–100;
Stephen J. Patterson, *Beyond the Passion: Rethinking the Death and Life of Jesus* (Minneapolis:
Fortress Press, 2004), pp. 70–82; Frank J. Matera, "Christ in the Theologies of Paul and John: A
Study in the Diverse Unity of New Testament Theology," *Theological Studies*, 67 (2006), p. 244;
and Finlan, *Problems with Atonement*, pp. 31–8. For a discussion of the death of Christ generally
in the gospel, see Raymond E. Brown, *The Death of the Messiah: From Gethsemane to the Grave –
A Commentary on the Passion Narratives in the Four Gospels*, 2 vols. (New York: Doubleday,
1994).
[11] Matera, "Christ in Paul and John," p. 241.

theological solution. The cross is "foolishness" and a "stumbling block" to Gentiles and Jews, but to those who have tasted eschatological salvation from God, the cross reveals the wisdom of God and God's strength (1 Cor. 1:18–25). Paul's presentation of this insight is internally pluralistic.[12] It is more evocative and provocative than it is systematic. Its coherence is not so much logical as it is affective, symbolic, and spiritual.

Christ died "for our sins"; clearly Paul understood Christ's death to be redemptive. The mechanism of redemption through Christ's death involves some sort of an exchange, through his humanity, with human sinners. The nature of this exchange is captured in various metaphors and allusions, rather than spelled out precisely. Christ died for "me," for us and for all, even the ungodly (Gal. 2:20; Rom. 5:8; 2 Thess. 5:9–10; 2 Cor. 5:14; Rom. 5:6). He gave himself for our sins to rescue us from the present evil age (Gal. 1:4), ransomed us from the curse of the law by becoming a curse in our stead (Gal. 3:13), and was set forth by God as the place of atonement or expiation for sins (Rom. 3:25).[13] Christ as God's Son was "sent in the likeness of sinful flesh" (Rom. 8:3), and was even made by God "to be sin,"[14] so that in Christ we could become God's righteousness (2 Cor. 5:21). The death of Christ is an interchange between God and humanity; humans can become a new creation (2 Cor. 5:14–15). The message of the cross is a message of reconciliation.[15]

The metaphor of Christ as sacrifice is central to Paul's view that salvation reconciles us to God. As a Jew, Paul drew on the meanings of Hebrew sacrifice. Yet, as one whose primary mission successes were with Gentiles, he was also well attuned to the sacrificial traditions and practices of non-Jewish peoples.[16] From Jewish tradition, he adapted the idea that the death of a martyr could be efficacious for many (1 Macc. 2–5; 2 Macc. 5:12–14, 24–26; 6; 7). Integral to his own religious environment was also the daily practice of temple sacrifice, intended to show respect and obedience to God, as well as to turn aside the effects of impurity and

---

[12] Elisabeth Schüssler Fiorenza discusses six "interpretive strategies" that are "embedded in the Pauline literature" about Jesus' death, and these are not exhaustive. Schüssler Fiorenza, *Jesus: Miriam's Child, Sophia's Prophet*, pp. 111–19.

[13] Matera, "Christ in Paul and John," p. 243.

[14] What is the meaning of this? Matera suggests that Christ either "fully entered into the human condition, which was under the power of sin and which he overcame," or that his death "was an offering for sin" ("Christ in Paul and John," p. 243, n. 18). Certainly both of these are true. Later I will develop the point that Christ enters fully into the human condition, accepting even to share with us the guilt, alienation, and desolation of sin.

[15] Frank J. Matera, *New Testament Theology: Exploring Diversity and Unity* (Louisville, KY: Westminster John Knox Press, 2007), pp. 140–1.

[16] Finlan, *Problems with Atonement*, p. 11.

sin, and open the way to God's favor. The Passover lamb was a special instance of sacrifice, alluding to the roots of Jewish identity in the exodus from Egypt. In the Jewish cult, and not only in the New Testament, the meanings of sacrifice are various and are dialectically related. Generally, sacrifice represents the people, striving to leave offenses behind and become "pure." The focus is not on God's demand or "anger," but on making offerings pleasing to God, and even on God's providing the sacrifice (cf. the binding of Isaac in Gen. 22; Rom. 3:25).[17] In Jewish tradition, there was already a development toward the "spiritualization" of sacrifice, in which motivations and moral transformation become more important than the ritual itself or the specific sacrificial offering.[18]

In referring to Christ as the place of expiation for sin, Paul is drawing on the imagery of the Day of Atonement (Lev. 16), when the high priest enters the Holy of Holies (referring not to the Jerusalem Temple but to the tabernacle of the desert wanderings) to expiate for his own sins and those of the people by sprinkling blood over the cover of the ark of the covenant. This sacrifice is neither a punishment nor a compensation given to God. It is an act of ritual purification or cleansing that expiates sin. Through the sacrifice, sins are "wiped away." Like the ancestors of old, Christians are a pilgrim people, waiting for God's final deliverance. Christ is the new place where God effects atonement for sins, now by sprinkling Christ's own blood. (Similar imagery is employed in Heb. 9:1–10:18 and in 1 John 2:2, 4:10.)[19]

Nowhere in the New Testament does forgiveness depend on punishment or retribution. "Wrath" is present as a minor note in the New Testament's symphony of salvation – albeit not absent. We are justified by Christ's blood and will "be saved by him from the wrath of God" (Rom. 5:9; see Rom. 1:18; 1 Thess. 1:10; Heb. 3:11, 10:31). God's wrath is God's refusal to accept alienation of God's beloved. God's wrath is God's opposition to suffering, not God's determination to cause it.[20] James Dunn suggests that for Paul "wrath" means the destructive consequences of sin (Rom. 1:18–22). In Paul's theology of sacrifice, "the primary thought is the destruction of the malignant, poisonous organism of sin," a process

[17] James D. G. Dunn, "Paul's Understanding of the Death of Jesus as Sacrifice," in S. W. Sykes (ed.), *Sacrifice and Redemption: Durham Essays in Theology* (Cambridge University Press, 1991), p. 49.
[18] Ibid., pp. 20–9. See also Sloyan, *Why Jesus Died*, pp. 80–100; and Peter Schmiechen, *Saving Power: Theories of Atonement and Forms of the Church* (Grand Rapids, MI: Eerdmans, 2005), pp. 20–7.
[19] Matera, "Christ in Paul and John," p. 244.
[20] Schmiechen, *Saving Power*, pp. 219–20.

to which the term "expiation" applies.[21] Atonement as expiation in this sense is necessary for the reconstitution of a community of God's beloved creatures in which all alienation and violence are overcome.

Many cultures in the ancient Near East, both Jewish and Gentile, utilized expulsion rituals, in which the sin or some other burden of the people, such as a plague, was transferred onto a victim to be driven out from the community. For Jews this ritual concerned a "scapegoat" associated with the annual Day of Atonement; for other religious cultures, other victims might be used – for example, a sheep, a bull, a male prisoner, or a woman.[22] The victim, innocent in itself, carried the sin or burden out, transferring it away from the community. Another operative metaphor in Paul is the practice of ransoming a slave or an indebted person by a payment of money or by providing another person who would serve in his or her stead (cf. Mark 10:45; Matt. 20:28). In the Hebrew Bible, ransom was used in connection with God's deliverance of his people from slavery or from exile (Isa. 35:10, 43:3). In addition to sacrificial death, Paul provides legal and economic models of Christ's suffering and death, as, for instance, ransoming or taking the place of a slave, debtor, or captive.

Not all New Testament models of salvation focus on the death of Christ, and the death of Christ should be interpreted dialectically with other models, not in isolation from them. An important alternative model, discussed in Chapter 4, is salvation through the incarnation, which unites humanity to divinity (Phil. 2:5–8). The models of incarnation (beginning with a preexistent divine being) and of death-resurrection (narrated from the perspective of a human, historical life) are both represented to some degree in almost every New Testament author. Though the incarnation of the Word is John's dominant model, John alludes to Jesus' sacrificial *death* by having John the Baptist compare him to the Passover lamb: "Behold the Lamb of God who takes away the sin of the world!" (John 1:29, 36). Paul is the first biblical theologian of Christ's saving death. Yet he comes close to the *incarnation* model when he suggests that Jesus Christ "was in the form of God" before he was born (Phil.

---

[21] Dunn, "Paul's Understanding," p. 50.
[22] Finlan, *Problems with Atonement*, pp. 31–8. See also Michael Winter, *The Atonement: Problems in Theology* (London: Geoffrey Chapman, 1995), pp. 80–6, for a discussion of theological appropriations of the scapegoat theme, including the work of René Girard. Christine Gudorf makes a lot of sense when she objects that scapegoat theories do not interrupt but rechannel violence, so that its original perpetrators are never confronted. This makes "scapegoat" atonement theories complicit at least in allowing perpetrators to evade responsibility, and even in upholding their unjust authority (Christine E. Gudorf, *Victimization: Examining Christian Complicity* [Philadelphia: Trinity Press International, 1992]).

2:6–8); when he connects the Spirit of God with Jesus Christ (Rom. 8); and when he sees Christ as a "second Adam" who restores creation and whose whole life saves by recapitulating human history (Rom. 5:12–21). As Frank Matera asserts, each of these two models "reveals something about God, the human condition, and the benefits of Christ, which the other does not, and perhaps cannot reveal. These differences remind us that the mystery of Christ is multifaceted and cannot be explained in only one way."[23]

Contemporary theologies of the cross can avoid sacralizing violence and making it ethically and politically acceptable if they integrate the symbols of incarnation and resurrection along with cross as saving death. Resurrection is a natural counterpart of cross because the two are narrated together in all four gospels. Building on Jewish traditions (Maccabees and Daniel), resurrection functions as a vindication of the righteous sufferer who gives his life for many. The theme of incarnation has closer parallels in Greek and Roman religions than in Judaism. The link of divine incarnation and cross is not as clear or overt in the biblical materials as is that between resurrection and cross. However, it is only on the basis of this very premise that the cross can be "God's solidarity with the victims" (Sobrino) and with oppressors (Moltmann) in a saving way, inspiring the church's politics of salvation.

A suffering death was not the major point of the incarnation. Christ was put to death on the cross as the result of the way he lived in unity with God and humanity, and it is the unity of the two through Christ that the incarnation most essentially signifies. Therefore, it is important not to overlook or minimize paradigms of salvation, in theology as well as the bible, that focus on the incarnation as enabling human divinization (the Cappadocians and Eastern Christianity); that revolve around Jesus' inauguration of the reign of God through his entire life, ministry, and teaching (feminist and liberationist theologies and ethics); or that see the cross as God's solidarity with innocent victims of malign power (liberation theologies, including new voices from Asia and Africa).

Before turning to the development of atonement theologies in the Christian tradition, we will consider how two of the later epistles, Hebrews and 1 Peter, combine incarnation and death-resurrection themes, and model the ideal enactment of cross soteriologies in the church.

---

[23] Matera, "Christ in John and Paul," pp. 255–6.

THE LETTER TO THE HEBREWS AND CROSS AS SACRIFICE

The most eloquent and well-developed New Testament interpretation of Christ's death as a sacrifice is the Letter to the Hebrews, probably composed toward the end of the first century CE, possibly for Jewish Christians in Rome.[24] Edward Schillebeeckx has lamented the fact that "for many Christians Hebrews has become an unknown text" and recommends the work as "the most subtle human document in New Testament literature."[25] Examining Hebrews helps provide a nuanced model of salvation as dependent on the sacrificial death of Christ. The early importance of such a model certainly derives in great part from the fact that Jewish sacrifice provided a ready framework for coming to terms with the unexpected death of Jesus.[26] In the Middle Ages, the idea of Christ's death as an atoning sacrifice became theologically ascendant due to the influence of Anselm.

A major aim of Hebrews is to revitalize the faith of a community that had undergone persecution. The central christological category of Hebrews is Christ as the "high priest," who, though God's Son and an instrument of creation (1:2), became human, "like his brothers and sisters in every respect," so that he might "make a sacrifice of atonement for the sins of the people" (2:17; cf. 2:11). While Hebrews assumes a "high" christology in which the Son of God was "for a little while made lower than the angels" (2:9), it also emphasizes the reality of the earthly, human Jesus, a man of "blood and flesh" (2:14). Through his humanity, Jesus is one with us and makes a sacrifice on our behalf. Just as does the high priest in the tabernacle on Yom Kippur (Day of Atonement), Christ as the people's representative effects atonement for sin.[27] Hebrews unites incarnation and death-resurrection as foundations of salvation, as well as the humanity and the divinity of Jesus Christ.

---

[24] See Harold W. Attridge, "Hebrews, Epistle to the," in David Noel Freedman (ed.), *The Anchor Bible Dictionary*, vol. 3 (New York: Doubleday, 1992), pp. 97–105, at 105–6. See also Harry W. Attridge, *A Commentary on the Epistle to the Hebrews*, Hermeneia Commentary Series (Philadelphia: Fortress, 1989); Fred B. Craddock, "The Letter to the Hebrews: Introduction, Commentary, and Reflections," in *The New Interpreter's Bible*, General Articles, vol. 12 (Nashville: Abingdon, 1998), pp. 101–16; and Raymond E. Brown, *An Introduction to the New Testament* (New York: Doubleday, 1996), pp. 683–704.

[25] Edward Schillebeeckx, *Christ: The Experience of Jesus as Lord* (New York: Crossroad, 1981), p. 238.

[26] Sloyan, *Why Jesus Died*.

[27] Attridge, "Hebrews, Epistle to the," p. 101.

"High priest," as a designation anchored in Jewish tradition, begins with the fact of humanity. This metaphor for Jesus' role "works" because it has a well-known human referent. Yet the author of Hebrews repeatedly contrasts the sacrifice of Christ's death with the sacrifices of the Levitical high priests, who must atone for their own sins as well as those of the covenant people and whose sacrificial acts must be repeated. Christ is a heavenly high priest (8:1–2), "after the order of Melchizedek" (6:20, 7:11, 17; cf. Ps. 110).

Melchizedek was revered at Qumran for his eschatological priestly role. The author of Hebrews is making an argument to converts from Judaism who may have had a Qumran association.[28] The Dead Sea Scrolls suggest that, in Jewish theology, the mysterious figure of Melchizedek is a supernatural being who rescues the righteous.[29] The allusion backs the point that Christ is no ordinary human priest. He "holds his priesthood permanently, because he continues forever." He "is able for all time to save those who approach God through him, since he always lives to make intercession for them" (7:24–5). Whereas the high priest of the desert tabernacle had to return yearly with the blood of goats and bulls, the sacrifice of Jesus' own blood wipes out sins forever.[30] The identification of Jesus with the high priest rather than the sacrificial animal marks a decisive difference between Jesus and the animal blood sacrifice and the scapegoat: Jesus is a voluntary victim, one who steps from a role of privilege and power to identify with the people and undertake a mission in their favor.[31]

Christ's sacrifice inaugurates a new covenant (8:13), in which believers are called to imitate Christ's fidelity and willingness to suffer (10:16, 24–5; 12:7). Christ's one sacrifice is of lasting efficacy (10:12); now glorified, he is our intercessor, asking for forgiveness on our behalf. In this regard, Hebrews confirms Paul's confidence in the prevenient mercy of God (Rom. 5:8; cf. Rom. 8:34). Also, because Christ eternally intercedes for us and for the church, every person is directly related to God in Christ, even without benefit of a human intermediary (7:25). "The privilege of approaching God, once reserved to priests, has become democratized and available to all."[32]

[28] Richard N. Longenecker, *Studies in Hermeneutics, Christology and Discipleship* (Sheffield: Sheffield Phoenix Press, 2006), ch. 9.
[29] Brown, *Introduction to the New Testament*, p. 687.
[30] Ibid., p. 688.
[31] Richard D. Nelson, " 'He Offered Himself': Sacrifice in Hebrews," *Interpretation* (July 2003), p. 254.
[32] Ibid., p. 260.

Christ's suffering and death are central to the effectiveness of his priesthood for our salvation and, in Hebrews, take on the aura of purpose and necessity. "Although he was a Son, he learned obedience through what he suffered; and having been made perfect, he became the source of eternal salvation for all who obey him" (5:8–9). Jesus "endured the cross, disregarding its shame," "for the sake of the joy that was set before him." The exaltation and resurrection language in Hebrews refer to Christ's humanity and suffering, and so offers hope for those who suffer after him: Christ "has taken his seat at the right hand of the throne of God" (12:2). God made Christ "perfect through sufferings" (2:10), and precisely because he himself was "tested by what he suffered, he is able to help those who are being tested" (2:18).

Very problematic as exemplary of Christian behavior are the ideas that God purposively inflicts suffering, that our "perfection" depends on suffering, and that obedient submission to the "test" of suffering is the path to Christ-like existence. Two feminist theologians voice the essential problem. Accusing Christianity of having a major role in the shaping of women's acceptance of abuse, they object: "If the best person who ever lived gave his life for others, then, to be of value we should likewise sacrifice ourselves. Any sense that we have a right to care for our own needs is in conflict with being a faithful follower of Jesus."[33] As a historical observation about a function that such texts have played in Christian piety, this complaint is well deserved. Christians must be accountable for the practical uses and meanings of sacred texts, even if these were not the "original" meanings or the only possible interpretations. Still, an appreciation of Hebrews in its own context may help counteract damaging uses and foster contemporary interpretations that are more closely analogous to the text's original purpose, or at least its function within a collection of sacred writings that upholds Jesus' option for the vulnerable and marginalized.

First, and most fundamental, Hebrews retains an incarnational framework for Christ's sacrifice and emphasizes its unique character, thus excluding too close a parallel between Christ's action and human action. For Hebrews (or, for that matter, the New Testament in general), Christ's death has the saving effect it does precisely because Jesus Christ is both an earthly human being and God's Son. His sacrifice cannot be repeated.

Second, the community is expected to emulate Christ in ways appropriate to their circumstances. The audience of Hebrews has, as a

---

[33] Brown and Parker, "For God So Loved the World?" p. 2.

community, undergone suffering in the form of persecution (10:32–4).[34] Here it is not a matter of whether any community members have the right to expect the submission of other members. Nor does the author seem to envision a situation where community members could remain steadfast in their faith and still escape or resist persecution. Rather, suffering is inescapable for the community as a whole, but with faith and endurance, believers will share in the glory that is now Christ's. They can rely on Christ's prior action and continual intercession to give them confidence and hope (6:11, 11:1).

Hebrews encourages those who suffer by stressing that suffering comes from the Father, has a purpose, and will work to the benefit of those who are steadfast. "Now discipline always seems painful rather than pleasant at the time, but later it yields the peaceful fruit of righteousness to those who have been trained by it" (12:11). Hebrews' starting point is the *reality* of unjust human suffering, and its goal is to endow that suffering with meaning and render it bearable. The idea that God wills that human persons should suffer is undercut by the idea that Christ has made the full and perfect sacrifice, sufficient for the remission of all sins. Even so, the author grants that his point, the purpose of suffering in relation to salvation, is "hard to explain"!

Hebrews' conclusion turns from logic and theology to the way of life Christians must live to exhibit the salvation established by the one sacrifice of Christ. Its description relegates suffering to a secondary, subsidiary place, compared with love and praise of God (13:15–16). Again, this qualifies the message that Christians ought to suffer in imitation of Christ. The primary goal of discipleship is love, not suffering. Sacrifice, of course, accompanies a truly loving way of life and practices of love within the community. Yet the ethical injunctions that mark a Christian lifestyle are concerned with the positive over the negative. "Let mutual love continue. Do not neglect to show hospitality to strangers ... Remember those who are in prison ... Keep your lives free from the love of money, and be content with what you have" (13:1–3, 5).

I PETER ON SACRIFICE AND THE COMMUNITY

Hebrews may be better understood if read in line with 1 Peter, with which it has many affinities.[35] Both documents see Christ's death as an atoning

---

[34] See Attridge, "Hebrews, Epistle to the," p. 97.
[35] Ibid., p. 104. On 1 Peter, see also Brown, *Introduction to the New Testament*, pp. 705–24; and Schillebeeckx, *Christ*, pp. 223–37.

sacrifice (1:2, 19; 2:12–15), giving access to an eschatological glorification attained through faithful endurance and sharing the sufferings of Christ (1:6–9, 2:20, 4:13). Both outline a practical Christian life of community virtues. 1 Peter exemplifies the contingency, fallibility, and even corruptibility of Christian attempts to name specific examples of what may turn out to be culturally bound "virtues." The appearance of a version of the "household code" in 2:18–3:7 illustrates the danger of associating sacrificial suffering with Christian identity in the real world, especially in relations within the community. Nevertheless, the letter captures a spirit close to Hebrews when it exhorts Christians to "give an accounting of the hope that is in you" with their deeds (3:15). It advises them to "have unity of spirit, sympathy, love for one another, a tender heart, and a humble mind. Do not repay evil for evil or abuse for abuse; but, on the contrary, repay with a blessing" (3:8–9; cf. 4:7–11). Christians of today should and will insist more strongly than either 1 Peter or Hebrews that these injunctions apply to all members of the community equally. Refusing to continue cycles of abuse must include resisting and ending abuse, particularly in the case of power imbalances detrimental to the needs of and "love for" the less advantaged party. In order to avoid distorted and even violent applications of the "sacrifice" model to justify oppression, Christians must interpret sacrifice in coordination with Jesus' teaching and the example of his ministry to those who suffer.

Hebrews and 1 Peter bear an important message for Christian social ethics. As a result of the death and exaltation of Christ, salvation is an eschatological reality with "cosmic or political dimensions." Salvation is "a process under way in the present as Christians, through faith, hope, and charity (Heb. 10:22–24), follow the 'new and living way' to God's presence opened by Christ (10:19–21)." This does not imply suffering for its own sake, but rather the willingness to accept "a life of prayer, service, and suffering" as the price of engagement with an often rejecting world.[36]

1 Peter gives up the cultic enactment of sacrifice in favor of collective behavior that "with gentleness and reverence" (3:15) seeks to win doubters and sinners over to Christ. An important spin on Hebrews is given by 1 Peter when it extends the royal priesthood of Christ to the whole community: "you are a chosen race, a royal priesthood, a holy nation, God's own people." By "your honorable deeds" you may lead others to "glorify God when he comes to judge" (1 Pet. 2:9, 12). The life of the community should reveal God's love and mercy and lead others to share in it. 1 Peter

---

[36] Attridge, "Hebrews, Epistle to the," p. 103.

displays "the distinctive communal identity of the Jesus movement, its solidarity in suffering, its radical promotion of social cohesion and fraternal love, and its offer of human dignity and place of belonging to society's dislocated strangers."[37]

The community reflects Jesus' sacrifice by overcoming every difficulty in bringing the outcast and the offender back into the community. Christ's sacrifice and intercession may be supposed effective even for those whose lives are not yet converted. Given the importance of the covenantal identity of Christians as a people in Hebrews, it may be assumed that the risen Christ intercedes for the community as a whole, including members whose fidelity has been so shaken by trials that they are unable to pray with trust and hope. This also sets a standard for the work of the church. 1 Peter regards costly communal efforts on behalf of others as an expiatory sacrifice in imitation of Christ.[38] A life of mutual love, forgiveness, hospitality, and willingness to suffer for those in greater need, even those who have done wrong, marks the church as a community that shares in Christ's priesthood of reconciliation and furthers his mission in the world.

LATER ATONEMENT THEOLOGIES

Just as in the New Testament, there is also a pluralism of models of salvation operative in Christian theological tradition. Church fathers such as Irenaeus and Athanasius use the incarnation, crucifixion, and other models simultaneously without attempting any systematic organization or explanation.[39] Some, most influentially Irenaeus, Origen, and Augustine, develop the redemptive meaning of the crucifixion along a model that Gustaf Aulen dubbed "Christus Victor,"[40] that he regarded as dominant in patristic sources, and that he wanted to recover for contemporary theology. In this model, Christ redeems by freeing sinful humanity from captivity to the devil, brought about by sin. The means by which this

---

[37] John H. Elliott, *Conflict, Community, and Honor: 1 Peter in Social-Scientific Perspective* (Eugene, OR: Wipf & Stock, 2007), p. 3.

[38] Schillebeeckx, *Christ*, pp. 228–9.

[39] See Irenaeus, "Against Heresies," in A. Cleveland Coxe (ed.), *The Apostolic Fathers with Justin Martyr and Irenaeus* (New York: Scribner's, 1985), pp. 309–567; Athanasius, "On the Incarnation of the Word," in Edward Rochie Hardy (ed.), *Christology of the Later Fathers* (Philadelphia: Westminster Press, 1954), pp. 55–110. See also Schmiechen, *Saving Power*, pp. 123–30, 169–85; and Winter, *Atonement*, pp. 38–60.

[40] Gustaf Aulen, *Christus Victor: An Historical Study of the Three Main Types of the Idea of Atonement*, trans. A. G. Herbert (London: SPCK, 1953).

is accomplished are interpreted variously. For instance, humanity is the devil's legitimate property, so that he has to be tricked into overreaching himself with the bait of Christ's humanity (an early version); or the devil commits an injustice by killing the innocent Christ, and so his rights are terminated (Augustine).[41]

Because this model seems naively mythological, imputes rights to the devil over against God, may attribute trickery to God, and has little space for God's mercy and forgiveness, it has been criticized for centuries and has become theologically marginal in theories of salvation since the Middle Ages. It does have some merit insofar as it conveys symbolically the power of evil forces in the world and encourages us to name and resist structural sin that seems to captivate human choice.[42] However, the final question is whether an explanation for the power of sin is needed that attributes causality to some force outside of human persons, societies, and histories; and whether such an explanation complicates unnecessarily or helps to resolve the already vexing problems of human free will and divine omnipotence.

Resistance to "bondage to the devil" explanations of atonement is behind the medieval rise to prominence of theories privileging the death of Christ, as a substitute, over the incarnation. Several contemporary authors have observed, with dismay and even outrage, that, despite biblical variety, one specific model of salvation, under the tenacious influence of the eleventh-century Benedictine Anselm of Canterbury, has attained hegemony in Western Christian theology and piety. This is the model of Christ's death as a substitutionary sacrifice for human sin, needed to repay a debt to God, whose infinite honor has been offended past the limit of any purely human act of compensation. A "God-Man" is called for, because only a man who is also God can make up for an infinite offense. Substitutionary atonement was reinforced by the Reformers, especially John Calvin, and came to be deeply formative of the popular religious imagination, both Protestant and Roman Catholic. In Calvin's striking phrases, the sinner (who is all of us)

was estranged from God by sin, an heir of wrath, exposed to the curse of eternal death ... doomed to horrible destruction and already involved in it; ... [so that] Christ interposed took the punishment upon himself, and bore what by the just judgment of God was impending over sinners; with his own blood expiated the sins which rendered them hateful to God, by this expiation satisfied and duly

[41] Augustine, *On the Trinity*, XIII.13, 15, 16; IV.17.
[42] See Winter, *Atonement*, p. 131; and Weaver, *Nonviolent Atonement*, pp. 210–15.

propitiated God the Father, by this intercession appeased his anger, on this basis founded peace between God and men.[43]

In the view of modern critics, the paradigm of Jesus' death as atoning sacrifice, especially if seen as penal substitution, seems to compromise God's mercy, to make God demand and even engineer innocent suffering, and to make a suffering death the entire purpose of the incarnation. It sets up violence as divinely sanctioned and encourages human beings to imitate or submit to it.

These are concerns with a long and respectable pedigree. Only a generation after Anselm, Peter Abelard complained "how cruel and wicked it seems that anyone should demand the blood of an innocent person as the price for anything, or that it should in any way please him that an innocent man should be slain – still less that God should consider the death of his Son so agreeable that by it he should be reconciled to the whole world!"[44] Indeed, Anselm himself puts the following in the mouth of his interlocutor in *Cur Deus Homo*, a former student named Boso, who, readers have sometimes felt, got the better of the argument: "If God could not save sinners except by condemning a just man, where is his omnipotence? If, on the other hand, he was capable of doing so, but did not will it, how shall we defend his wisdom and justice?"[45]

The soteriology of Anselm does provide clues for a view of the cross as not in itself the purpose of the incarnation or willed by God, even though Anselm's theology also includes aspects that stand in need of correction, at least for modern-day believers. His position will here be complemented by that of Julian of Norwich, then tested by global theologies of liberation, reconciliation, and social change. First, following Richard Southern, it is necessary to question some understandings of Anselm in light of what he actually said and of his context.

ANSELM RECONSIDERED

Anselm maintained that in offending God's honor, human sin upset divine order in the universe. The death of Jesus satisfies divine honor and

[43] John Calvin, *Institutes of the Christian Religion*, trans. Henry Beveridge, vol. 1 (Grand Rapids, MI: Eerdmans, 1946), II.16.2.
[44] Peter Abelard, "Exposition of the Epistle to the Romans," in William C. Placher (ed.), *Readings in the History of Christian Theology*, vol. 1: *From Its Beginnings to the Eve of the Reformation* (Philadelphia: Westminster Press, 1988), pp. 150–1, at 150.
[45] Anselm, *Cur Deus Homo* (*Why God Became Man*) 1.8, in Brian Davies and G. R. Evans (eds.), *Anselm of Canterbury: The Major Works* (New York: Oxford University, 1998); pp. 260–356, at 275. Hereafter, citations to *Cur Deus Homo* will include the book and chapter number followed in parentheses by the parallel page number(s) in *Major Works*.

restores cosmic harmony. Anselm's theory was a rejoinder to the Christus Victor model, which was dominant in the early Middle Ages. In this model, Christ's death resolves a contest between God and the devil over sinful humanity. In all versions of the model, God ultimately gains victory over the devil through the resurrection.[46] Anselm rightly discerned that the devil could never have legitimate rights before God. His theory is an attempt to explain the biblical symbols of salvation through the cross of Christ in terms of the relationship between God and humanity alone. Humans are responsible to God, not to the devil. Hence Anselm's emphasis is on finding an explanation for the cross as necessary within the terms of this relationship.

Anselm himself did not prioritize the idea that Christ substitutes for humanity in bearing the punishment or penalty for sin, as in the "penal substitution" theory later developed by Luther, Calvin, and their interpreters and embraced by many Roman Catholics. Instead, Anselm focused on the determination of God to restore the harmony of creation disrupted by sin. God's "honor" refers not to individual personal dignity, but, as in feudal society, to an integrated system of relationships revolving around an authoritative benefactor. According to Richard Southern, "God's honour is the complex of service and worship which the whole Creation, animate and inanimate, in Heaven and earth, owes to the Creator, and which preserves everything in its due place."[47] The incarnation and the suffering and death of Jesus Christ must be understood in terms of God's mercy as undeterred love for creation and in terms of God's justice as the will and power to make creation right.

"*Beauty* is a new word in Anselm's theological vocabulary, that first comes into prominence in the *Cur Deus Homo*. In using it, he refers not to poetic or pictorial beauty, but to the beauty of a perfectly ordered universe."[48] God's mercy and God's justice meet in God's determination to restore to the entire creation the beauty, harmony, and rectitude for which it has been created and which participates in God's own supreme goodness.[49] In Anselm's words, God's reason for the incarnation is that "the human race, clearly his most precious piece of workmanship, had been completely ruined; it was not fitting that what God had planned for mankind should be utterly nullified, and the plan in question could not

---

[46] See Aulen, *Christus Victor*; Weaver, *Nonviolent Atonement*, pp. 14–16.
[47] Richard W. Southern, *Saint Anselm: A Portrait in a Landscape* (Cambridge: Cambridge University Press, 1990), p. 226.
[48] Ibid., p. 212. Southern cites *Cur Deus Homo* 1.15.
[49] Ibid., p. 214.

be brought into effect unless the human race were set free by its Creator in person."[50]

Boso presses the question of whether God cannot save humanity from ruin and restore order simply by merciful forgiveness, particularly since Christ urges continual forgiveness on his followers.[51] It is easy to sympathize with Boso's feeling that "it is a surprising supposition that God takes delight in, or is in need of, the blood of an innocent man."[52] Yet Anselm continues to insist that the ability to give recompense for sin and unload the burden of guilt is essential to the eventual happiness of the repentant sinner, to whom he refers as "wretched little man."[53]

A key point for Southern is that, in producing *Cur Deus Homo*, Anselm was likely to have been replying to criticism of Christian doctrine that had come from learned and pious Jews, whose communities were increasingly numerous in Western Europe in the late eleventh century.[54] Chief among their questions was whether the incarnation offends a monotheistic sense of God, as well as trust in God's goodness, impassability, and dignity.[55] "Honor" was a term that for Anselm captured the dignity of God. Anselm's project, revolving around God's honor, was to show not only that the incarnation and death of Christ were *necessary*, but also that they were "fitting" to the character of God and to the fulfillment of the purposes for which God created the universe and specifically humanity.

As Southern outlines it, Anselm's argument begins from the fact that humanity was created for eternal blessedness (or I would say "unity") with God, expressed as the complete "submission" (or conformity) of the human will to God's. By rejecting this relationship, the human race has deprived the whole creation of harmony with God. Since it is impossible that the purpose of God's creating and uniting love should be frustrated, a means of redemption – supplied by and "fitting to" the nature of God – must exist. As Anselm says, God would not accept "that the human race, that so precious product of his hand, had been totally lost," and "it was not fitting that all that God had planned for man should

---

[50] Anselm, *Cur Deus Homo* 1.4 (p. 269); see also 2.4 (pp. 317–19).
[51] Ibid., 1.12 (pp. 284–5).   [52] Ibid., 1.10 (p. 282).
[53] Ibid., 1.11 (p. 283); 1.24 (pp. 309–13, at 312).
[54] A point of some interest, perhaps indicating that Anselm respectfully envisioned a Jewish audience, is that he argues that no one could possibly knowingly and intentionally put God to death. Those who did so acted in ignorance of such great evil, and so they are not guilty of it (*Cur Deus Homo* II.15, in Anselm of Canterbury, *Why God Became Man and the Virgin Conception and Original Sin*, trans. Joseph M. Colleran [Albany, NY: Magi Books, 1969]. Subsequent direct citations of *Cur Deus Homo* will be from this edition).
[55] Southern, *Anselm*, pp. 198–200.

come to nothing."[56] The answer is a supreme offering of obedience, that is, an act of union with and love of God. While humanity certainly *ought* to offer such an act of reconciling obedience and love, only God *can* do so. Hence, the incarnation: "a God-Man is necessary for the Redemption of the whole Creation."[57]

As Southern grants, Anselm's solution (a God-Man pays humanity's debt) has been continually dogged by suspicion. Anselm does not actually resolve Boso's objection to the idea that "God so derives delight from, or has need of, the blood of the innocent, that he neither wishes nor is able to spare the guilty without the death of the innocent."[58] Instead, he merely gets Boso to agree that neither of them will attribute anything "unsuitable" to God. Yet for this very reason, as critics beginning with Abelard argue, the incarnation must be an act of love – not payment of a debt to God.

Unfortunately, Anselm's favorite analogy to the relation between God and humanity – a lord and his vassals – emphasizes a rigorous and even repressive regime of hierarchical subordination that is alien to the Christian experience of reconciliation in Christ.[59] Southern's reinterpretation of Anselm does not legitimate this hierarchy or try to rescue Anselm's attempt to show logically why Jesus Christ's death must repay a debt to God. Instead, he exposes and elaborates Anselm's larger concern with the dignity or honor of God as including God's creative and reconciling love.

Unlike the stereotype of "Anselmian" atonement theory, Anselm does not see the cross or suffering as the main point of the incarnation, much less as necessary to mollify an angry, unforgiving, and violent God. In some ways, his approach is more like the recapitulation ("Second Adam") model of Paul and Irenaeus, for it is Christ's unbreakably close relation to God throughout his life that rectifies the human situation and leads to his rejection and death. Anselm uses the language of "obedience" to name Jesus' intimacy with the Father and the concordance of their wills. Christ's suffering and death "were inflicted on him because he maintained his obedience," an obedience "consisting in his upholding of righteousness so bravely and pertinaciously that as a result he incurred death."[60]

From the standpoint of today's religious and moral sensibilities, Anselm can be faulted for speaking repeatedly of Jesus' life and death as a "debt"

[56] *Cur Deus Homo* I.4.   [57] Southern, *Anselm*, p. 206.   [58] *Cur Deus Homo*, I.10.
[59] Southern, *Anselm*, p. 222.   [60] *Cur Deus Homo*, I.9.

owed by sinners, if not by Jesus himself, and for setting up too great a contrast between the roles or perspectives of the Father and Son, so that Jesus Christ seems to supply something that God demands. This tendency is exacerbated by the language of "obedience," since to us it can suggest submission to an external authority rather than a unity in love. Moreover, Anselm does not always maintain the focus on obedience rather than on death as the primary axis of salvation, as when he opens with the question "By what logic or necessity did God become man, and by his death, as we believe and profess, restore life to the world?"[61] These issues notwithstanding, Anselm does not write violence into the heart of the divine, set up God as a destroyer whose almighty wrath must be appeased, or Jesus as a superman who withstands an ungodly amount of violence to rise again unscathed. To avoid such problems, it is salutary to keep in mind that the agenda of *Cur Deus Homo* is to explain the incarnation, not only the cross. And, as keys to the saving significance of Jesus Christ, it is necessary to balance soteriologies that focus on the cross and suffering with those highlighting recapitulation, divinization, inauguration of the reign of God, and resurrection.

JULIAN OF NORWICH: ANOTHER VISION

Alternative readings of Anselm reveal, then, that the sacrificial death of Christ on the cross is best understood as an act of God's love and the outcome of a complete identification with the human condition. It is nevertheless true that the feudal and transactional elements in Anselm's soteriology connote a God whose justice overrides God's mercy. A more straightforward vision of the embrace of humanity in God's reconciling and healing love may be found in the fourteenth-century English anchoress and mystic, Julian of Norwich. Beginning during an illness when she was thirty years old, Julian enjoyed revelations or "showings" from God that included vivid depictions of Christ's sufferings on the cross but that also led Julian to appreciate that the Trinity and the incarnation are included in the cross as their true meanings. Behind or within Christ's suffering is the love of God that unites all creation with God's own being. Though a theology of the cross is certainly warranted by Julian's visions and piety, she reinforces the idea that the incarnation is more central than

---

[61] Ibid., I.1. Yet on the next page, Anselm allows Boso to restate the question, without rebuttal, as follows: "By what necessity or logic did God, almighty as he is, take upon himself the humble standing and weakness of human nature with a view to that nature's restoration?" (I.1).

the cross to the reality of salvation. Julian attests that within medieval atonement theologies, the biblical model of incarnation continued to have a place alongside cross and resurrection.

As a young woman, Julian prayed that she might see Christ's sufferings on the cross, have full compassion for them, and even share in those bodily sufferings herself. Eventually her wish was granted in the form of a paralyzing illness that brought her close to death. But in the event, she realizes that the sufferings of Christ are in some mysterious way the embodiment of God's tender love and mercy for humanity. She does not attempt to explain the mechanism of salvation through the cross and does not turn to categories of satisfaction, punishment, or substitution.

In a vision of Christ's passion Julian sees "the red blood trickle down" from the crown of thorns, "hot and freshly and right plenteously."[62] Suddenly, in the same "showing" she grasps that in the passion "was comprehended and specified the Trinity, with the incarnation, and unity betwixt God and man's soul."[63] All the help of salvation we have in the cross: "it is of His Goodness." Yet the cross is not the only, or even the primary, means. "For God of his goodness hath ordained means to help us, full fair and many: of which the chief and principal mean is the blessed nature that He took of the Maid."[64] God has created humanity for unity in love with God; by a union of divine and human natures, God restores fallen humanity, entering into our sinful condition with transforming love. "He that made man for love, by the same love He would restore man to the same bliss, and overpassing." Just as "we were like-made to the Trinity in our first making," so "we should be like Jesus Christ, Our Savior … by the virtue of our again-making." For love of humanity, God makes himself "as like to man in this deadly life, in our foulness and our wretchedness, as man might be without guilt."[65] Through Christ, God the Trinity and Creator is preserving the human soul, "us mightily and wisely saving and keeping for love; and we shall not be overcome of our Enemy."[66]

The centerpiece of Julian's experience of God is the divine love, with its assurance that "all shall be well." God's "Might, Wisdom and Goodness" shall "make well all that is not well."[67] God shows Julian that through "His homely loving," God is "everything that is good and comfortable for us: He is our clothing that for love wrappeth us claspeth us, and all

---

[62] Julian of Norwich, *Revelations of Divine Love* (Grand Rapids Ethereal Library, Grand Rapids, MI; accessed July 21, 2006, at www.ccel.org), ch. 2.
[63] Ibid., ch. 1. [64] Ibid., ch. 6. [65] Ibid., ch. 10.
[66] Ibid., ch. 1. [67] Ibid.

encloseth us for tender love." Though the entire universe and "all that is made" is shown to Julian as a tiny, vulnerable ball the size of a hazelnut, God assures her, "It lasteth, and ever shall last for that God loveth it."[68]

What is the origin and impact of sin for Julian? Joan Nuth compares a story Julian tells to illustrate the nature of Adam's fall to a similar story found in the *Cur Deus Homo*. Julian may have been familiar with Anselm's teachings and writings, particularly if she had once been a Benedictine nun, as some historians hypothesize.[69] Anselm compares Adam to a slave who is given a command by his master, warned not to "throw himself" into a ditch, "despises" the master's command, inexplicably ignores the warning, and hence is thoroughly to blame for not having carried out the assigned task. Julian compares Adam to the "respectful" servant of a lord who regards him "lovingly, sweetly and mildly." The servant runs off on a task, "loving to do his lord's will," but falls inadvertently and cannot get up again, upon which the lord looks on his pain and struggle "with great compassion and pity."[70]

Although Anselm might fairly object that there is something about Julian's version that misses the reality of deliberate wrongdoing and the human experience of guilt, she might just as fairly rejoin that acknowledgment of guilt has already been well served by Christian theology and that the enfolding wonder of divine love deserves compensatory attention. This would have been particularly true in light of the growing interest in the human, suffering Jesus in the Middle Ages and the spirituality of preparation for death in the face of the Black Plague during Julian's time. She tells us that she has long known from the teaching of the church as well as from her own experience that the blame of sin hangs upon us continually, causing great dread.[71]

Julian certainly gives time to the vileness and foulness of sin. But her message is that sins are forgiven "by mercy and grace," as soon as the soul turns to God. Then the soul will be welcomed in kindness: "My darling I am glad thou art come to me: in all thy woe I have ever been with thee; and now seest thou my loving and we be oned in bliss."[72] Sin causes great suffering and lack of consolation for those who are blind to the nearness

---

[68] Ibid., ch. 5.

[69] Joan M. Nuth, "Two Medieval Soteriologies: Anselm of Canterbury and Julian of Norwich," *Theological Studies*, 53 (1992), pp. 611–45. Julian's version of the story is found in *Revelations*, ch. 51; Anselm's in *Cur Deus Homo*, I.24. See also Joan M. Nuth, *Wisdom's Daughter: The Theology of Julian of Norwich* (New York: Crossroad, 1991); and Jane Ellen McAvoy, *The Satisfied Life: Medieval Women Mystics on Atonement* (Cleveland: Pilgrim Press, 2000).

[70] Nuth, "Two Medieval Soteriologies," p. 611.

[71] Julian, *Revelations*, ch. 50.   [72] Ibid., ch. 40.

of God. But the most damaging effect of sin is that it prevents one from trusting in the mercy of God and relying on God's ever-present love. The idea that God is wrathful and must forgive is a human perception, but God in reality already surrounds the fallen and despairing soul with maternal care.[73]

The mother may suffer the child to fall sometimes, and to be hurt in diverse manners for its own profit, but she may never suffer that any manner of peril come to the child, for love. And though our earthly mother may suffer her child to perish, our heavenly Mother, Jesus, may not suffer us that are His children to perish: for He is All-mighty, All-wisdom, and All-love; and so is none but He – blessed may He be![74]

In life-threatening illness, Julian learned that God's love is stronger than the power of evil. Rather than "fear of eternal damnation," she "learned that her attitude towards God, even in the midst of suffering, should be trust" and that this holds true for all Christians.[75] Both Anselm and Julian rely on a Pauline Adam–Christ typology. Anselm sees the entire life of Christ as more important than the cross alone, and sees both the incarnation and the cross as part of the one will and love of God that creates and restores. Because he also emphasizes the destructiveness of Adam's sin, he depicts restoration of divine honor and harmony as payment of a "debt." In contrast, Julian stresses not only the continuity between the creating and redeeming will of God, but also the continuing oneness of God and the human creature.[76] She is thus disposed to envision salvation as available by virtue of the close unity of God and humanity in Christ – an incarnational model.

ETHICAL CRITERIA OF ATONEMENT THEORIES

A fundamental point is that "atonement" does not *of itself* denote punishment or sacrifice. "Atonement" simply means to bring into unity, and in a Christian theological context it refers to the creation of a mutual relationship of love between God and humanity.[77] Insofar as a prior state of alienation is presumed, atonement is also "reconciliation." As accounting for reconciliation after sin, atonement theory in general is characterized

---

[73] Ibid., ch. 46.
[74] Ibid., ch. 61. For references to God and Christ as a mother, see chs. 60–2.
[75] Nuth, "Two Medieval Soteriologies," p. 620.   [76] Ibid., p. 633.
[77] Winter, *Atonement*, p. 2. The word has roots in Middle English, signifying to be "at one" or "in harmony" (*Webster's New Collegiate Dictionary*). See also Gerald O'Collins, S.J., *Jesus Our Redeemer: A Christian Approach to Salvation* (Oxford: Oxford University Press, 2007), pp. 10–11.

by a positive reading of Christ's death, if not in its own right, then as an expression or consequence of God's atoning love.[78] "Atonement" is still a soteriological paradigm with explanatory value for Christian experience within certain ethical-political parameters.

An adequate atonement theory must accomplish at least five goals:

1. It must portray the cross as a consequence of love, a love that includes sacrifice but is not defined primarily by it. What fundamentally defines salvation granted by God is not that Christ died but that, out of love, God is incarnate in our full humanity, including suffering and death.[79]

2. It must affirm that sinners and victims alike are saved by the cross, again on the premise of the incarnation. The salvation of sinners results from Christ's full humanity, his endurance of the worst kinds of suffering and alienation that humanity knows. The redemption of all forms of human suffering requires the incarnation; in Christ, God shares human "forsakenness."

3. It must affirm both salvation or "justification," and transformation or "sanctification." To do this, it must keep cross close to incarnation and resurrection. The one who dies is human and divine, linking our humanity with his resurrection life. In the Spirit of Christ, a new existence has already begun.

4. It must issue in a politics of salvation that is coherent with Jesus' ministry of the reign of God and option for the poor. Moreover, this is a "public" politics, not only an inner-ecclesial "community ethic."

---

[78] A very useful overview of types of atonement theory is Schmiechen, *Saving Power*.

[79] A contested point in Christian theology past and present is whether it is appropriate to say that God suffers on the cross. The consensus of liberation theology is that God does. I believe that this view is not only appropriate but also required by the incarnation as uniting full humanity and full divinity. As discussed in Chapter 4, the interpretation of Chalcedon holding that the person of Jesus Christ is the Word and that he has no human person has been used as a strategy to "protect" God from experiences (being born, suffering, and dying) that seem incompatible (from a human standpoint) with God's enduring and reliable character as creating, sustaining, and saving love (God's impassibility or aseity). Under this rubric, Christ or the Word suffers in his human nature only, and not in his divine nature, although it can be said metaphorically that "God suffers." It seems to me that to say that Christ is a divine person only and that God does not fully assume full human nature undermines the incarnation, the possibility of salvation from evil, and the formulation of Chalcedon that Jesus Christ is both fully God and fully human. However, as with all descriptions of God in human terms, the suffering of God must be affirmed *analogously*. Divine characteristics, dispositions, and experiences are *never* literally the same as human ones. God must suffer in a way that does not undermine God's constancy and ever-uniting love. In other words, both God's personal involvement in human suffering and what used to be called "divine aseity" are aspects of the complex and ineffable reality of salvation in Christ.

5. It must issue in a theology and practice of the church that partake in this ministry. It must support and nurture a church that does justice. The public, political justice mission of the church is affirmed by and affects Christian liturgy.

The following require emphasis as especially important to atonement theologies today: the salvation of both oppressors and oppressed through the compassionate love of God; the importance of seeing cross through resurrection (not neglecting incarnation) in order to empower resistance to injustice and confront sinners with the demand for change; the public, political role of the church based on the reality of salvation in Christ; and the role of liturgy in carrying out the "ministry of reconciliation" entrusted to the church, that all creation may "become new" (1 Cor. 5:17–18).

First, Christ brings into the community of love not only the victims of violence, but also those who have perpetrated that violence. Jesus is no mere scapegoat or casualty of historical forces. Jesus is an agent who acts with purpose, going to whatever lengths necessary to forge a community of friends who will live out of love and hope in God.[80] Christ's death is a death for sinners, who need transformation more than the innocent. This point has been submerged in some feminist and liberationist soteriologies that rightly draw attention to the oppressed who have no voice, or struggle to find one. But the reality of sin and the need to redeem it are evident to those who most suffer its effects. The lyrics of a slave spiritual cry, "Sinner, do you love my Jesus? / Sinner, do you love my Jesus? / Sinner do you love my Jesus? / Soldiers of the cross."[81]

The argument from the standpoint of the "sinner" becomes psychologically and emotionally persuasive in the hands of Jürgen Moltmann, drafted into the German army at age seventeen during World War II and only later realizing the atrocities he had served. He grasps that Christ is not only the brother of history's victims, but "the one who delivers us from the guilt that weighs us down and robs us of every kind of future."[82] The compassion of God atones for the guilty. As a result of personal experience Moltmann came to realize that in order to live with a burden of guilt

---

[80] Reid, *Taking Up the Cross*, pp. 46–8.

[81] M. Shawn Copeland, "To Live at the Disposal of the Cross: Mystical-Political Discipleship as Christological Focus," in Anne M. Clifford and Anthony J. Godzieba (eds.), *Christology: Memory, Inquiry, Practice*, College Theology Society Annual Volume 48, 2002 (Maryknoll, NY: Orbis Books, 2003), p. 189.

[82] Jürgen Moltmann, *Jesus Christ for Today's World*, trans. Margaret Kohl (Minneapolis: Fortress Press, 1994), pp. 2–3.

like Auschwitz, "expiation is needed." Without forgiveness based on some real possibility of atonement, "the guilty who recognize their guilt cannot live, for they have lost all their self-respect." In the cross, God is on the side not only of the victims but also of the guilty. In the person of Jesus Christ, humanity and divinity are united in such a way that evildoers are allowed to make amends. Justice lies within the work of divine compassion and, together with it, creates new hope. "Compassion is the love that overcomes its own hurt, love that bears the suffering which guilt has caused, and yet holds fast to the beloved."[83] It is not necessary to see God as the "cause" of Christ's suffering, or Christ as "the meek and helpless victim." Instead, through the life of Christ that ends on the cross, "God seeks out the lost beings he has created, and enters into their forsakenness, bringing them his fellowship, which can never be lost."[84]

• As Paul and Anselm recognize, Christ's passion and death on the cross do more than put him "on the side of the victims." He is a guilty one among the perpetrators, taking on responsibility for the burden of evil their sin has caused. "God proves his love for us in that while we were still sinners Christ died for us" (Rom. 5:8). Christ even shares the terror of the damned. Between the crucifixion and resurrection, according to the Apostles' Creed, Christ "descends into hell" (see 1 Pet. 4:6, 3:18–20).[85] This "descent" indicates his thorough identification with the human condition, especially death. It might also be read to indicate Christ's sharing of our most hopeless guilt and despair, as well as his saving presence among the lost and corrupt, even among the dead.[86] The human Christ in hell suffers the pains of hell, and the divine Christ dispels its terrors with his light. After all, Christ suffers the worst that human existence can offer.[87]

Marilyn McCord Adams even proposes that Christ in fact is not "utterly sinless" because as a human being he participates in practices and structures that perpetuate sin's patterns.[88] Christ, like other human

---

[83] Ibid., p. 68.   [84] Ibid., p. 178.

[85] 1 Peter depicts Christ preaching the gospel to the dead, so that even they might live in the Spirit (1 Pet. 4:6); and going to "make proclamation" to spirits "in prison" who had been "disobedient" during "the days of Noah" (3:18–20).

[86] Moltmann, *Jesus Christ for Today's World*, pp. 66–7, 144. A similar theory is advanced by Hans Urs von Balthasar. See, e.g., Hans Urs von Balthasar, *Theo-Drama: Theological Dramatic Theory – The Dramatis Personae*, 3 vols. (San Francisco: St. Ignatius Press, 1990), vol. 2, p. 54; and *Does Jesus Know Us? Do We Know Him?* (San Francisco: Ignatius Press, 1983), pp. 32–3.

[87] Moltmann, *The Way of Jesus Christ*, p. 173.

[88] Marilyn McCord Adams, *Christ and Horrors: The Coherence of Christology* (Cambridge: Cambridge University Press, 2006), pp. 69–71. "The Gospels give us a Jesus who was not only a victim, but also an occasioner and perpetrator of horrors. What scripture does not show is Jesus perpetrating horrors with malicious intent or outside a Divinely purposed framework within which those very horrors may be defeated" (p. 71).

beings, is constituted by his personal and social relationships, as well as by his relation to his Father in heaven and to the Word. Christ is in solidarity with the human race, sinful and innocent alike.

⌈God's uniting love for all creatures reaches into every dark, lonely, and tormented corner of existence and brings God into every place, not excluding the suffering of the wicked and the damned.⌋ In that darkness and with unfathomable self-emptying, God becomes "guilty" and dies in Christ, in a radical act of maternal aching and yearning for the child who has been "disappeared" by evil.[89] God invades the despair of her child with the consolation of her absolute presence and sustenance⌈ In Jesus Christ, God enters all of the human condition, save sin – and human beings enter completely, if eschatologically, into God.⌋ ⌈God, who is rich in mercy, out of the great love with which he loved us, even when we were dead through our trespasses, made us alive together with Christ" (Eph. 2:4–5).

Wonhee Anne Joh provocatively engages maternal imagery to illuminate the redemption of the "wounded subject" suffering *han*, abjection, and marginalization. The "maternal trace" in the semiotics of the cross presents the overcoming of alienation through a love that is prior to and does not rely on separation. Divine love on the cross can be compared to "pregnancy when the mother–child relationship is so intertwined." In a mother's love, love for the child, love for herself, and "willingness to give herself up" are not mutually exclusive. The mother's love of the cross is the basis of a "new ethics" of oneness among God and all created beings.[90] Moving outward from the image of the mother, a Trinitarian theology also sets the cross in the context of inclusive, relational personhood, that creates, nurtures, and overcomes "horrors."[91]

While human mothers long in impotent grief to take on the suffering and even guilt of their children, so to heal them by their love, the insurmountable vulnerability of mothers lies in the fact that their love will always surpass their power. Traditional discourses of the "aseity," "impassibility," and "omnipotence" of God are obstacles to faith and salvation

[89] This is a reference to the Mothers of the Plaza de Mayo, Buenos Aires, who courageously joined in demonstration against a repressive government that had abducted their children – "the disappeared." See Regina M. Anavy, "Hope Ends 29-Year March of Mothers of the Plaza de Mayo: 1,500th Demonstration over Disappeared Children," *San Francisco Chronicle*, February 26, 2006, www.sfgate.com/cgi-bin/article.cgi?file=/chronicle/archive/2006/02/26/ING5RHDJ471. DTL (accessed March 6, 2007); and Marguerite Guzman Bouvard, *Revolutionizing Motherhood: The Mothers of the Plaza de Mayo* (Wilmington, DE: Scholarly Resources, 1994).
[90] Wonhee Anne Joh, *Heart of the Cross: A Postcolonial Christology* (Louisville, KY: Westminster John Knox Press, 2006), p. 112.
[91] Adams, *Christ and Horrors*, pp. 148, 53, 56, 163.

when used to remove God from the human condition or to locate a will to cause suffering scandalously within the divine dispositions. Yet this language can be recovered if taken in the context of divine surmounting love: "God is love, and he who abides in love abides in God and God in him" (Eph. 3:21). Jesus captures for us the unity of God's unchanging and reliable love and God's suffering with wayward, disconsolate children in the parable of the Prodigal Son (Luke 15:11–32).

God's aseity and suffering are pictured as one in the moment in which the father aches to embrace the son in whose approach his love already rejoices: "But while he was still far off, his father saw him and was filled with compassion; he ran and put his arms around him and kissed him" (15:20). It is the security of parental love that has drawn back the erring child, and it is this same unfailing love that continually endears the child to his father's heart and makes separation so intolerable for the father.

The force of God's uniting and healing love endures. Its constancy is unsurpassed. It is always powerful enough to reconcile, is never defeated by grief and sin. It is abiding, faithful, and victorious. "Neither death nor life nor angels nor rulers, nor things present, nor things to come, nor powers, nor height, nor depth, nor anything else in all creation, will be able to separate us from the love of God in Christ Jesus our Lord" (Rom. 8:38–9). God herself enters unfailingly into the very place and heart of her child. Her child is being raped, is committing rape; is in prison, is torturing the prisoner; is dead on a dark road, is in the electric chair. A beloved child of God demands just vengeance with cold eyes; a beloved child of God weeps inconsolably for her own justly condemned and executed son. The mysterious God loves in tender vulnerability and in sustaining power.

As mothers' hearts rend with their children's suffering more readily than with their own, so God's unsurpassed love for humans is narrated scripturally as a love both that *is* and that *gives up* the beloved one who dies in compassion for us. "For God so loved the world that he gave his only begotten Son" (John 3:16). The Lord Jesus Christ "gave himself for our sins to set us free from the present evil age, according to the will of our God and Father" (Gal. 1:4). "He who did not withhold his own Son, but gave him up for all of us, will he not with him also give us everything else?" (Rom. 8:32). The point here is not that God "wants" the death of Jesus, but that God is with and in our human situation, into and beyond death and hell. "Only a suffering God can help."[92]

---

[92] Dietrich Bonhoeffer, *Letters and Papers from Prison*, ed. Eberhard Bethge, trans. Reginald Fuller (New York: Macmillan, 1953), p. 220.

In the divine-human Christ, God enters into human suffering. God is in solidarity with the victims, promising resurrection. God also bestows upon sinners the resources to repent, rectify wrongdoing, hold up our faces to God's gaze, and accept the forgiving and restoring love that already surrounds us. Jesus' death is "necessary" insofar as death is the place of our ultimate desolation, where the infinite love of our Mother-Father God comes to meet us and lift us up.

Next, atonement for both victims and sinners, as a concretely and practically transformative event, returns us to the ultimate interdependence of cross and resurrection. There is no New Testament gospel of the cross, but rather a "gospel of Emmanuel," a gospel of the reign of God and a gospel of salvation through Christ's death and resurrection. [93] In the gospels, cross and resurrection form one story; Paul is insistent that faith is meaningful only because Christ is risen (1 Cor. 15:14). Resurrection and its effects on disciples are communicated in the vivid biblical stories of empty tomb, appearances, and Pentecost. Resurrection speaks especially well to those whose human existence is threatened with annihilation by evil.

To live within the resurrection is the very definition or constitution of Christian discipleship, as personal, ethical, and political transformation.[94] Yet despite rich narrative resources in the New Testament, resurrection is not only neglected by proponents and adversaries of atonement theories, but also muted in many liturgical reenactments of Jesus' passion. According to Virginia Fabella of the Philippines, Catholics in her country "have developed (or inherited) a dead-end theology of the cross with no resurrection or salvation in sight." Many women "look upon the passion and death of Jesus as ends in themselves and actually relish being victims." Clergy reinforce this attitude. She cites one priest who says he does not preach the resurrection in his homilies because " 'the people are not prepared for it.' "[95] This kind of attitude has personal and political consequences. For example, says Fabella, "a woman who is raped will invariably commit suicide rather than allow her husband and family to suffer the ignominy of living with a raped woman."[96]

---

[93] Moltmann, *The Way of Jesus Christ*, p. 185.
[94] See Oliver O'Donovan, *Resurrection and Moral Order: An Outline for Evangelical Ethics*, 2nd edn. (Grand Rapids, MI: Eerdmans, 1994); Rowan Williams, *Resurrection: Interpreting the Easter Gospel*, rev. edn. (Cleveland: Pilgrim Press, 2002); James Alison, *Undergoing God: Dispatches from the Scene of a Break-In* (New York: Continuum, 2006).
[95] Virginia Fabella, "Christology from an Asian Woman's Perspective," in R. S. Sugirtharajah (ed.), *Asian Faces of Jesus* (Maryknoll, NY: Orbis, 1993), p. 215.
[96] Ibid., p. 216.

The South African theologian Takatso Alfred Mofokeng maintains that "it is common knowledge in black churches that Good Friday celebrations occupy a position of prominence in the black Christian church calendar while the resurrection event comparatively remains in the shadows." The story of Jesus' passion and death is narrated by "sweating, crying and sometimes even fainting 'witnesses' " before congregations "packed with young and old people … In fact it is their own painful life story that they are reliving and narrating. Jesus of Nazareth is tortured, abused and humiliated and crucified in them. They are hanging on the cross as innocent victims of white evil forces. Jesus' cry of abandonment is their own daily cry. They experience abandonment by their own God, who they believe is righteous and good."[97]

The hour of forsaken death must be recognized as a truly pervasive human reality, one in which we are joined to the love of Christ. Those in the throes of suffering rightly embrace God's solidarity in the suffering of the cross. Nevertheless, the resurrection is a premise of the cross, the guarantee of our assurance that solidarity in Jesus' suffering will not be in vain.

As Moltmann observes, "If the resurrection event is an eschatological one, then the risen Christ cannot be what he is only from the time of his resurrection. He must also have this same identity in his suffering and death on the cross, in his proclamation and ministry, in his whole life from the very beginning."[98] The cross is endowed with salvific meaning because it is always already understood from the perspective of faith in the risen Lord in the Christian community. The risen Lord is the crucified Jesus. Resurrection experience is an experience of " 'the impossible becoming possible,' analogous to life and justice triumphing over death and injustice."[99]

Like Wonhee Anne Joh, Mary Grey likens the cross to women's birth experience. But while Joh pursues the metaphor of "oneness" (incarnation), Grey highlights "rebirth" (resurrection). She suggests that Jesus be viewed not as "innocent lamb, delivered up to slaughter as ransom payment," but in terms of birth, change and transformation. As in the birth process, the cross may be seen as "a 'letting go' of self – in pain and

[97] Takatso Alfred Mofokeng, *The Crucified Among the Crossbearers: Towards a Black Christology* (Kampen: Uitgeversmaatschappij J. H. Kok, 1983), pp. 27–8.
[98] Moltmann, *The Way of Jesus Christ*, p. 170.
[99] Jon Sobrino, *Christ the Liberator*, trans. Paul Burns (Maryknoll, NY: Orbis, 2001), p. 72. See also Schmiechen, *Saving Power*, pp. 17–18. The cross and resurrection are mutually interpreting. In light of the resurrection, the disciples had to rethink everything in their experience of Jesus.

struggle – for the creation of new being."¹⁰⁰ This image does not capture the human experience of desolation, much less of despair and guilt, as redeemed in the cross. However, it provides a complementary metaphor that speaks to the way promise is already beheld in the suffering because new life is already beginning.

According to Mofokeng, the resurrection must become operative in the experience of the faithful, so that they are motivated "to seek life in a struggle against forces that deny and destroy life."¹⁰¹ Mofokeng's point is as true of theologies of salvation as it is of the existential experience of suffering black people: Jesus' sacrificial death is our salvation, because it is God's act of compassion and renewal of life. The good news bestows hope and possibilities. As an ethical model, the cross properly inspires resistance, not acquiescence. Jesus' death, precisely as the death of the Son of God, is an example of power assuming vulnerability (Phil. 2:6–11); it does not model behavior to be emulated by those who "suffer 'innocently,'" as Mofokeng puts it.¹⁰²

Jacquelyn Grant reminds us that the cross empowers black women also because Jesus is "God incarnate" and "Jesus' suffering was not the suffering of a mere human."¹⁰³ According to a Korean theologian, Christ's "passive" suffering as a suffering servant is important because it convinces them that he is the one who knows their plight, for he has been in their situation of helpless suffering. Yet there is also an "active" dimension of the suffering of Jesus, the solidarity that makes "the struggle for liberation" and "the doing of justice" possible.¹⁰⁴ "Through Jesus Christ, Asian women ... see life-giving aspects in their suffering and service that create a new humanity for the people they serve."¹⁰⁵ This includes resistance to colonial legacies, patriarchal structures, economic exploitation, sexual abuse and enslavement, and all distortions of the cross that tell women to suffer silently. As Katie Geneva Cannon attests on the basis of the experience of black churchwomen who fought slavery and segregation in the United States, God's true union with humanity and resurrection life give us strength to battle structural evil with faith and hope, in the power

¹⁰⁰ Mary Grey, *Feminism, Redemption and the Christian Tradition* (Mystic, CT: Twenty-Third Publications, 1990), p. 186.
¹⁰¹ Mofokeng, *Crucified Among the Crossbearers*, p. 29.
¹⁰² Ibid., p. 28.
¹⁰³ Jacquelyn Grant, *White Women's Christ and Black Women's Jesus: Feminist Christology and Womanist Response* (Atlanta: Scholars Press, 1989), p. 212.
¹⁰⁴ Chung Hyun Kyung, "Who Is Jesus for Asian Women?" in Sugirtharajah (ed.), *Asian Faces of Jesus*, p. 228.
¹⁰⁵ Ibid., p. 229.

of the Spirit. "God's sustaining presence is known in the resistance to evil."[106]

It is clear, then, that theologies of the atonement require public social action for change, a personal and corporate politics that reaches from the church into the world. Yet the cross has gained visibility in depictions of Christian politics in the past half-century, in large part to check overly optimistic assessments of the potential of Christianity to be a catalyst for progressive social change. Despite the successes of the U.S. civil rights movement, in which religious leaders and churches were centrally involved, radical Christians later in the century saw how the churches had colluded and were still colluding in militarism and economic neo-colonialism. Moreover, despite the hopeful social theologies of the early and middle twentieth century, global conditions continued along lines of racism, violence, and exploitation. Therefore, cross theologies backed away from rather than sought political activism.

Christians stressed the obligation to take a stand against the corruptions of political power and to accept that suffering and likely defeat would be the price of a cruciform way of life in fidelity to Christ. American ethicists such as John Howard Yoder and Stanley Hauerwas,[107] writing in the wake of World War II and during the Vietnamese–American war, sounded this message loud and clear for more than a generation. Their clarion call for greater fidelity to the gospel has been exceptionally powerful and continues to resonate with a new generation of ethicists because of its success in evoking a strong sense of Christian identity, community, and way of life. This strand of thinking has taken especially deep roots in theologies and theological ethics rooted in the cultures of North America and Western Europe, where the churches' incorporation of liberal norms of justice had risked a diminished capacity to denounce fascism, militarism, materialism, and global economic exploitation. It should be remembered that North America and Western Europe offer contexts for countercultural protest in the form of denouncement and refusal, in which the larger

---

[106] Katie Geneva Cannon, "The Wounds of Jesus: Justification of Goodness in the Face of Manifold Evil," in Emilie M. Townes (ed.), *A Troubling in My Soul: Womanist Perspectives on Evil and Suffering* (Maryknoll, NY: Orbis Books, 1993), pp. 219–31, at 229.

[107] These two have been prolific, especially Hauerwas. Exemplary works are John Howard Yoder, *The Politics of Jesus*, 2nd edn. (Grand Rapids, MI: Eerdmans, 1994); and Stanley Hauerwas, *The Peaceable Kingdom: A Primer in Christian Ethics*, 2nd edn. (London: SCM Press, 2003). An audience beyond the Christian church is implied in works such as John Howard Yoder, *For the Nations: Essays Public and Evangelical* (Grand Rapids MI: Eerdmans, 1997); and Stanley Hauerwas, *War and the American Difference: Theological Reflections on War and National Identity* (Grand Rapids, MI: Baker Academic, 2011).

culture itself secures the protestors' basic needs and human rights. In situations of extreme poverty, violent civil conflict, or government repression, the option of "cruciform" nonresistance or nonparticipation is much less compelling.

In new theologies and christologies from around the globe, the cross has taken on different meanings. The cross, especially as God's transforming solidarity with those who suffer, calls Christians to act on behalf of the poor. It empowers people who actually suffer injustice to resist and to work confidently for social and political changes. In these contexts, the danger is not so much the watered-down or superficial politics of liberalism. It is that cross-oriented atonement theories can either feed resignation to violence or embrace it in service to idolatrous ends. They can discourage investment in participatory, socially engaged politics because discipleship and public life are seen as nonintersecting spheres. The stance of the cross as a faithful "witness against" still has a place. In fact, it will always have a place as long as Christian symbols and loyalties can be co-opted to serve domination systems. But this is not the only, or globally the most important, meaning of Jesus Christ in the twenty-first century. As Virginia Fabella has said, "The mission of preaching the gospel demands our participation in the transformation of the world. Thus active solidarity with the people against sexism, racism, ethnic discrimination and economic injustice is truly missionary."[108]

Even as Christians conform to the way of Christ's cross, they hope and strive for a way of life free from all violence and suffering. A new manner of existence – not just spiritually but socially and politically – is already available to those willing to take on the consequences of commitment to divine love and justice. This new existence will include sacrifice. Christians will not underestimate the power of evil forces and structures or the likelihood that disciples will be captive to or complicit in these same evils. Yet salvation depends on Jesus' inauguration of the reign of God, confirmed in his resurrection and the sending of the Spirit.

The politics of salvation has, first, an inner-ecclesial dimension. Within communities, salvation is transmitted in several ways: faith as a relation of trust to God in Christ; rebirth in the Spirit sent to the church; participation in a reconciled community of celebration and mission; liturgical, sacramental participation in Christ; and acts of love and justice. Ongoing practices transmit Christ's solidarity with the poor and oppressed, as well

---

[108] Fabella, "Christology from an Asian Woman's Perspective," p. 221.

as with those needing forgiveness and conversion.[109] The church makes Jesus' saving power accessible to real people in real relationships and structures. This brings us to the extra-ecclesial dimension of salvation. Works of service have been a key part of Christian calling from biblical times to our own. Yet these works are not limited to church members, but extend to all "neighbors" in need. In fact, when Christians enact renewed being and relationship, they touch everyone with whom they interact in families, workplaces, local civil society, economic behavior, and political participation. They have an effect on "distant neighbors" through voluntary organizations, structures of international governance, educational and professional networks, and economic structures that link all of us to myriad other people nationally, regionally, and globally.

Christian works of love and justice must today involve a commitment to social and structural justice for all peoples, which requires engagement of individual believers, of Christian organizations, and of the church itself as a community and as an institution. Christians will work with other persons, groups, organizations, and networks, nationally and internationally, to transmit salvation as restored humanity and restored creation. In these alliances, Christians will both contribute to and learn from non-Christian and nonreligious partners. Christian social ethics and the Christian mission for justice will be the primary subject matter of the final two chapters.

From a Catholic perspective, Kristin Heyer offers that common cultural symbols or philosophical concepts and arguments often provide language for public justice work, yet sometimes specifically Christian symbols, narratives, and arguments can enrich civil discourse too. When religious people link social commitment to their highest values, it shows the depth of that commitment. Religious stories and symbols from one tradition can even strike a responsive chord in other people's imaginations, appealing to their own deepest values and formative narratives, as long as religious resources are used with "tolerance and humility" and an attitude of mutual invitation.[110]

Just as Christ saves sinners, so the church must communicate social reconciliation, repentance, and reform to public transgressors, including but not limited to its own members. It is perhaps easier to see how the churches should be committed to "the poor" – to resist HIV/AIDS, rape

---

[109] See Schmiechen, *Saving Power*, pp. 356–8.
[110] Kristin E. Heyer, *Prophetic and Public: The Social Witness of U.S. Catholicism* (Washington, DC: Georgetown University Press, 2006), p. 15.

as a weapon of war, grinding poverty in the "two-thirds world," inequit-
able exploitation of natural resources, human trafficking, and ethnic violence. Compassion for and solidarity with the victims of such conditions
inspire many in the churches to work for their human dignity, human
rights, and structural justice.

It is equally important that, as the body of Christ, the church owns
Christ's work of interceding for those who are personally responsible for
evil and those caught up in predatory social structures. Christ calls us to
unite them (or us) to the love of God, even while they (we) are "still sinners" (Rom. 5:8). Writing of the South African Truth and Reconciliation
Commission (TRC) and of its support by religious leaders and churches,
John de Gruchy calls the church to be "in solidarity with the world
in its sin, its suffering, its struggles and its hopes."[111] "It is through the
mediation of human beings, fallen and fallible, but also seeking to be a
community of vicarious love in the world, that reconciliation becomes a
reality," a social and political reality, not just the practice of a community
of believers.[112]

A historical precedent is the Stuttgart Confession of Guilt, published
by the German Confessing Church in 1945. Although many of the authors
actually opposed the Nazi regime and suffered for it, they acknowledged
solidarity with the nation and the church in sin and suffering, they confessed guilt, and called for a new beginning.[113] As de Gruchy notes, "It is
seldom the case that those who perpetrate violence and evil are prepared
to confess their guilt."[114] Therefore, these leaders, on behalf of the church,
called for and exemplified repentance as a step to action and real change.
He draws comparisons to the South African post-apartheid TRC, which
reminds us that any reconciliation process is tenuous and fallible. This
does not diminish the obligation to take steps ahead.

The importance of corporate atoning actions was borne out for me
personally at a conference on Catholic peace-building initiatives held in
Burundi in the summer of 2006.[115] Like other peoples in the Great Lakes
region of Africa (including Rwanda, Congo, and Uganda), communities
in Burundi have experienced ethnic violence in which great numbers on

[111] John W. de Gruchy, *Reconciliation: Restoring Justice* (Minneapolis: Fortress Press, 2002), p. 94.
[112] Ibid., p. 95.   [113] Ibid., pp. 108–9.   [114] Ibid., p. 112.
[115] This conference – one of a series – was sponsored by the Catholic Peacebuilding Network of the
Kroc Institute, University of Notre Dame; and by Catholic Relief Services. For more information, see the website of the Catholic Peacebuilding Network at cpn.nd.edu (accessed May 27,
2012). An outcome of the series is Robert J. Schreiter, R. Scott Appleby, and Gerard F. Powers
(eds.), *Peacebuilding: Catholic Theology, Ethics, and Praxis* (Maryknoll, NY: Orbis Books, 2010).

both sides have participated. Yet communal reconciliation and rebuilding are necessary for life to go on. Churches have an essential role to play in confessing sin, avowing repentance, and uniting all in a shared narrative of hope. This role will require a theology of salvation in which the guilty are included along with the innocent and in which expiation, forgiveness, reparations, and restoration are counterparts. As de Gruchy observes, the community can play a role in these processes, both liturgically and through exemplary social action, that goes beyond the ability of any one individual to repent, forgive, or make amends.

LITURGY AND THE POLITICS OF SALVATION: AN ILLUSTRATION

Liturgy defines the church as the place where restorative justice and reconciliation are encountered, not only personally but politically. The primary Christian ritual, the eucharist, commemorates Jesus' final meal with his disciples, presents his death as mediating salvation, and also celebrates incarnation and resurrection. The eucharist is a vital point of contact between the church's self-understanding and its mission in and for the world. In the eucharist, community is enacted, disciples are formed, and the ecclesial missions of service, work for justice, and reconciliation are taken up and carried forward.

Liturgy reflects the community's understanding of the mystery of the atonement and of the human relationships that follow. Yet, while it is true that morality, ethics, and politics flow from liturgy, it is equally or even more true that liturgy flows from these activities, since it is in our moral, ethical, and political relationships that the reality of salvation is made personal, historical, and concrete. Biblical confessions such as Galatians 3:28 reflect a basic Christian experience of inclusion and equality that reveals God as mercy, forgiveness, generosity, and love. Authentic liturgical and especially eucharistic celebration comes out of, represents, and continues the transformative process of living communities (1 Cor. 11). "The Eucharist presupposes a community engaged in action for justice, a praxis of liberation from violence and injustice ... members of these communities possess the strong sense of freedom that comes with the gift of the Spirit and helps them develop community structures that are participatory and respectful of a variety and multiplicity of gifts."[116]

---

[116] David Power, "Eucharistic Justice," *Theological Studies*, 67 (2006), p. 879.

The dialectical relation of transformed relationship and liturgy is just as present in the case of nontransformed, nonsalvific communities, when liturgies reflect disordered relationships. The Christian ability to grasp the mystery of atonement as reconciliation is dependent on the new relationships that an authentic confession of salvation in Christ presupposes. The local church, participating in its social milieu, may fail to embody divine justice and mercy. In that case, liturgy will not celebrate these realities either. "Family conflict, racial prejudice, economic injustice, sexism, civil disorder and violent international aggression are all challenges to the effective faith of those who gather for public prayer in Jesus' name," particularly when these disordered relationships infect the liturgy itself.[117] This does not mean that eucharistic participation must be personally and morally perfect, for we come before God to seek forgiveness, strength, and healing. But it does require that we approach the eucharist in humility, repentance, and good faith.

To the extent that old relationships of exclusion or domination remain and are not repented, our knowledge of God will be distorted and our liturgies will be inauthentic conveyors of salvation. A glaring example is celebration of the eucharist with words that reflect and perpetuate centuries of unjust derogation and persecution of the Jewish people. This is an appropriate example to consider here, in light of the trajectory of the reign of God, the Jewish identity of the earliest followers of Jesus, the gradual extension to Gentiles, and the subsequent "othering" of Jews that emerged early in Christian history (see Chapter 3). Anti-Semitism and supercessionism continue to be problems for the church today, despite the courageous actions of the German Confessing Church.

This can be illustrated with recent liturgical changes and disputes that have occurred within my own communion, Roman Catholicism, over the attitude of Christians to the Jewish people and their faith. These debates exemplify ambiguities in the dialectic of liturgy, theology, and changing ethical practices. The theology of Israel and its covenant have evolved in Catholicism along with relations among Jews and Christians after the Holocaust, or Shoah. Following the violence of the Third Reich against the Jews, abetted by the cooperation, collusion, or indifference of millions of Christians and their leaders, Roman Catholics and other Christians have been forced to confront the legacy of centuries of anti-Semitic and supercessionist theologies.

---

[117] Mary Collins, "Liturgy," in Joseph A. Komonchak, Mary Collins, and Dermot A. Lane (eds.), *The New Dictionary of Theology* (Wilmington, DE: Michael Glazier 1987), p. 595.

One result is the theology of the Vatican II document *Nostra Aetate*, according to which God's covenant with the Jewish people is everlasting.[118] A symbolic reaffirmation of the bond between Christians and Jews, and of Christian repentance for sins against the Jews, was John Paul II's prayer at the Western Wall in Jerusalem in 2000. The pope's action was a public ritual expression of changing theology and practice. His gesture reflects a more general trend in Europe and North America to affirm politically and legally the ethnic and religious identity of Jews, their human rights (as at Nuremburg and in the Universal Declaration of Human Rights), the basic legitimacy of the state of Israel, and the repudiation of anti-Jewish attitudes and behavior in every locale.

The path toward full Christian acceptance of Israel and Judaism has not been smooth, however. In 2001, the Vatican document *Dominus Iesus* reiterated that all salvation is through Christ, that Christianity is the only true religion, and that Catholicism is Christianity's most complete embodiment.[119] Many people have commented on the tension if not contradiction between *Nostra Aetate* and *Dominus Iesus*.

What factors might explain the turn represented by *Dominus Iesus*? A first issue is general concern among Vatican officials about the growing acceptance by many Christians of the faith of members of other religions. This is the product of greater exposure to other faiths, both Christian and non-Christian; of the recognition of holiness in adherents of these faiths; and in the experience of striving with these peoples toward common goals. In the decades since the council, Catholics have been intensively engaged in dialogue with non-Christians. Particularly in Asia, where Christians are a small minority, Catholic theologians have been wary of any triumphalistic theological tendencies and have become increasingly open to the possibility of truth and even salvation in multiple traditions.

Meanwhile, secularity continues unabated among formerly Christian nations in Europe. To some European Catholic leaders, the strength and even existence of Christianity appear to be under siege. The development of interreligious acceptance is manifestly worrisome in the eyes of the Vatican, which has issued various warnings to and strictures against theologians who are perceived to stray too far from the

---

[118] *Nostra Aetate (Declaration on the Relationship of the Church to Non-Christian Religions)*, no. 4, in Walter M. Abbott (ed.), *The Documents of Vatican II* (New York: America Press, 1966).
[119] Congregation for the Doctrine of the Faith, *Declaration 'Dominus Iesus' on the Unicity and Salvific Universality of Jesus Christ and the Church*, www.vatican.va/roman_curia/congregations/cfaith/documents/rc_con_cfaith_doc_20000806_dominus-iesus_En.html (accessed May 27, 2008).

maxim "Outside the Christian chui ːh – or at least outside the grace of Christ – there is no salvation." Examples include Jacques Dupuis, Aloysius Pieris, Roger Haight, Raimon Panikkar, Michael Amaladoss, and Peter Phan.

Another factor that has contributed to Christian perceptions of Jews is the growth, in the twenty-first century, of Israel's influence, along with its military might. And despite the just complaint of Israelis that they are under constant threat of attack by Islamic militants, many outside Israel (and some within it) are sympathetic to the plight of the displaced Palestinians, economically deprived, under Israeli-imposed travel and work restrictions, and subject to Israeli military retaliation. Not least of all, Jewish settlements in the West Bank continue to expand, even though the international community considers them illegal. These politically ambiguous developments may be affecting Christian attitudes, theologies, and practices.

In the minds of some Catholic leaders, the memory of the murder of 6 million Jews at Christian hands has dimmed, while anxiety about Christian uniqueness has grown. The Vatican II ethic of receptivity and rapprochement toward members of other religious traditions, especially Jews, has diminished in favor of a defensive ethic of Christian exclusivity, expressed theologically, liturgically, and practically. Pope Benedict XVI drew media attention and criticism when he baptized a prominent Muslim leader in Rome during Easter week, 2008. His book on Christology, *Jesus of Nazareth*, expounds at length on the decisive and insurmountable theological differences between Christianity and Judaism.[120]

One salient instance of the liturgy, theology, and ethics connection and its bearing on the Christian–Jewish relationship is the controversial expansion of access to the Tridentine Mass. In 2007, Benedict XVI issued a papal order allowing wider use of the "Latin Mass," in the form of the 1962 (pre-Vatican II) Roman Missal, published three years before *Nostra Aetate*. The notorious phrase "the perfidious Jews" had been removed from the Good Friday rite of the Latin Mass in 1959 by Pope John XXIII. However, the 1962 Missal still refers to the "blindness" of the Jews, calls for their conversion, and asks that they "be delivered from their darkness." Moreover, the rite prays for the conversion of "pagans" or "infidels,"

[120] Joseph Ratzinger, Pope Benedict XVI, *Jesus of Nazareth: From the Baptism in the Jordan to the Transfiguration*, trans. Adrian J. Walker (New York: Doubleday, 2007).

to whom it refers as worshipping "idols," an unnecessary insult to other world religions, not least of all Islam.[121]

Greater permissiveness toward the use of the 1962 Missal has had serious consequences in the theological and practical orders. According to the Statement of the "Jews and Christians" Discussion Group of the Central Committee of German Catholics (April 2007), the reintroduction of the Catholic Tridentine Mass has disrupted Jewish–Christian relations and dialogue in the political and cultural setting most affected by the Holocaust, an effect that is especially egregious but not limited to that context. "To revive the 1962 Missal with the old Good Friday intercession means the denial of a substantial theological paradigm change made by the Council: in fact, the biblically-justified new understanding of the relationship of the Church to Judaism with the accompanying change to the Church's own self-understanding."[122] The document concludes, "It is clearly obvious what ensues with the reacceptance of the Tridentine Missal: a lasting disruption to the Catholic–Jewish Dialogue that began so hopefully at the Second Vatican Council."

In response to such criticisms, and presumably to the practical and political consequences they predicted for Jewish–Christian relations, the pope in February 2008 further adapted the Good Friday prayer for the Jews. He removed negative characterizations of the Jews and commended them as having first heard the word of God. Nevertheless, the prayer still calls for Jews to recognize Jesus Christ as Savior and specifies that Israel will be saved through inclusion in the Christian church. This amounts to reversion to the pre-Vatican II theology of Christian–Jewish relations. Its adequacy has not been accepted by those engaged in serious dialogue between the two traditions. A deterioration of Catholic–Jewish relations reflects and is reflected in the reintroduction of an adapted Tridentine Good Friday liturgy. To worsen the situation, in January 2009 Benedict XVI revoked the excommunications of four schismatic bishops, members of the Society of St. Pius X, which rejects the reforms of Vatican II, and in 2012 he began a series of talks on reconciliation.[123] One of the

---

[121] For this and other information, as well as access to the primary texts, responses, and commentaries, see the website of the Boston College Center for Christian–Jewish Learning, www.bc.edu/research/cjl/meta-elements/texts/cjrelations/topics (accessed May 19, 2008). For a critical discussion of *Nostra Aetate* and recent events, see John R. Donahue, S.J., "Trouble Ahead? The Future of Jewish–Catholic Relations," *Commonweal* (March 13, 2009), pp. 19–23.

[122] This is the first of three numbered objections in the document, accessed at the website given in the preceding note.

[123] David Kerr, "Vatican Splits Negotiations with Pius X Society," Catholic News Service, May 16, 2012, www.catholicnewsagency.com/news/vatican-says-no-deal-reached-yet-with-pius-x-society/ (accessed June 22, 2012).

four, Richard Williamson, has denied the Holocaust, saying he does not believe 6 million Jews died in Nazi gas chambers.

In *Jesus of Nazareth II*, Benedict XVI rejects the notion of Jews bearing collective guilt for the death of Jesus, attributing it instead to the sin of all humanity. Benedict also clarifies that the characterizations of "the Jews" in John's gospel refer to the Temple aristocracy. Since there was a custom at Passover of pardoning one criminal, the Temple elites are joined in the condemnation of Jesus by a crowd of Barabbas's supporters. The pope explicitly affirms the position of *Nostra Aetate* that neither the Jewish people as a whole nor Jews today can be charged with the death of Jesus.[124] This is a marked advance. It still does not amount to a full endorsement of the Vatican II theology of the enduring and saving divine covenant with Israel.

In conclusion, the atonement paradigm of salvation should be tied to resurrection and incarnation, and complemented by an ethics of the reign of God. So conceived, it can inspire the communities of service, work for structural change, and vicarious sacrifice for others that can make a difference in the world around us. Political and liturgical embodiments of the inclusive reign of God convey the mystery of God in Christ, while exclusive atonement theologies and liturgies obscure it at the practical level. Soteriological, liturgical, and political truths are mutually reinforcing.

The image of Christ on the cross has disclosive power regarding our salvation from sin, a reality that escapes systematic analysis but enduringly informs Christian ritual and prayer. The cross is a powerful religious symbol of divine solidarity with suffering humanity. It is also a symbol of transformation, both because it is God who suffers on the cross and because we experience the cross through the resurrection. Far from sabotaging the radical Christian social impetus with symbolic mediations of violence, the atonement paradigm can bridge the distance between sinful humanity's violent social structures and the transformed life to which Jesus calls us. Atonement enables human persons and societies to grow in conformity to the love and justice of God that engender harmonies among all creatures and their divine source of life.

The next chapter will consider how and why the specific content of Christian ethics is accountable to the standard of justice, as implied, for example, in calls for respect for the Jews or economic opportunities for the global poor. It will argue that the meanings of justice are both

[124] Joseph Ratzinger, Pope Benedict XVI, *Jesus of Nazareth*, part 2: *Holy Week: From the Entrance into Jerusalem to the Resurrection* (San Francisco: Ignatius Press, 2011).

particular to specific contexts and at a deeper level defined by the contours of human nature and of the natural world that extends beyond human beings. The chapter will elaborate how human understanding of and commitment to justice is interdependent with religious identity and enhanced by an experience of salvation in Jesus Christ.

CHAPTER 7

Nature

The chapters thus far have been primarily biblical and theological in orientation, but ethical ideals and standards have played a key part in readings of scripture, doctrines, and theologies. In fact, the recognition of evil and suffering as unjust, wrong, and unacceptable shaped the very first chapters, not only as a driving force in humanity's religious quest or as setting compelling political goals, but as in fact a product of already given experiences of salvation.

The argument has been that the Genesis creation narratives call humans to responsibility; that Jesus' ministry of the kingdom of God makes possible a new way of existence and shows what it looks like; that humans are redeemed and empowered through the incarnation, cross, and resurrection of Jesus Christ; that the action of the Spirit in the church converts persons and communities to faith and love; and that Christian action must be simultaneously personal, ecclesial, and political.

Within all of these theological claims, ethical values, virtues, and norms are at least implicit. Often they are very overt. Genesis calls us to form relationships in "the image of God" that renounce alienation, violence, and domination. Jesus' practice of table fellowship constitutes inclusion, forgiveness, and special care for the poor. The events of Jesus' life, death, and resurrection make it possible for us to share the new reality he embodies, but those events must not be interpreted in a way that sacralizes violence. Christian ecclesial and political action should be guided by the virtue and norm of love, but the practical meanings of love must be further specified in terms of what dispositions, practices, relationships, and actions do or do not serve human welfare.

Parts of this chapter are based on the following works: "Toward Global Ethics," *Theological Studies*, 63/2 (2002), pp. 324–44; "Nature, Change, and Justice," in David Albertson and Cabell King (eds.), *Without Nature? A New Condition for Theology* (New York: Fordham University Press, 2009), pp. 282–303; "Nature and Natural Law," in Jacques Haers, S.J., and Lieven Boeve (eds.), *To Discern Creation in a Scattering World* (Leiden: Peeters, forthcoming).

In other words, both the practice of love and the theology of Christian
practice must be structured by justice. This is an essential point for
Christian social ethics.[1] But it would be too narrow to see the ideal of
Christian love and the ethical norm of justice as related in only one direction: from love to justice. As the first chapter, I hope, made clear, Christian
concepts of grace, salvation, and virtue are already embedded in the new
personal and social, which is to say moral and political, relationships of
God's reign. And those relationships are never just "Christian" or among
Christians, but are also always "human," joining people who participate
in many types or layers of community at once, especially in our pluralistic and global age. The consequence is that we always bring to our discernment of scripture, tradition, and theology the ethical lenses provided
by our own experiences of the human reality and those of our communities. The normativity of scripture and tradition and the normativity of our
existential experiences of evil and good are mutually informing. Ethics is
thus a criterion of theology, just as theology is of ethics.

To ethics, bible and theology bring the conviction that, since all are
made in the image of God and approached by God in Christ with infinite mercy and compassion, so must we build reconciling communities
that make the plight of the poor a special priority. Ethics, in turn, elucidates the moral and social renewal that is part and counterpart of the
reality of salvation. To biblical and theological traditions, ethics brings
the identification of basic goods that all require and the reinforcement
of basic human equality as a fundamental guide to moral action. Today's
interconnected world offers opportunities and creates responsibilities to
augment access to goods and equality across communities, cultures, and
regions, by means of institutions and networks that expand the range of
political agency. The agency of Christian love, structured by justice, must
permeate this global expanse.

WHY NATURAL LAW?

A theory of justice that can help structure and expand the work of love
must be able to account not only for basic goods and equality, but also

[1] See Reinhold Niebuhr, *Nature and Destiny of Man*, vol. 2: *Human Destiny* (Louisville, KY: Westminster John Knox Press, 1996), p. 251. This requirement is key to Christian feminist ethics, a point that has been made frequently by Margaret Farley. See Margaret A. Farley, "A Feminist Version of Respect for Persons," in Charles E. Curran, Margaret A. Farley, and Richard A. McCormick, S.J. (eds.), *Feminist Ethics and the Catholic Moral Tradition* (New York: Paulist Press, 1996), pp. 164–83; originally published in the *Journal of Feminist Studies in Religion*, 9 (1993); and *Just Love: A Framework for Christian Sexual Ethics* (New York: Continuum, 2006).

for how practical moral decision making occurs and for why there is both great variety and some basic similarities in how goods are perceived and decisions assessed over time and worldwide. In addition, an adequate theory of justice must be able to explain the roles played by religious commitment and community in forming ethical insight and practice.

⌈The purpose of this chapter is to present a revised version of Thomistic natural law, which I believe to be a theory capable of meeting these demands⌋Augustine, Luther, Calvin, and others endorsed versions of natural law, as have many other thinkers. Related concepts that have wide currency are "common morality," "respect for persons," and "human rights."[2] The basic concept of natural law may prove fruitful for diverse conversation partners, particularly if it is revised to incorporate an explicitly inductive and dialogical epistemology. In addition, normative discourse about "nature" today must be broadened from the human to the whole of nature.

The theology and ethics of Thomas Aquinas, which provide a basis here, were introduced in Chapter 5. The objective of that discussion was to show how, for Aquinas, salvation and sanctification in Christ involve a transformation of human nature through a participation in divine nature, allowing friendship with God and consistent love of God and neighbor. This transformation should not be thought of in terms of a static change in nature (through the "infusion" of the virtues), but as a dynamic relation to God through the Holy Spirit. Ecumenical validation of this view was provided by recourse to the thought of Martin Luther and his modern interpreters.

The present discussion returns to the question of "nature" itself, granting that the theologian will always see "human nature" and "the natural world" through the lenses of Christian identity and biblical and theological themes, such as creation, sin, redemption, and sanctification. The concept and language of "human nature" is a way to express what constitutes us as distinctively human, what connects us to other human beings, how humans are related to the rest of the natural world, what justice

<hr>

[2] These have been incorporated in recent versions of Thomistic ethics, including the modern papal social encyclicals. See Craig A. Boyd, *A Shared Morality: A Narrative Defense of Natural Law Ethics* (Grand Rapids, MI: Brazos Press, 2007); Kenneth R. Himes (ed.), *Modern Catholic Social Teaching: Commentaries and Interpretations* (Washington, DC: Georgetown University Press, 2005); Thomas Massaro, S.J., *Living Justice: Catholic Social Teaching in Action* (New York: Rowman & Littlefield, 2000); David Hollenbach, S.J., *The Common Good and Christian Ethics* (Cambridge: Cambridge University Press, 2002); and David Hollenbach (ed.), *Refugee Rights: Ethics, Advocacy, and Africa* (Washington, DC: Georgetown University Press, 2008).

requires in those relations, and how and why conversation about justice can be carried on across distances of time, space, culture, and religion.

As the Catholic International Theological Commission recognizes, the concepts of nature and natural law provide a resource for twenty-first-century ethics, since "the great problems that present themselves to human beings have a more international, planetary dimension." The moral ideal of "global solidarity ... has its ultimate foundation in the unity of the human race."

This translates into a planetary responsibility. Thus the problem of ecological equilibrium, of the protection of the environment, of the resources and of the climate have become a pressing concern, which calls upon all humanity and whose solution goes quite beyond national boundaries.[3]

Natural law ethics no doubt needs to be updated and revised in a global, postmodern context. Nevertheless, the moral realism at its center is worthy of a vigorous defense. "Periodic disclosures of human wickedness and horrors – lynchings, secret police abductions or death squad assassinations – reawaken our sense of the importance of objective moral standards to which evil-doers can be held accountable."[4] Women, ethnic and cultural minorities, victims of political violence, and those excluded from basic necessities because of others' greed often appeal to basic justice and common humanity. They demand that their own humanity be recognized and patent injustices reversed. These appeals reveal the existence and the importance of our common human nature and the moral claims it exerts. An ethics of common nature and humanity is a way of calling the powerful to account. Natural law ethics also can support a global ecological ethics, an ethics of justice toward the natural world.

The reconstructed vision of natural law that I will propose is different from that of Aquinas, in that it does not depend on a conception of reality as consisting in a static hierarchy of beings, whose essences, functions, and purposes never change. What I see as most characteristic and most worth recovering in natural law tradition is a view of human existence and of morality as purposeful (teleological); a conviction that basic moral values are "objective" and shared among culturally different human beings (moral realism); a moral epistemology of inductive,

---

[3] International Theological Commission, "The Search for Universal Ethics: A New Look at Natural Law," July 2009, available at the Vatican website (www.vatican.va) in French and Italian. Unofficial English translation by Joseph Bolin, www.pathsoflove.com/universal-ethics-natural-law.html (accessed March 18, 2011).

[4] Stephen J. Pope, "Reason and Natural Law," in Gilbert Meilaender and William Werpehowski (eds.), *The Oxford Handbook of Theological Ethics* (Oxford University Press, 2005), pp. 148–9.

experience-based, critical practical reasoning (a connection between the "is" and the "ought"), in which contingent contexts are highly influential in discerning priorities among goods and concrete choices about them. Supporting this last point is Aquinas's view of practical reason, which depicts moral knowledge and choice as relying interdependently on the reason and will, as well as on the virtues that orient both to action that rightly respects goods in the concrete. Among these virtues prudence is key. At the practical level, all knowledge of the natural law and all applications of its requirements of justice are perspectival and include the influences of historical and social location, including religious identity.

I propose that an important implication of a view of practical reason as always operating contextually is that what is known by reason and what is known by faith cannot easily be separated, nor should they be. Both reason and faith work within the agent's whole context and engage the agent's multifaceted identity. Moreover, salvation from God in Christ is mediated historically, by the Spirit in the church, made up of people with multiple communal memberships. What is important to consider are not the independent counsels of reason and faith, church and society, but the ways in which different persons and communities order priorities among goods differently. It is the job of the ethicist to examine these orderings critically, and the job of the Christian ethicist to recommend how priorities should be established on the basis of membership in the body of Christ *and* on the basis of insights that wider experiences and other communal identities may provide as to the concrete meanings and political relevance of gospel values.[5]

I want to focus on three components of a revised and credible natural law theory. The first is the definition of human "nature," or at least the identification of the aspects of nature that are relevant to moral obligation. I sort these aspects into three categories: species-typical characteristics; basic human goods; and basic equality. The second component is an explanation of how we come to know what defines human nature and how nature relates to morality, that is, an epistemology of natural law. Building on but going beyond Aquinas, I propose that knowledge of nature and the natural law requires inductive consensus building that includes experiences of God, takes into account cultural differences, corrects bias, and envisions the possibility of change in nature itself, in

[5] Jean Porter applies a similar characterization to Thomistic social ethics, and to the ethics of Aquinas himself, in "Making Common Cause with Men and Women of Our Age: A Thomist Perspective," *Studies in Christian Ethics* 25 (2012), pp. 169–73.

the moral requirements of nature, and especially in knowledge of those
requirements. The third component is a concept of moral virtue that,
elaborating on the epistemology of natural law, explains how agents learn
to recognize human goods and equality and how to act consistently to
realize those values.

After laying out the definition of nature, the inductive character of
practical reason, and the role of virtue in moral knowing and acting, I will
offer Aquinas's analysis of "just war" to exemplify contextual thinking
about what justice requires, then consider briefly how the scope of natural
law ethics extends from human nature to the whole natural world.

A NORMATIVE CONCEPT OF HUMAN NATURE

Human nature includes human *characteristics*, human *goods*, and basic
human *equality* or *"equal respect."*

First of all, then, all species-typical or "normal" human beings have
certain characteristics in common.[6] Traditionally and in Thomistic perspective, humans possess the characteristic capacities (or "faculties") of
intellect and will. Aquinas tends to privilege intellect over will in discussing the natural law (even though charity, an orientation of the will to
God in love, is the "form" or "root" of the theological virtues and directs
us to our highest good [*ST* II-II.23.8]).

The framework that grounds natural law morality in intelligence and
freedom should be expanded in five ways. First, contemporary philosophy, psychology, and epistemology would not separate intellect and will
so clearly into sequential moments or phases as Aquinas implies when
he says that the will cannot choose something unless it is already known
(*ST* II-II.4.7). All knowledge and inquiry are already "interested," or
committed to understand certain realities and answer certain questions rather than others. The will is involved in the process of coming to
knowledge.

Second, not only do reason and will operate together, they operate in
conjunction with additional human capacities: the emotions, affections,
and imagination. Aquinas himself recognizes that reason operates under

---

[6] I am assuming a definition of "the human" based on characteristics of the species as a whole and
of adult members within the range of "normal" or "healthy" functioning. I do not intend this
definition to establish the parameters of "normality" or to rule out the humanity of humans who
do not measure up to the norm or ideal. How to defend the inclusion of anomalous members
within the categories "human" and "human person" is an additional theoretical and practical
problem that is important but not undertaken here.

the influence of the passions, or what we today might call the emotions.[7] Though the passions are often presented by Aquinas as disorderly, he rejects the idea that they are evil in themselves. The passions are a problem only when not moderated by reason (*ST* I-II.24).[8] But emotions and reason are interrelated, not separate capacities. For Aquinas, the emotions are forms of appetitive motion that have complex relations to other powers or capacities by which we see and experience ourselves and the world.[9] Emotional responses are not automatic; they are shaped or mediated by cultural (and religious) symbols, narratives, and practices.[10] In turn, the emotions can lead to an intellectual evaluation of the usefulness, dangerousness, or beauty of an object or a course of action.[11]

Theorists today recognize that sometimes emotions can lead to knowledge, that they have a sort of "cognitive" function that attunes the reason, rather than just the other way around. Passions or emotions can draw reason to recognize and the will to choose what one's emotive response has already flagged as right or "fitting."[12] According to Diana Fritz Cates, "Moral understanding has an emotional component," and the emotional dimension of knowledge gives it both a relational and a bodily quality.[13] "Understanding the act may include understanding its moral dimensions and reaching moral understanding may include feeling and reflecting upon certain moral emotions like grief and guilt."[14] Jean Porter points

---

[7] For Aquinas, the passions are movements of the sensory appetite, a bodily experience of attraction or aversion, occurring as a result of a cognitive evaluation of an object. If the passions are taken together with the judgments that give rise to them, they come close to what we mean today by the emotions. See Claudia Eisen Murphy, "Aquinas on Our Responsibility for Our Emotions," *Medieval Philosophy and Theology*, 8 (1999), pp. 167–8.

[8] For Aquinas, "the completed intellectual power of the human soul as an intellectual substance is constituted by intellect, senses, will, and sense-appetite together." Kevin White, "The Passions of the Soul (Ia IIae, qq. 22–28)," in Stephen J. Pope (ed.), *The Ethics of Aquinas* (Washington, DC: Georgetown University Press, 2002), pp. 103–115, at 105.

[9] Diana Fritz Cates, *Aquinas on the Emotions: A Religious-Ethical Inquiry* (Washington, DC: Georgetown University Press, 2009), pp. 10, 121–2.

[10] See Paul Lauritzen, "Emotions and Religious Ethics," *Journal of Religious Ethics*, 16 (1988), pp. 308, 312–16.

[11] Cates, *Aquinas on the Emotions*, p. 115. Cates cites Aquinas, *Summa Theologiae*, I.78.4., including ad.5.

[12] See Martha C. Nussbaum, *Upheavals of Thought: The Intelligence of Emotions* (New York: Cambridge University Press, 2003); Diana Fritz Cates, *Choosing to Feel: Virtue, Friendship, and Compassion for Friends* (University of Notre Dame Press, 1997); and Maureen H. O'Connell, *Compassion: Loving Our Neighbor in an Age of Globalization* (Maryknoll, NY: Orbis Books, 2009).

[13] Diana Fritz Cates, "Caring for Girls and Women Who Are Considering Abortion: Rethinking Informed Consent," in Diana Fritz Cates and Paul Lauritzen (eds.), *Medicine and the Ethics of Care* (Washington, DC: Georgetown University Press, 2001), pp. 168, 172.

[14] Ibid., p. 183.

out that Aquinas's own view that the virtues are interconnected in moral action entails that "intellectual judgement and passion or sensibility are inseparably linked."[15]

Third, it follows that human embodiment both sets conditions on and enables human knowing and choosing. In our human nature, rational self-consciousness and voluntary decisions are involved with and dependent on the corporeal existence we share with animals and other beings. Intellect, will, imagination, and emotions are all embodied capacities. According to Aquinas, all knowledge comes through sense impressions (*ST* I.78.4.ad 4), although the intellect infers more than the senses directly convey.

To speak of the embodied, material nature of human beings is already to imply a fourth point, humans are relational and social. In fact, relationships and sociality may be more constitutively human than characteristics ascribable to human individuals, such as rational intellect and free will. The human is "a social and political being," for whom the good life is not lived in isolation, but in relationship "with parents, children, a wife [spouse], and friends and fellow citizens generally."[16] Aquinas reappropriates this insight of Aristotle when he envisions every individual person as a part of the whole community, and thus always related with and to others in the common good (*ST* II-II.64.2). Of course, for Aquinas, the "body politic" is not humanity's ultimate end, which is fellowship with God, the universal common good (I-II.21.4.r.ad. 3; I-II.109.3).[17] As we saw in Chapter 2, the sociality of the person is supported by the Genesis creation stories, which portray the "image of God" in humanity as inhering in relationships rather than (as Aquinas implies) in individual characteristics such as reason and freedom.

Fifth, the capacity for self-transcendence, spirituality, or religiosity is also characteristically human. This capacity may be called the "religious affections" or "sense of the divine."[18] Christian natural law theories, deriving from Augustine and Aquinas, understand human activity to be directed ultimately by the "supernatural" (divinely bestowed) good of loving union with God, termed by Aquinas "friendship" with God (II-II.23.1; 23.2.ad.1; 23.7). But modern authors suggest that hunger for

[15] Jean Porter, *Moral Action and Christian Ethics* (Cambridge University Press, 1995), p. 196.
[16] Aristotle, *Nicomachean Ethics*, trans. Martin Ostwald (Upper Saddle River, NJ: Prentice Hall, 1999) book 1, 7.
[17] Ibid.
[18] Building on the Calvinist tradition, especially Jonathan Edwards, see James M. Gustafson, *A Sense of the Divine: The Natural Environment from a Theocentric Perspective* (Cleveland: Pilgrim Press, 1994).

unity with the divine and an ability to glimpse God's presence are universal human capacities. In the words of Edward Schillebeeckx, "Religion is an anthropological constant without which human salvation, redemption, and true liberation are impossible." Even beyond Christianity, there is a religious or spiritual dimension of human consciousness that gives a "utopian" edge to diverse human quests for meaning amidst the realities of suffering and change.[19] Religion conveys a vision of reconciled community through the power and love of God, but religion also urges the dispositions of humility, gratitude, repentance, and compassion that are necessary to reconciliation.

Transcendence and spirituality do not separate us from our natural environment or other nonhuman living beings. A sense of these beings' own ineffable mystery and uniqueness rules out any expectation of complete human control or of unlimited human use. Our consciousness and spirit are formed interactively with other creatures, and they provide conditions and images through which we approach the infinite. As Bonaventure wrote in praise of Francis of Assisi:

> Aroused by all things to the love of God,
> He rejoiced in all the works of the Lord's hands
> And from these joy-producing manifestations
> He rose to their life-giving
> Principle and cause.
> In beautiful things
> He saw Beauty itself.[20]

To this philosophical and theological construal of human nature as having consistent characteristics, including a religious capacity for union with God, a historical and empirical objection may be raised. This line of critique is based on the observation that human nature *changes*. Will species-typical characteristics evolve into something different, to a "nature" that would be unrecognizable to humans today? Even if human goods have been more or less the same historically up to now, will they necessarily remain so? By what rationale can equality, for example –admittedly a recent and still culturally limited ideal – be defended as a human

---

[19] Edward Schillebeeckx, *The Schillebeeckx Reader*, ed. Robert J. Schreiter (Edinburgh: T & T Clark, 1984), pp. 36–7; originally published in Edward Schillebeeckx, *God Among Us: The Gospel Proclaimed*, trans. John Bowden (New York and London: Crossroad and SCM Press, 1980), pp. 250–3.

[20] Saint Bonaventure, *The Life of Saint Francis*, IX, 1, trans. Ewert Cousins, p. 263; as cited by Regis J. Armstrong, O.F.M. Cap., and Ignatius C. Brady, O.F.M., Introduction to *Francis and Clare: The Complete Works* (New York: Paulist Press, 1982), p. 19.

"universal" rather than as a recent regional development? Certainly human nature has always interacted with its environment and continues to do so. Nature is not static but pliable and metamorphosing. In an age of genetic technology, nanotechnology, and biomechanical hybridity, it could be argued that nature is changing past the bounds of our descriptive and moral categories.[21] This arguably obliterates any possibility of a natural moral law. If nature changes, then there can be no stable morality based on "nature."

To the contrary, "nature" requires recognizable identity over time, not static sameness. Aristotle defined nature not in terms of the unchanging traits of beings, but as their propensity to change while maintaining their identity.[22] Human nature certainly includes change as well as continuity, because human beings and societies are historical, and their very existence is dynamic and open. Ecological theologian Peter Scott rightly calls human nature "the temporal emergence of embodied selves-in-relation," including relation to the rest of nature and now to technology. These relations are not "external" to human beings but help constitute what being human is.[23]

Human nature is necessarily "developmental" not only because of these changing relationships, but also because within these relationships, humans pursue goods that are specified in different ways at different times, that may be more or less completely realized, and that will vary at the level of particular instantiations.[24] Natural law as a moral law indicates "an unfolding developing process."[25] Natural law theories require not that humans or the human species be unchanging, but that human beings have characteristics that perdure within change and that among these distinctive characteristics are those that constitute humans as moral beings. These

[21] For a discussion of the stability of nature and change, see Hilary Rose and Steven Rose, "The Changing Face of Human Nature," *Daedalus* (Summer 2009), pp. 7–20; David Albertson and Cabell King (eds.), *Without Nature? A New Condition for Theology* (New York: Fordham University Press, 2010); and Lisa Sowle Cahill, Hille Haker, and Eloi Messi Metogo (eds.), *Human Nature, Human Goods and Natural Law* (London: SCM Press, 2010), especially the articles by Ludwig Siep and Jean-Pierre Wils. On humanity's "hybrid" nature in a technological age, recreated in the image of the incarnation, see Peter Manley Scott, *Anti-Human Theology: Nature, Technology and the Postnatural* (London: SCM Press, 2010), pp. 130–9.

[22] Aristotle, *Metaphysics*, trans. Richard Hope (Ann Arbor: University of Michigan Press, 1952), V; Aristotle, *Nicomachean Ethics*, I.7.4–5.

[23] Peter Scott, *A Political Theology of Nature* (Cambridge University Press, 2003), p. 192. What we need is "an account of *Nature-inclusive-of-Humanity-which-is other-than-Nature*" which requires that all three nouns be accented" (ibid., p. 57).

[24] Boyd, *Shared Morality*, p. 183. See also Cristina L. H. Traina, *Feminist Ethics and Natural Law: The End of the Anathemas* (Washington, DC: Georgetown University Press, 1999).

[25] Ibid., p. 191.

very same characteristics that constantly define the species – intelligence, imagination, contextual freedom, social and material relationality – also enable human nature's dynamism. Natural law ethics can accept the reality of change; recognizable continuity of "the human" still remains, and makes it possible to speak of human characteristics and goods.

Having outlined some basic and relatively invariant human characteristics (intellect and will; emotions, affections, and imagination; embodiment and materiality; historicity and relationality; a religious sense of the divine), I will consider the *basic goods* that constitute human flourishing. As Aquinas puts it, "The good is that which all things seek after." Aquinas's first precept of morality and of the natural law is: "Good is to be done and pursued, and evil is to be avoided" (*ST* I-II.94.2). But to say that good is to be done and evil avoided, the first principle of practical reason, does not move us very far toward action. What specifically *is* good for human beings?

Goods beyond the human constitution itself guide human desire, deliberation, choice, and action. But goods can include human states and relations, as well as nonhuman entities. For instance, food is a good, and so is a system of food production and equitable distribution. An edible plant is a good for humans, and it is also good in its own right as a being with an integral nature and a characteristic form of flourishing, and as such it demands human respect. No list of human goods will ever be complete and unrevisable, particularly when it reaches into the more detailed aspects of human life that vary from culture to culture. Nor will any system of norms specifying the ways in which goods should be respected. As Aquinas cautions, practical reason "is busied with contingent matters, about which human action is concerned" (I-II.94.4). While the general principles of the natural law do not change, "the more we descend to matters of detail," the more we encounter variation, both in practical rectitude and in knowledge (I-II.94.4), both of goods and of how to realize them.

Aquinas does not give a complete, systematic treatment of all the human goods and bads or of the precepts guiding us toward them. Aquinas's distinction between primary and secondary precepts of natural law introduces the possibility of claiming more stability for basic human inclinations and ends than for more concrete specifications of their fulfillment.[26] Aquinas does not enumerate the primary principles or precepts

---

[26] Aquinas writes of widely recognized basic inclinations and the general precepts based on them in *ST* I-II.94.2. In *ST* I-II.100, he affirms that "every judgment of practical reason proceeds from principles known naturally" (a.1), but also states that some of the more particular precepts of

completely, nor does he draw a clear line between primary and secondary principles. Yet he does begin his discussion of the practical content of the natural law by naming three fairly basic spheres of morality, known to all cultures, with their constitutive goods. First, just like every other creature, humans seek self-preservation by protecting their own lives. Second, like other animals, humans seek sexual intercourse, then nurture and educate their offspring. Finally, human beings, through their distinctively human intelligence, seek "to know the truth about God and to live in society."[27] Life is a good and so are measures that protect it; children are a good and so are family bonds and education; sociality is a good and so are systems of just government; God is the ultimate Good, and good also are human paths to the divine.

Aquinas derives precepts of the natural law teleologically, that is, from observation of our natural inclinations as directing us to ends that are naturally apprehended as good. Lying, cheating, aggressive dominance, and adultery are also common human behaviors, and in this sense they are natural to human beings and societies. Yet they do not constitute the goods that humans ought to pursue, because they are destructive of human well-being. The purpose of moral and political activity is to seek human and social flourishing and happiness.

In distinguishing good from bad inclinations, Aquinas appeals for the reader's consensus about things that everyone presumably can see. His premise is that it is generally clear what harms the human good and what supports it, although he also presupposes and is shaped by Christian doctrine. Agreement is possible not just because different traditions coincidentally arrive at similar values, but because all traditions are at a deep level grounded in the same human and earthly reality. Nevertheless, to say all persons and societies procreate and educate the young is not yet to specify the best or acceptable ways of doing so, to deal with exceptional cases, or to answer the problem of perversion and injustice in sex, gender, family, or education. Also, factual information, or understandings about the facts, can be mistaken or can change. Aquinas had a different view of

---

the natural law are better known by the wise and are clarified by revelation (a.1, a.3, a.5). For a discussion, see Stephen J. Pope, "Knowability of the Natural Law: A Foundation for Ethics of the Common Good," in James Donahue and M. Theresa Moser, R.S.C.J. (eds.), *Religion, Ethics, and the Common Good*, College Theology Society Annual Volume 41 (Mystic, CT: Twenty-Third Publications, 1996), pp. 57–9. Daniel Daly makes a case for an inductive epistemology of the natural law, at least or especially where the secondary precepts are concerned. The general principles are virtually self-evident, but they are few and quite formal ("The Relationship of Virtues and Norms in the *Summa Theologiae*," *Heythrop Journal*, 51 [2010], pp. 214–29).

[27] Ibid., I-II.94.2.

the "facts" of procreation than modern people, which influenced how he then interpreted procreation's good and its moral parameters. He shared cultural assumptions about the status of women. And he had no idea that human overpopulation could some day threaten planetary disaster.

Still, Aquinas's basic observations are uncontroversial. Protection of human life and health, the institutionalization of procreation to socialize children, the economic and political organization of society, and the formalization of religious expression are defining elements of every major culture. These *are* acknowledged human goods; good societies *do* seek and protect them; and moral and social behavior *ought* to respect them. Certainly Aquinas is right that people in all cultures understand and value these goods, on the basis of their experience and by observing human life.

Recognition of basic human goods is necessary for any program of social justice in a global era. Rebutting the idea that women and men have two different "complementary" natures, feminist theologian Colleen Griffith asserts that "there is a natural givenness to human bodiliness," calls the body *"common ground,"* and mentions shared biological stages, such as birth, growth, continued life, aging, and death.[28] The philosopher Martha Nussbaum furnishes a contemporary list of basic goods, the goods that constitute a life with dignity. Nussbaum's goods ("capabilities") include life; bodily health; bodily integrity; senses, imagination, and thought; emotions; practical reason; affiliation (relationship to others, including participation in social institutions); relationship to other species; play; and political and material control over one's environment.[29] Ana María Díaz-Stevens affirms the reality of gender, race, and age differences, as well as differences in culture, life experience, education, profession, and health and ability. Nevertheless, certain things are the same for everyone:

The need to be cared for and loved and to reciprocate in kind; the need for family and friends; the need for a means of livelihood; the need for a roof over our heads, clothes on our backs, and education for ourselves and our children; the need for a means of maintaining our health; the need for a healthy environment where we can live peaceful and meaningful lives, where we can recreate and share gifts and present our needs, cares, and aspirations without fear of

[28] Colleen M. Griffith, "Human Bodiliness: Sameness as Starting Point," in Elizabeth A. Johnson (ed.), *The Church Women Want: Catholic Women in Dialogue* (New York: Crossroad, 2002), pp. 64–6.
[29] Martha C. Nussbaum, *Women and Human Development* (New York: Cambridge University Press, 2000), pp. 78–80.

discrimination or refusal. We all need a place to meet each other with not just tolerance but acceptance.[30]

Although these goods are understood and sought differently in different cultures, "there is much family relatedness and much overlap among societies," according to Nussbaum. Although human experiences and their related goods are "experienced differently in different contexts, we can none the less identify certain features of our common humanity."[31] In life as it is actually lived, "we do find a family of experiences, clustering around certain focuses, which can provide reasonable starting points for cross-cultural reflection."[32] In other words, the goods identified as most basic by natural law theories are not seriously in dispute.

Stipulating human characteristics and naming the goods fundamentally important for human flourishing is not nearly as difficult, however, as arguing that all persons are entitled, in principle, to *equal access* to basic goods. Stated differently, equality itself is a basic human characteristic, and equal respect a basic good and moral obligation. Although recognition of equality can take different forms in different spheres (the legal, political, economic, or social, for instance), the core meaning of equality is that "human beings are entitled to be treated with respect because they are of equal worth, independently of their ability, contribution, success, work or desert." Differential treatment can be justified but requires defense in light of the premise of basic equality.[33]

The greatest source of disagreement and "cultural diversity" in ethics is conflict over whether human beings in general are essentially equal, and hence equally deserving of the basic goods all value. Recognition of the equal dignity and rights of other human beings, "mutual respect," or "respect for persons" is a modern value that seems in modern cultures

---

[30] Ana María Díaz-Stevens, "The Divine Danger of Diversity: A Hispanic Catholic Perspective," in Johnson (ed.), *The Church Women Want*, p. 92.

[31] Martha C. Nussbaum, "Non-Relative Virtues: An Aristotelian Approach," in Martha C. Nussbaum and Amartya Sen (eds.), *The Quality of Life* (Oxford: Clarendon Press, 1993), p. 263. An earlier version appeared in Peter A. French, Theodore E. Uehling, and Howard Wettstein (eds.), *Midwest Studies in Philosophy* (Notre Dame, IN: University of Notre Dame Press, 1988) vol. 13.

[32] Nussbaum, "Non-Relative Virtues," p. 265.

[33] Duncan B. Forrester, *On Human Worth* (London: SCM Press, 2000), p. 31. Forrester believes that equality is difficult if not impossible to defend without a Christian theological rationale, and offering such a defense is the main objective of his project (ibid., pp. 135, 250). See also Duncan B. Forrester, *Christian Justice and Public Policy* (Cambridge: Cambridge University Press, 1997). While I have likewise shown grounds in bible and tradition for recognizing equality, I believe it is important to realize that equality was not in fact a general Christian social norm before modernity and to try to make a case that there is a human ability to recognize the basic equality of others without the support of Christian theology.

self-evidently to define justice. But equality is not taken for granted in all cultures. Indeed, even within cultures that endorse general equality and rights in theory or in law, the practical equality of some is effectively denied by practices and ideologies that define them as "less than equal" for spurious, deceptive, and self-interested reasons. Glaring examples are sexism, ethnic and racial discrimination, and class-based systems of exclusion. Getting consensus on lists of goods is easy; getting agreement on equal access is much more difficult.

The strength of Aquinas's approach to the basic human inclinations and to derivative basic precepts of the natural law is his appeal for an inductive but general consensus about the things that people in all cultures do seem to seek and respect: the preservation of life, procreation and education of children, and cooperative social existence (*ST* II–II.94.2.). The weakness of Aquinas is that he does not assume basic equality. For instance, he (like Aristotle) assumes that slaves and women occupy subordinate rather than equal positions of access to goods. In deriving more specific conclusions from the basic precepts, he is inadequately sensitive to the perspectives and experiences of other cultures and of nonelite groups within his own culture.

Equality as a human characteristic and good that demands moral recognition is a new arrival on the natural law scene. Recognition of human equality does have ancient historical precedents, especially in religious ideas that all persons are created by God, embody a spark of the divine, or are equally redeemed by God. But equality as a political ideal or norm arrived with the Enlightenment and with modern movements for rights, democracy, and liberation. The global expansion of the ideal of equality as an ethical ideal demanded by the "reality" of human being and existence is also a modern phenomenon. It has been enabled by anticolonial movements and by communications media that bring alien cultures into contact with one another, show commonalities in human lives and aspirations across cultures, and make it possible to join forces in working for change.

To discover how or on what philosophical basis equality can be defended remains a significant challenge. A Kantian approach might argue that the structure of moral reason in and of itself or a priori dictates that every human being should be regarded as an end in him- or herself, and never simply as a means to the ends of others.[34] Some see Kant's principle of equal respect as especially amenable to theologically grounded

[34] See Immanuel Kant, *Foundations of the Metaphysics of Morals*, ed. Robert Paul Wolff, trans. Lewis White Beck (Indianapolis: Bobbs-Merrill, 1969), pp. 44, 64 (2nd sec.).

ethics, and even as itself indebted to theology.[35] One weak point of this argument is that the majority of human societies in human history have not in fact made equality the basis of their exercise of moral reason. Kant's "categorical imperative" assumes human equality, but does not show why it is really self-evident.

The argument that, to be consistent, any rational agent must will any of his or her actions to become a universal law is problematic if one is attempting to persuade people who are not in fundamental agreement that all other agents are equal to oneself (or one's group) in basic worth and agency. If one does not accept this premise, one will not accept that differential treatment of lower-status groups of people in relation to basic goods is actually exploitation. And higher-status groups will be regarded with fear and defensiveness, rather than with the assumption of mutual, equal accountability.

Another tactic in defense of equality might be to refer the idea to a common tradition, such as the biblical narratives of humanity's divine creation and redemption or a political tradition of democracy and human rights. Religious defenses of "human dignity," such as Catholic social teaching or Jean Porter's *Nature as Reason*,[36] tend to appeal to the first type of argument; in the former case, to bolster the claim that human equality is self-evident to reason. Jeffrey Stout's *Democracy and Tradition* and the later work of John Rawls are examples of the second type of appeal, to a shared political tradition.[37] The obvious problem with a tradition-based approach is that it forfeits epistemological universality and, with it, the possibility that equality can be understood as a generally compelling social and political ideal.

Theologian Margaret Farley – informed by Christian beliefs, modern political traditions, and Kantian respect for persons – argues that justice as equal respect can be inferred from "the shared concrete reality of persons."[38] Her argument is that it is possible for and even morally incumbent

---

[35] Forrester, *On Human Worth*, p. 130.

[36] According to *Gaudium et Spes*, no. 28, "Since all men possess a rational soul and are created in God's likeness, since they have the same nature and origin, have been redeemed by Christ, and enjoy the same divine calling and destiny, the basic equality of all must receive increasingly greater recognition" (Vatican document, Pope Paul VI, December 7, 1965: "Pastoral Constitution on the Church in the Modern World"). See also Jean Porter, *Nature as Reason: A Thomistic Theory of the Natural Law* (Grand Rapids, MI: Eerdmans, 2005), especially pp. 358–78 on natural rights.

[37] Jeffrey Stout, *Democracy and Tradition* (Princeton, NJ: Princeton University Press, 2005); and John Rawls, *Political Liberalism* (New York: Columbia University Press, 1996).

[38] Farley, *Just Love*, p. 210.

upon persons to recognize that other persons are unique but are also sharers in common humanity, with parallel potential for flourishing and vulnerability to diminishment. In addition, persons can and should recognize in other persons a capacity for freedom and self-determination, and a capacity and need to be in interpersonal relationships of knowledge and love.[39] Freedom and relationality ground ethical responsibility to the other, insofar as we recognize others as subjects like ourselves, capable as we are of self-possession and self-transcendence, of flourishing and suffering. From a religious standpoint, genuine community requires not only knowledge of interdependence, but also the recognition that the life of "the other" shares in a "mystery and greatness" that we cannot fully understand from our own vantage point and should not seek to control.[40]

Arguments in favor of equality can be supported by sociological and economic evidence that societies in which there is greater equality are more successful societies, while wide inequality is socially dysfunctional. Like other species, human beings share the same needs and require the same resources. This inspires competition. But human beings have a greater capacity than other species to be for one another sources of care, protection, assistance, nurturance, and love. This provides an unparalleled "potential to be each other's greatest source of comfort and security."[41]

When there are vast disparities between the very wealthy and the shrinking middle and growing lower classes (as in the United States in the first decade of this century), distrust and cynicism abound. The rich are corrupted by a sense of inalienable advantage. Those of lower status give up hope of affecting the economic system and displace their anger onto people who are even more vulnerable. The expectations and virtues upon which democracy rests are eroded. The resulting social problems affect the whole society, not just those on the bottom. In more egalitarian societies, by contrast, more people are oriented by empathy toward inclusive social relations.[42]

Ultimately it may be that recognition of human equality requires more than an intellectual argument, or even a demonstration of equality's social benefits. Writing on universal human rights, Grace Kao hypothesizes

---

[39] Ibid., pp. 212–13.
[40] Reinhold Niebuhr, *The Irony of American History*, intro. Andrew J. Bacevich (University of Chicago Press, 2008), p. 139.
[41] Richard Wilkinson and Kate Pickett, *The Spirit Level: Why Greater Equality Makes Societies Stronger* (London: Bloomsbury Press, 2010), p. 198. See also Joseph E. Stiglitz, *The Price of Inequality: How Today's Divided Society Endangers Our Future* (New York: W. W. Norton, 2012).
[42] Ibid., pp. 166–8, 173.

that perhaps there is no definitively persuasive logical defense of the equal inviolability of all human persons. Rather, "we encounter others as coming into our presence bearing legitimate claims upon us about how we are to treat them," just as we bear claims upon our treatment by others.[43] Compassion and solidarity depend not on logic alone, or on empirical evidence about beneficial effects, but on imagination and emotion, usually nourished by community narratives and practices in which the virtues of mutual respect and respect for the most vulnerable are taught. A sincere and lasting personal commitment to equality requires a movement of compassion or solidarity in which one recognizes the other as not only like oneself, but as eliciting and claiming the practical respect that we ourselves desire and believe we deserve.

The key to recognizing equality lies in the practical intensification and extension of the human capacities for empathy and compassion. Philosophers like Paul Ricoeur and Emmanuel Levinas appeal to our human ability and obligation to recognize the humanity of "the other" and to respond to the subjectivity, situation, and needs of the other with the same dedication we have to our own welfare.[44] Maureen O'Connell urges that compassion perceives reality truly, interprets reality by including overlooked perspectives, and then strives actively to empower the excluded and gain more inclusive patterns of social participation.[45] These themes are reinforced by the commands found in many religious traditions, to the effect that we ought to regard others as other selves, out of love of God. Greater recognition of equality is supported by the expansion of social narratives, movements, structures, and practices premised on equality and encouraging practical respect for equality. Religious narratives and practices, such as eucharistic fellowship, hospitality, and care for the poor, can enlarge the human capacities for empathy and altruism.

Philosophers and theologians who adopt an inductive approach to a common morality or to the justice of "liberation" often rely on narratives, personal histories, anecdotes, aesthetic media like the visual arts and poetry, and even photographs to bring home the humanity and dignity of those who suffer due to social inequalities. Martha Nussbaum, for

[43] Grace Y. Kao, *Grounding Human Rights in a Pluralist World* (Washington, DC: Georgetown University Press, 2011), p. 163.

[44] See Emmanuel Levinas, *Totality and Infinity: An Essay on Exteriority*, trans. Alphonso Lingis (Pittsburgh: Duquesne University Press, 1969; originally published in French in 1961); and *Otherwise Than Being, or Beyond Essence*, trans. Alphonso Lingis (Dordrecht: Kluwer Academic, 1978; originally published in French in 1974). Sese also Paul Ricoeur, *Oneself as Another*, trans. Kathleen Blamey (University of Chicago Press, 1992).

[45] O'Connell, *Compassion*, p. 2.

instance, sprinkles her writings on the capabilities approach with stories of women she has met in India and Bangladesh. Religious narratives can have a similar function, as illustrated by the powerful parables of Jesus, challenging those who want to enter God's reign to behave with the compassion of the Good Samaritan, Prodigal Son's father, or shepherd in search of a lost sheep. Religious art can reach across and unite communities to battle common problems of poverty, racism, and violence.[46]

The interdependence of knowledge of the natural law with narratives, practices, and virtues is the focus of the next two sections, on moral epistemology and on natural law and the virtues. This discussion interfaces with and expands the argument of the first chapter, that moral knowledge and knowledge of God are practically and communally engendered and tested.

KNOWLEDGE OF THE NATURAL LAW

The epistemology of natural law must be developed in terms of inductive consensus building that identifies patterns of continuity within change; that incorporates new insights, especially the fact of human equality; and that recognizes that bias and vested interests will work against recognition of equality and must be countered.[47] Knowledge of the natural law is always perspectival and partial, even when it is also true and accurate. Knowledge is never detached from the particular contexts, identities, and interests of knowing subjects. An inductive epistemology is demanded by the practical nature of moral knowledge, and if it is also collaborative, it will help counteract the ever-present reality of bias. Knowledge of human needs, goods, and obligations approaches universality only to the extent that the reasoning process behind it is extensive, inclusive, and critical.

The deductive method of neoscholasticism, and its claim to timeless certitude in the specific conclusions proposed on the basis of its principles, are clearly now untenable, a point already well established.[48] Moral

---

[46] Maureen O'Connell, *If These Walls Could Talk: Community Muralism and the Beauty of Justice* (Collegeville MN: Liturgical Press, 2012) offers a theological interpretation of a public art movement that has inspired social change in Philadelphia.

[47] See Cahill et al. (eds.), *Human Nature and Natural Law*, especially the essays by Ludwig Siep, Cristina Traina, and Maria Christina Astorga. See also Susan Frank Parsons, *Feminism and Christian Ethics* (Cambridge University Press, 1996), p. 199, on an "appropriate universalism" in feminist moral reasoning.

[48] See, e.g., Michael B. Crowe, "The Pursuit of the Natural Law," in Charles E. Curran and Richard A. McCormick, S.J. (eds.), *Natural Law and Theology* (New York: Paulist Press, 1991), pp. 296–332 (originally published in the *Irish Theological Quarterly*, 44 [1977]); and Daniel Daly,

truth as practical truth is a truth of action, true "about" action's conformity to the reality of goods as they are available concretely and interrelated.
As Josef Pieper explains, "Realization of the good presupposes that our
actions are appropriate to the real situation, that is to the concrete realities
which form the 'environment' of a concrete human action; and that we
therefore take this concrete reality seriously, with clear-eyed objectivity."[49]
Practical moral decisions also involve an "inevitable choice between competing options."[50] Thus, according to Aquinas, "the intellect cannot be
infallibly in conformity with things in contingent matters" (I-II.57.a.5; see
also 94.a.4 on the natural law and contingent truth).

The central thesis of Daniel Westberg's *Right Practical Reason* is that
intellect and will are interactive in the process of action and of discernment of right action; it is a misconception to think that the reason
first knows goods that the will subsequently does or does not choose.[51]
Westberg affirms that, for Aquinas, moral "truth" is found not in apprehension as such but in judgment leading to action. Acting is the chief end
of practical reason as well as the central aspect of moral virtue;[52] reason,
will, and action are simultaneous in moral relationships and in the attainment of moral truth.

Because of the practical nature of moral knowledge, "we learn the
natural law, not by deduction, but by reflection upon our own and our
predecessors' desires, choices, mistakes, and successes."[53] This assumes
membership in a community or communities where people together and
in institutions seek goods. A point to be stressed, then, is that human
nature, its ends, its flourishing, and its moral standards are not "discovered" as already existent and unchanging entities. Insofar as basic human
goods are the prerequisites of human bodily survival and health, of aspects
of psychological well-being that are relatively invariant, and of the human
ability to cooperate socially and form peaceful societies, the basic goods

"The Relationship of Virtues and Norms in the Summa Theologiae," *Heythrop Journal*, 51 (2010),
pp. 214–29.
[49] Josef Pieper, *The Four Cardinal Virtues*, trans. Richard Winston, Clara Winston, Lawrence E.
Lynch, and Daniel F. Coogan (University of Notre Dame Press, 1966), p. 10.
[50] Daniel Westberg, *Right Practical Reason: Aristotle, Action, and Prudence in Aquinas* (New York:
Oxford University Press, 1994), p. 139.
[51] Ibid., pp. 82, 84, 246–7.
[52] Ibid., pp. 61, 65, 195.
[53] Pamela M. Hall, *Narrative and the Natural Law: An Interpretation of Thomistic Ethics* (Notre
Dame, IN: Notre Dame University Press, 1999), p. 94. Jean Porter, *The Recovery of Virtue: The
Relevance of Aquinas for Christian Ethics* (Louisville, KY: Westminster John Knox Press, 1990),
p. 122, affirms the relevance of individual circumstances to the exercise of prudence.

are to that degree stable and invariant across cultures. However, insofar as these dimensions of human being can either change (e.g., through technology) or be implemented variously in different cultural contexts, both the basic goods and knowledge of them must develop inductively and communally. In historical, human contexts, neither bias nor error can be eliminated.

The recognition of equality is particularly vulnerable in this regard, both because it is not obviously in the interest of those at the top of social hierarchies to recognize the equality of those at the bottom and because the cultural ascription of differential status affects perceptions of the mutual interrelation of social members (as it did for Aquinas). It is easier for those in power to deny that the equality of all is important to the well-being of all and to successful social functioning than it is to deny that everyone needs food, clean water, and an end to war. Particularly in view of competition for basic material and social goods, equality is a casualty of self-interest. The alacrity and universality with which human dignity and equality are recognized in principle attest to a tacit and growing consensus about its real truth and value, despite hypocrisy and abuse in its practical observance. "Hypocrisy is the homage vice pays to virtue."[54] Because of the interdependence of moral knowledge and the virtues, the topic of moral epistemology leads into and depends upon an understanding of moral virtue.

MORAL KNOWLEDGE, ACTION, AND THE VIRTUES

Natural law ethics, then, must entail more than theoretical knowledge of goods and norms. It requires prior dispositions to know reality, persons, and goods truthfully and in their right relationships. It also requires good judgment about what to do in a given situation. Perhaps even more important, it requires the practical determination to put judgment into effect. To judge and act well, one must be disposed to or desire the particular goods or ends that would be reasonable, not letting one's judgment be swayed or destroyed by concupiscence or disordered desire (*ST* I-II.58.5). The tendency to act in favor of goods and of fair access to them for all is called virtue. A virtue is a character-forming habit, often called "a disposition to act in a certain way" (I-II.49.3; 55.2–3), that is, toward a good that is objective and real, and is seen in the proper relationship to

[54] François de La Rochefoucauld (1613–80), *Maxim 218*; as cited in John Bartlett, *Familiar Quotations*, 10th edn. (Boston: Little, Brown, 1919).

other, possibly competing goods. Aquinas says that virtue is "like a second nature, in accord with reason," "directed to man's good" (I-II.58.1). A virtue (or vice) is a sort of bridge or connector among agent, actions, objective goods, and community.

Virtue, as operative in Aquinas's ethics, builds on a concept absolutely crucial to the moral theories of Plato and Aristotle, as well as to their Christian heirs: happiness.[55] The classical Greeks approached virtue with a question of human purpose and meaning that still resonates powerfully today: What is happiness, and how can I secure it? Realizing that we have limited control over the circumstances of our lives and the goods available to us, the philosophers proposed that true happiness lies not in goods like power, property, fame, or even friendship, but ultimately in the good of virtue itself: the individual's ability to order his or her own life reasonably and to live according to his or her highest moral, intellectual, and religious values. The good life is the virtuous life, and the virtuous life is the only life that will guarantee genuine happiness. While Plato stressed that true knowledge of the good requires a sort of "breakthrough" insight unattained by most people, Aristotle was more confident that virtue can be learned through education, practice, and imitation of the wise.

Augustine, as a Christian, took the classical virtue framework an important step further. The highest and only true good is God, the *summum bonum* and sole source of humanity's lasting happiness. The virtuous person attains the only good that truly matters. With Plato, Augustine agreed that true virtue requires a vision of the good, but a vision of the true and highest good, God, must be enabled by grace. Grace confers the virtues that unite us to God; love of God as the *summum bonum* brings together union with the Good above all goods and the perpetual happiness of perfect human virtue. With Aristotle, Augustine agrees that virtue can be taught or acquired through human efforts, but this applies only to human virtues and the natural goods to which they dispose us. And even then, the natural virtues are ultimately perverted because they are not oriented to the *summum bonum*. As William Spohn acknowledges, "Virtue ethics is generally better at depicting formation than transformation,"[56] which helps explain why Christian authors create a second category of

---

[55] Consult Plato's *Republic*, Aristotle's *Nicomachean Ethics*, and Augustine's *On the Morals of the Catholic Church*. For an overview, stressing theological renditions of virtue theory, see Porter, "Virtue," in Meilaender and Werpehowski (eds.), *Oxford Handbook of Theological Ethics*, pp. 205–19.

[56] William C. Spohn, *Go and Do Likewise: Jesus and Ethics* (New York: Continuum, 1999), p. 29.

virtues, the theological virtues, to account for conversion to love of God. Taking these virtues outside the framework of habituation is one way for a theory of the theological virtues to explain how virtues can constitute a person's character as something radically new.

For Augustine, love of God as our true good brings the only lasting happiness, and love of God is always a gift. Love of God, or charity, reorders all the natural or cardinal virtues so that they become forms of love of God.

As to virtue leading us to a happy life, I hold virtue to be nothing else than perfect love of God ... temperance is love giving itself entirely to that which is loved; fortitude is love readily bearing all things for the sake of the loved object; justice is love serving only the loved object, and therefore ruling rightly; prudence is love distinguishing with sagacity between what hinders it and what helps it. The object of this love is not anything, but only God, the chief good, the highest wisdom, the perfect harmony.[57]

As we saw in Chapter 5, Aquinas appropriates Augustine's theological paradigm of virtue, though not his view that the virtues of non-Christians are little more than vicious perversions of true virtue (*ST* I-II.85.1).[58] The natural virtues, acquired through habituation, are inadequate to bring humans to their final destiny, but they are imperfect rather than disastrously off-base (I-II.54.3; 58.1–3; 62.1). The natural virtues, assisted by the "grace of creation" (I.95.1), are capable of leading us to the goods for which we are suited naturally, and even to God, understood as "First Cause" if not yet as Friend (I.95.3; I-II.2.8; 3.4; 4.4).

The virtues, as human dispositions or character traits, are important because they speak to the reality of goods, and especially of God and salvation, as present, apprehended, desired, and embraced within the historical process. To live virtuously is to conform to these goods and to participate in them. Rightly understood, the virtues also display humanity's social interconnectedness and need for social relationships.

[57] See Augustine, *On the Morals of the Catholic Church*, in Whitney J. Oates (ed.), *Basic Writings of Saint Augustine* (New York: Random House, 1948), vol. 1, pp. 331–2.
[58] Eberhard Schockenhoff distinguishes Aquinas from Augustine on this point. Whereas Augustine sees any act without charity as merely an act of sinful self-love, for Aquinas, "the virtues of the natural human being in their orientation to the particular ends of human practice deserve their own human significance, which is not destroyed by the absence of charity." Though imperfect, the natural virtues are sinful only when they prevent one from pursuing the final end of love of God (*ST* II-II.23.7): Schockenhoff, "The Virtue of Charity (IIa IIae, qq. 23–46)," in Pope (ed.), *Ethics of Aquinas*, p. 251. The point is confirmed by James Keenan, S.J., "The Virtue of Prudence (IIa IIae, qq. 47–57)," pp. 266–7 and Clifford G. Kossel, S.J., "Natural Law and Human Law (Ia IIae qq. 90–97)," pp. 176–8, both in Pope (ed.), *Ethics of Aquinas*.

The cardinal or moral virtues are prudence, justice, fortitude, and temperance. Aquinas sees all four as interdependent and mutually necessary. Justice, fortitude, and temperance are determinations of the will, helping agents to rightly order their desires for goods. Prudence, uniquely, is a moral virtue of the intellect, helping agents to know which goods to choose and how to realize them concretely (II-II.47.2).[59]

For Aquinas, all moral reasoning is perfected by the virtue of prudence (I-II.47–56); although prudence is an intellectual virtue, it is not directed at speculative truth but at action. Prudence is "right reason about things to be done" (I-II.57.a.4). Justice, fortitude, and temperance, the virtues that direct the will rightly, are also necessary to prudential choice (I-II.58.4–5), since the will influences intellectual discernment of goods. Will and reason acting together particularize and specify the goods at stake in any concrete circumstance, giving rise to action, which in turn situates or resituates reason and will. For both Aristotle and Aquinas, this results in a certain circularity.

For reason to be correct, the appetite needs to be properly ordered, seeking after proper goals, with contrary or excessive desires properly regulated, fear, anger, and so on under control, and proper regard for other persons' good held in the will. When reason and appetite are mutually regulated in this way, then the agent may be seen as virtuous.[60]

Among the cardinal virtues, justice receives the longest treatment in the *Summa*. The virtue of justice (II-II.57–122) governs right relations among persons, in respect both of the natural order of beings and their needs, and of agreements undertaken voluntarily. General justice disposes the agent to act for the common good (II-II.58.6), while particular justice is a disposition to act for particular goods, either in relations among parts in a whole (commutative justice) or in the relation of a part to the whole (distributive justice; II.61.1–2). Fortitude (II-II.123–140) and temperance

[59] For an overview of all four, see, in addition to Pieper, *Four Cardinal Virtues*, Stephen J. Pope, "Overview of the Ethics of Thomas Aquinas," in Pope (ed.), *Ethics of Aquinas*, pp. 39–46. In addition, in the *Ethics of Aquinas*, there are separate chapters on all the cardinal and theological virtues.

[60] Westberg, *Right Practical Reason*, p. 247. Similarly, according to Keenan, "the mutual dependency of prudence and the moral virtues (this is not a vicious circle but rather an evolving spiral [the metaphor is attributed to Thomas Kopfensteiner]) incorporates and integrates moral reasoning into an evolving vision of the human person" ("The Virtue of Prudence," p. 259).

(II-II.141–169) order the internal desires of agents so that the will follows right reason.

As we saw in Chapter 5, Aquinas has a strong doctrine of sanctification, since he believes that justification (which he calls "sanctifying grace") is a participation in the divine nature (through the theological virtue of charity). If our natures are changed, then we will of necessity act differently. In addition to the theological virtues, wisdom, and the gifts and fruits of the Spirit, Aquinas connects the moral virtues to grace even more directly, through the infused moral virtues. Since charity requires expression in works of moral virtue, God infuses new moral virtues to help the natural ones along. "All the moral virtues are infused together with charity." Because of these infused moral virtues, a person is able to perform "each different kind of good work" (I-II.65.3).[61]

In addition, Aquinas admits that if recipients of saving grace have not previously cultivated moral virtues, the regenerating work of grace is actually impeded by the consequences of their former recalcitrance. The fact that justifying grace and the virtue of charity are in no way dependent on human merit or bestowed on those of better character implies that there will be an existential gap between charity as an essential change and the moral habits people already have. Even though moral virtues are infused, they do not always work well, "by reason of certain contrary dispositions remaining from previous acts." This difficulty obviously does not occur with acquired virtues, since the effort required to have cultivated the virtue will have countered any bad habits that formerly stood in their way (I-II.65.3.r.ad.2).

So we see that for Aquinas (and confirmed in human experience) grace is necessary to overcome the impediments of fallen nature; but nature can help or hinder the outworkings of grace. "Sanctification is effected by all the virtues," not just the theological and infused ones (I-II.70.4.r.ad.1), and sometimes the natural virtues are lacking even in believers. Of course, if, as was suggested in Chapter 5, grace is actually infused or bestowed through participation in the body of Christ, this makes the theological virtues more like the moral virtues – not in that their origin is human, but in that they are communally habituated, thus gradually overcoming contrary dispositions. The moral regeneration of believers is gracefully but gradually accomplished by their participation in the church.

---

[61] On the relation of the theological virtues to the infused moral virtues, see Thomas F. O'Meara, "Virtues in the Theology of Thomas Aquinas," *Theological Studies*, 58 (1997), pp. 265–7.

Virtue has enjoyed quite a renaissance in recent moral thinking, among both philosophers and theologians.[62] According to William Spohn, a spirituality and ethics of virtue is the best way to appropriate the gospel. It provides the most comprehensive account of moral experience, and it is most amenable to the narrative presentation of the life, death, and resurrection of Jesus in the New Testament.[63] This is also the thesis of Daniel Harrington and James Keenan, in *Jesus and Virtue Ethics*.[64] Virtue ethics takes the concern with moral living to the deeper levels of moral identity, including intentions, emotions, and the imagination.[65] Virtue ethics can also recognize that even our deepest personal identity is formed in community and is dependent on it.[66] For Jean Porter, it is impossible to understand Aquinas's theory of natural reason apart from his theology of the virtues.[67] Virtue as an organizing category can connect Christian ethics to the moral and political aspects of other branches of theology and church life, such as spirituality and liturgy.[68]

Without doubt, the most prolific and influential twentieth-century promoter of virtue theory in Christian ethics is Stanley Hauerwas.[69] Hauerwas, however, does not bring along Aquinas's idea that the virtues

[62] See Alasdair MacIntyre, *After Virtue: A Study in Moral Theory*, 2nd edn. (University of Notre Dame Press, 1984); Rosalind Hursthouse, *On Virtue Ethics* (Oxford University Press, 1999); Romanus Cessario, *The Moral Virtues and Theological Ethics* (University of Notre Dame Press, 1991); Joseph J. Kotva, Jr., *The Christian Case for Virtue Ethics* (Washington, DC: Georgetown University Press, 1997); Stanley Hauerwas and Charles R. Pinches, *Christians Among the Virtues: Theological Conversations with Ancient and Modern Ethics* (University of Notre Dame Press, 1997); James F. Keenan, "Virtue Ethics," in Bernard Hoose (ed.), *Christian Ethics: An Introduction* (London: Cassell, 1998), pp. 84–94; James F. Keenan, "Proposing Cardinal Virtues," *Theological Studies*, 56 (1995), pp. 709–29; Porter, "Virtue"; William B. Spohn, "Scripture," in Meilaender and Werpehowski (eds.), *Oxford Handbook of Theological Ethics*, pp. 93–111; Jennifer A. Herdt, *Putting on Virtue: The Legacy of the Splendid Vices* (University of Chicago Press, 2008); William C. Mattison III, *Introducing Moral Theology: True Happiness and the Virtues* (Grand Rapids, MI: Brazos Press, 2008); and Charles E. Curran and Lisa A. Fullam (eds.), *Virtue: Readings in Moral Theology No. 16* (New York: Paulist Press, 2011).

[63] Spohn, *Go and Do Likewise*, pp. 28–9.

[64] Daniel Harrington, S.J., and James Keenan, S.J., *Jesus and Virtue Ethics: Building Bridges Between New Testament Studies and Moral Theology* (New York: Rowman & Littlefield, 2005); see also Daniel Harrington, S.J., and James Keenan, S.J., *Paul and Virtue Ethics: Building Bridges Between New Testament Studies and Moral Theology* (New York: Rowman & Littlefield, 2010).

[65] Spohn, *Go and Do Likewise*, p. 30.

[66] Spohn, "Scripture," pp. 104–7.   [67] Porter, *Nature as Reason*.

[68] See Bruce T. Morrill, *Anamnesis as Dangerous Memory: Political and Liturgical Theology in Dialogue* (Collegeville, MN: Liturgical Press, 2000).

[69] A few of Stanley Hauerwas's numerous works touching on Christian virtue ethics are *A Community of Character: Toward a Constructive Christian Social Ethic* (University of Notre Dame Press, 1981); *Character and the Christian Life: A Study in Theological Ethics*, 2nd edn. (San Antonio, TX: Trinity University Press, 1985); and *Vision and Virtue: Essays in Christian Ethical Reflection* (University of Notre Dame Press, 1981).

are active responses to goods that are commonly and naturally known. Hauerwas adopts a more radical Augustinian view of sin's effects than does Aquinas, and therefore focuses his ethics on Christian virtues rather than also on natural virtues. In addition, Hauerwas is heavily influenced by the virtue theory of the philosopher Alasdair MacIntyre, who maintains that virtue – and indeed, ethics – are possible only in a community united in a particular vision of the good, a condition that no longer obtains in contemporary liberal societies and one that in the nature of the case can never amount to a universal ethics.[70] Hauerwas's basic thesis is that Christian character or virtue is formed in and only in the church as a countercultural community constituted by the vision, narrative, and practices of Jesus Christ and his cross. (Hauerwas endorses an absolute stance of Christian nonviolence).[71]

Aquinas, in contrast, would certainly see the gift of the theological virtues by the Spirit in the church as essential to Christian identity. Yet Aquinas retains a positive and constructive view of reasonable human morality, and of a social and political ethics oriented by the common good. The goods that constitute human flourishing can be generally known across communities; this is the source of an ethics of the natural moral law (I-II.94).

PRACTICAL REASON, VIRTUE, AND PRAGMATISM

At this point similarities emerge between Aquinas's ethics and the realist version of pragmatism presented in Chapter 1. Aspects in common are that, to know things, one has to be open or disposed to them, to desire to know; the self, knowledge, and agency are social and practical; practices shape and validate knowledge's correspondence to reality; true knowledge is not detached but issues in consequences. What natural law theory emphasizes more clearly than pragmatism, however, is the objective nature of the good as a normative criterion of moral realities and of true proposals or practices that correspond to them. The intellectual virtues, including prudence, are "directed to the apprehension of truth (see Ia, q.79, a.11, ad 2)."[72] Yet it is not enough that moral knowledge be true in

[70] See MacIntyre, *After Virtue*.
[71] See Stanley Hauerwas, *The Peaceable Kingdom: A Primer in Christian Ethics* (University of Notre Dame Press, 1991).
[72] Gregory M. Reichberg, "The Intellectual Virtues (Ia IIae, qq. 57–58)" in Pope (ed.), *Ethics of Aquinas*, p. 134.

the sense of corresponding to reality; it must also be virtuous in the sense of corresponding to and acting for the reality of the good.

The pragmatist approach can create the impression that moral truth simply means correspondence of proposals and practices to realities that those statements have helped to generate and are now reinforcing. The upshot would be a relativistic view of morality and truth in which separate moral worlds could have their own internal truths of correspondence, with no accountability to truths as constituted elsewhere. Yet there is a continuity among moral worlds and their goods that is guaranteed by the underlying realities of human embodiment, human interdependence with the natural world, and basic human experiences of suffering and well-being. Different moral realities can be good or evil, whatever the accuracy of moral statements that correspond to and validate them. The moral justification of torture, for example, generates a moral world in which torture is acceptable and enacted. In that sense, the proposal that torture is morally acceptable may be true just in the sense that it corresponds to the reality occurring. But that practice and the worldview that sustains it are subject to broader criteria of moral judgment, which derive from the goods that define human well-being and justice in general, and are not fundamentally relative from culture to culture. Torture is wrong no matter what the political rationale because it aims to destroy the personal and moral integrity and identity of human beings. The objectivity of some basic goods, priorities among them, their amenability to reasonable yet inductive inquiry, and their appeal across cultures despite local variations are the contributions of natural law ethics.

For societies as for individuals, knowledge, will, and action are entwined, with "truth" emerging at the point of their convergence around shared goods. Thus moral agreement is made more likely when practical objectives and strategies are also shared. For instance, ethical and political common ground is enlarged when communities or cultures participate in cooperative political institutions or agreements. Conversely, the public recognition of cross-cultural, even "global" values, such as human rights, the UN Millennium Development Goals, or treaty provisions on global climate change, is already a sort of action or practice that disposes will and emotions to solidarity at the practical level. Theoretical recognition of goods, affirmative judgment, solidaristic choice, and action are always already preceding and informing each other in the concrete, making any one a reasonable point of entry for analysis or for practical reinforcement.

The dialectical and social nature of ethical knowledge, commitment, action, and truth is reflected in the pluralistic way moral responses to globalization actually arise. While the diversity in focus and location of such responses can be interpreted as testifying to their fragmented and ultimately incommensurable nature, I am convinced such a reading is a mistake. More credence need not be given to postmodern agnostic theory about the possibility of a common morality than to evidence of a convergence of ethically motivated action in the present global system.

Margaret Keck and Kathryn Sikkink identify "complex global networks" that reform ideas, influence policy debates, pressure domestic policy, and enforce or seek to renegotiate international norms and rules. What they see as distinctive about such networks "is their transnational nature and the way they are organized around shared values and discourses." What stimulates network formation is "core values – ideas about right and wrong."[73] But it is not just any values or ideas of right and wrong that motivate these activists. Their main and shared agenda is to promote greater human equality in relation to basic material and social goods, as well as respect for the natural environment. The most important and visible areas of change – human rights, women's rights, and the environment – display a unity of moral vision, a common commitment to redressing imbalances of power and well-being so that marginal persons, groups, and nature can flourish. Inclusiveness, equality, and solidarity are uniting values. Institutions, practices, and norms that give solidarity life will in large part be specified contextually and culturally. This does not rule out some cross-cultural continuities in core values, their opposites, and congruent norms (e.g., no terrorism, torture, rape, genocide, or unlimited emissions of ozone-destroying gasses).

PRACTICAL CHRISTIAN ETHICS – WAR AS A TEST CASE

Aquinas bases the substantive content of his ethics primarily on natural law, as a realist moral system known through practical engagement with one's environment, other persons, the communities in which one participates, inherited traditions of moral wisdom, and one's knowledge of other communities and their traditions. The natural law indicates normative moral values and obligations that are shared. In addition to recognizing that legitimate variation in ways of respecting these values and obligations will increase in proportion to the specificity and hence contingency

[73] Margaret E. Keck and Kathryn Sikkink, *Activists Beyond Borders: Advocacy Networks in International Politics* (Ithaca, NY: Cornell University Press, 1998), pp. 199, 200, and 201 respectively.

of the situations in which they claim us, Aquinas also recognizes that the ostensible universality of the natural law is affected by partial and ambiguous moral knowledge, and by inevitable bias and self-interest that corrupt how moral obligations are discerned and fulfilled.

Nevertheless, it is still possible, according to Aquinas, for individuals and societies to know what is reasonable to do, to actually do it a significant amount of the time, and to acquire the virtues that facilitate acting for the good cooperatively with others. In addition, Christian virtues suffuse the whole process with the gift of divine friendship, healing human nature and creating new possibilities. A debated point in Aquinas's ethics is what these new possibilities are, and how they relate to humanity's natural goals and virtues. Another point, often made over against Aquinas and Thomistic ethics (including Catholic social thought), is that if the reality of sin is taken seriously, both the reliability and the universality of natural law reasoning fail. Even if one believes, as I do, that the redeeming presence of God's empowering Spirit is everywhere in creation and history, one must still confront the continuing irrational and destructive power of evil.

Aquinas's thinking about killing in war is a good illustration of his basic natural law method, its concrete interdependence both with Christian tradition and with a particular cultural context, and the questions to which natural law leads. Both following and changing Augustine, Aquinas defends and limits war for the common good on the basis of natural law reasoning. The theological virtue of charity changes the ultimate framework and the motivation for following what natural justice demands regarding war. In addition, both the theological virtues and the infused moral virtues can affect the normative content of the ethics of war and killing so that the result is apparently at odds with justice as usually understood. Thus a tension results between the practices that follow from Christian identity and those required for justice. Aquinas resolves this by assigning the special obligations of charity to a separate, smaller realm of Christians who compensate for the failure of the majority to enact pacific biblical ideals. He does not, however, adequately address the probability that just-war reasoning itself will become perverted and fail the common good, a possibility of which twenty-first-century Christians are all too well aware.

First of all, Aquinas places the entire realm of political ethics, including the justifiability of killing, under the aegis of the common good (II-II.64, especially a.2, 5, 6, 7). Regarding war, the primary frame of reference is the good of one's own political community, but outsiders and adversaries are held accountable to and protected by mutual norms of justice that further cooperative social living. Because the common good requires peace and the protection of life, there is a prima facie obligation to abjure violence and killing. Hence, Aquinas titles the first article of his question on war "Is It Always Sinful to Wage War?" (II-II.40.a1) – assuming that it *usually* is. His answer is that the prima facie wrongness of war is overridden in cases in which there is a dire threat to the common good that cannot be averted in any other way. Then killing is justified. Sometimes it will be necessary to justify war. Although Aquinas's point of departure is apparently the common sinfulness of war, it is war's reasonable justification that occupies his attention primarily.

Aquinas's own assessment of war is indebted not only to reason but also to Christian tradition and formation. The three main criteria for a just war, adapted from Augustine, are lawful authority to defend the common good against enemies, the just cause of defending against injury or attack, and the right intention of advancing peace (II-II.40.1). Aquinas does not elaborate much on the specific applications of these criteria, except to say that ambushes are a legitimate means in war, as long as they are accomplished by concealment of strategy rather than outright deception, which would violate justice (40.3). Further specification would get into the "contingent" areas in which prudence necessarily guides and in which different cultures and eras may accept different practices.

Although basic just-war criteria are defensible in terms of reason and the cardinal virtues, the interdependence of Christian insight and practical reasonableness in Aquinas's own thinking is evident from the way he sets up the question. Not only is the proposal of the three criteria backed with references to Augustine, it is formulated in response to scriptural objections: the Lord says not to take up the sword (Matt. 26:52); the Lord says not to resist evil (Matt. 5:39; cf. Rom. 12:19); the church forbids killing in tournaments (40.1.ad 1, 2, 4). Revealingly, however, Aquinas replies not by engaging the internal dynamics of scripture and tradition, but by interpreting or qualifying the biblical message in light of requirements of the common good. Church belonging does not abrogate the relevance of justice and political responsibility to Christian decision making, though Christian values will sensitize reason to discern better what is just.

Aquinas shifts from the biblical and ecclesial grounds on which he poses the objections to a common good basis for the responses, which he does not make contingent on explicitly Christian premises. He answers the objections as follows: to "take the sword" means to take it without valid authority, though we should be mindful of the obligation of nonresistance and ready to obey it; this obligation can be set aside "for the common good, or the good of those with whom [one] is fighting"; killing for the sake of war exercises and not the real thing is "inordinate and perilous" (40.1.1–2, 4). Similarly, Aquinas approves fighting on holy days if the common good demands it (40.4).

Though it might seem that Aquinas has dispensed with biblical condemnations a little too readily, he reinscribes the Christian obligation to live nonviolently in the vocations of those explicitly dedicated to Christian prayer and eucharistic celebration, that is, clergy and bishops. The reasons are that "warlike pursuits … hinder the mind very much from the contemplation of Divine things, the praise of God, and prayers for the people;" and that killing is incompatible with representing the passion of Christ on the altar (40.2). But for Christians in leadership roles or military service, wars to seek the peace also can be seen as serving "the Divine spiritual good" fulfilled more directly by clerics (40.2.r.ad.3). In other words, a life lived toward friendship with God can be expressed in acts against injustice that do not conform at the material level with the prima facie moral meaning of the evangelical ideals of nonviolence and forgiveness.

Aquinas does commend nonresistance in the face of death in a different context, martyrdom, where the expression of explicitly Christian identity becomes the controlling factor (II-II.124.2). Although the natural, civic virtue of fortitude is aimed at securing justice, gratuitous fortitude, directed by charity, strengthens faith in Jesus Christ (124.2.r.ad.1, 2). So while allowing oneself to be killed might seem incompatible with justice and the common good, it can be an expression of charity, faith, and the infused moral virtue of fortitude. (Aquinas similarly says that fasting can be an expression of the infused moral virtue of temperance, though eating moderately is an expression of the parallel cardinal virtue [I-II.65.5]; that total abstinence from sex can perfect chastity; and that voluntary poverty can perfect liberality, in the context of religious commitment [I-II.64.1.ad 3, r.ad.3].)

These higher expressions of charity are, however, not absolutely required, even for believers. One reason would be that the requirements of justice do not disappear; another and related reason is that historical human life is filled with broken and sinful situations in which the cardinal virtues must be manifest in conditionally appropriate ways. Relevant to war, Aquinas says that enemy love need not always mean actually showing enemies "the signs and effects of love" (II-II.25.9). Though we should not exclude enemies from the goodwill with which we should regard people generally, it is not necessary to favor enemies individually, except "in a case of urgency," where they lack basic needs such as food and water (ibid.) – a contingency that would also create a requirement of justice.

The upshot is that Aquinas grounds his applied ethics, especially his social ethics, primarily in the natural law, considered as discernment of human goods, the common good, and justice. Practically speaking, however, he approaches ethics as a Christian and looks at goods and justice from a vantage point that includes formation in scriptures, tradition, liturgy, vowed religious life, and the ecclesial, political, and social institutions of his era. Aquinas does envision some ways in which Christian commitment might provide substantive content to the moral life that goes beyond the natural moral law. He does not specify all the cases in which this might be so, nor does he draw a clear line or connection between the cardinal virtues and the infused moral virtues. Their interaction seems to depend on individual narratives, commitments, and circumstances. Aquinas does clarify, however, that perfect charity all the time is not expected even of those dedicated to the Christian life. Christians are motivated by charity; by the infused virtue of justice, which orients all decisions about relationships to God as highest good; and by natural justice, which identifies and prioritizes relations among human persons in respect to temporal goods. He seems to allow substantial latitude for decisions about how this will play out in the concrete.

The ethics of Aquinas is reasonable, situationally sensitive, flexible, and open to convergences with other traditions about goods and justice, given basic human values like life, family, and society. Nature for Aquinas is God's creation, and it orients humans and other creatures toward God's will as expressed in the ordering of creation and the destination of all things for the universal common good. Aquinas also keeps the profile of Christian identity in clear view, though its practical impact changes. A critic may well say that, as a Christian ethics, this is not adequately prophetic and pro-active or critical enough of customary social and political behavior. Aquinas views war, for example, from the perspective of elite decision makers and as an event on which key players are able to have a clear and objective perspective, taken outside of and prior to any exchanges of violence. He does not fully acknowledge the tension or even conflict that arises when immediate justice demands measures that contradict the ostensible moral meaning of the gospel.

Aquinas does recognize sin as a nefarious ingredient in human affairs. He does not spend much time identifying and attacking the ways sin commonly shows itself in "reasonable" governmental and military strategies or in the construction of group identities, the dynamics of competition among groups, and the rationalization of political and military power plays or attempts to grab resources as just on generalizable grounds. In my view, critiques of this sort are not fatal to the natural law project, but they do call for a more critical and self-critical approach to endeavors with tremendously high human and moral stakes, such as the conduct of civil conflict and war.

The first decade of the twenty-first century alone was replete with horrific examples of the human and environmental costs of violence in Iraq, Afghanistan, Sudan, Congo, Myanmar, Mexico, and numerous other places. In addition, racism and economic oppression constitute "structural violence" responsible for the deaths and suffering of millions more people. The next chapter will feature peacebuilding as a Christian and interreligious response to such evils. Before constructive and hopeful solutions can be proposed, however, it is necessary to grasp the depth of evil; the complicity of those, including "good Christians," who claim to be opposed to it; the necessity and difficulty of radical conversion; and the inevitability of conflict in the process of dismantling distorted power structures. These problems have been broached in Chapter 2 and have been recurrent themes throughout this book. They shall be reemphasized at the end of this chapter.

Now we will consider nature as the whole of the natural world and investigate the relevance of natural justice and Christian salvation to problems of nature and ecology. Though I will not assess specific examples, the magnitude of an environmental problem like climate change is enough to signal the urgency of a creation-wide extension of moral responsibility.[74]

NATURAL LAW AND ECOLOGY

I have argued that certain goods for humans can be universally known, most obviously those based on the physical conditions of human survival and on our natural sociality and need for cooperative relationships. Moreover, basic human equality yields an obligation to ensure that all have access to the minimum conditions of human sustenance. This

---

[74] See the issue titled "Theological Reflections on Climate Change," *Studies in Christian Ethics* 24/1 (2011), with major essays by Susan Parsons, Celia Deane-Drummond, Timothy Gorringe, Michael S. Northcott, Peter Manley Scott, Cathriona Russell, and Byron Smith; Michael S. Northcott, *A Moral Climate: The Ethics of Global Warming* (London: Darton, Longman & Todd, 2007); and Sallie McFague, *A New Climate for Theology: God, the World, and Global Warming* (Minneapolis: Fortress Press, 2008).

implies, at the very least, that our common human environment be protected as a prerequisite of human flourishing. Environmental degradation wreaks suffering on the poor first and most of all.[75] The process of naming ecological goods and responding to ecological dangers should be inclusive of all those affected.

A natural law approach to the characteristics and goods of "nature" can be extended analogously from human to nonhuman beings. We can know some universal ecological goods, such as interdependence, balance of ecosystems, openness to the new, clean water and air, and species survival.[76] As public goods or global common goods, these are at one level *human* goods. But they are also goods for *nature itself* and for the variety of beings that constitute the nonhuman natural world. Reasonable reflection on our experience of nature, accompanied by responses of the emotions, imagination, and senses, inspires wonder, awe, and respect. Nature has value in its own right, and not only as beneficent or threatening to human beings and their interests.[77] As a biblical ecologist asserts, though nature suits many of humanity's needs, those needs "are an insufficient frame of reference entirely to explain creation. Only God can supply such a frame of reference."[78]

Noninstrumental respect for nature can be referred back to Aquinas, even though Aquinas's view of creation was definitely hierarchical, with lower animals existing for human use, their suffering sublimated into the well-ordered good of the whole (II-II.64.1; 1.22.a2). According to Aquinas, only humans, as rational and free, participate in divine wisdom through the natural law (I–II.91.2). Only humans are called to enjoy the personal "friendship" with God made possible by grace (II–II.23.1, 5). This gives them a priority over nonpersonal creatures.

Nevertheless, all beings participate in the divine being in their own way, through their created natures, their natural inclinations, acts, and ends (I-II.91.2). Therefore, each being has value and is related to God in its own right. Moreover, each being finds its ultimate destiny in God as its final end, in a way suited to its own nature, even if that is not humanity's way of personal friendship. According to Aquinas, humans "attain

---

[75] See Leonardo Boff and Virgil Elizondo (eds.), *Ecology and Poverty* (Maryknoll, NY: Orbis Books, 1995).

[76] See John Hart, *Sacramental Commons: Christian Ecological Ethics* (Lanham, MD: Rowman & Littlefield, 2006), part II; and Scott, *Political Theology of Nature*, pp. 45–8.

[77] See Gustafson, *Sense of the Divine*.

[78] Michael A. Bullmore, "The Four Most Important Biblical Passages for a Christian Environmentalism," *Trinity Journal*, 19 n.s. (1998), 145. The four passages are Psalm 104, Genesis 1–2, Genesis 9:8–17, and Romans 8:18–23.

to their last end by knowing and loving God." But other creatures also "share in the divine likeness, inasmuch as they are, or live, or even know" (I-II.1.8; cf. I-II.91.a.1, 2). God is the "universal good" of all of nature, not just humans (I.60.5.r.ad.3–5); and is "loved by everything with natural love" (I.60. r.ad.4; cf. r.ad.5). Taking these themes beyond what Aquinas himself explicitly argues, it is possible to suggest that all creatures are destined for union with God, even "deification," in ways suited to the goodness of their own natures.[79] And insofar as humans enjoy everlasting friendship with God through the resurrection of the body (not disembodied immortality of the soul), humanity's embodied nature, as inherently and definitively interconnected with other creatures, will presumably survive, if in an altered state. This may imply that the entire universe coheres and persists everlastingly in the common good of God.

Aquinas himself says that the body is in fact not necessary for "perfect Happiness," that is, the "vision of God" (I-II.4.a.5). His reasoning is that the vision of the divine essence is attained by the intellect, and the intellect needs only sensibly mediated "phantasms" in order to know earthly realities, not the essence of God, which in eternal life the intellect will know directly. Aquinas also takes as a point of departure the traditional idea that "the souls of the saints" are after death "separated from their bodies" until the last judgment.

But this rationale for dispensing with a bodily component to knowledge of God as Friend may be questioned on two counts. First, it is not biblical; Christ himself after death appears in a changed bodily form, the "first fruit" of human resurrection. Second, friendship with God in God's essence may not require the mediation of the senses as we experience it in this life, but there is no reason to exclude the possibility that just as our bodies are changed by resurrection, so is the way they participate in relationships, including relationship to God. So the question becomes whether it is intrinsic to the meaning of human embodied personhood to be a self in relation to a variety of other creatures, and if so, then their eternal life accompanies ours. In addition, as previously noted, all creatures relate to God in their own right, and God as the "universal common good" of every creature persists eternally.

Just as with human society, however, neither respect for nature in its own right nor hope of creation's "eternal life" means that all

---

[79] Citing Athanasius and Karl Rahner, Denis Edwards argues for involvement of the whole creation in "deification through incarnation" ("Sketching an Ecological Theology of the Holy Spirit and the Word of God," in Paul Murray, Diego Irarrázaval, and Maria Clara Bingemer [eds.], *Lord and Life-Giver: Spirit Today* [London: SCM Press, 2011], p. 20).

competition and conflict can or will be replaced by earthly, natural harmony. James Gustafson believes that "conflict or dissonance, as well as harmony and consonance are part of nature and our place in it."[80] Celia Deane-Drummond discerns "overall patterns" in natural processes but warns that "the discovery of ecological instability and apparent flux betrays the fragile nature of any ordering that seems apparent to the casual observer."[81] Moreover, "we deceive ourselves if we think that we have the necessary wisdom and knowledge to intervene for the good of the biosphere" as a whole.[82] The sciences and the natural sciences warn us that some goods are limited; that predation, suffering, and death are part of nature's evolved condition. The suffering of some seems essential to the flourishing of others. In fact, there is a shocking, even grotesque, level of suffering in the natural world, not all of it "abnormal." Consider animals that "naturally" survive by consuming the newborn offspring of other species, and predators who eat their victims alive.

We must seek to know and do justice for nature in much the same way as we do for humans. Because practical reason deals with "contingent matters" in both human justice and ecojustice, we must strive pragmatically to limit and rectify environmental troubles even when we are unable to attain an ideal of "wild" and unimpeded harmonious coexistence. There is no stable harmony of nature as a whole, or even of large systems within nature, just as there are no stable harmonies for all human life, or even for large geographical or historical systems, such as ethnicities, tribes, empires, or regional alliances of peoples. Yet there clearly do exist relatively stable goods for various natural kinds, such as animals, plants, oceans, and forests, as well as goods and evils for individual beings, classes of beings, or ecosystems that exist in particular places and times.

Several decades ago, Gustafson warned that God does not create a comprehensive "order" in which all conflicts of need and interest can be resolved. Rather, nature, history, and culture offer "possibilities for different patterns of well-being," as well as God-given "new possibilities for well-being" to occur.[83] If we lack certitude in many decisions, it is

---

[80] Gustafson, *Sense of the Divine*, p. 49.
[81] Celia E. Deane-Drummond, *The Ethics of Nature* (Malden, MA: Blackwell, 2004), pp. 40 and 39, respectively.
[82] Celia Deane-Drummond, *Eco-Theology* (London: Dartman, Longman & Todd, 2008), p. 125.
[83] James M. Gustafson, *The Contributions of Theology to Medical Ethics* (Milwaukee, WI: Marquette University Theology Department, 1975), pp. 38–9.

important to maintain attitudes of respect for life, openness to new possibilities, and self-criticism, due to the realities of finitude and sin.[84]

As in human affairs, practical wisdom or prudence is key to ecological morality. Specific decisions must and can be gauged to the conditions, needs, capabilities, and well-being of concrete beings and relationships. Deane-Drummond agrees that prudence is necessary to make decisions in the face of uncertain future scenarios, to adjudicate between the human needs of the poor and species extinction, to decide specific policies that will reduce climate change, and so on.[85] She suggests that, although the market-based political economy that has led to poverty and environmental injustice needs radical reform, it might be best to seek interim mediating strategies that will address the more pernicious effects of liberalism and capitalism, while not giving up on deeper long-term changes.[86]

It is inevitable that some circumstances will be difficult and some needs will conflict. It is not only inevitable, it is obligatory, to decide priorities among needs and, in the natural world, to prefer the good of some creatures to that of others in cases of conflict. Yet respect for the goods proper to every creature, and the value in principle of the access of every being to the goods proper to it, create a moral obligation to reduce suffering and enhance well-being as much as possible. The virtue of humility will lead humans to acknowledge limits and repent of failures.

CREATION AND NEW CREATION

What is added to the natural law perspective by a theology of creation? To talk about "creation" is to put "nature" in a faith perspective, the perspective of divine sovereignty, providence, and salvation. The biblical narratives of creation make an essential point about nature: it is not of the essence of nature to be "red in tooth and claw" or of humans to be violent and self-promoting.[87] Creation defines evil and suffering as non-normative, not the way things ought to be.

---

[84] Ibid., pp. 56–72.
[85] Deane-Drummond, *Ethics of Nature*, pp. 284–5.   [86] Ibid., p. 27.
[87] Alfred Lord Tennyson's *In Memoriam A.H.H.*, 1850. The quotation comes in canto 56 and there refers to humanity and human nature:

> Who trusted God was love indeed
> And love Creation's final law
> Tho' Nature, red in tooth and claw
> With ravine, shriek'd against his creed …

Still, while conflict, competition, and suffering may not be good they are inevitable. Their presence is paradoxical and puzzling. As we saw in Chapter 2, the creation stories in Genesis do not actually explain why evil exists, nor do they eliminate all disorder from the original creation. The Genesis narratives project disharmony from before humanity's disobedience. Before the fall, the humans are commanded to "subdue" nature (Gen. 1:28), as if there is already a sort of potential unruliness, multi-purposiveness, or disruptive natural vitality that they are responsible for ameliorating. The symbol "creation" constitutes a mandate to deem unnecessary suffering unacceptable and to resist it. To live in "the image of God" (Gen. 1:28) means to exist in relationship to God and to other creatures, healing misery and exercising providence for the well-being of all to the extent that we are able.

The words of the American poet Mary Oliver convey a profound truth: "If God exists he isn't just butter and good luck. / He's also the tick that killed my wonderful dog Luke."[88] The creation stories do not tell us why God creates a world where suffering and evil are inevitable, but they convey a moral duty: alleviate suffering insofar as it is in our power to do so. Oliver, always attentive to the concrete mysteries and beauties of her immediate surroundings, continues, "I pray for the desperate earth. / I pray for the desperate world. / I do the little each person can do, it isn't much."[89] The narratives of creation advise us both to invoke *God's* care and to actively *take* care, of ourselves and other creatures.

The process of redemption already begins in the Pentateuch, through the covenant with Noah, the call of Abraham, and God's forming of a covenant people through Moses, the Exodus, and Sinai. The Hebrew Bible also sees creation as blessed even before the advent of humans, and creation itself praises God (Isa. 42:10; Ps. 19:1, 69:34, 96:11–12, 98:7–8, 103:22, 150:6), a depiction continued in the New Testament (Phil. 2:10; Rev. 5:13).[90] The first covenant, God's covenant with Noah, should perhaps be called the "Creation covenant," because it is not only with humans but with all living creatures (Gen. 9:8–17).[91] God's creative Sophia (Lady Wisdom) is active throughout creation, "the creative and freeing power of God let loose in the world" (Prov. 1:20–33, 8:35).[92] Eastern Orthodox

[88] "At the River Clarion," in Mary Oliver, *Evidence* (Boston: Beacon Press, 2009), p. 51.
[89] Ibid., p. 53.
[90] Deane-Drummond, *Eco-Theology*, p. 86.
[91] Bullmore, "Biblical Passages for a Christian Environmentalism," 157.
[92] Elizabeth Johnson, *She Who Is: The Mystery of God in Feminist Theological Discourse* (New York: Crossroad, 1996), p. 83.

theologians use biblical imagery of Word and Sophia to make similar points.[93] In the vision of the prophet Isaiah, who is a major source for the Christian interpretation of redemption in Jesus Christ (Luke 4), God's healing and restoring covenant is not with Israel or even humanity alone, but with all of God's creatures. "And the wolf shall dwell with the lamb, and the leopard shall lie down with the kid; and the calf and the young lion and the fatling together; and a little child shall lead them" (Isa. 11:6). If God's covenant includes all of nature, then that puts humanity in covenant with all of nature too, in one community of life.[94]

The Christian New Testament continues the trajectory of redemption in the incarnation, the life and ministry of Jesus, the gift of resurrection life in the Holy Spirit, and the formation of communities that strive to overcome divisions among human beings and between humans and other creatures. According to Paul, "If anyone is in Christ, there is a new creation: everything old has passed away; see, everything has become new!" (2 Cor. 5:17; cf. Gal. 6:15; Eph. 2:15). Though humans are Paul's primary referent, he knows that "the whole creation has been groaning in labor pains until now" (Rom. 8:22) and, with us, awaits "the redemption of our bodies" (8:24). "Creation itself will be set free from its bondage to decay" and will somehow participate in "the freedom of the glory of the children of God" (Rom. 8:21). Creation is "eager for the revealing of the children of God" (Rom. 8:19) "who have the first fruits of the Spirit" (Rom. 8:19, 23), in which all creation may share.

According to the christological hymn of Colossians, Christ is the "first born from the dead," but also and at the same time "the first born of creation" (1:15, 18), hinting that creation is included through Christ in the resurrection. Modern authors like Jürgen Moltmann maintain that all of nature is redeemed in Christ.[95] According to Moltmann, Christ "died in solidarity with all living things." Thus, in raising Christ, "God brought not merely eternal life for the dead but also the first anticipatory radiance of immortal being for mortal creation."[96] For Elizabeth Johnson, "the Creator Spirit dwells in compassionate solidarity with every living being that suffers, from the dinosaurs wiped out by an asteroid to the

---

[93] See Deane-Drummond, *Eco-Theology*, ch. 5, for a discussion.
[94] Michael S. Northcott, *The Environment and Christian Ethics* (Cambridge University Press, 1996), pp. 129–30.
[95] See, e.g., Jürgen Moltmann, *The Source of Life: The Holy Spirit and the Theology of Life*, trans. Margaret Kohl (Minneapolis: Fortress Press, 1997), ch. 10: "… 'And Thou Renewest the Face of the Earth': The Ecology of the Creative Spirit," pp. 111–124.
[96] Jürgen Moltmann, *The Way of Jesus Christ* (Minneapolis: Fortress Press, 1993), p. 253.

baby impala eaten by a lion ... Thus the pattern of cross and resurrection is discerned on a cosmic scale."[97]

The redemption of creation through the incarnation and resurrection of Christ also makes sense when we realize that the incarnation unites God with human embodiment, and human embodiment unites humans with the rest of the natural world. Deane-Drummond reminds us that Christ is the "last Adam," in whose image we are remade, and Adam is made from the dust of the earth.[98] Christ is one with humanity and with all creation in his birth, life, bodily death, descent into the hell of extinction and despair, and resurrection in the body. The incarnate God in Christ is one with the suffering of all creatures and takes on suffering to transform it.

Creation, as argued in Chapter 2, depends on God's children to "subdue" (not eliminate) the suffering generated by the vigorous proliferation of life forms. The children of God "till and keep" other natural kinds, bringing them closer to the ideal but elusive harmony symbolized in Genesis as "garden" (Gen. 2:15). In the "new creation" in Christ, natural evil and the evil wrought by human hands are alike redeemed and their victims resurrected. Even now, Christ's resurrection establishes a new order of relationships among humans and other creatures.[99]

Human relationality and embodiment mean that there can be no sharp line between humans and other beings. If humans are inherently social, and their sociality includes relations to other creatures, then the union of humanity in God as our ultimate good and destiny implies the union in that same good of all else that exists. Humans exist as material, embodied, evolved, living, and social only in their ecological niche; they have a place in the world that is really a point in a network of indefinitely extenuating relations. Human existence will not be resurrected fully without its constitutive relations to other creatures.

The integrity of every life and the harmony of all lives were never "original," but they are eschatologically promised. They are also historically anticipated. Christ incarnate and resurrected inaugurates "a new heaven and a new earth" (Rev. 21:1, 2; Pet. 3:13). Those who call themselves "children of God" must strive to imitate divine providence, mercy, and care in their relationships to all human beings and to earth's other inhabitants;

[97] Elizabeth Johnson, "Creator Spirit and Ecological Ethics: An Ancient Frontier," in Murray et al. (eds.), *Lord and Life-Giver*, p. 27.
[98] Deane-Drummond, *Eco-Theology*, p. 100.
[99] Oliver O'Donovan, *Resurrection and Moral Order* (Leicester: Intervarsity Press, 1986), p. 13.

and to embody resurrection's "first fruits" by enlarging the spheres of their harmonious coexistence.

Situations of ongoing oppression, suffering, and hopelessness shadow basic assumptions of natural law social ethics – general human reasonableness, goodwill, and likelihood of progressive reform. Christian social ethics must confront the seriousness and intransigence of evil, as well as the necessity to convert, not just convince, the unjust beneficiaries of social power. The celebration of creation and the encouragement of human participation in God's redeeming action cannot proceed on firm and honest ground until human agency in and complicity with evil and horror are confronted fully. Undemanding sympathy that is apathetic about meaningful change is cheap grace. An Augustinian sensibility should imbue Christians with an appreciation of their involvement in structural sin and the ambiguity of many of their choices. We are entangled in "miserable necessities" even while trying to do good, to achieve "the tranquility of order" over against war, conflict, and poverty.

Along with sexism, racism and ethnic discrimination are excellent examples of the practical denial of the politics of salvation and of the supposedly universal recognition of basic human goods and equality. Racial and ethnic hatreds are at the root of multiple forms of personal and social violence, especially war and civil conflict. These sinful phenomena invade the mutual formation of Christian identity and particular cultural identities, as well as the interface of Christian politics and broader social structures. Bryan Massingale takes the U.S. Catholic Church to task for having unrepentantly aided and abetted slavery and subsequent racism. But he also sees the church as a possible agent of repentance, conversion, and reform, not just of the church, but of social and civic life.[100]

As opportunities to heal racism, Massingale names the sacraments of baptism and eucharist, celebrated as though they really represent the inclusion of all in one body of Christ; practices of interracial solidarity and the option for the poor; and liturgies of lament and compassion.[101] However, these avenues of reconciliation will not lead to results unless they are based on hard truth telling that unsettles the stories privileged groups relate to account for their privilege by erasing responsibility for the

[100] Bryan N. Massingale, *Racial Justice and the Catholic Church* (Maryknoll, NY: Orbis Books, 2009).
[101] Ibid., p. 85.

injustices on which it is built. This obviously must go beyond the church to other groups and institutions in society .

True and lasting healing of divisions, hatred, and violence requires concrete, affirmative steps to redress harms by means of reparations, both personal and social. It is the responsibility of Christian communities to foster genuine reconciliation in their internal relationships and to advocate (both as individual members and as a body) for the gradual forging of new social narratives that include practical, meaningful access for all to basic goods and opportunities. The Christian values and practices of forgiveness, redemption, repentance, inclusive solidarity and preferential option for the poor sensitize Christians to the needs and sufferings of others, and give hope that change will arrive. Christians can be seeds of change in larger or different communities as they expand transformative practices and engage the imaginations of other people with images and narratives of changed relationships.

The final brief chapter, on hope, offers examples of Christian resistance to some of the oldest, most widespread, and most destructive forms of suffering humans perpetrate against their fellow human beings. It will show that political and ecclesial efforts at amelioration and transformation can be hope-filled and effective, even when widespread success is far from guaranteed. As the Nigerian theologian Agbonkhiameghe Orobator proclaimed in an address to the Catholic Theological Society of America, "Grace is everywhere, and at all times, unconditionally."[102] Religious peacebuilding, for example, moves in partnership across ethnic, racial, political, and religious divides to bring reconciliation, social reconstruction, and a more just future.

---

[102] Agbonkhiameghe Orobator, S.J., "A Global Sign of Outward Grace: The Sacramentality of the World Church in the Era of Globalization," Plenary Address to the Catholic Theological Society of America, St. Louis, MO, June 8, 2012.

CHAPTER 8

Hope

The hope of building just and peaceful societies, contrasted with the historical realities of poverty, racism, ethnic hatred, sexism, and war, presents the biggest conceivable challenge to the thesis of this book: violence and domination distort a more fundamental goodness of human nature, sustained, fulfilled, and renewed by God incarnate in Jesus Christ, who through his kingdom ministry and the sending of his Spirit enables a new politics of salvation. It is right to beware of

exaggerated religious rhetoric that makes promises that God probably cannot keep; assurances of a cosmic hope, but not much attention to the small possibilities for some tiny improvements in the complexities of individual, interpersonal, and public life; proclamations that all things are made new in Christ when nothing significant changes in human actions and events.[1]

The present chapter takes on the difficult enterprise of granting the ineradicable nature of war and conflict, while testifying to the spiritual and political power of actions and movements to overcome divisions and reconcile enemies. It will offer the example of peacebuilding as a strategy to reduce conflict and its causes and as a Christian expression of the politics of salvation, advocacy for inclusive human flourishing.

Peacebuilding also demonstrates how hope is engendered from within human suffering. In his 2007 encyclical, *Spe Salvi*, Pope Benedict XVI wrote: "All serious and upright human conduct is hope in action."[2] Not only do human solidarity and practical action to change conditions of violence express hope, they nourish hope and make hope for a better future possible. Mary Grey illustrates the "outrageous" virtue of hope with the story of Acholdeng, a Sudanese refugee who with her starving

---

[1] James M. Gustafson, *An Examined Faith: The Grace of Self-Doubt* (Minneapolis: Fortress Press, 2004), p. 107.

[2] Benedict XVI, *Spe salvi* (2007), www.vatican.va/holy_father/benedict_xvi/encyclicals/documents/hf_ben-xvi_enc_20071130_spe-salvi_en.html (accessed May 17, 2012), no. 35.

child walked four days until finding a feeding center that would admit her. Lying exhausted and dehydrated on a blanket, she heard other desperate women slowly arise one by one and begin to sing, "even as babies were dying." "'They sang courting songs, songs of prosperity and hope, songs of praise to the cows they didn't have and to the life they only half had ... It was light in the darkness. Slowly Acholdeng hobbled over to join them, taking up the rhythms and the dance ... It was a great act of defiance,'" which Grey places at "the heart of a spirituality of resistance."[3]

This story portrays women at the bare minimum of human existence, with marginal agency for change. Their action consists only in the reenactment of memories of happiness, a dramatic and affective liturgy of immersion in a past reality that hints at what might be possible still. To embrace even the slim possibility of change is to hope, and hope is seeded in the foretaste of God's kingdom that arrives with Spirit-inspired solidarity. As Jürgen Moltmann writes, "In the community of Christ we experience *God's spirit* as a power of life which makes us live."[4] The divine Spirit is also present in the community of these women, inspiring in them a resistant hope.

Throughout his long and prodigious theological career, Moltmann has been a prophet of hope.[5] A keynote of his theology is that we live in the present eschatologically, out of God's future as already tangible. In a later work on ethics and hope, Moltmann draws the constitutive connection between hope and transformative action. When the second letter of Peter (3:12) urges Christians to be " 'waiting for and hastening the coming of the Lord's future,' " this means "crossing the frontiers of the present reality." "If we take up the cause of 'widows' and 'orphans', a fragment of life comes into our own life."[6] Echoing (or foreshadowing) Benedict XVI, Moltmann announces that salvation is hope in action. [7] Kwok Pui-lan puts the accent on the power of advocacy to inspire hope. She takes up the challenge articulated at the beginning of this chapter: "When we look at the complexity of global issues and the dense matrices of structural

[3] Mary C. Grey, *The Outrageous Pursuit of Hope: Prophetic Dreams for the Twenty-First Century* (New York: Continuum, 2001; first published 2000 by Darton Longman and Todd), p. 40. Grey is citing John Vidal, "A Dance in the Shadow of Death," *Guardian* (September 22, 1998).

[4] Jürgen Moltmann, *In the End – the Beginning: The Life of Hope*, trans. Margaret Kohl (Minneapolis: Fortress Press, 2004), pp. 164, 94.

[5] Jürgen Moltmann, *Theology of Hope: On the Ground and the Implications of a Christian Eschatology*, trans. James W. Leitch (London: SCM Press, 1967).

[6] Ibid., pp. 6, 8.

[7] "Salvation Is Hope in Action" is a heading in a report Moltmann authored in 1972–3 (ibid., p. 37).

oppression, we might sometimes wonder whether an alternative world is possible." Kwok attests that the solidarity and collaborative efforts of faithful Third World and indigenous women offer "a rare gift – hope abundant."[8]

Perhaps surprisingly, Thomas Aquinas validates in his treatment of hope the hypothesis of Chapter 7 that the gift of the theological virtues is practical and communal in origin. He also confirms the opening claim of this chapter that even the theological virtue of hope is born in action for change. As Dominic Doyle shows, Aquinas underlines the necessary role of worldly hopes and their corresponding actions for justice in leading to, not only following from, eschatological hope for the fulfillment of human goods in God.[9] The theological virtue of eschatological hope can in fact be willed and approached only through actions seeking this-worldly objects of hope. Citing Romans 8:24 ("We are saved by hope"), Aquinas asserts that we hope for an end only when we are "fittingly moved to the end, and coming near it: which indeed happens through some action," that is "through the operations of virtues" (*ST* I-II.69.1).[10] Actions for justice in the world move us toward our ultimate end of friendship with God and increase in us the virtue of hope, of both the "secular" and the eschatological varieties. The virtue of eschatological hope is in fact contingent on practices that bring us existentially nearer to the end of union with God.

Just as Jesus' resurrection is a historically "impossible" act of God, so the resurrection life of Christians in history must express what is "historically impossible." Christians must bring about the impossible, albeit partially, testifying that "the impossible has become possible." In carrying out Jesus' mission, in hope, we ourselves live the kingdom he ministered and thus grasp in our own lives and actually verify the truth of the resurrection.[11]

Hope is not the same thing as optimism about general upward trends in global justice. Hope is not unrealistic about what can be accomplished. Yet hope takes root in actual work to change conditions, work in which we find solidarity with others, experience successes as well as discouragements and failures, and develop the fellowship and the courage that enable

[8] Kwok Pui-lan, "Introduction," in Kwok Pui-lan (ed.), *Hope Abundant: Third World and Indigenous Women's Theology* (Maryknoll, NY: Orbis Books, 2010), p. 13.
[9] Dominic Doyle, "*Spe salvi* on Eschatological and Secular Hope," *Theological Studies*, 71/2 (2010), pp. 350–79.
[10] Ibid., 369–370, Doyle's translation from the Latin.
[11] Jon Sobrino, *Christ the Liberator: A View from the Victims*, trans. Paul Burns (Maryknoll, NY: Orbis Books, 2001), pp. 48–9.

us to go on working toward the better future we envision. This kind of
work – hope in action – is well illustrated by Christian peacebuilding.

Peacebuilding evolved in response to a kind of human misery that
is causally complex, bowed down under deadly violence, corrupting of
virtually all sectors and levels of society, entangling international and
transnational actors, blurring lines between innocent and guilty, and of
unbearable duration. Most wars in the modern period have been between
nation-states. There has been a decrease in violent conflict among or
between states since its peak in the mid-1980s. At the end of 2009, the
rate of interstate conflict was at its lowest point since 1960.[12] Yet, even
though the global prevalence of international wars has decreased, the
level of conflict within nations has not. So-called societal warfare – that
is, civil, ethnic, and communal conflict *within* nations – has been the
predominant form of warfare since the mid-1950s. This is one reason most
war deaths today are civilian, a distinguishing feature of late modern, as
opposed to early modern (but not ancient), warfare. During World War I,
civilians made up fewer than 5 percent of all casualties. Today at least 75
percent of those killed in war are noncombatants.[13]

There are about four new societal wars each year, and they follow a
trend in becoming longer and more protracted, often receiving military
and/or monetary aid from outside, as happened with the "superpow-
ers" during the cold war.[14] Intra-state conflict – now more frequent and
lethal than wars between states – is often or usually economically motivated, with ethnic, religious, or ideological differences exploited to validate and accomplish economic ends. Africa, to a greater extent than any
other continent, has been and is being afflicted by the ravages of war,
having suffered more than twenty major civil wars since 1960. Rwanda,
Somalia, Angola, Sudan, Liberia, Congo, and Burundi are among those
that have endured serious armed conflict, including genocide. These conflicts almost always are inspired and driven by economic inequality and
competition.

In protracted conflicts, differentiations among pre-violent, violent, and
post-violent phases are not easy to maintain. Peacebuilders must engage
all sectors of society, from local perpetrators and victims, to government, business, educational, and religious elites, to international lawyers,

[12] Monty G. Marshall and Benjamin G. Cole, *Global Report 2009: Conflict, Governance, and State Fragility* (Center for Systemic Peace and Center for Global Policy, 2009), www.systemicpeace.org/ (accessed November 5, 2010) 4.
[13] www.globalsecurity.org/military/world/war/index.html (accessed January 19, 2007).
[14] Marshall and Cole, *Global Report 2009*, 4.

scholars, leaders of finance and industry, regulators, government officials, and religious leaders.[15] Peacebuilding goes forward in the practical and active hope that it is possible to transform conflict and build sustainable peace, fed by the existential experience of change occurring, beginning with bonds of solidarity among those committed to a different future.

Christian peacebuilding or peacemaking is an ecumenical movement and theory that bridges traditional just war and pacifism. Some practitioners and theologians, notably Glen Stassen and allied proponents of his just peacemaking theory,[16] take as their point of departure the challenge of biblical nonviolence. Others, like most members of the Catholic Peacebuilding Network,[17] begin from a qualified and stringent acceptance of the necessity of force to control some violations of justice. However, the two sides meet in peacebuilding as a practical commitment to build or restore conditions of peace by working for structural justice and reconciliation at the grassroots level; by involving interreligious partners; and by seeking networked reinforcement of conditions of peace among local, national, regional, transnational, and international organizations, both civic and governmental.

A sad but important fact about peacebuilding is that it is an imperfect process. Results are always ambiguous, even if a marked improvement on the status quo. Daniel Philpott says rightly that violations of human dignity and rights create deep social and personal wounds that are extremely difficult to remedy. One major reason is that restorative goals and practices are necessarily in tension with one another. For example, some measures that restore justice, like the punishment of human rights violators and reparations to their victims, may delay regime transition and the establishment of democratic institutions. Criminal trials and punishment may also stand in tension with social processes of forgiveness and reconciliation. Yet amnesty is in turn at odds with the goal of building a society in which all are held to the same standards of justice.[18] Therefore, peacebuilding is not so much about conforming to theoretical criteria of justice and peace as it is about finding very practical ways to discover

---

[15] R. Scott Appleby, "Peacebuilding and Catholicism: Affinities, Convergences Possibilities," in Robert J. Schreiter, R. Scott Appleby, and Gerard F. Powers (eds.), *Peacebuilding: Catholic Theology, Ethics, and Praxis* (Maryknoll NY: Orbis Books, 2010), p. 3.

[16] Glen Stassen, *Just Peacemaking: The New Paradigm for the Ethics of Peace and War* (Cleveland: Pilgrim Press, 2008).

[17] cpn.nd.edu/ (accessed May 17, 2012).

[18] Daniel Philpott, "Reconciliation: A Catholic Ethic for Peacebuilding in the Political Order," in Schreiter et al. (eds.), *Peacebuilding*, pp. 92–124.

and create opportunities to reduce violence and strategize for better social conditions.

The South African theologian Denise Ackerman captures the way that religious and interreligious peacebuilding represents the "politics of salvation." Effective and lasting reconciliation that transforms unjust and evil structures amounts to an "embodied praxis for change" constituted by five components: recognition of the true nature of an unjust situation; public acknowledgment of real injustice; collective lament for the evils perpetrated and suffered; forgiveness of wrongdoers; and social reconstruction that is inclusive, participatory, and reparative.[19] Yet sometimes the "unjust situation" is an ongoing situation of outright violence, the "public acknowledgement" must take the form of prophetic denunciation, the "reconstruction" consists in solidaristic action in the face of a death-dealing regime, and "forgiveness" must defer to the urgency of condemnation, resistance, and survival.

In 2011, the Liberian peace activist Leymah Gbowee won the Nobel Prize for spearheading a grassroots women's movement against the civil war in which the corrupt regime of Charles Taylor and ruthless warlords tore apart the country and terrorized its entire population. The documentary *Pray the Devil Back to Hell* tells their story and offers a practical example of "hope in action" and of resurrection life despite "impossible" odds.[20]

PRAY THE DEVIL BACK TO HELL

Liberia is a country of 3 million people, founded in 1847 by freed American slaves who formed an elite class that dominated the indigenous peoples. A combination of factors, including disparities between rich and poor, ethnic tensions, and a fight for control of natural resources, led to civil war in 1989. In 1997 Charles Taylor was elected president, beginning a reign of tyranny and terror during which he played a key role in Sierra Leone's diamond trade. Opposition by a faction of rebel warlords, ironically calling themselves "Liberians United for Reconciliation and Democracy" (LURD), precipitated another outbreak of war in 1999. By 2002, approximately 200,000 people had died, and by 2003, Taylor had

[19] Denise Ackerman, "Reconciliation as Embodied Change: A South African Perspective," *Proceedings of the Fifty-ninth Annual Convention, Catholic Theological Society of America*, 59 (2004), pp. 60–5.
[20] *Pray the Devil Back to Hell*, by Abigail E. Disney and Gini Reticker (Fork Films, USA, 2008, 72 minutes); www.PraytheDevilBacktoHell.com (accessed June 13, 2012).

lost control of many of the rural areas. The country was overwhelmed
by turmoil and violence, with armed insurgents causing as much blood-
shed as Taylor. Both factions plundered villages, raped women, and killed
and mutilated men, women, and children. Both enlarged their bands of
militants by conscripting child soldiers, forcing them to kill their parents,
then keeping them high on drugs so that they were willing to carry guns
and use them wantonly.

The main narrator in *Pray the Devil Back to Hell* is a social worker,
Leymah Gbowee, who was forced to flee her village on foot when she
was five months pregnant, with her three-year-old son and two-year-old
daughter. A Lutheran Christian, Leymah had a dream in which she was
told to bring the women of the church together to pray for peace. Taylor
himself professed to be a Christian and used the pulpit as a platform
from which to rouse support. As Leymah puts it, "Taylor could pray the
Devil out of hell." Leymah preached her own demand for "peace now" in
her congregation and joined with other churches to start the Christian
Women's Peace Initiative. Along with the Muslim police officer Asatu Bah
Kenneth, Leymah and fellow activists created the first Christian–Muslim
women's initiative in Liberia. Leymah: "Does the bullet know Christian
from Muslim?" Asatu: "We're all serving the same God."

The women tirelessly engaged the male religious leaders, exhorting
them to exert pressure on political leaders. In the spirit of the heroines of
Aristophanes' *Lysistrata*, the women resorted to what they regarded as a
uniquely female tool: a sex strike. The message to their husbands was serious (and effective): "If you have any power to put a stop to the war, you
go and do it!"

Beginning in April 2003, the women organized mass street protests.
Janet Johnson Bryant, a journalist with the Catholic news station Radio
Veritas, broadcast a call for women to meet in a field near her house.
The women tied up their hair, set aside jewelry and makeup, dressed in
white, and gathered in the local fish market under a banner announc-
ing "The Women of Liberia Want Peace Now." Their numbers rose to
2,500. "We want peace, no more war. Our children are dying and we are
tired of suffering – we want peace." Charles Taylor ominously declared,
"*Nobody* will go into the streets to embarrass my administration," but
as his car made its daily pass by the market where the women demonstrated, Taylor merely slowed down, then returned home. The violence
in and around the capital, Monrovia, escalated, however. Calls by the
international community for peace talks were met by refusal from Taylor
and LURD.

International demands for peace negotiations emboldened the women. In April 2003 Leymah Gbowee and hundreds of white-clad companions presented to Parliament and to the president the "Women of Liberia Position Statement on the Liberian Crisis," which read in part, "Stop the carnage and engage in fruitful dialogue." Seeing popular support on their side, Taylor finally agreed to attend peace talks in Accra, Ghana. The difficulty of bringing LURD to the other side of the table still loomed. The women sent two delegates, Etweda "Sugars" Cooper, a longtime activist and community organizer, and Asatu to the rebel strongholds in Sierra Leone. The women were determined and relentless, traits that served them well and soon would be needed even more. They met with individual leaders, insisting, "Your mothers and sisters have come this far to talk to you." "If you don't go [to the talks] you will be responsible for the deaths of all these people." The rebels finally acceded to the women's demands. Thousands of ordinary Liberians contributed money to send women to Ghana to keep up the pressure on the negotiators. More women were recruited in Sierra Leone. Still uniformed in their white tee shirts, they monitored the proceedings from outside the peace hall.

The violence was far from over. Talks in Accra dragged on for six weeks without progress. Meanwhile, Charles Taylor was indicted by a war crimes tribunal in Sierra Leone and fled back to Liberia. The violence in and around Monrovia escalated. Women still sat in the fish market, while trucks carrying young boys going to fight passed by and returned late in the day with loads of wounded. In Accra the combatants resisted serious negotiations, enjoying the international notoriety and plush hotel life financed by the negotiations' sponsor (ECOWAS). Behind the scenes, Liberian women tried to persuade various warlords to work out peace positions. The men were holding out for guarantees of power, position, and control of resources in the form of government jobs that would give them unfettered access to goods and capital.

Finally, in frustration, the women formed a human wall around the peace hall, declaring that no one would have food or drink or leave the site until progress had been made. When a security guard threatened Leymah with arrest and a captive general tried to jump out over the women, Leymah (as she recalls) "went wild." Using a weapon of high cultural significance (it is considered a curse if a mother strips naked in front of her son), Leymah began to take off her clothes, starting with her head wrap. Leymah's righteous wrath and serious purpose were not lost on the chief mediator, General Abdulsalami Abubakar, a former Nigerian president, who knew that the Liberian women were justifiably "trying to make their men see reason." To the would-be escapee he retorted, "Go and sit down! If you were a real man you would not be killing your people. That is why they are treating you like boys." Having won the battle and with renewed courage for the contest ahead, the activists gave the combatants two weeks to conduct real peace talks and come up with a resolution – or the confrontation would be repeated.

The mood changed. Agreements were made. Charles Taylor would go into exile in Nigeria. UN peacekeepers would enter Monrovia. A transitional government would be established in preparation for democratic elections. The price paid was positions in the transitional government for many of the warlords. The women returned home to acclaim, trailed by a throng of children singing the movement's trademark "We want peace, no more war!" Now it was time not to rest but to mobilize forces to monitor the implementation of the peace agreement, especially the disarmament of thousands of young men still in a haze of drugs and alcohol. When UN officials failed to control the situation, the women stepped in and arranged an orderly collection of weapons.

The reintegration of perpetrators was a special dilemma, given the horrific atrocities suffered by many of the women and their families. Vaiba Flomo, with Leymah Gbowee a founder of the Christian Women's Peace Initiative, tells of one mother who was forced to sing and dance while rebels raped her twelve-year-old daughter and slit her husband's throat. This account is one of the most gripping and devastating moments of the film. As Leymah remembers:

Women had become the 'toy of war' for over-drugged young militias. Sexual abuse and exploitation spared no woman; we were raped and abused regardless of our age, religious or social status. A common scene daily was a mother watching her young one being forcibly recruited or her daughter being taken away as the wife of another drug emboldened fighter.[21]

Vaiba asks, "How can we move on if we do not forgive?" yet confesses, "But really I tell you no lie, with the stories from the women, I find it hard." She does not hide her anger at child soldiers and other perpetrators but concedes that "a lot of them were victims as much as we were."

In January 2006, Ellen Johnson Sirleaf was elected president of Liberia, the first woman president in Africa. In 2011, Leymah Gbowee and President Sirleaf received the Nobel Peace Prize, along with a Muslim peace activist from Yemen, Tawakkol Karman. In April 2012, Charles

[21] Leymah Gbowee, Nobel Lecture, Oslo, December 10, 2010, www.nobelprize.org/nobel_prizes/peace/laureates/2011 (accessed May 12, 2012).

Taylor was convicted of multiple charges of war crimes and sentenced to fifty years in prison by the UN-sponsored Special Tribunal for Sierra Leone, meeting in The Hague. In her Nobel lecture, Leymah reflects, "We used our pains, broken bodies and scarred emotions to confront the injustices and terror of our nation. We were aware that the end of the war will only come through non-violence, as we had all seen that the use of violence was taking us and our beloved country deeper into the abyss of pains, death, and destruction."[22] She connects the struggle of Liberian women to that of women worldwide, in Zimbabwe, Congo, Uganda, Cote d'Ivoire, Egypt, Afghanistan, Tunisia, Yemen, Palestine, and Israel, urging that genuine equality of women and men will not be realized until women are equally represented in decision-making roles.

Despite the victory of the Liberian women's peace initiative, serious difficulties remain in their country and worldwide. The conclusion of peace talks and the conviction of Taylor were victories for social stability and justice. Yet in order to negotiate peace it was necessary to make concessions to warlords, underwriting the ethos of impunity that had made their depredations possible in the first place. Charles Taylor is destined to spend the rest of his life in prison, but holding him accountable for war crimes may make it more difficult to negotiate termination of power with other despots.

Certainly Leymah's aspiration to full political authority for women has not been fulfilled. In fact, powerlessness and abuse of women continue barely abated, not only in situations of outright conflict, but even during and after the signing of peace accords, the establishment of transitional governments, and the formation of ostensibly democratic institutions. The formal conclusion of hostilities under such measures as the introduction of UN peacekeepers tends to go forward according to a paradigm in which human security is equated with state security or military security. The importance of engaging nonstate actors and civil society in the construction of peaceful, fair, and participatory institutions is inadequately addressed. Sanam Anderlini laments that "the question of security and peace for whom is often left hanging."[23] Equality for women will not result simply from more stable and peaceful conditions if exclusionary gender norms remain in place. And bringing economically productive work to women is also insufficient if unaccompanied by changes in

---

[22] Ibid.
[23] Sanam Naraghi Anderlini, *Women Building Peace: What They Do, Why It Matters* (Boulder, CO: Riener, 2007), p. 197.

structural inequalities, such as women's exclusion from political power, lack of access to education, disadvantage before the law, and cultural norms that make women subordinate to men.[24]

These problems are forcefully illustrated by the history of UN Resolution 1325.[25] In 2000, the UN Security Council recognized through this resolution that civilians are directly and specifically targeted in contemporary warfare and that, among them, women are subject to multiple, degrading, and permanently harmful forms of sexual violence and other atrocities simply by virtue of the fact that they are women. Moreover, violence against women continues during and after peace negotiations, in which formal roles for women are a rarity. Resolution 1325 calls not only for an end to gender-based violence, but also for full inclusion of women in power structures and in efforts to maintain peace and security.

Even though 1325 was unanimously adopted by the Security Council, its implementation depends on ratification by individual states. Signatories must devise comprehensive, coherent, and consistent processes of compliance that include necessary efforts to create ownership and "buy in" by all actors at every level of society, from high-level government and military to local community and religious leaders. The UN as such cannot enforce compliance or penalize noncompliance. Thus legal ratification of 1325 by national governments is meaningless without serious and sincere commitment on their part – backed up by adequate financial, personnel, and program resources – to make sure that the provisions of 1325 become reality. "Regardless of the policies and the seemingly heartfelt speeches, the inaction and the lack of leadership within major institutions [at both state and international levels] set a tone that women are not important."[26]

For example, despite the election of President Sirleaf, a joint investigation by the government of Liberia and the UN was forced to conclude in 2010 that "sexual and gender-based violence (SGBV) is not only prevalent in Liberian society; it is unfortunately accepted as an integral part of gender relations." During the civil war, violence against women was a weapon of war. In 2009, Liberia launched a national action plan to implement

[24] Ibid., p. 200.
[25] See "What Is U.N. Security Council Resolution 1325 and Why Is It So Critical Today?" United States Institute of Peace, www.usip.org/gender_peacebuilding/about_UNSCR_1325#What_is_U.N._Security_Council_Resolution_1325_ (accessed June 13, 2010).
[26] Anderlini, *Women Building Peace*, 214.

Resolution 1325 with the participation of all stakeholders, decision making by women, and consideration of the real needs of local communities.[27] Yet as of 2010, rape was still Liberia's most frequently reported serious crime, and almost half of rape victims were under eighteen. Perpetrators are not limited to armed combatants; they include family members, husbands or partners, and teachers.[28] An innovative "rape court" in Monrovia has still not succeeded in bringing timely justice to alleged victims and defendants, due in part to an inadequate budget and a backlog of complaints.[29]

Nevertheless, women have made progress since the war. Leymah Gbowee credits much of it to President Sirleaf's integrity and leadership style, as well as to the simple fact that a woman president holds out a different image of women's capabilities to both sexes. Just as women's peace initiative members campaigned in villages and markets to "get out the vote" among women in the nation's first democratic election, so women continue to take leadership and inspire other women at national and local levels. In the first years after the war, the West African regional Women Peace and Security Network–Africa, headed by Leymah Gbowee, conducted leadership projects with girls in three rural regions of Liberia and secured "fantastic" results in two.[30] The ratio of girls to boys enrolled in school has risen; more women are enrolled in adult literacy programs; many more girls aspire to attend high school and go on to university. Leymah in fact interprets the continuing high rates of violence against women as a backlash against women's new empowerment.

The resolution of situations of extreme and protracted conflict will never be easy or clear-cut. To resolve one situation does not rule out the possibility or even likelihood of future outbreaks of violence, or even a cycle of outbreaks and cease-fires, in the same locale or elsewhere. Yet religious peacebuilders are uniquely well-positioned to gain access to local leaders, build trust in communities, and advocate for women's voices. Christian images and narratives such as creation, image of God, reign

---

[27] "Liberia Launches UN-Backed National Action Plan on Women, Peace and Security," U.N. News Centre (March 8, 2009), www.un.org/apps/news/story.asp?NewsID=30117&Cr=liberia&Cr1=women (accessed June 14, 2012).

[28] "Fact Sheet: *Combating Sexual and Gender–Based Violence in Liberia*," A Joint Programme of the Government of Liberia and the United Nations, stoprapenow.org/uploads/features/SGBVemail.pdf (accessed June 13, 2012).

[29] Jina Moore , "Liberia's 'Rape Court': Progress for Women and Girls Delayed?" *Christian Science Monitor* (October 10, 2010), www.csmonitor.com/World/Africa/Africa-Monitor/2010/1010/Liberia-s-Rape-Court-Progress-for-women-and-girls-delayed (accessed June 14, 2012).

[30] Michael Fleshman, "Even with Peace, Liberia's Women Struggle: A Conversation with Activist Leymah Gbowee," *Africa Renewal* (April 2010), p. 8, www.un.org/en/africarenewal/vol24no1/liberia.html (accessed June 14, 2012).

of God, solidarity in cross bearing, repentance, conversion, power of the Spirit, and resurrection to transformed existence can encourage church members to reach out to others in steps toward social healing.

These images can correlate with symbols of ultimacy in other traditions. When such symbols are interpreted and reinforced by personal risk taking and solidaristic action for peace and justice, they can evoke responses in kind from other social actors and communities. Religious peacebuilding can serve as a powerful counterweight to the political conscription of religious narratives and symbols to serve partisan interests and validate violent means. The credibility of religious peacebuilders stems from and relies on their personal and communal integrity of purpose, good-faith efforts to increase mutual understanding, solidarity with all groups suffering violence in a community, and willingness to make personal sacrifices to serve the politics of salvation.

Myla Leguro is a Catholic Relief Services representative who works to end conflict among Christians, Muslims, and indigenous peoples in Mindinao, the Philippines. She reminds us that peacebuilding is never a linear process, nor are its results ensured. Nevertheless, healing and reconciliation are necessary expressions of Christian identity and an integral part of the mission of Christian organizations and churches, a mission that must be continually re-envisioned in light of new opportunities and obstacles. Building Catholic impetus to engage in dialogue, build solidarity, and lend support for the demands of Muslims and indigenous peoples "is not an easy task. But we continue to hope." Peacebuilders "are not certain of when they will arrive at their envisioned destination and uncertain of what they will encounter along the way. But they have owned this as a mission – a mission that will be sustained because of God's guidance and blessing."[31]

Peacebuilding practices reflect the vision of Christian politics that has shaped the previous chapters of this project. First, peacebuilding expresses an experience of God in Jesus Christ that has an active political dimension and interfaces with critical human needs and possibilities. The practical dimensions of faith and salvation shape an explanatory theological vision, confirmed in political action to enhance human flourishing and justice.

Second, the image of "creation" supports the struggle against evil, by holding up the possibility of an alternative way of being, by probing the

---

[31] Myla Leguro, "The Many Dimensions of Catholic Peacebuilding: Mindanao Experience," Fifth Annual Catholic Peacebulding Conference, University of Notre Dame (April 14, 2008), http://cpn.nd.edu/topics-in-catholic-peacebuilding (accessed September 23, 2012).

origins and dynamics of sin, and by invoking God's sustaining presence as the ground of renewed relationships. Peacebuilding as embodied, reconciling praxis replaces violent and exploitative practices and institutions with concrete alternatives that reshape personal and social habits so that a different society can emerge.

Third, peacebuilding goes forward in a practically grounded and realistic awareness that violence will never be eradicated completely. Yet it thrives in expectation of concrete historical changes. Peacebuilding embodies Jesus' politics of the reign of God, insofar as it understands that reconciliation is in some ways a present reality, in other ways an ambiguous process, and in every way dependent on the eschatological gift of resurrection life.

Fourth, peacebuilding displays the truth and the practical meaning of Christians' affirmation of the genuine humanity and divinity of Christ. Human limits and failures are overcome because God has entered the human condition and completely shared the human dilemma; in Christ, human joys and sufferings are fully united with the divine.

Fifth, the Spirit of God at work in the Christian community and its members enables the new way of being that is called resurrection life, divinization, or membership in Christ's body the church. The Spirit is our guarantor of Christ's real presence in lives and communities, of the possibility of overcoming violence, reconciling enemies, and moving toward a more just and peaceful future. The renewing power of the Spirit moves among all peoples and all creatures.

Sixth, Christ on the cross unites with the victims of violence, survivors of violence, and perpetrators of violence. The crucified Christ is in solidarity with all the alienated and forsaken sufferers who despair of a future. He empowers the church to exist hopefully in the midst of evil, to begin the reconciliation of weapons bearers, and to promise resurrection to those crushed by evil's weight.

Seventh, peacebuilders know that the life of Christian discipleship is structured by justice and seeks justice across boundaries of cultures, ethnicities, religions, nations, and continents. Peacebuilders are respectful of distinctive identities that lead to different worldviews, practices, and priorities. Yet they are also convinced that people everywhere value basic respect, access to the essential conditions of a dignified life, political participation, and social organization that facilitates peaceful coexistence. For peacebuilders, the politics of salvation moves from local communities of faith to regional and global societies, joining Christian faith with experiences of God in other religious traditions.

Index

Abelard, Peter, 220
Ackerman, Denise, 295
Adams, Marilyn McCord, 230, 231
Adeney, Frances, 12
Albertson, David, 256
Alcoff, Linda Martin, 29
Alison, James, 233
Allison, Dale C., Jr, 83
Amaladoss, Michael, 243
Ambrose, Glenn, 160
Anatolios, Khaled, 141
Anavy, Regina M., 231
Anderlini, Sanam, 299, 300
Anselm of Canterbury, 204, 207, 213, 220–4,
    226–7, 230
anti-Semitism, 116
apocalyptic, 77–8, 90–4, 122, 138, 156
    modified apocalyptic dualism, 97, 99
Appleby, R. Scott, 239, 294
Aquinas, Thomas, 4, 29, 45, 133, 164, 170, 172,
    174–9, 186, 190, 200–2, 249–3, 257–9, 261,
    266–9, 278, 282, 292
    basic human goods, 257–9
    common good, 276–9
    embodiment, 252–5, 282
    emotions, 252–4
    ethics, 280
    fruits of the Holy Spirit, 176
    natural law, 275–80
    nonhuman nature, 282
    salvation, 170–9
    sanctification, 169
    virtue, 169, 170–5, 178, 254, 267–71, 276, 292
Archer, Margaret S., 8, 13
Arendt, Hannah, 41–3
Aristotle, 171, 254, 256, 261, 268, 270
Armstrong, Regis J., 255
Ashley, J. Matthew, 99
Astorga, Maria Christina, 265
Athanasius, 130, 133, 140, 149, 187, 218, 282
atonement theory, 227–40

biblical perspectives, 207–12
in Christian theology, 220
criteria, 207, 227–9
models of, 218–20
resurrection and, 235
for sinners, 231
Attridge, Harold W., 213, 216, 217
    Augustine, 9, 37–9, 59, 130–1, 133, 141, 143,
        175, 180–3, 184, 189, 191, 193, 218–19, 249,
        254, 268–9, 276, 277
    politics, 181–3
    virtue, 181–3
Aulen, Gustaf, 218, 221
Ayer, A. J., 11–12
Ayres, Lewis, 9, 10, 126, 130, 138, 140–1, 149–50,
    193

Baillie, D.M., 131
Balch, David L., 128
Barclay, John M. G., 153
Barth, Karl, 46, 51
basic human goods, 23, 171, 257–9,
    266–7
    equal access to, 259–61
beauty, aesthetics, 7, 221–2, 253, 255
Bell, Catherine, 26
Benedict XVI, 243–5, 290–1
Berger, Peter L., 21
Biggar, Nigel, 19
Billings, J. Todd, 170
Billy, Dennis J., 127, 175
Bingemer, Maria Clara, 161
Bird, Phyllis A., 78
Birmingham, Peg, 41
Blenkinsopp, Joseph, 58, 93
Boeve, Lieven, 247
Boff, Leonardo, 281
Bonaventure, 255
Bonhoeffer, Dietrich, 232
Bordeyne, Philippe, 160
Borg, Marcus, 84, 115

Made in the USA
Middletown, DE
15 May 2018